# The Complete Book of FENCES

# The Complete Book of FENCES

DAN RAMSEY

FIRST EDITION
FIRST PRINTING



Library of Congress Cataloging in Publication Data

Ramsey, Dan, 1945-
The complete book of fences.
Includes index.
1. Fences. I. Title.
TH4965.R35 1983 631.2'7 82-19343
ISBN 0-8306-0508-8
ISBN 0-8306-1508-3 (pbk.)

Cover design by Carol Stickles.

# Contents

# Introduction

ROBERT FROST REMINDS US THAT, "GOOD FENces make good neighbors." The opposite is also true: good neighbors make good fences.

Fences come in all shapes, sizes, colors, and purposes from the Great Wall of China to the little white picket fence around the roses. Fences are built from wood, metal, wire, iron, steel, glass, fiberglass, plastic, clay, brick, and scrap. They can be simple or ornate, functional or aesthetic.

*The Complete Book of Fences* is a fully illustrated book on how to choose, design, prepare, build, and maintain all types of fences for all sorts of reasons. Both the first-time and veteran fence builder will find practical and useful information on tools, posts and framing, corners and ends, bracing, gates, maintenance and repair, landscaping, as well as on dozens of other important subjects together with step-by-step how-to instructions and hundreds of illustrations.

There's also a section on designing and building other outdoor structures: decks, sunshades, gazebos, engawas, aeries, tree houses, greenhouses, and much more. Plus, there is a section on landscaping to enhance the beauty and function of your fence and special sections on how to choose the right fence materials.

# Acknowledgments

Many people in the fence industry contributed to this book. They include Ginny Blair, Director of Public Relations of the Chain Link Fence Manufacturers Institute; Jan Bradford, Membership Manager of the International Fence Industry Association; Charles N. Farley, Director of Marketing, and Maureen M. Cunningham, Marketing Assistant of the Brick Institute of America; Doug McNeill, Product Sales Manager or Weyerhaeuser Company; Raymond W. Moholt, Manager of Product Publicity of Western Wood Products Association and the Western Red Cedar Lumber Association; Stacey Graham Wilson, Publicity Manager, Building Products, of Georgia-Pacific Corporation; Gerald B. Wellner, Manager of Public Information, Koppers Company, Inc.; Pamela Allsebrook of the California Redwood Association; Builders Fence Company, Inc.; the U.S. Department of Agriculture; Washington State Cooperative Extension Service; Cliff Pluard of Pluard & Sons Fence Service, Inc., Ken Downing and Jerry O'Dell of The Fenceman Fence Co., and Paul Larison of Parr Lumber Company, all of Vancouver, Washington; and especially to Val Ramso for his excellent photography.

To the memory of my father,
Clarence Allen Ramsey.

**Other TAB books by the author:**

No. 1263 *How To Be A Disc Jockey*
No. 1458 *Building a Log Home from Scratch or Kit*
No. 2339 *Student Pilot's Solo Practice Guide*

# Chapter 1

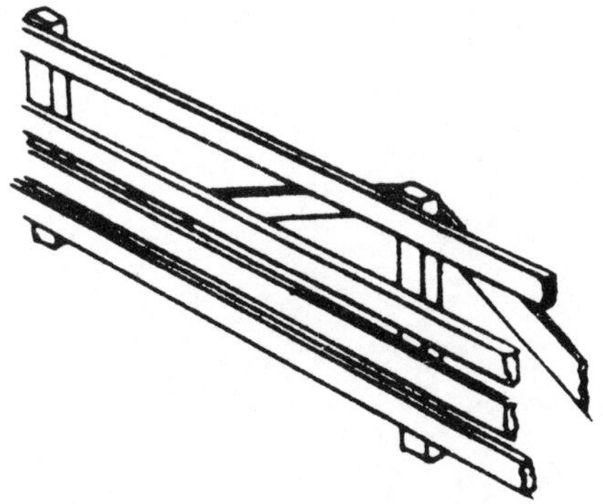

# All About Fences

IN OUR EFFORTS TO DEFINE OUR OWN SPACE WE have dug moats, hand-built a 1500-mile wall over mountains, and planted a flag on the moon. Psychologists say it stems from "primordial" territorial instincts. Whatever the basis for this need to stake out our turn, we're building more fences today than ever before. And we're putting them to work for us in new ways (Fig. 1-1).

A fence is a barrier enclosing or bordering a field, yard, or other area. Its purpose is to prevent entrance, confine animals or people, or to mark a boundary. A newer function is controlling the environment. You can control effects of the sun, wind, and the earth with fencing and walls.

## HISTORY

No one knows when the first fence was built, but the largest is still, at least partially, in place. The Great Wall of China was begun during the third century B.C., and many sections still stand. Its base was 15 to 30 feet thick, and its height averaged 25 feet. Its length was approximately 1500 miles.

Fences of biblical times were actually walls built around cities for protection. Normally a dozen or more feet thick, the walls were built to withstand almost anything.

Fences took on a new function during the Victorian era: beauty. Fences short enough to step over were built with ornate whorls and arabesques to impress the passersby. In America everyone's desire to live near the centers of commercial activity reduced the size of property on which each home was built. With everyone living face-to-face on 100 × 100-foot lots, individuality was expressed by the art of landscaping and fences. Fences began to function as landscaping. Fences became structures of beauty and expression (Fig. 1-2).

Fences retained their original purposes down on the farm: to keep people out and animals in. The invention of barbed wire, woven wire, and electric fences was a great help to farmers.

## PURPOSES

Let's take a closer look at the reasons why people build fences. All reasons can be lumped together under the overworked phrase "environ-

Fig. 1-1. Fences are as creative as their designers (courtesy California Redwood Association).

mental control." More specifically, people build fences to:

- Mark property boundaries.
- Mark area boundaries.
- Keep people out.
- Keep people in.
- Keep animals in or out.
- Control visibility for privacy.
- Control the sun.
- Control the wind.
- Control snow.
- Control water.
- Control soil and erosion.
- Reduce or control noise.
- Control landscaping.
- Control the visual effect.

Most fences are built for a combination of reasons. A chain link fence may be erected to mark boundaries, keep some people and animals in, keep others out, control landscaping, and improve the home's visual effect. The fence has also added value to the property by making the home a better place to live.

### Property Boundary

Many fences are built to define the boundaries of a property. As homesteads become smaller and smaller, many people express their territorial rights nonaggressively by marking out property lines with a fence.

Property boundary fences need not be large or expensive. Many are simply rail or picket fences erected along the front and sides of the property. They can also serve as landscape controls by keeping others off lawns and away from shrubs and flowers. A boundary fence can be combined with a privacy fence to shield vision of others from private areas of a yard or to shield vision of unattractive sights from the homeowner. Simple property boundary fences also serve as animal control fences in the country.

### Area Boundary

Smaller properties also mean that yards must be more efficient. They must serve as recreation areas, service areas, and storage and garden areas. This is often done by segmenting a yard with purpose-designed fences. A pool area may be fenced by a movable security fence. A garden area will need a security fence that doesn't block the sun's rays. A privacy area will have a large opaque fence that insures visual control. A dog run can be fenced for both security and visibility.

### Exterior Security

Fences can reduce or eliminate the opportunities for intruders to enter your property. Some fences may only slow them down. Others reduce visibility into the yard and reduce intrusions into an unknown area. Still others can be wired to set off an

Fig. 1-2. Fences can be a work of art (courtesy Western Red Cedar Lumber Association).

Fig. 1-3. Fences can offer privacy even in small backyards (photo by Val Ramos).

alarm whenever someone tries to enter.

### Interior Security

Fence builders want to keep others, primarily children, on the property or within a defined area. Interior security fences can be anything from a 4-foot-high chain link fence to a 2-foot-thick concrete wall depending on your needs, budget, and skills.

An interior security fence for children or animals must be both high enough and difficult to scale. If you're building a fence to keep your 2-year-old child out of the street, make it tall enough to retain a 10-year-old child. Build it from materials such as large-weave chain link or a basket weave wood fence. These same rules apply if you're building a prison fence.

### Animal Control

Fences are also constructed to keep animals in or out. A rancher may build a two-strand wire fence to contain his cattle. A pet owner will build an enclosure to keep his animal away from cars and postmen. An amateur landscaper might build a fence to keep neighborhood dogs from damaging plants.

### Visual Control

Privacy is the primary reason why many sub-

Fig. 1-4. This fence offers privacy and beauty (courtesy California Redwood Association).

Fig. 1-5. Good neighbors make good fences (courtesy International Fence Industry Association).

urban fences are built (Fig. 1-3). The easiest way to achieve total privacy is to rim your property with a high, solid fence. Once the the fence is up, you may discover that you've created a rigid environment with a confined, boarded-up feeling. You may also have alienated yourself from your neighbors.

An alternative is to use a combination of plants, screens, and opaque and semiopaque fences to control visibility. You can install a solid board or panel fence in areas where you want complete privacy and low rail fences where visibility isn't as important as property boundary definition.

In areas where you must erect a solid fence to insure privacy, do your best to make it handsome from both sides (Fig. 1-4). Your neighbor has to look at it, too. It can either be a pleasant view or an unpleasant reminder of your unfriendliness. Be a good neighbor with your "good neighbor" fence (Fig. 1-5).

A privacy fence doesn't have to be at the edge of your property line. You can build an 8-foot-high privacy fence around your pool or patio much more easily, less expensively, and more neighborly than a full 6-foot perimeter fence (Figs. 1-6 and 1-7). You can also use translucent glass or plastic to obscure vision while allowing light into your yard.

### Sun Control

Your fence can control the sun's heat and glare in many ways. Shade can be produced with solid wood, masonry, or other fence materials. Glare can be reduced with plastic or glass panels. Your choice of design and materials depends on what other purposes the fence must fulfill. If it must also screen an area from winds, a solid fence material is preferred. If light breezes are desired, a louvered fence will be best.

Other structures can be built to help control the sun's effects within your yard. Chapter 11 will show you how to choose and build many sun controls including the gazebo, pavilion, sun trap, screens, and arbors.

### Wind Control

The wind is not as easy to control as the sun because its behavior is less predictable. Before building a fence for wind control, you should study

Fig. 1-6. Fences are often built to enclose pools for both safety and privacy (courtesy International Fence Industry Association).

Fig. 1-7. A patio fence extends the living space of a home (courtesy Western Red Cedar Lumber Association).

and understand the wind's behavior in your yard. The direction of the prevailing wind is not necessarily the direction it will blow across the patio. Your house, trees, and other structures can change the direction of the wind. You can divert and direct the wind.

To discover the wind's direction at your proposed fence location, simply attach colored yarn or strips of cloth to stakes set in the ground. As the prevailing wind blows, you can check the stakes to see how other structures will deflect the wind. You can then plan your fence to either capture or release the wind as you desire (Fig. 1-8).

### Snow Control

If you're building a fence in Florida, you can pass over this section. Most parts of the country get at least some snow each year. In northern climates snow can be a headache to the fence builder. Snow wants to drift against solid fences and pile up, producing a fence's two greatest enemies: moisture and pressure.

The solution is in both planning and design. Find out the direction of the prevailing winter wind and whether any nearby structures will change that wind to predict where snow will accumulate quickly if stopped by a fence or wall. Then decide whether snow buildup is desirable at that location. In most cases it's undesirable and can be reduced or eliminated with a fence that allows wind flow. It may be desirable to have a snow-stopping fence where the snow would normally drift onto plants or patios. A solid, well-constructed fence will do the job.

### Water Control

Fences can also control rainwater, standing water, or running water. Livestock ranchers build water fences across creeks to dam up or control water flow. Homeowners in areas of high wind and heavy rains can control rain and divert it away from

Fig. 1-8. A well-planned fence can diffuse wind and make a yard more comfortable (courtesy California Redwood Association).

doorways, windows, and other areas. Fences can also keep standing water away from lawns, flowers, etc.

### Soil Control

Fences and walls can reduce erosion and control soil. A solid fence can divert water runoff and help protect the root systems of trees and plants. Larger fences used to hold back earth are called retaining walls and can be built from heavy timbers, brick, concrete, blocks, or stone.

In building any fence or wall on a slope, carefully consider the direction, path, and amount of drainage. A fence or wall cannot stop drainage, only divert it safely. Retaining walls should have "weep holes" every few feet to allow moisture in the retained dirt to drain off. Dammed water can freeze and damage the wall. There is more information on constructing walls for soil control in Chapter 9.

### Noise Control

Fences can control noise both physically and

Fig. 1-9. A decorative outdoor room is formed by this unique wood fence (courtesy Western Wood Products Association).

Fig. 1-10. Fences can be functional or decorative (courtesy Western Red Cedar Lumber Association).

psychologically. In an area where noises are a problem, such as near a major highway or factory, a tall, thick fence can physically reduce the noise level by absorbing and reflecting the sound. Living fences such as hedges, trees, and climbing vines are also effective.

Psychologists say that removing a sound from sight can also seemingly reduce the noise. It isn't physically reduced, but often becomes a background noise if it's removed from the line of sight. This fact can be used by homeowners bothered by highway traffic, industrial plants, and noise from nearby schools.

## Landscape Control

Fences can separate your outdoor living area into rooms (Fig. 1-9). You can then use them to develop moods with landscaping. A recreation area will have open fencing and low-maintenance plants. The garden area will have an animal security fence enclosing the vegetables and fruits. A sunbathing area can be contained with a solid high fence surrounding grass. A flower garden will be separated from the recreation area with a louvered board fence or picket fence.

Fences can also serve as vertical gardens for climbing plants and flower boxes. Ivy or sweet peas can be crisscrossed on strings attached to wooden, chain link, or brick fences. They can also be a natural backdrop for annual flowers or perennial plants.

## Decoration

Fences can also be completely decorative in themselves (Fig. 1-10). They can be outdoor canvases for a myriad variety of colors and designs. Fences can be sided and painted to blend in with the color and design of your home or other structure.

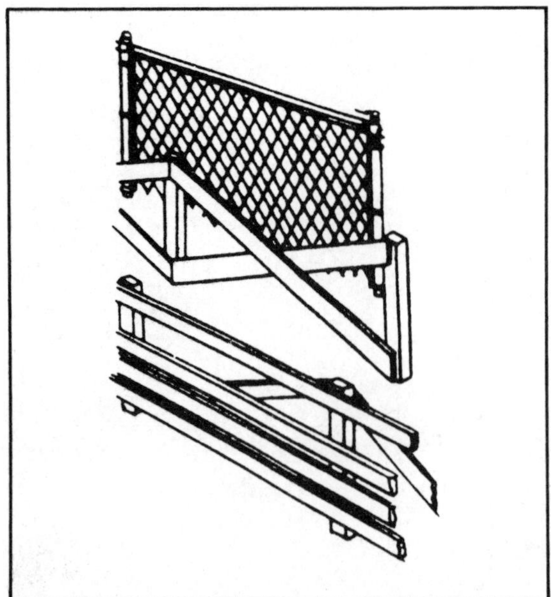

Fig. 1-11. Unique fencing designs and materials.

They can be used to display fountains, wood designs, or unique planters. They can serve primarily as art.

There are literally dozens of reasons why people build fences and walls, from the practicality of a livestock fence to the purely decorative fence. The fences are all designed and built to control the environment of the owner.

## TYPES

Fences have been made in every imaginable form with every possible material (Fig. 1-11). Fences have been built from lumber, railroad ties, plywood, hardboard, aluminum, iron, steel, logs, wire, brick, stone, poured concrete, split wood, glass, plastic, bamboo, asbestos board, canvas, fiberglass, bottles, cans, adobe, dirt, clay, living plants, and many other natural and man-made materials (Fig. 1-12).

Solid fences are built to stop things: vision, sun, wind, water, humans, animals, noise, dirt, etc. Most are made of wood or masonry such as brick or stone.

Open fences are designed to either reduce vision, elements, or entry, or to enhance the beauty of property. The variety of building materials is wider and includes nearly all types of wood, metal, stone, and larger plants.

Walls are simply solid fences with an additional element: strength. Walls are built to hold back dirt or other elements, or to add security to property. Walls are also built solely for beauty.

Screens are short width fences designed to shield an area from view or elements. Screens are used to separate a property into areas or rooms.

Fences can also be broken down into low fences of 4 feet high or less and high fences of 5 feet high or more (Fig. 1-3). The sizing is general as a high picket fence may only be 4 feet high, and a short board fence can be 5 feet high.

To simplify things, this book separates all fences, walls, and screens into seven categories: rail fences, picket fences, board fences, chain link fences, livestock fences, masonry fences, and other fence materials. These fences are covered in Chapters 4 through 10. Chapters 2 and 3 explain how to plan and build fences in general. Later chapters cover other outdoor structures, gates, maintenance, and landscaping.

### Rail Fences

The so-called "rail" fence is actually a "post and rail" fence: the post being the vertical member

Fig. 1-12. A retaining wall of railroad ties.

Fig. 1-13. Fences come in all sizes and shapes (courtesy California Redwood Association).

and the rails running horizontally. Rail fences are as unique as their applications.

Most rail fences are low, 2 to 4 feet high and open. They were originally built by the pioneers to contain livestock and were constructed of small logs and split wood. The first rail fence was the zigzag or snake fence built by early settlers from available timber. The fence was simple to construct and maintain, but it required more wood than today's rail fences.

As fence materials became more scarce and property lines needed to be more defined, the post and rail fence evolved to the two- and three-rail fence. The two-rail fence is used as a landscaping element in suburban settings, while the three-rail fence can serve as a livestock security fence in rural areas.

Modern rail fences are usually constructed of 4×4-posts and 6 to 8-foot-long rails of logs, split rails, 4×4's, or 1×4-board rails (Fig. 1-14). You'll learn more about how to design and build rail fences in Chapter 4.

### Picket Fences

Picket fences are rail fences with evenly spaced horizontal pickets attached to the rails (Fig. 1-15). Picket fences are both practical and decorative (Fig. 1-16). Nearly all picket fences are 4 feet high or less.

The picket fence has many advantages over other types of fences. First, it defines a property line without obstructing vision and the feeling of openness. Second, the picket fence has become an art form and suggests a friendly owner. Pickets are simply boards that have had their tops cut to a uniform design. Third, picket fences are also prac-

Fig. 1-14. A rail fence of 4×4 posts (courtesy Western Wood Products Association).

tical control fences for children and small pets, the natural enemies of all growing things. Fourth, they are easy to construct and maintain. Picket fences can still be purchased in 4 and 6-foot sections, painted and ready to install.

Picket fences seem to go best with older homes on small city lots. Chapter 5 shows you how to design your own picket fence and build it with basic tools.

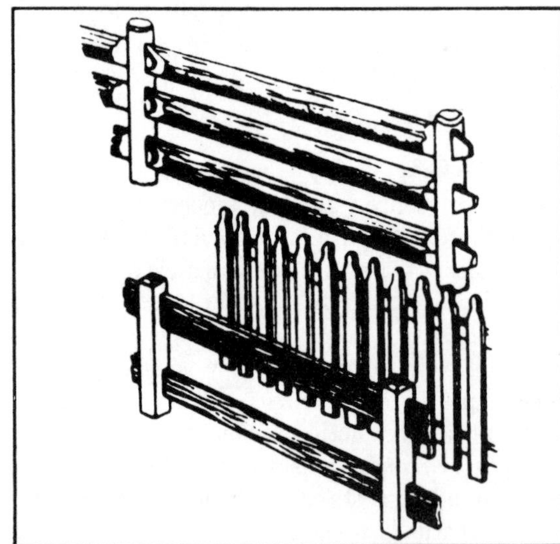

Fig. 1-15. Common rail and picket fences.

## Board Fences

Board fences comprise all types of high wood fence designs from board-on-board to slat, louver, and grape stake fences (Fig. 1-17). Construction of the post and rails is basically the same. The difference is in the "siding" placed on the fence (Fig. 1-18).

Board fences are useful and easy to build, but they require a large amount of wood and can be expensive (Fig. 1-19). Careful planning can overcome the cost factor and many design problems to make board fences highly efficient.

Most board fences are designed for security and privacy. They are the most common "backyard" fences and isolate your yard from the view of others. Some good neighbors build a modified board fence, shorter or more open, to reduce visibility without eliminating friendliness (Fig. 1-20).

Planning, material selection, construction techniques, and step-by-step instructions for

Fig. 1-16. A "fence" means a picket fence for many people (courtesy Western Wood Products Association).

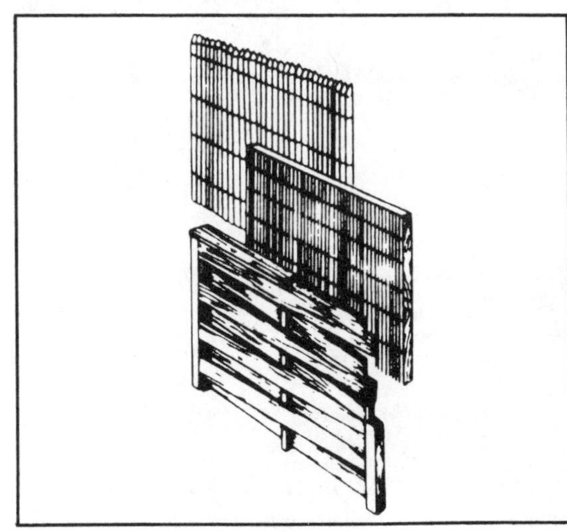

Fig. 1-17. Popular board fences.

building all common board fences are offered in Chapter 6.

## Chain Link Fences

Chain link fences offer many advantages: maximum visibility, security, long life, and ease of construction (Fig. 1-21). They don't offer privacy in themselves. This can be overcome with wood, metal, or plastic inserts.

Wire fence contractors are very competitive, so you may want to get several bids before you tackle the project yourself. They may be able to do it cheaper than you can. Remember, though, that there's a wide range of quality in chain link fence materials.

Chain link fences consist of metal posts, fabric,

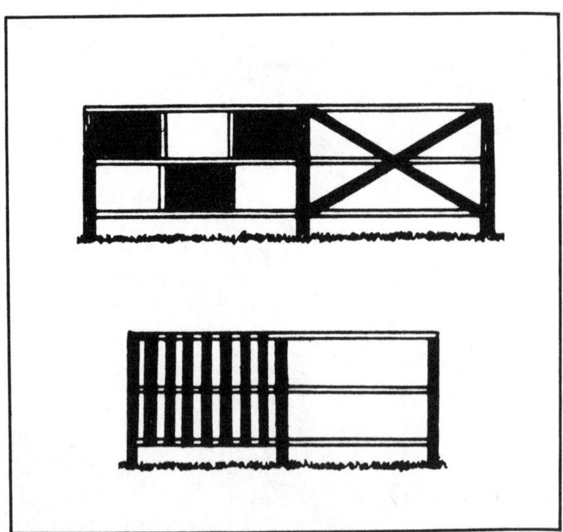

Fig. 1-18. There are many ways to "side" a fence.

tension bars and bands, top rails, and fittings. The posts are set in concrete. The chain link fabric is stretched between posts and attached with the tension bar and bands. Gates are hung separately. Chapter 7 offers complete instructions on how to select and install chain link fences.

### Livestock Fences

Livestock fences must be both efficient and economical at their purpose: to contain valuable animals. Livestock fences include those made with barbed wire, woven wire, poultry netting, cable, electric fences, and wooden corrals.

Productive farmland is often fenced with woven wire or a combination of woven wire and barbed wire. Marginal, cutover, or other less productive land is usually fenced with less expensive

Fig. 1-19. A horizontal board fence can weather to blend with its natural surroundings (courtesy Western Red Cedar Lumber Association).

Fig. 1-20. A good neighbor fence (courtesy Western Wood Products Association).

Fig. 1-21. The chain link fence is increasingly popular for low-cost protection.

Fig. 1-22. Brick fences can also be used as retaining walls for beauty and function (courtesy Brick Institute of America).

Fig. 1-23. A fence can be combined with other outdoor structures to add livability to your backyard (courtesy California Redwood Association).

materials such as single strand wire. Woven wires are used to confine livestock. Electric fencing is convenient where more permanent fencing would be too expensive or perhaps undesirable.

Chapter 8 tells how to design and build all types of wire and wood livestock fences.

## Masonry Fences

Fences and walls can also be built with masonry materials: brick, concrete, stone, etc. They enclose outdoor space and offer security and privacy.

Concrete masonry walls are built with blocks made of portland cement, graded rock, and water. Blocks with a quarter or more of their cross-sectional area open are called "hollow" blocks. They are easy to construct with minimal tools and basic knowledge.

Fig. 1-24. A fence can be combined with other outdoor structures to enhance the entryway of a home (courtesy Western Red Cedar Lumber Association).

Fig. 1-25. Wood fences can be a decorative element of landscaping (courtesy California Redwood Association).

Bricks are solid masonry, often red in color from the inclusion of clay. Bricks usually require a little more skill to lay, but the technique can be quickly learned by the do-it-yourselfer.

Stone is more difficult because the stones are usually of varied sizes and shapes. Selection and placement are important. The results are more natural and decorative than fences and walls of man-made materials.

Chapter 9 will show you step-by-step how to build straight, pier and panel, and serpentine masonry fences along with garden and retaining walls (Fig. 1-22). It gives you information on buying the basic materials and tools, how to locate your masonry fence or wall, how to pour footings, how to mix mortar, and how to cut brick. You'll also learn how to design and plan unique masonry walls and fences to fit your individual needs.

## OUTDOOR STRUCTURES

There are many outdoor structures that you can build to complement your fence and increase the usefulness of your property (Figs. 1-23 and 1-24). You can build decks, railings and benches, walks and engawas, screens, enclosures, arbors and treillage, gazebos, pavilions, aeries, a tree house, planters, greenhouses, storage items, and dozens of other useful structures with basic skills and tools. That's what Chapter 11 is all about. Chapter 14 illustrates how you can use your fence as a landscaping tool to increase the beauty of your property (Fig. 1-25).

# Chapter 2

# Planning Your Fence

EVERY GOOD FENCE IS BUILT TWICE—ONCE ON paper and once on the ground. Fence building would be simple if everyone lived on a perfectly level 100 × 100-foot lot. Most property is not typical. Slopes have to be descended. Trees must be passed. Soils must be considered. Styles must be chosen.

The first thing to do in planning your fence is to make a study of your property: size, shape, soil, drainage, trees, ground cover, utilities, local weather conditions, and appropriateness of your fence.

Then draw up plans (Fig. 2-1). This involves reviewing as many ideas as possible, learning about local building regulations, considering height and length requirements, locating the fence, talking with neighbors, and then picking your fence.

Choose the best type of fence to solve your problem: closed, tall, short, wood, masonry, etc. Pick the style, list the materials you'll need, and consider the gates and related hardware. Review your plans for function and appropriateness. Finally, you solve any special problems: slopes, trees, curves, banks, water, soils, and strength. Your fence is built on paper, where problems can be easily solved and errors can be corrected.

## STUDYING PROPERTY

Before you decide which fence is best, take a good look at the property you're going to fence. It may be a backyard fence for privacy, a quarter section for cattle, or a fence around a new in-ground pool. Make a rough measurement of the fence line. If possible, plant a few stakes and run a string showing the proposed fence. Write down your measurements and special requirements or angles.

Make a rough sketch of the shape; a full drawing isn't necessary yet. If your lot is rectangular, you don't have to draw it to scale. Your sketch should have two sides longer than the other.

Mark "north" on your rough sketch and draw in the relationship of nearby properties and fences. Draw in any grades, banks, berms, trees, or other elements that may affect your fence. Pay special attention to *topography*, the lay of the land. Wind direction, sun orientation, and shade from outside

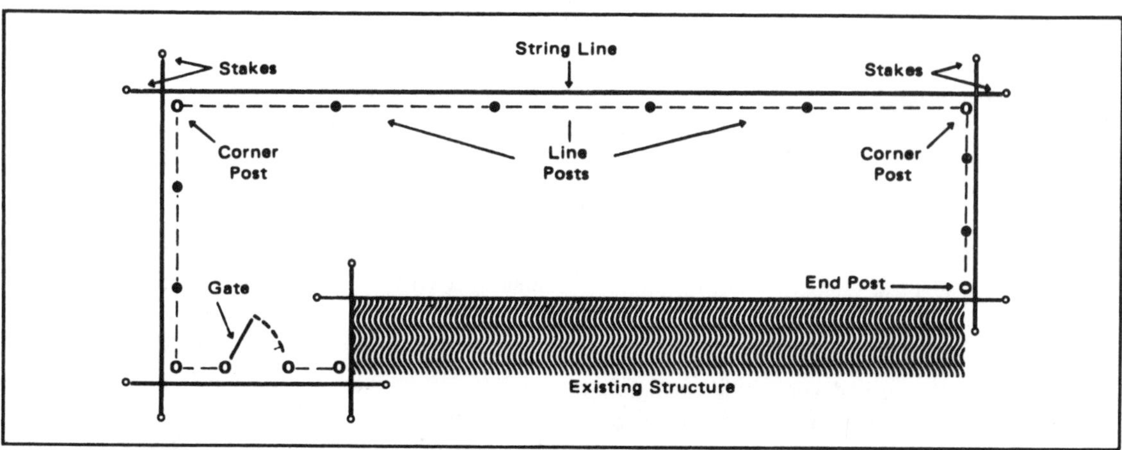


Fig. 2-1. Typical fence plan.

property lines should be put on your map.

The soil is important to the fence builder for two reasons. Soil type indicates how the ground will drain, and some soils are easier to dig for postholes and wall footings. You can have your soil tested at little or no cost through the local cooperative extension service (in the phone book) or a soil laboratory. They will analyze the soil and make recommendations about digging and trenching, post materials, hole or footing depth, and recommended digging equipment. They can also tell you whether concrete or gravel will be the most efficient hole filler for your fence. Make sure you take soil samples along your proposed fence line. In some areas soil types are mixed and can be found in ribbons just a few feet wide.

Draining will also be important to the planning of your fence. It's usually best to plan your fence along the highest elevations to allow water to run off away from your fence. Fences built in low spots, especially wood post fences, quickly deteriorate and must be replaced more often. If necessary, you can change the direction of natural drainage and keep standing water away from fences and walls with catch basins, contouring, and dry wells.

Living plants are also important in planning your fence. If your landscaping is already established, you'll probably want to disturb as little as possible. If it isn't in yet, you can use your fence as a part of your landscaping plan. What type of ground cover do you have or plan to have—grass (what type), ivy, sandwort, juniper, or potentilla? Are there shrubs you want to plant or keep? How will they be affected by your fence? How about hedges? Can you integrate them into your fence?

Trees can be a point of beauty or a pain for fence builders. You may be able to blend existing trees into your fence plans. Don't try to move them as most won't take the change. Work around them or cut them down. Be careful of damaging the root systems, especially in rainy parts of the country, as the roots are probably near the surface and can easily be damaged.

There's a man-made element to planning your fence that many builders often forget until it's too late: utilities. Newer subdivisions have underground utilities—phone, gas, water, and electrical lines—running under the property. For convenience, many of these lines run along a *utility easement* on the property lines—right where you want to build your fence. To make sure that you won't damage these lines, check with local utilities before digging. In many areas the utilities have banded together and offered a single telephone number where information on underground utility location can be found. They have property maps available and can quickly locate your parcel and notify you of any underground hazards. Some utility companies will place stakes over utility lines to help you in planning your fence or wall. Rural fence builders should also use this service as primary utility lines run along fence lines, roads, and even through fields where easements have been purchased.

As you study your property and plan your fence, consider local weather conditions and what part your new fence will play. Your fence can deflect or stop winds, soften or eliminate sunshine, or deflect rains as needed. Questions to ask include:

- Will this fence throw a shadow? Will it give too much shade to nearby plants?
- What change will this fence have on the wind? Will it break it up and send it off in another direction? Which direction? Will it affect another landscaping element?
- How will this fence affect and be affected by rain and snow? Is there proper drainage?
- Does this fence need special preservatives or treatment to combat adverse sun or weather bleaching?
- Should this fence be open or opaque considering the weather conditions in your yard?

Finally, ask yourself, "How appropriate is this fence?" Will it serve its intended purpose? Will it be an integral part of your landscaping, or will it detract?

A short brick wall may be an attractive addition to your yard, but it may not offer the security and privacy you need. A barbed wire fence may be efficient for containing animals, but it may detract from the beauty of your landscaped backyard. A tall fence may keep animals out of your azaleas, but it may make your neighbors feel you're unfriendly. Make your fence both effective and appropriate (Fig. 2-2).

## DRAWING PLANS

By now you've studied your property and have some good ideas on how to place and build your fence. You've even made a rough sketch of your lot and proposed fences and walls. Now it's time to get serious.

Most stationery stores will have graph paper to help you draw a diagram of your property and amenities to scale. The best scale is one square per foot. If your lot is 100 feet wide, find graph paper with at least a 100-square width. Whatever scale you decide, make it consistent.

Find a map of your property if possible. Check for a title insurance policy you received when you purchased your property. It may be called a *plat map, subdivision map,* or section map depending on the type of land and the part of the country. If you can't find your map, request one from a local title insurance company or from the country courthouse. It may even have a legal description on it such as "Lot 42, Mill Plain Acres" or "SW¼, SE½ of Section 16" to help you locate lines.

With your drawing of your property, talk over your fence plans with others. You can hold a family conference to decide what type and location would be best. Consult with neighbors to see if you can share fences or tie into another fence. Speak with local officials about fencing regulations. See Table 2-6.

## FENCE LAWS

There's a law for just about everything, and fences are no exception. Fence laws are usually practical: don't build a fence on someone else's property, don't build a fence where it will obstruct the safe view of drivers, and don't build a fence that will detract from the value of neighboring properties.

The problem is that laws involving fence construction are not standard. They vary from state to state, city to city, and even neighborhood to neighborhood. Here's how to find out what laws govern the construction of fences in your area:

- Check your title insurance policy to see if there are any restrictions or reservations that might apply such as "No fences shall be built in the area in front of the home." Check for easements for utilities or roads. Fences can't be built on most easements without written permission from the holder.
- Contact the county or city building department to see what regulations they may have on building fences. Some have basic regulations and a small fee based on the fence's value. Others have specific and detailed requirements.

**Table 2-1. Fence Plan Sheet for a Chain Link Fence.**

| Posts | O.D. Size | Length | Kind |
|---|---|---|---|
| | | | Corner Posts |
| | | | End Posts |
| | | | Gate Posts |
| | | | Line Posts |

| Amount | Size | Fence Line Sketch |
|---|---|---|
| Tension Bands | | |
| | | |
| Brace Bands | | |
| | | |
| Rail Ends | | |
| | | |
| Post Caps | | |
| | | |
| Nuts and Bolts | | |
| | | |
| Eye-Tops | | |
| | | |
| Top Rail | | |
| | | |
| Top Rail Sleeves | | |
| | | |
| Chain Link Fabric | | |
| | | |
| Tension Bars | | |
| | | |
| Tie Wires | | |
| | | |
| Post Hinge | | |
| | | |

| Gates | | | |
|---|---|---|---|
| Width | Height | Width | Height |
| | | | |

- Make sure other regulations aren't violated. Your area may restrict fences on corner lots to a height of 4 feet for traffic visibility (Fig. 2-3). Other local governments may not allow you to build your fence within a specific distance of a sidewalk. Your county courthouse or city hall can direct you to any departments that may have jurisdiction.
- Talk with a government official or title officer in your area to find out how close you can locate your fence and other structures to property lines. If you're building a common fence, you may be able to straddle the line. If lines aren't clear, you may offset your fence a foot or two inside the probable line location.

One problem that some fence builders face can be easily solved. Local codes may not allow a fence taller than 6 feet at the property line (Fig. 2-4). That's a problem if your house sets high and you need at least an 8-foot fence for privacy. The solution is often the *45-degree rule*. That is, a higher fence can be built within the property as long as it isn't higher than a 45-degree angle from a point 6 feet above the property line. You can simply build a taller fence within your property as long as it doesn't break this rule. Check if your area has the 45-degree rule.

As you draw your fence plans, consider the length of your fence, both sectional and overall. The overall length of your fence should be checked to make sure it will be structurally sound. Solid fences of more than 30 or 40 feet in length often need extra bracing in windy areas depending on the design, components, and height. The length of fence sections is also important for the planning of post locations. Posts can be separated by 4, 6, 8, 10, or 12 feet of rail and siding or other cover depending on the height of the fence, the weight of the materials, and the strength of the posts and the rails. Most board fences have 8-foot center-to-center posts. Chain link fence posts are often spaced 10 feet apart, and picket fences are built with a typical 4-foot spread between posts (Fig. 2-5). This should be reflected in your drawings.

You may be able to save plenty of time, labor, and money by tying your fence into that of a neighbor's. The problems to overcome are few: an agreement of ownership, style, maintenance, and location. You may have a written agreement to attach your fence to his at a corner. You still own and maintain your fence, or you may build a common fence along the property line. You'll want a written agreement stating that you are "tenants in common," that you will share the erection and maintenance costs equally, and that the style of the fence will be one agreeable to both parties. Keep this agreement with your important papers and let subsequent owners know about it.

## CHOOSING YOUR FENCE

You can use your plans to draw out the specific

Fig. 2-2. This fence serves many purposes (courtesy Western Wood Products Association).

Fig. 2-3. Local laws may allow you to "step" your fence for traffic visibility in the front yard and privacy in the backyard (photo by Val Ramos).

type of fence or fences you'll be building. You may decide to use one type around your garden area, another as a dog run, and a third for privacy around your patio (Fig. 2-6). You may simply run a perimeter fence around your property as in the case of livestock, pets, and for children.

Among solid wood fences you can choose a basket weave, panel fence, board fence, board-on-board, diagonal board, plastic fence, or other style (Figs. 2-7 through 2-17). You can then draw a construction diagram or *elevation* or your fence to scale on another sheet of graph paper. It will show the dimensions of the fence, the width between posts, the size of materials used in the construction, and can even include a materials list. Styles are dis-

Fig. 2-4. Local fence laws may restrict fence height (photo by Val Ramos).

cussed further in Chapters 4 through 10.

Your materials list will be helpful in estimating the cost of construction. Here's a partial list of materials you may need in building your fence:

### Wood Fences

*Posts:* 3×4, 4×4, or 4×5-inch milled or split wood; 5, 6, or 7-foot-long steel posts in L, T, or U shape.

*Stringers:* 2×3 or 2×4-rails in 4, 6, 8, 10 or 12-foot lengths.

*Siding:* 1×4, 1×6, 1×8-boards, of 4, 5, 6, or 8-foot lengths; 1×1, 1×2, or 1×3 pickets of 3, 4, or 5-foot grape stakes; ⅜×2×4, 6, or 8-foot lath for battens of lattice; ¼ to ¾-inch exterior plywood in 4×8-foot sheets; other solid panels (tempered hardboard, cement asbestos, aluminum, galvanized steel, fiberglass, acrylic plastic, plastic-filled screening, reed screen, plate glass, wire glass, etc.).

### Chain Link Fences

*Posts:* 1⅜ to 2⅜-inch outside diameter galvanized steel posts, 2 to 3 feet longer than the wire height.

*Top rail:* 1⅜-inch outside diameter galvanized steel rail (usually in 21-foot lengths).

*Fabric:* 1½ to 9 gauge in widths of 3, 3½, 4, 5, and 6 feet, standard length of 50 feet per roll.

*Miscellaneous:* Post caps, rail ends, top rail sleeves, brace bands, eye-tops, tension bars, tension bands, tie wires, post hinges, nuts, bolts, scrolls, gates, gate latch, etc., as needed.

### Wire Fences

*Posts:* (same as wood fences, above).

Fig. 2-5. Front yard visibility regulations may be met with a spaced picket fence (photo by Val Ramos).

Fig. 2-6. Fencing materials such as wood and brick can be combined for decoratively functional fencing (photo by Val Ramos).

*Stringers:* (same as wood fences, above).

*Fabric:* 9, 11, 12½, 14½-gauge galvanized strand, or woven field wire, 12½ to 15½-gauge barbed wire; ½, 1, 2, 3×4 mesh wire; poultry netting or fence, etc. See Figs. 2-18 through 2-20.

### Masonry Fences

*Brick:* standard, normal, SCR, Roman.

*Block:* cinder, concrete, cement.

*Mortar:* portland cement, Sakrete concrete, other.

You'll also need a list of tools for the job. They are listed in Chapter 3 and in the chapter on your specific type of fence. Many of the tools you'll have on hand, while others may be purchased, rented, or borrowed.

## PLANNING THE GATE

Nearly every fence needs a gate. The gate allows entrance to the fenced area; its practical. A gate can also be a design element; it's aesthetic.

Fig. 2-7. Common types of board fences: good neighbor, alternate panel, solid panel, and louvered (courtesy Weyerhaeuser Company).

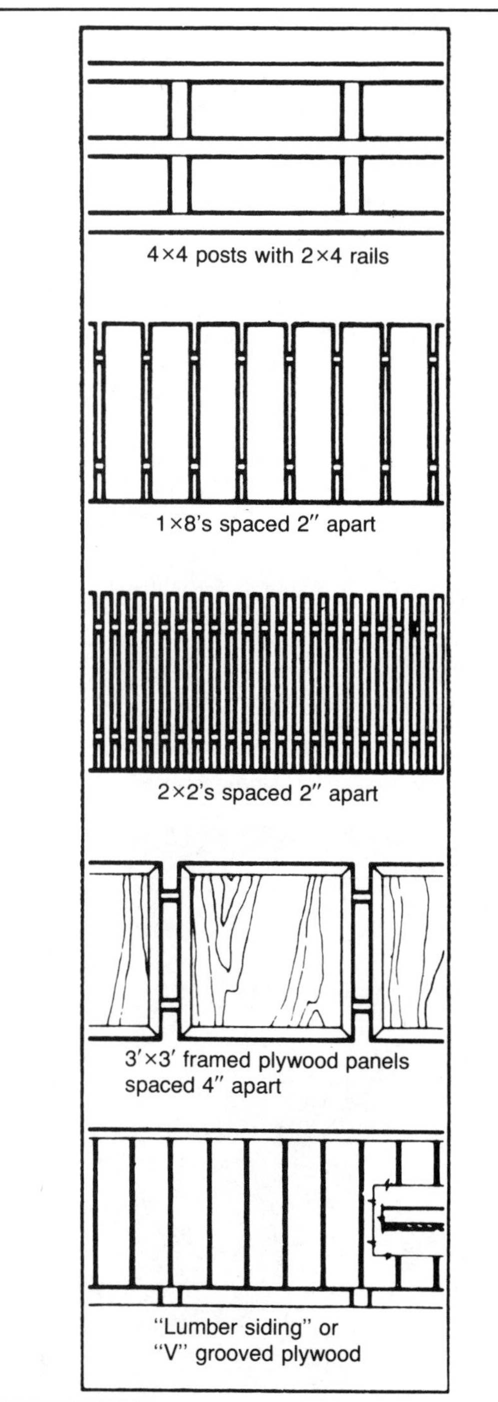

Fig. 2-8. There are many types of siding you can install on a wood fence.

Fig. 2-9. "Dog-eared" board fence (photo by Val Ramos).

The first consideration in planning your gate is its location. You may decide to install a "good neighbor" gate for a friend living in an adjoining house, or your gate may allow you to back your trailer into a fenced area. A gate can be the door from one part of your yard to another, such as from the recreation area to the garden. A gate may allow easy access to a pet area. The gate for a livestock fence may be for vehicles to pass or for animals to enter an adjoining pasture. Take a look at your design and review the purposes of your fence and the areas it severs.

You also want your gate to be an integral part of your fence. You can design it to either blend in with your fence, such as a solid board fence gate, or be decorative, such as a short picket fence with overhead trellis. It can be built of either similar or contrasting materials. A chain link gate can be installed

Fig. 2-10. Alternate board fence (photo by Val Ramos).

Fig. 2-11. Post and rail fence (photo by Val Ramos).

Fig. 2-12. Horizontal board fence (photo by Val Ramos).

Fig. 2-13. Split rail fence (photo by Val Ramos).

Fig. 2-14. Decorative slat fence (photo by Val Ramos).

Fig. 2-15. Fence boards can be tight or spaced (photo by Val Ramos).

Fig. 2-16. Picket fences can become more decorative with height variations (photo by Val Ramos).

with a wooden fence. A wooden gate can complement a brick wall. A rail gate can break a woven wire fence.

Another gate design consideration is how it will open and close. You may want a left or right swinging gate, one that opens in or out from the primary area, or a double door gate.

Chapter 12 is devoted entirely to building and installing gates. You may want to look ahead to this chapter for some ideas on how to plan the best gate for your fence.

## REVIEWING YOUR FENCE PLANS

Now that you've drawn your fence plans to scale, set them aside for awhile and take a look at other fences. This will either sell you on your plan or give you ideas for improving it.

You have probably noticed that whenever you get a new interest, it opens your eyes to its commonness. If you buy a Hotzinger automobile because you want to be unique, you'll probably see four of them driving home from the dealer. You may take up coin collecting and learn that, to your surprise, half of your friends are numismatists. It's the same with fences. As you seriously consider planning and building a fence, your eyes will be open to hundreds of fences you never even noticed.

Take advantage of this human condition by looking for fences and considering them as a solution to your fencing problems. You may have your heart set on a 6-foot board-on-board fence, but look at how other homeowners have used concrete walls, grape stake siding, and even chain link fencing to achieve the same purposes. Your study of other fences will help you refine your own fence plan and give you design ideas that can improve the

Fig. 2-17. An angled slat fence can offer visual privacy while allowing the entry of sun and wind (photo by Val Ramos).

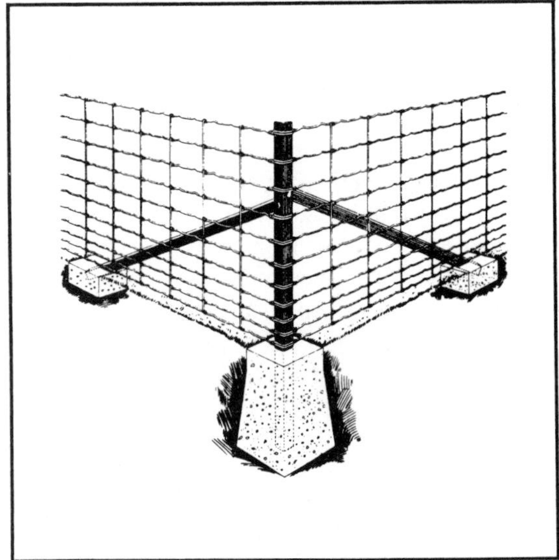

Fig. 2-18. Planning the corner of a wire fence is important to its longevity.

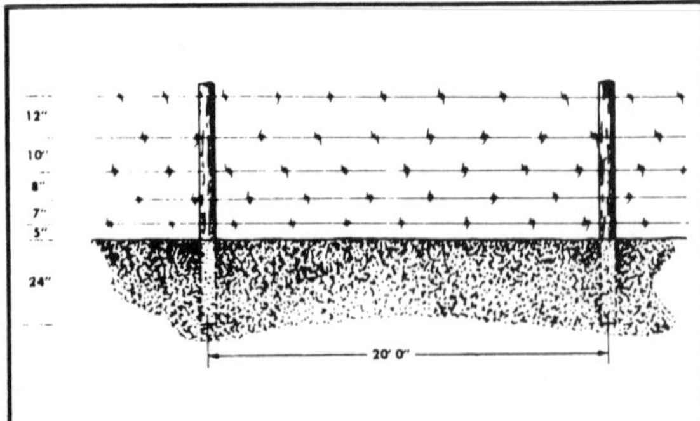


Fig. 2-19. Planning a barbed wire fence. This five-wire fence is primarily for sheep and medium-size livestock.

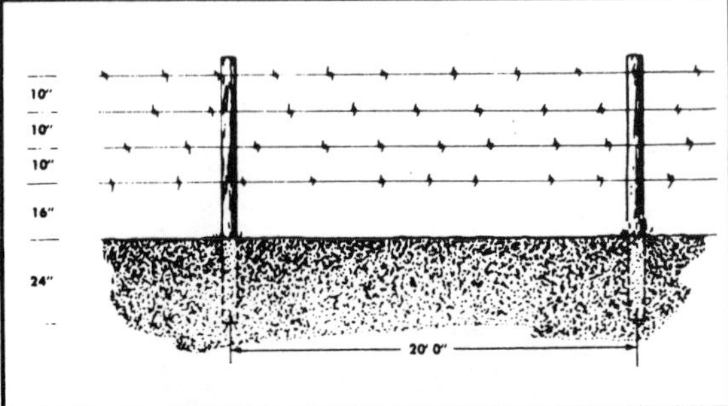


Fig. 2-20. This four-wire boundary fence is designed for cattle control.

value of your property or reduce construction costs.

Your fence may be a large investment, costing $500 or more to construct. If so, you may want to invest $20 to $30 in the services of a landscape architect before you settle on your "final" plan. The architect can review your plans and make design and construction suggestions that can increase your fence's efficiency and value. He or she may suggest that you replace a section of your solid concrete block fence with a decorative concrete block screen or colored concrete section. The landscape architect may be able to suggest unique picket designs or give you the address of a local home with a fence similar to the one you're constructing. If you're using a fence contractor, the architect may be able to give an opinion of his work or suggest an alternate contractor.

You can find professional help in building your fence through personal recommendations or list-ings in the Yellow Pages of the phone book under "Landscape Designers," "Landscape Architects," and "Architects." Get a fee quotation over the phone, then make an appointment with the one most experienced in designing fences. Make up two lists of questions: important and not as important. Cover the important ones first. If you still have time, get answers to the less important questions. Get your money's worth.

## SOLVING FENCE PROBLEMS

As you have designed and planned your fence, you may have run into problems that must be solved before you build: problems like going around a tree, descending a slope, edging a bank, making your fence curve, or crossing water. It's much cheaper to solve these problems on paper rather than in the field. Let's take them one at a time and see how other fence builders have turned a problem into a solution.

### Trees

Fence layout can be complicated by one or more trees growing right on the proposed fence line. If the tree is small, it can be moved or removed. If it's large, you'll probably have to work around it. You can bring the fence right up to it and stop a couple inches short of the trunk, then begin the fence a couple inches on the other side. The tree becomes part of the fence. Don't place the last post so close to the tree that you injure the root system when you dig the posthole. The fence should also be designed so that its edge next to the tree can be remodeled occasionally to accommodate the growth of the tree trunk.

Fig. 2-21. Windscreens can be built as decorative objects (photo by Val Ramos).

Fig. 2-22. Windscreens can be functional, protecting an entryway from harsh sun and wind (photo by Val Ramos).

Don't use the tree as a fence post, if possible. It may be injured by nails and boards. The nails usually don't do any damage to the tree, but they do make holes in the outer skin of the trunk that permits disease and bacteria to enter. If too many nails are embedded in the bark or if wire mesh restricts growth, the tree's sap flow may be stopped, which can injure or kill the tree.

If you live in a high wind area, allow more space between the tree and adjoining fence. The wind will make the trunk sway and twist, possibly damaging the fence (Figs. 2-21 and 2-22).

### Slopes

A sloping hillside stops many fence builders.

Fig. 2-23. There are many ways to take a fence down a slope.

They think that hillside fencing is just too difficult to design and build. This is not true. The small amount of extra effort and planning it takes to run your fence down the slope will be compensated by the additional beauty and design it issues (Figs. 2-23 and 2-24).

There are two basic ways you can build a hillside fence: contoured or stepped. Some fences look better built one way rather than the other, so your choice may depend on the purpose and materials (Fig. 2-25). Loose fencing such as post and rail, picket, and chain link is often used as contour fencing. Solid boards are more commonly used as stepped fencing.

Less flexible are the more geometric forms such as solid board, plywood, fiberglass panel, louver, and basket weave. These can be canted to fit a hillside, but they require careful cutting and fitting (Fig. 2-26).

The first step in laying a fence along a slope is to figure how steep the rise is. There are many ways to do this, but the easiest may be to use a line level and a chalk line. Run the string from a stake at the high point in your fence line. Tie the string to the stake at ground level and stretch it to a tall stake at the lowest point. Draw the string taut, hang the line level on the center of the string, and shift the

Fig. 2-24. Careful planning and construction can result in a beautiful sloping fence (courtesy Weyerhaeuser Company).

Fig. 2-25. Typical slope fence (photo by Val Ramos).

Fig. 2-26. Combining sloping and level fences (photo by Val Ramos).

Fig. 2-27. A fence can be built above a ledge to control soil erosion and security (photo by Val Ramos).

string up or down on the tall stake as necessary until the bubble is centered. Then you can calculate the slope's drop by dividing the height of the string above the grade on the tall stake into the length of the line between the stakes.

To plan fence steps along the slope, simply divide the drop by the number of fence sections you have between the top and bottom of the slope. If your sloping sections of fencing cover 24 feet in a drop of 6 feet and you plan to build your fence in 8-foot sections, each section must drop 2 feet.

## Banks

Fences built along or to contain banks need some engineering because of the earth's natural stresses. It's best to have a landscape architect or engineer draw up the plans. The problem is that banks are unstable ground, subject to shifting and erosion (Fig. 2-27). Any structure built on a bank is subject to the same elements.

An engineer will suggest that footings and posts be installed deeper than normal to counter the erosion and shifting of earth around them (Figs. 2-28 and 2-29). Bank erosion can also be slowed down or stopped by planting ground covers that have thick root systems.

## Curves

If your fence plan calls for a curve, there are a couple ways to build. You can build the fence in a

Fig. 2-28. This fence is built on a concrete foundation to reduce soil movement (photo by Val Ramos).

Fig. 2-29. Short banks can be controlled with stone walls (photo by Val Ramos).

Fig. 2-30. A rail fence can easily make the turn (photo by Val Ramos).

ture arc or fudge and build in angled sections.

To plot a true arc curve, simply place a stake where the curve begins, one where it ends, and a pivot stake at a 90-degree angle from the point halfway between the two end stakes. Tie a string to the pivot stake. Run the other end out to one of the end stakes and attach a pointed stick. Make sure that the pivot stake is the same distance from the other stake. Finally, use the pointed stick to scribe a line on the ground in an arc between each end stake. That's your curved fence line.

You can set posts and rails along this line and make the curve in short angles or use a pliable fence siding such as thin hardboard or basket weave to make a true curve (Fig. 2-30).

## Water

Sometimes a fence, especially a livestock fence, must cross standing or running water. This can present a problem for the fencer builder, but not one that can't be overcome.

When fences cross ditches, streams, or dry washes that flood in winter, the problem is that the fence must serve its primary purpose of security or control without creating a barrier that can become choked with debris and cause a flood. One solution is to install a *floodgate*. It is a simple, rugged device that opens automatically at flood stage. It pivots on posts at each side of the stream and swings upward as the water rises. Floodgates can also be slung on cables. See Chapter 8.

## Chapter 3

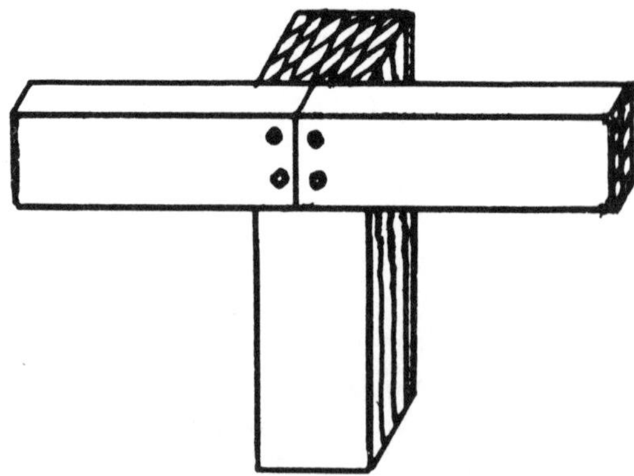

# Building Your Fence

THOUSANDS OF MILES OF FENCE ARE BUILT each year by people who have never before driven a nail, dug a posthole, or set a block. The required skills are easy to learn and apply.

You may decide to build your own fence or have an experienced contractor do it. In either case you should talk with a contractor who can give you an estimate of costs and possibly some pointers.

Consider the tools you'll need to build your fence: basic building tools, tools for working the ground, woodworking tools, tools for metal and wire, and concrete-masonry tools (Fig. 3-1).

You also need to know how to select and buy fencing materials: lumber, boards, chain link fabric and posts, woven wire, brick, stone, concrete, nails, and other supplies (Figs. 3-2 through 3-6). You'll also need to know the basics of fence construction: how to locate your fence, dig holes and set posts, run rails and stringers, attach siding, and preserve and coat your fence.

## CHOOSING A CONTRACTOR

Price must be an important consideration in choosing a fence contractor,but there are shysters in every industry. You want to be sure that the contractor you select can and will deliver and, just as important, that he will be around later to back up his promises. There are things to consider when selecting a reliable fence contractor.

### Advertising

Watch out for claims of unbelievable discounts. It may be a setup for the "bait-and-switch" routine where you'll hear, "Sorry, we're all out of that, but let me show you this." Read the small print in the ad. You may get the discount on the material, then find yourself paying an inflated price for labor or other items necessary to build the fence.

There is no such thing as "something for nothing." Business can't continue to exist without profits. The reputable contractor deserves a reasonable profit. He can't stay reputable without it.

### Salesperson

Ask for and check the information on his busi-

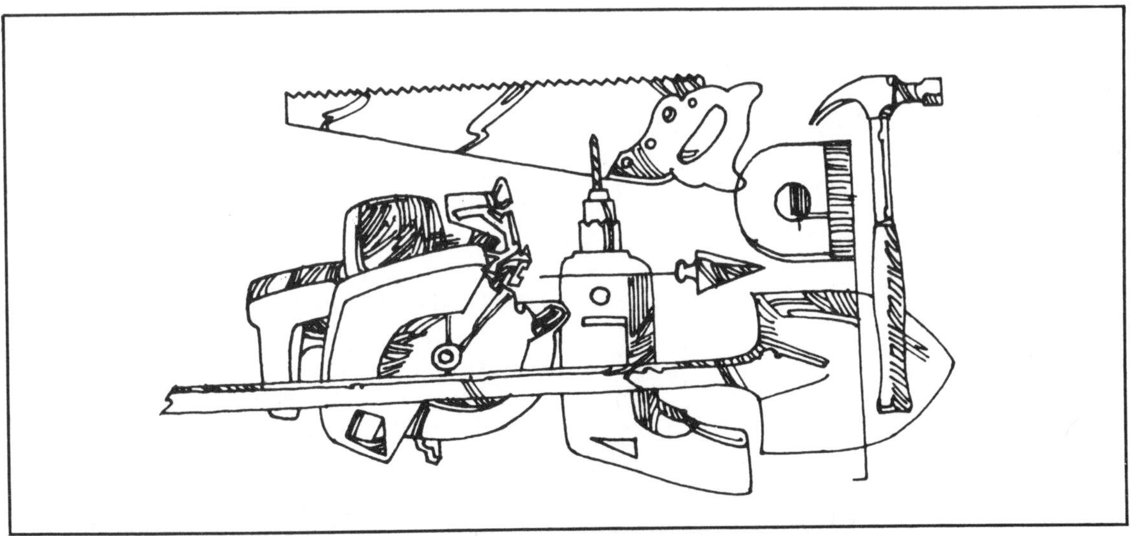

Fig. 3-1. Basic wood fence building tools (courtesy Wolmanized pressure-treated lumber).

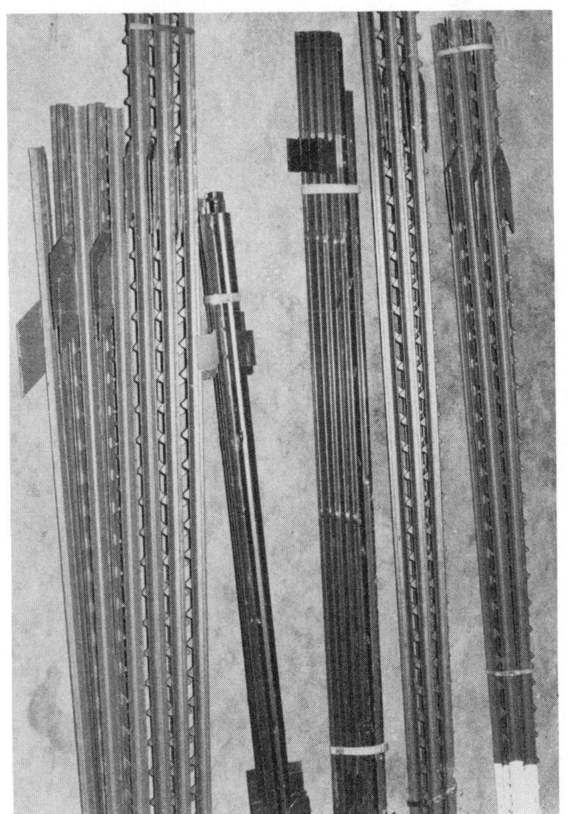

Fig. 3-2. Common steel fence posts for wire fences (photo by Val Ramos).

Fig. 3-3. Posts for chain link fences (photo by Val Ramos).

Fig. 3-4. A wide variety of wire fence fabrics is available (photo by Val Ramos).

ness card. Check out his firm's reputation with the Chamber of Commerce or Better Business Bureau. A long-time operator will honor his guarantees. Beware if a firm's name has been changed several times.

Ask about other fences his firm may have installed nearby and for addresses of satisfied customers. Request samples of materials to be used. Ask for the names of suppliers, banks, credit references, and professional business associations.

Be wary of an estimate over the telephone or one by a salesman who doesn't personally inspect and measure the job. Fear tactics, price threats, knocking competitors, and sudden large price cuts are practices that may well arouse your suspicions.

## Contract

Get everything in writing. Most reputable firms use a printed estimate form that gives all the details of the contract and often serves as a contract when signed by both parties.

First, don't settle for a mere mention of dimensions on the contract. Get all the specifications—the number and size of gates, the gauge or quality of materials to be used, heights, maximum post spacings, number of gate and corner posts, size and depth of postholes, whether concrete or other stabilizing materials will be used, and whether the fence will be level or will follow the contour of the yard.

You may want to ask for a copy of published industry standards to give you some basis for com-

Fig. 3-5. Square fence posts with brackets already attached (photo by Val Ramos).

Fig. 3-6. Four-foot chain link fence fabric (photo by Val Ramos).

parison. When comparing price, be sure the specifications are also comparable.

The contract should state who (you or the contractor) is responsible for clearing the fence line before the job and who will clean up afterwards. It should also state who will pay for any locally required permits.

If local and state licensing is required, has the contractor complied? If not, he may be lacking legally in the area of adequate insurance. You could be liable.

The contract should state the starting and completion date, even though weather and other things may cause understandable delays.

The contractor is obligated to advise you of your rights. You generally have three days to change your mind, and this should be in the contract.

Warranties and guarantees may be important to you. If so, ask for them in writing.

### Deciding

Compare every aspect of the estimates and contracts. Look at one or more fences that each competitive firm has installed.

It all comes down to your own confidence in the firm based on the information you have in hand. Even if you decide to have the contractor build your fence, you should understand the facts in this book on how and why fences are built to get your money's worth.

## DECIDING TO DO IT YOURSELF

You may decide to build your own fence. Finances may rule out the hiring of a contractor, or perhaps you simply have the urge to create and build it yourself.

If you have a feeling for tools and a capacity for doing reasonably careful work, you should be able to erect a fence that's as sturdy and attractive as any professional job. Fence building is not one of the most difficult skills to learn. Materials are easy to obtain. Standard lumber can be used to build many types of fences. Masonry work is simple to learn.

The only really tough part of building a fence is digging the postholes and setting the posts so they are firmly embedded and precisely aligned. You can solve this problem by renting a posthole digger or hiring a young worker who enjoys exercise. Your helper may even be available for "Tom Sawyer" work once the fence is up.

To decide whether it's worth your while to build your fence, make an estimate of costs and compare it with an estimate from a contractor. Here's how you make a do-it-yourself cost estimate:

■ **Lumber.** Using your fence plan, count up the number of posts, rails, and pieces of siding you'll need and their size. Make sure the posts are long enough. Then add 10 percent to your total to allow for waste and error.

■ **Hardware.** Fencing hardware includes

gate hinges and latches, stringer brackets, fasteners, screws, bolts, and nails (Figs. 3-7 through 3-9).

■ **Masonry.** Estimate the number of blocks, bricks, or stones you'll need for your fence or wall, along with the size and grade.

■ **Concrete.** Posthole concrete requirements depend on the width and depth of the hole. Estimate two tight 2-foot-deep holes per 90-pound bag of ready-mix—one loose 3-foot-deep hole per bag.

■ **Stain.** Estimate square footage of coverage, then check against the coverage table on the can.

To order your fencing materials, find the dealer with the lowest overall prices and purchase them through him. Larger orders often earn discounts of 10 percent or more, or credit is given towards related materials: tools, paints, and hardware. Cash also earns a discount with some dealers. Don't be afraid to ask for a discount; it could mean a savings of $50 or more.

Fig. 3-7. "Hangers" or brackets for attaching 2 × 4 rails to wood fence posts (photo by Val Ramos).

Fig. 3-8. Square steel post with premounted brackets (photo by Val Ramos).

## BASIC TOOLS

A *carpenter's level* should be at least 24 inches long and contain three vials, so it can be used to check both horizontal and vertical planes. Some have a special vial on one end intended for checking 45-degree angles and slopes (Fig. 3-10).

*Chalk line* is 50 to 100 feet of strong string encased with a quantity of chalk dust (Fig. 3-11). Stretch the string tightly between two points, then snap it. The chalk on the string marks the line. Better ones are refillable with chalk dust and do double duty as a *plumb bob* which is useful for making vertical lines.

A *combination square* is used to check corners and cuts for squareness and lay out lines for 45-

Fig. 3-9. Corner posts must have brackets on adjoining sides (photo by Val Ramos).

degree cuts. Use it as a depth gauge and as a bench rule.

*Flexible tapes* are useful. Both a short (6 to 12 feet) and long (50 to 100 feet) tape should be in your toolbox. They come in different widths. A ¾-inch tape is a good choice, even though it's bulkier than others. It has the rigidity to span openings without buckling. Better tapes have locks. Longer tapes should be thinner and more pliable.

*Screwdrivers* should include both straight tip and Phillips-head in many sizes.

A *claw hammer* is an important tool to the wood fence builder for driving and pulling nails. The striking surface should be slightly convex (ball-faced) and allow you to drive a nail flush without damage to adjacent surfaces. The handle may be hardwood or rubber-sheathed fiberglass or steel. Some prefer wood because it doesn't get cold to the touch in inclement weather. Others prefer steel because the head is more securely attached.

A *crosscut saw* has small teeth with knifelike points. The saw is designed for cutting across the grain of lumber, but it's also good for sawing all types of plywood. A saw that's "taper ground," which usually indicates a quality product, has 8 or 10 teeth per inch and is 26 inches long.

A *keyhole saw* has a narrow blade that tapers to a small point. The saw is useful for sawing curved lines. A single handle with three different blades is often available as a *nest of saws*, one of which can be used to saw metal.

*Backsaws* have teeth like a crosscut saw and a

Fig. 3-10. Check for square every few boards (photo by Val Ramos).

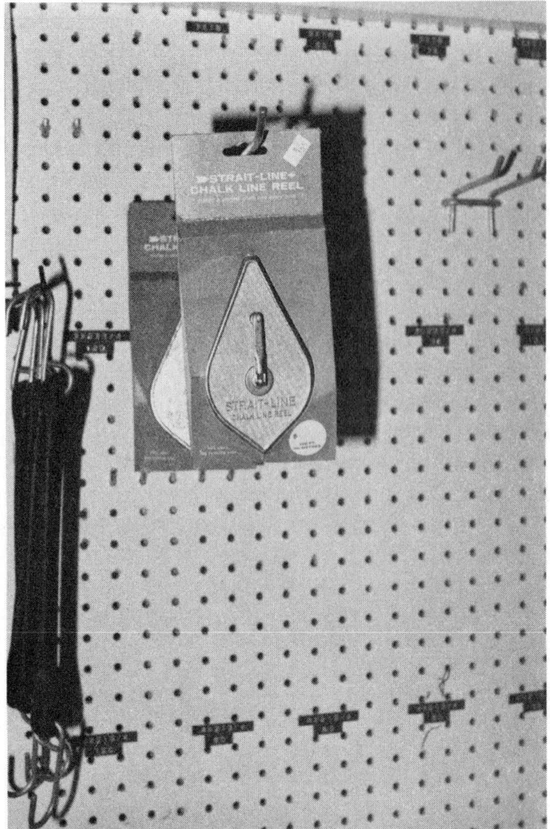


Fig. 3-11. Chalk line for marking a fence line or cutting fence tops (photo by Val Ramos).

rectangular blade that is stiffened with a length of steel or brass along its top edge. A backsaw is for more precise work than can be accomplished with other saws, such as making plywood cutouts as fence decorations.

*Hand drills* look and work like eggbeaters. With a set of bits or "points," they can be used to drill pilot holes for screws or other uses.

*Brace and bits* are for making holes larger than those possible with a hand drill. The brace is essentially U-shaped, with a chunk at one end and a flat, knob-type handle at the other. Bits range in size from ¼ to 1 inch, but there are adjustable *expansive bits* that allow the forming of holes as large as 3 inches. Bits used in a brace have screw points so they draw themselves into the wood as they turn.

*Slip-joint pliers* are made of drop-forged steel and are 8 inches long. They are called slip-joint because the jaws can be adjusted to grip objects of various sizes. They're excellent for general-purpose gripping, bending, and even occasional nail pulling. Good ones have a nice pivot action and include a short, sharp section in each jaw so the tool can be used to cut wire.

*Clamshell diggers* are two-handled shovels used for digging postholes. With this tool the fence builder plunges the blades into the soil and chews his way out by working the handles back and forth. It's difficult to use for digging holes deeper than 2 feet because the sidewalls interfere with the spreading of the handles.

*Augers* dig holes with a circular motion. There are two types of augers. One uses a screw blade and operates as a twist drill. The other has cutting blades combined with a scoop arrangement that holds the loose soil as it is bored out. Either type is best used in rock-free ground.

*Circular saws* are often called "cutoff" saws and are used for crosscutting, ripping, beveling, mitering, and other routine operations that are done much faster with circular saws than handsaws. Capacity is often judged in terms of blade diameter. Generally, the larger the blade, the heavier and more expensive the tool will be. Replacement blades will also cost more. Common blades are: *combination blade*, good for both crosscutting and ripping lumber; *plywood blade* for cutting plywood; *hollow ground blade*, which leaves a smooth edge on both lumber and plywood; and *crosscutting* and *rip blades*.

A *fence stretcher* is a block-and-tackle arrangement that pulls the wire or chain link fabric tight between posts so that it can be secured (Fig. 3-12).

*Cutting pliers* are used to cut wire both off the roll and once it is stretched. Heavy-duty cutting pliers are safest.

When building masonry walls and fences, a *concrete mixer* is used for larger jobs to mix concrete for walls, footings, or other structures. Mixers come in all sizes. Most can be rented.

*Concrete shovels* are used to mix the ingredients. You can buy or rent a concrete shovel, or

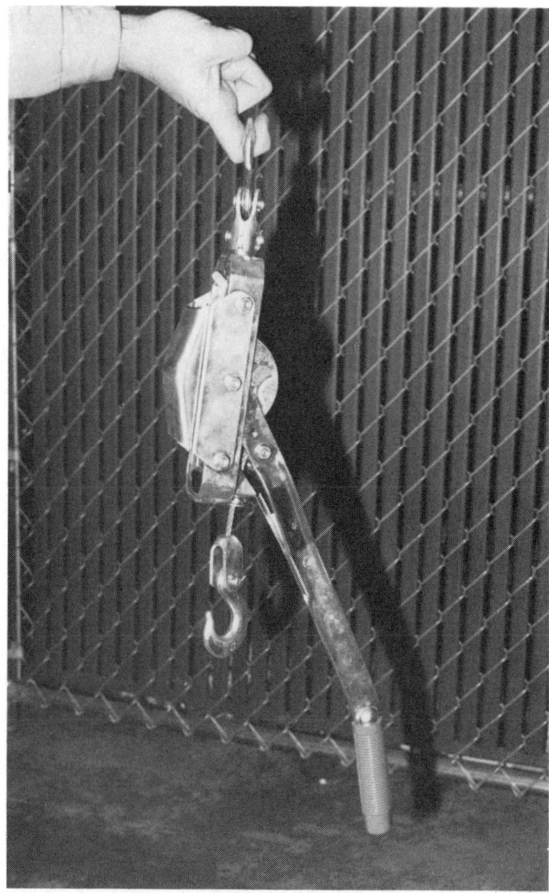

Fig. 3-12. Chain link fence fabric stretcher (photo by Val Ramos).

you can make one by straightening out a garden hoe or spade.

*Wheelbarrows* are useful. Rubber-tired metal wheelbarrows used for concrete work have a high body in the front to prevent spillage when the handles are lifted. Wheelbarrows used in the garden can be sufficient.

*Concrete working tools* include tampers, floats, groovers, edgers, trowels, pails, and hoses.

## SELECTING MATERIALS

Most fences are all or at least partially of wood. Knowing something about wood and related materials can save you time and money and make your fence more attractive (Figs. 3-13 and 3-14).

Wood is either hard or soft, a designation which has nothing to do with the actual density of the wood itself. These are botanical terms which indicate that the wood has come from either a broad-leafed deciduous tree (*hardwood*) or a cone-bearing or evergreen tree (*softwood*). Some popular hardwoods are birch, maple, walnut, mahogany, and oak. Common softwoods include pine, fir, redwood, and cedar. Nearly all wood fences are made of softwoods (Table 3-1).

Basic fences can be built from logs and saplings cut on the site, but most fence builders rely on dressed lumber and prefabricated fencing sold in most lumberyards. Fence kits usually include all the materials you need for the complete installation down to the nails. The kit includes fence posts that have been treated, cut to the proper length, notched

Fig. 3-13. Choosing your fence materials (photo by Val Ramos).

Fig. 3-14. Hand-selecting materials take more time, but it can pay off in a better fence (photo by Val Ramos).

or mortised as necessary to accommodate rails, the rails themselves, shaped pickets, woven wire, or other fence siding. A fence kit saves you from estimating, ordering, and cutting the lumber to fit your plans. The cost of a fence kit may be higher or lower than the individual materials depending on labor involved and local competition for business.

## Sizing Lumber

Familiar terms like 2×4 and 1×8 are used to designate different sizes of lumber as *nominal* sizing rather than actual sizing (Table 3-2). A 2×4 is actually 1½ by 3½ inches. All western woods and other softwood lumber that move from mills to building sites are ordered by these nominal sizes. Widths and thicknesses are slimmer than nominal. Most slimming down occurs in the drying out process and in planing or finishing. These sizes for seasoned lumber are uniform throughout the country (Table 3-3).

## Grading Lumber

Whether the lumber is purchased in a fence kit or direct from the lumber dealer, it should conform to certain standards.

Construction lumber is sold in a variety of grades. The best quality is smoothly finished and generally free of knots and blemishes. Unless the appearance of the wood itself is vital to the fence design, there is nothing to be gained by buying the topmost grades at what may be three times the price you would pay for lesser grades that are satisfactory for fence construction. Knots and other defects that make lumber unsuitable for finishing work do not interfere with the usefulness of a fence, especially if the surface is painted or otherwise covered.

**Table 3-1. Common Woods and Their Uses.**

| Species | Properties | Outdoor uses |
|---|---|---|
| Cedar | natural resistance to decay<br>not resistant to insects<br>resists shrinking, swelling, warping<br>easy to work with | decks<br>walks<br>fencing |
| Cypress | natural resistance to decay<br>natural resistance to insects<br>strong; finishes well<br>easy to work with | decks |
| Fir<br>Pine<br>Spruce | not resistant to insects<br>low resistance to decay<br>strong; finishes well<br>easy to work with<br>does not weather well without a sealer | decks<br>fencing |
| Hemlock | low resistance to decay<br>not resistant to insects<br>lightweight; uniform grain<br>easy to work with | decks |
| Redwood | natural resistance to decay<br>natural resistance to insects<br>easy to work with; finishes well<br>weathers well | decks<br>fencing<br>furniture |

Table 3-2. Lumber Scale: Board Feet per Timber.

| Length of Timber | 8 | 10 | 12 | 14 | 16 | 18 | 20 | 22 | 24 |
|---|---|---|---|---|---|---|---|---|---|
| 1×4 | 2 2/3 | 3 1/3 | 4 | 4 2/3 | 5 1/3 | — | — | — | — |
| 1×6 | 4 | 5 | 6 | 7 | 8 | — | — | — | — |
| 1×8 | 5 1/3 | 6 2/3 | 8 | 9 1/3 | 10 2/3 | — | — | — | — |
| 2×4 | 5 1/3 | 6 2/3 | 8 | 9 1/3 | 10 2/3 | 12 | 13 1/3 | — | — |
| 2×6 | 8 | 10 | 12 | 14 | 16 | 18 | 20 | — | — |
| 2×8 | 10 2/3 | 13 1/3 | 16 | 18 2/3 | 21 1/3 | 24 | 26 2/3 | — | — |
| 2×10 | 13 1/3 | 16 2/3 | 20 | 23 1/3 | 26 1/3 | 30 | 33 1/3 | — | — |
| 2×12 | 16 | 20 | 24 | 28 | 32 | 36 | 40 | | |
| 4×4 | 10 2/3 | 13 1/3 | 16 | 18 2/3 | 21 1/3 | 24 | 26 2/3 | — | — |
| 4×6 | 16 | 20 | 24 | 28 | 32 | 36 | 40 | — | — |
| 6×6 | 24 | 30 | 36 | 42 | 48 | 54 | 60 | 66 | 72 |

The function of lumber grade is to provide identification so that the user can purchase wood for the use intended. The official grading agency mark on a piece of lumber is assurance of its assigned grade. Grading practices of these agencies' member mills are supervised to assure uniformity. Figure 3-15 is a typical grade stamp. Here's how it's read:

—A is the mark for the Western Wood Products Association (WWPA), the grading agency whose standards are used on this lumber.
—B is the mill number; each mill is assigned a permanent number for grade stamp purposes.

Table 3-3. Nominal and Dry Sizes for Seasoned Lumber.

| Nominal Size (inches) | Actual Dry Size (inches) |
|---|---|
| 1 × 2 | ¾ × 1 ½ |
| 1 × 4 | ¾ × 3 ½ |
| 1 × 6 | ¾ × 5 ½ |
| 1 × 10 | ¾ × 9 ¼ |
| 1 × 12 | ¾ × 11 ¼ |
| 2 × 4 | 1 ½ × 3 ½ |
| 2 × 6 | 1 ½ × 5 ½ |
| 2 × 10 | 1 ½ × 9 ¼ |
| 2 × 12 | 1 ½ × 11 ¼ |
| 3 × 6 | 2 ½ × 5 ½ |
| 4 × 4 | 3 ½ × 3 ½ |
| 4 × 6 | 3 ½ × 5 ½ |

—C is an example of an official grade name abbreviation. The official grade name, as defined by the association, gives positive identification to the grade of lumber.
—D identifies the wood species.
—E denotes moisture content of lumber when unseasoned or "green" lumber.

You'll find other grading and wood association marks on wood. Figure 3-16 is a grade stamp for the American Wood Preservers Bureau. "LP-22" means the wood is treated to a minimum retention of .40 pounds per cubic foot and can be used in ground contact. LP-22 is recommended for all outdoor home projects.

Figure 3-17 illustrates the redwood grade marks of the California Redwood Association. "Clear All Heart" is the finest grade of redwood and is used for siding, paneling, and cabinets. "Clear" is nearly as good, but it includes some cream-colored sapwood. "Construction Heart" is general purpose redwood where clearness (freedom from knots) is not a prime factor. "Construction Common" is similar to Construction Heart except that it contains sapwood. "Merchantable" has loose knots. Other redwood grades include "Select Heart" and "Select."

## Buying Lumber

The success of your fence begins with using

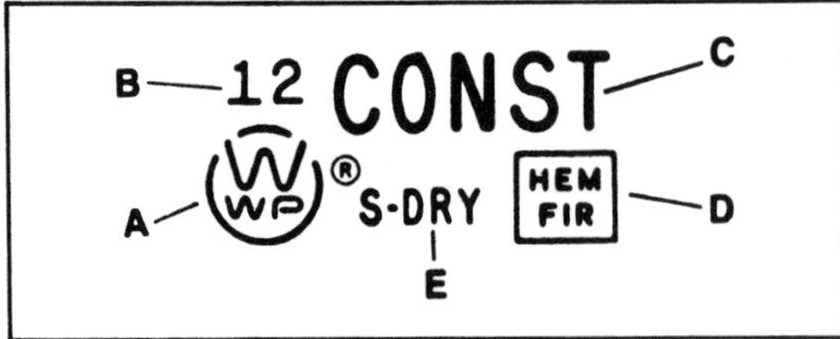


Fig. 3-15. Grade stamp (courtesy Georgia-Pacific Corp.).

Fig. 3-16. Grade stamp for pressure-treated wood (courtesy Western Wood Products Association).

Fig. 3-17. Redwood grade stamp (courtesy California Redwood Association).

the right lumber grade for the purpose. With the infinite variety of grain color and natural characteristics, wood affords its own uniqueness.

Most building supply home improvement retailers feature extensive lumber departments. In some centers lumber is stored or packaged for specific uses in small units for customer convenience. You will often find fencing materials displayed together.

As you plan your fence, remember the best ways to prevent overspending for lumber are to know how much you need and to buy the lowest grade of lumber that will do the job.

Boards are graded by "Common"—No. 1 Common, No. 2 Common, and No. 3 Common. The No. 1 has tight knots and is the best. The No. 3 has coarse knots and even knotholes, but it can still be used for fencing.

Dimension lumber is graded "Construction," "Standard," or "Utility" for light framing, "Stud" grade for studs in walls, and "Select" and "Structural" for higher strength (Table 3-4).

Some varieties of wood are better suited to fence building because they are naturally decay-resistant. Lumber cut from the heart of redwood, cedar, or cypress trees is strongly rot-resistant. Lumber cut from areas close to the bark of these trees will rot almost as quickly as lumber from more decay-susceptible woods like pine and fir.

Although entire fences are commonly built of decay-resistant wood, the main need for this immunity is in the posts, which are vulnerable to attack by fungi and wood-destroying insects. Other parts of the fence such as the rails, pickets, and boards are exposed to sunlight and air. They do not succumb as easily to decay. Many fence builders use heartwood for the posts and sapwood for the rest of the fence. Redwood or cedar posts and pine and fir stringers and boards are also used.

It's not always possible to find enough redwood, cedar, or cypress for your fence at a reason-

**Table 3-4. Dimensional Lumber Grades.**

| Material | Grades | Comments |
|---|---|---|
| Boards (commons) Siding, Paneling, Shelving, Sheathing, and Form Lumber | No. 1 Common No. 2 Common No. 3 Common | No. 1 Common boards are the ultimate in small-knot material for appearance uses, but less expensive No. 2 and No. 3 Commons are most often used in housing for paneling, siding and shelving. Boards are generally available at building material dealers in 1x2 through 1x12. |
| Light Framing | Construction Standard Utility | This category is for use where high strength values are not required such as studs, plates, sills, cripples, blocking, etc. |
| Studs | Stud | A popular grade for load and non-load-bearing walls. Limited to 10 ft. and shorter. |
| Structural Light Framing Joists and Planks | Select Structural No. 1 No. 2 No. 3 | These grades fit engineering applications where higher strength is needed, for uses such as trusses, joists, rafters and general framing. |

Fig. 3-18. Corner post and gateposts (photo by Val Ramos).

able cost. The alternative is to either treat wood with a preservative before installation or purchase pressure-treated wood that can last up to 20 years.

Here are some hints on buying lumber for your fence.

*Posts* should be 2 to 2½ feet longer than the height of the fence (Fig. 3-18). A 6-foot fence will require 8 to 8½-foot posts (Fig. 3-19). High, solid board fences need extra long posts to permit a deeper foundation. You can figure the length as 40 percent longer than the height of the fence in these instances, with 25 to 30 percent for normal applications.

Round posts made from peeled logs should be slightly larger than squared posts. Use a peeled 6-inch diameter post in place of a 4×4.

*Stringers* should be attached to a post every 8 to 10 feet depending on the weight it will carry. You can use 2×4s as standard rails for board fences.

*Pickets* come in many sizes and styles. Standard thickness as 1-inch nominal (¾-inch actual), and width ranges from 2 to 6 inches nominal.

*Boards* are typically 1 inch (nominal) thick and 6 to 12 inches (nominal) wide (Fig. 3-20).

Information on choosing plywood and hardboard for fencing material is in Chapter 10.

## Nails

Nails are graded or made by size, type, and surface. Sizes are referred to in terms of "penny," written "d" such as in "8d" or "8 penny." The 2d nail is 1 inch long, and each succeeding two "d's" adds ½ inch to the length. An 8d nail is 2½ inches long (Figs. 3-21 and 3-22). The nail type means its purpose and design: "common" for most applications, "concrete," "shingle," etc., for special nailing jobs. The surface is the finish on the nail. *Bright* nails are cleaned and uncoated. *Galvanized* are zinc-coated. *Cement-coated* nails have an adhesive for increased

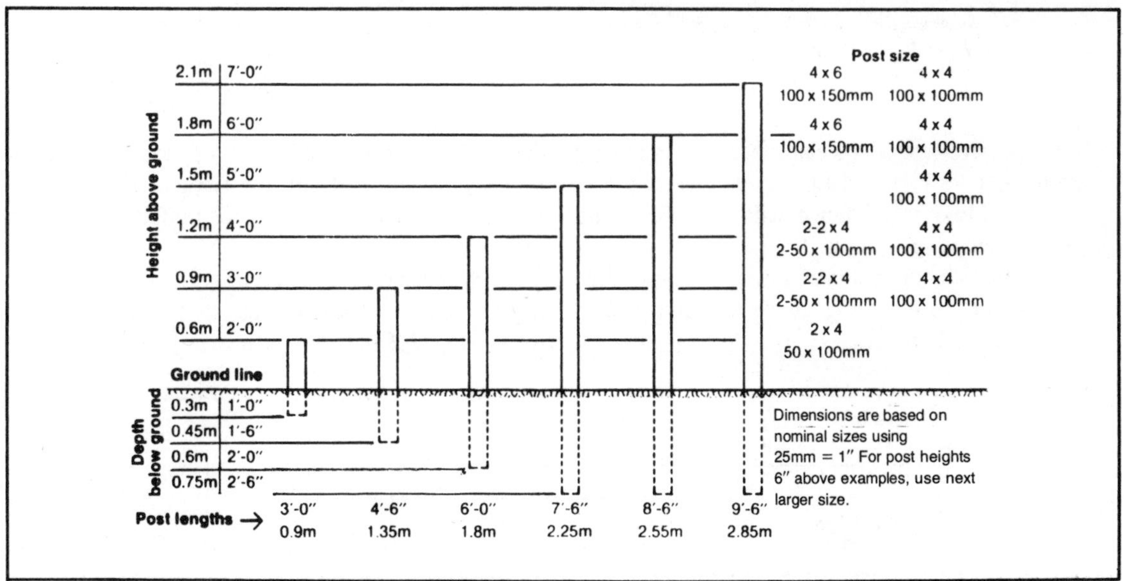


Fig. 3-19. Typical post size and embedment.

Fig. 3-20. Dog-eared fence boards (photo by Val Ramos).

holding power, and *blued* nails are sterilized by heating them until an oxidation layer, blue in color, is formed. Most wood fence nails are 6d or 8d galvanized common or box.

Information on selecting wire, chain link, brick, and concrete for your fence will be found in the appropriate chapters.

## BASIC FENCE CONSTRUCTION

There are five basic steps to building nearly all fences of whatever material.

- Locate the fence.
- Dig holes and set posts.
- Add rails or stringers.
- Install fence siding if appropriate.
- Coat and protect the fence.

Some fences will modify one or more of the steps, but they are all built around this system.

### Locating the Fence

The first thing you want to know is, "Where is this fence going to go?" You somehow want to mark it out on the ground, so it's both legal and straight. This is simple if you are building within your property, but it should be more precise if you're building a boundary fence as you may be building it for someone else.

If the original survey stakes are still in place, you can probably use them as boundary markers (Fig. 3-23). If you can't find them, you may want to invest in a survey or at least come to an agreement with adjoining neighbors as to where your common lines are.

To lay out the line you'll need a 50 to 100-foot tape, a carpenter's square, a ball of mason's twine or good string, a few stakes, a hatchet, and a piece of chalk for markings (Fig. 3-24).

Mark the corner or end points with a stake. Then run the string or mason's twine between the stakes, drawing it tight and tying it firmly to the stakes. Trim or go over any bushes or other obstructions.

Measure off the width of each section of fencing and place a stake. You can do this either with a measuring tape or by laying a stringer on the ground

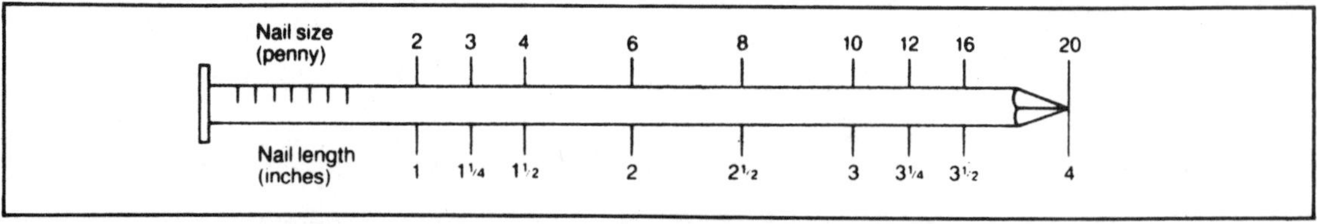


Fig. 3-21. Sizing nails (courtesy Wolmanized pressure-treated lumber).

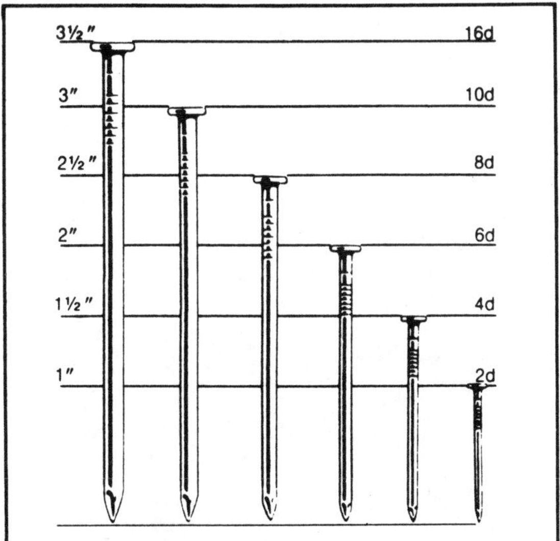


Fig. 3-22. Comparing common nail sizes (courtesy Georgia-Pacific Corp.).

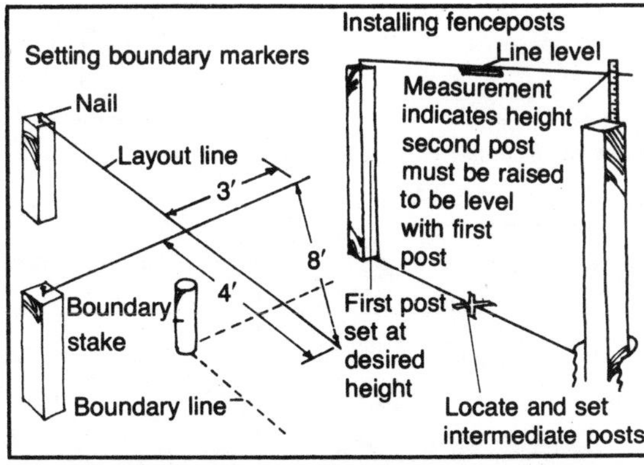


Fig. 3-23. How to set boundary markers and install fence posts (courtesy Wolmanized pressure-treated lumber).

under the fence line, placing a stake, then advancing the stringer again to mark the next stake (future post) position.

If you're building a long livestock fence, you can use a transit—bought, rented, or borrowed—to sight down your proposed fence line.

## Holes and Posts

Once your fence line is strung and the posthole sites are staked out, you're ready to start digging. The best size hole to dig depends on the kind of soil on which your fence is being built. The hole should be of a size that will give firm support to the post while permitting water to drain awav from around it (Figs. 3-25 through 3-28). In open, sandy soils make the hole only slightly bigger than the post. In heavy clay or adobe make the hole much larger and pack it with gravel. The gravel packing encourages water to drain away instead of remaining trapped around the post and allowing dry rot to begin (Figs. 3-29 and 3-30). If posts are to be set in concrete, dig the hole 2½ to 3 times the diameter of the post—about 10 by 10 inches for a 4×4 post.

Dig your holes with a posthole auger or clamshell digger as introduced earlier in this chapter. An auger won't be much good in rocky soil; a clamshell digger will work much better. A digging bar and a spoon-bladed shovel may be necessary in very rocky soil. If necessary, you can drill into the rock (star drill) and set a pin in the rock that will then be inserted into a drill shaft in the post. If the rock is shale, you can break it up with a sledge and pick.

The easiest way to make sure that your fence will follow a straight line is to set opposite corner posts first (Fig. 3-31). Set them permanently, then stretch a string or line between them and start setting intermediate posts. First, shovel 3 or 4 inches of gravel into the bottom of the posthole, tamp it down, then place the post on top of it. Fill in about a third of the hole with gravel, soil, or concrete. Tamp it down to hold the post upright, then true up the post with a carpenter's level or plumb bob before filling and packing the rest of the hole (Figs. 3-32 through 3-34).

## Rails or Stringers

Rails are the horizontal members of the fence running from post to post. There may be one, two, three, or more rails per section—usually two. Here's how they are installed (Figs. 3-35 through 3-39).

Set the top rail into position inside, outside, or within the frame. If within the frame, it's better to use a metal hanger for the stringer than to toenail it.

Set the middle and bottom stringers in the same way. Use a spirit level to keep the rails level. If descending a slope, the top rail can either be level

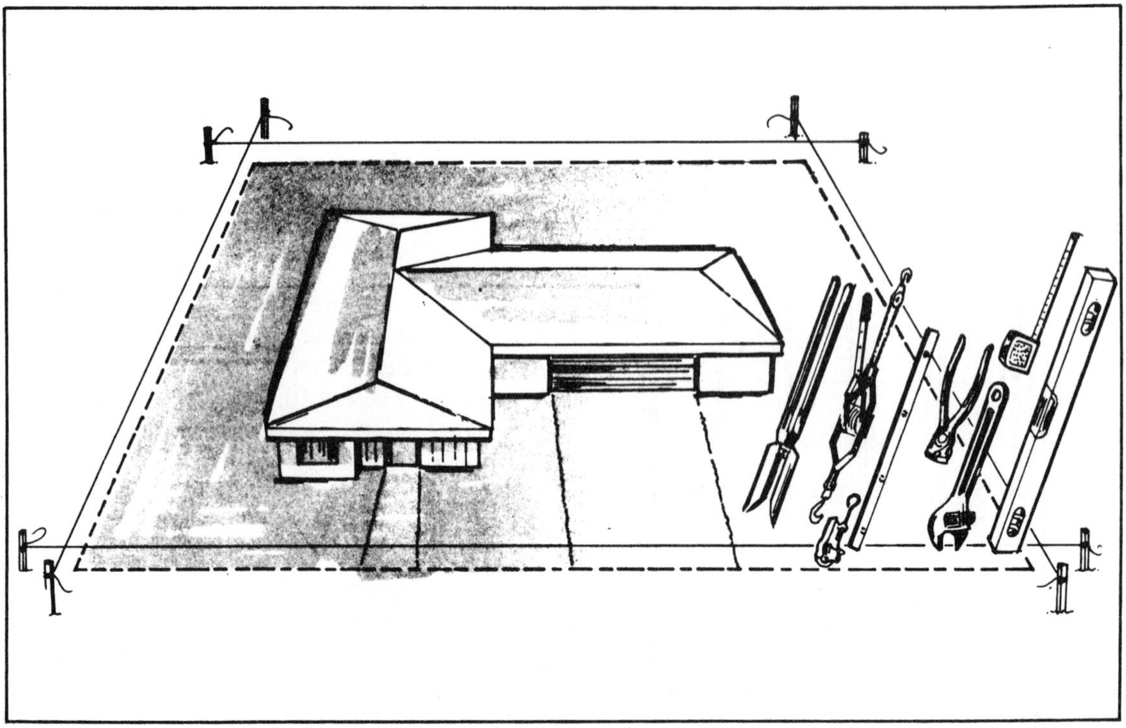

Fig. 3-24. Laying out the fence line and common chain link fence tools (courtesy Builders Fence Co., Inc.).

or descending, but the lower rail should generally follow the contour of the ground.

Post and rail fences may use larger dimensional lumber or split wood as rails—installed through the post or between a double post.

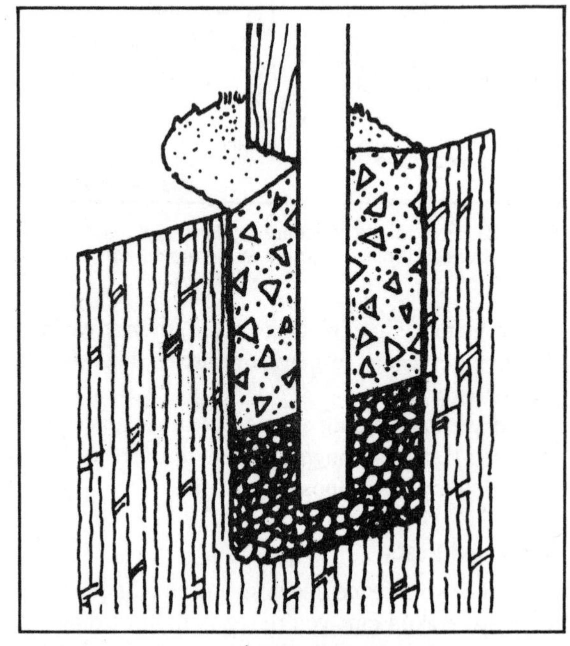
Fig. 3-25. Cement and gravel posthole.

## Siding

Siding is anything that's attached to the fence rails to cover the fence such as pickets, boards, laths, grape stakes, plywood, or other materials. Attaching siding is the easiest, yet most tedious job (Fig. 3-40).

If pickets, slats, or boards are to be attached with an opening between each, cut a slat to the exact width of the opening as a spacer. Nail a cleat to one end so that it can hang on the rail and butt the previous piece of siding. Then nail the next piece in place, shift the cleated spacer over one, and start again (Figs. 3-41 through 3-43).

A technique I've used to install siding is to nail

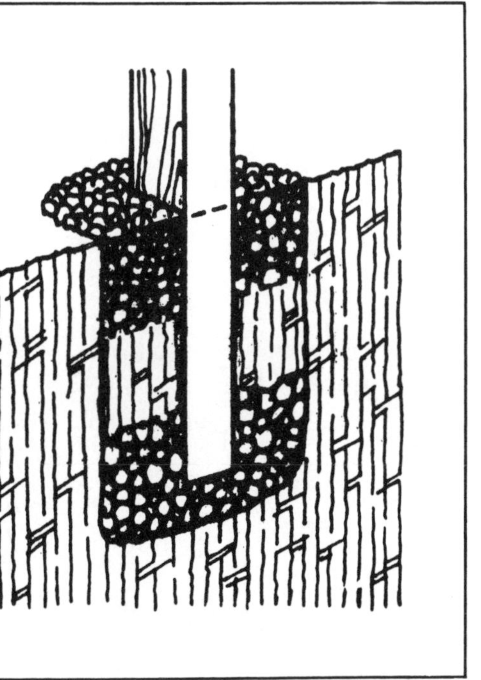

Fig. 3-26. Alternate gravel-cement-gravel posthole.

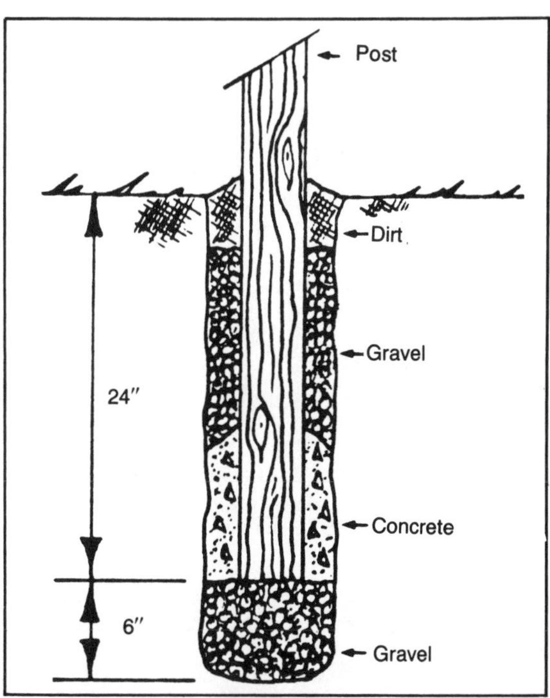


Fig. 3-28. Alternate posthole filling.

Fig. 3-27. Gravel and bracing posthole.

Fig. 3-29. Cement posthole fill must be crowned to keep water away from the wood (photo by Val Ramos).

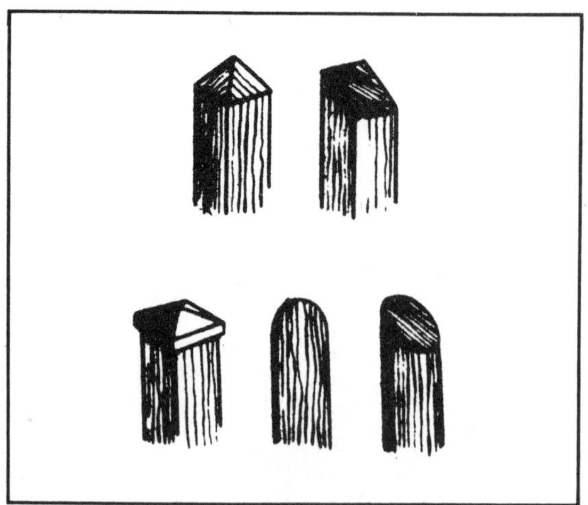

Fig. 3-30. Capping and angling posts will reduce rot due to water standing on the top of the post.

Fig. 3-32. Lighter steel posts don't need bracing to set up in concrete (photo by Val Ramos).

Fig. 3-31. Lining up the posts (photo by Val Ramos).

Fig. 3-33. Posts can be attached to cement foundations with steel plates (photo by Val Ramos).

Fig. 3-34. Note the steel post plate and the rail bracket (photo by Val Ramos).

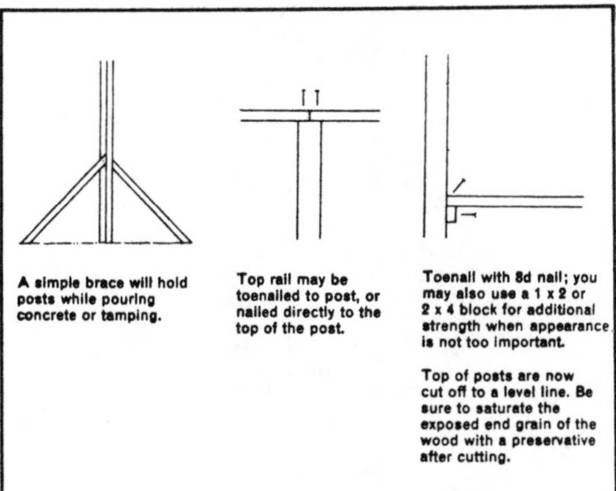


Fig. 3-35. Steps to installing the post and rails (courtesy Western Wood Products Association).

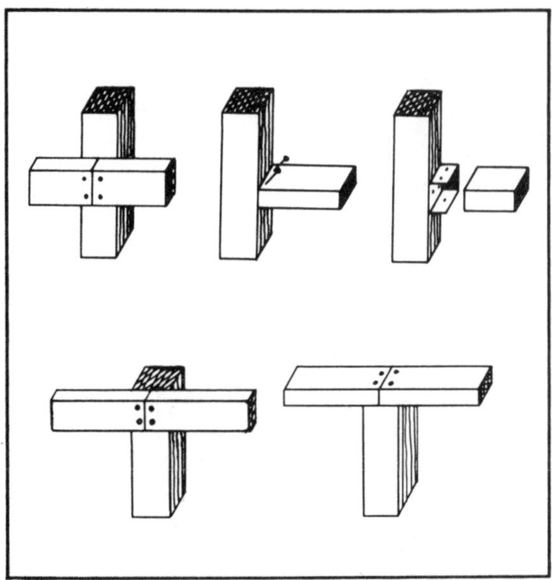

Fig. 3-36. Rails can be either lap-joined on outside of the post or toenailed or set in fence brackets. The top rail can be lap-joined on the side or butted on top of the post (courtesy Weyerhaeuser Co.).

a rail to the top of posts so that the boards butt up to it and against the previous board. Then the new board is nailed into place over the rails. To make this system go faster, have a helper place the boards. Drive a set nail, then finish nailing while the next board is placed into position. A section of fence goes up quickly this way.

## Coating

There are many ways of coating your fence. The reasons for doing so are to beautify and to protect.

Paints can both beautify and protect. Tell your paint dealer what you're planning to do, and he can recommend the right paint for the job. White is the traditional color for fences because it looks neat and clean—for awhile. Many fences are treated with stains for both protection and color. Some prefer only preservatives that allow the natural discoloration of the wood while protecting it. Common preservatives include penta, creosote, and copper sulfate. Fence coatings are commonly applied by

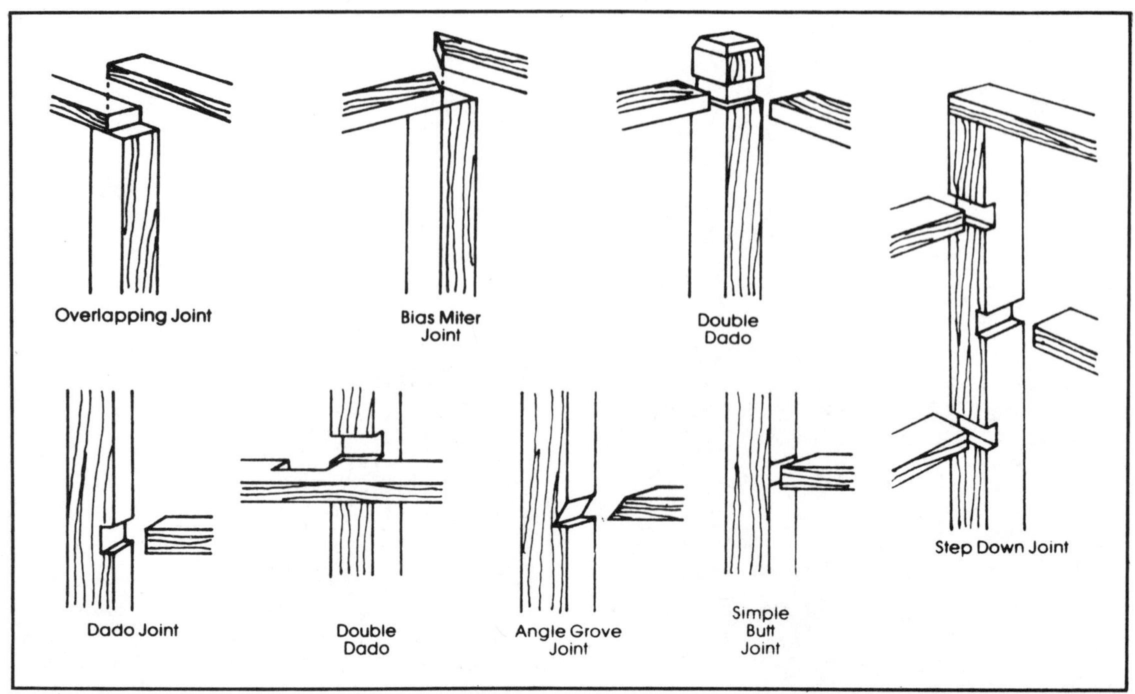


Fig. 3-37. Joining rails to posts.

Fig. 3-38. Attaching rails to posts with a rail bracket (photo by Val Ramos).

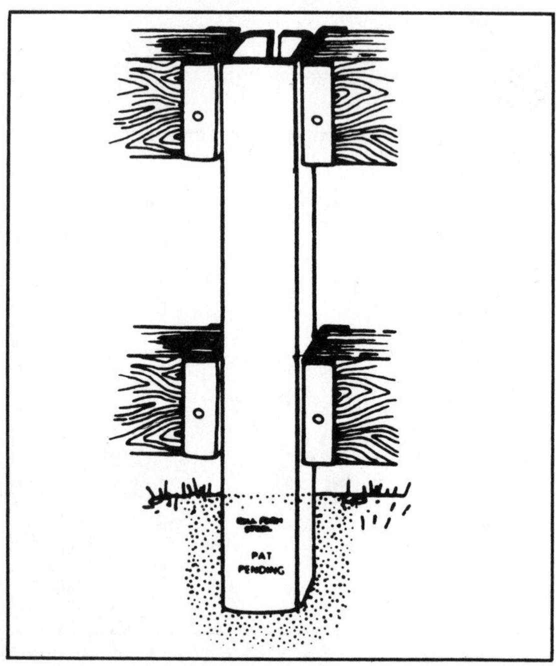


Fig. 3-39. Attaching rails to square steel posts with built-in brackets (courtesy Rollform, Inc.).

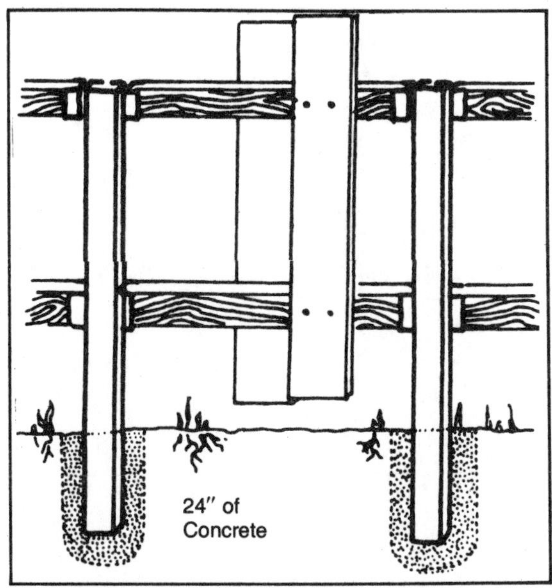


Fig. 3-40. Adding siding after rails are installed (courtesy Rollform, Inc.).

Fig. 3-42. Chain link fences can be beautified and made more opaque with plastic insert strips (photo by Val Ramos).

Fig. 3-41. When installing siding, butt the board to the top and check for square before nailing (photo by Val Ramos).

Fig. 3-43. Wood insert strips can also be used (photo by Val Ramos).

brush, roller, spray, or dipping. Information on coatings and application is given in Chapter 13.

Fences can be easy to build, even for the novice, with a knowledge of how to gather and use the correct tools, how to choose materials, and how to apply the five steps in fence construction.

# Chapter 4

# Rail Fences

RAIL FENCES ARE ABOUT THE EASIEST TO BUILD. Most are built with lower grade materials (Fig. 4-1). They require only basic tools and serve their purpose for many years.

Rail fences can be seen everywhere: around residences, parks, playgrounds, and businesses, as corrals, and as other farm animal fencing. Some clearly define property lines and keep larger animals in or out. Others are simply decorative. If a rail fence is properly built, of good material, on a clear, solid bed, and kept free from bushes and other growth, the rail fence is as cheap as any fence and often just as effective.

That's why the rail fence is often called a "pioneer fence." The fence is simple and inexpensive to build in areas where wood is plentiful. Some versions can be moved as new pasture fencing is needed.

The first rail fence was the picturesque zigzag, named for its shape. It was a by-product of the forest-clearing days when wood was plentiful and boundary lines were flexible enough to take a broad-gauge fence. As timber and land became more valuable, the kinks began to disappear from the zigzag fence, and it straightened itself out. As the market for timber increased, the fence shedded rails, eventually becoming the two- and three-rail fence of today.

The rails evolved from split wood to sawed lumber. Posts were added for a more efficient use of the wood.

The rail fence is more popular in rural settings. Its horizontal lines follow either rolling or flat terrain gracefully. The fence is economical in lumber usage, especially if it's built with wood at hand. It is also sturdy for holding larger animals.

There are some varieties of the rail fence that can easily be adapted to the suburban homesite. Light rail fences go best with ranch style homes, but they can improve the looks of any yard. The low post-and-board or split rail fence makes an excellent definition fence for the front yard. These fences discourage people from walking across the lawn or plants, but they don't block the view or shut off sunlight to plants. Rail fences are decorative, versatile, and easy to build.

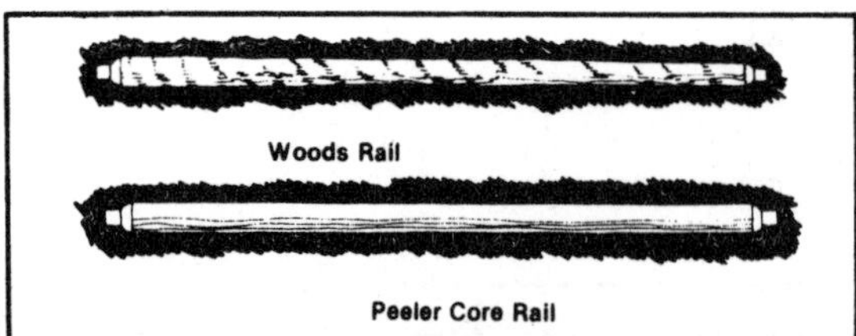


Fig. 4-1. Two types of rails available through lumberyards (courtesy Weyerhaeuser Co.).

## ZIGZAG FENCES

The *zigzag* rail fence is simplest to build, so let's start with it (Fig. 4-2). If you have a surplus of timber on your property or would like to create a rustic effect in your garden, you can install a zigzag fence with little effort.

The most common zigzag rail lengths are 6, 7, and 8 feet and about 6 inches thick. Smaller rails are 4 inches thick.

Traditionally, the rails of a zigzag fence simply overlap each other on the end. A rock or concrete block can be used under the overlapping point to keep the bottom rail off the ground. You can strengthen your fence by toenailing spikes into the rails, driving dowels or steel pins down through rails, or by setting posts with the rails.

Zigzag fences are an excellent landscape addition to a large garden. They can provide support for climbing vegetables such as beans and tomatoes.

## POST AND RAIL FENCES

The next logical step in the evolution of the fence is the *post and rail* fence (Figs. 4-3 through 4-8). Early posts and rails were made of small logs and split wood, but most of today's fences are built with dimensional lumber (Fig. 4-9). With such a variety of materials, the fence builder can create a barrier that is efficient, attractive, and easy to construct and maintain.

Posts are made of many styles and sizes of wood: rough-hewn, square dimensional, round peeled logs, and double posts. Their sizes range from 4 to 8 inches in diameter.

Posts can be set in dirt, gravel, concrete, or any combination of these materials. The depth is based on the height of the fence, the local frost line, and type of soil. The deeper the post, the better it generally is. Most rail fences have posts set 2 feet into the ground to provide support for the rails. Dig your hole deeper and set the post on gravel or a base stone to encourage drainage and prevent decay.

To align the posts, set the corner posts in place first. Put a little dirt or gravel around the post at a time, tamping it down so that water drains away from the post. If you're using concrete in the hole, finish it so the concrete slopes down from the post and the water drains away. Make sure the posts are plumb as you add hole material and compact it tightly. Let concrete cure a few days before you attach rails or, if you're filling the hole only with dirt and gravel, water and tamp the hole for a snug post (Fig. 4-10). If necessary, you can attach temporary supports to the posts.

Rails can be attached to the posts in many ways

Fig. 4-2. Zigzag fence (photo by Val Ramos).

Fig. 4-3. Post and rail fence (photo by Val Ramos).

Fig. 4-4. Another post and rail fence (courtesy Weyerhaeuser Co.).

Fig. 4-5. A post and rail fence can be used for beauty or some animal security (courtesy Weyerhaeuser Co.).

(Fig. 4-11). The easiest is to nail the rail directly to the post. You can also cut a notch or hole in the post—called a *mortise*—and insert the rail (Fig. 4-12). If the rail is also notched, it's called a mortise

Fig. 4-6. Post and rail fences are less expensive to build and maintain than most types (courtesy Weyerhaeuser Co.).

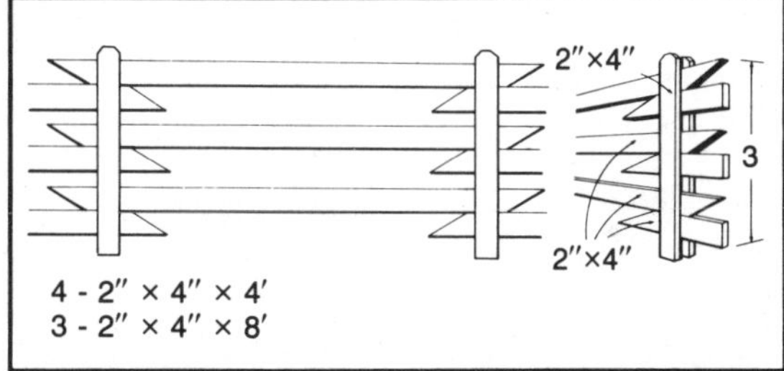

Fig. 4-7. Plans for a unique post and rail fence (courtesy Georgia-Pacific Corp.).

and tenon. You can build a double post system with rails between the posts and spacers to keep them separated. You can tie the rails to the post with baling wire. The methods are as diverse as the builders.

## POST AND BOARD FENCES

The *post and board* fence is the next step in the evolution of the rail fence (Figs. 4-13 and 4-14). It's similar in style and construction to the post and rail, but it uses the more efficient and more readily available dimensional lumber.

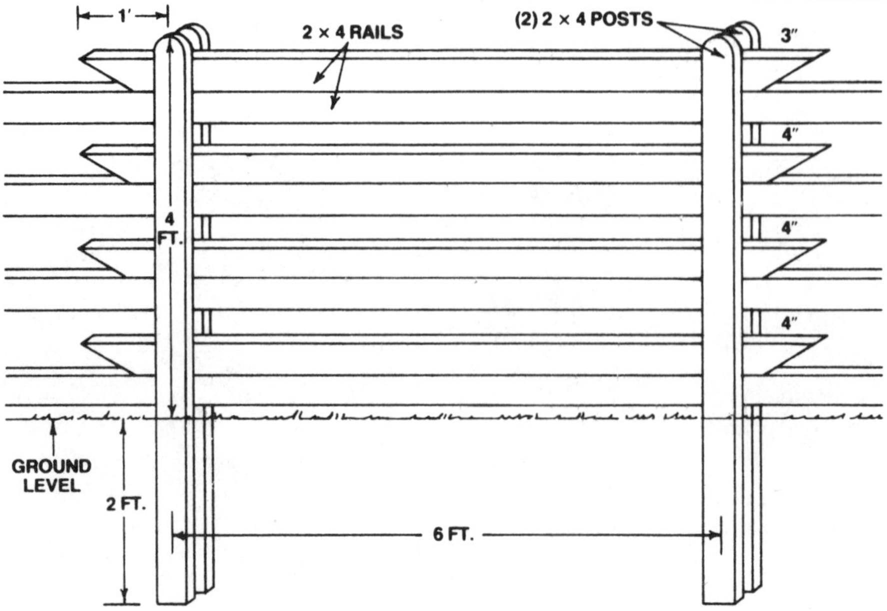

1'
2 × 4 RAILS
(2) 2 × 4 POSTS
3"
4"
4"
4"
4 FT.
GROUND LEVEL
2 FT.
6 FT.

**Materials List (Per Section)**
**Lumber:**
4 Pcs. 2 × 4 × 6' Posts
4 Pcs. 2 × 4 × 12' Rails
4 Pcs. 2 × 4 × 8' Rails
w /Shaped Ends

**Hardware:**
Post to Rails 80-10d
Common Nails
**For Section Add:**
2 Pcs. 2 × 4 × 6' Posts
48-10d Common Nails

*Note: Use Galvanized Hardware*

Fig. 4-8. Detailed plans for a unique post and rail fence (courtesy Wolmanized pressure-treated lumber).

Fig. 4-9. Dimensional rail fence.

Post and board fences are very popular both on the farm and ranch, where they commonly serve as corrals, and in the city where they are both functional and decorative. Figure 4-15 shows the two most common designs of post and board fences. These designs can be varied by increasing or decreasing the number of boards, their width, or the spacing between them.

For suburban fences, boards 1 inch thick (¾ inch dressed), 6 inches wide (5¾ inches dressed), and 6, 8, 10, 12, or 16 feet long are generally used. When the posts are spaced the usual 8 feet, the use of 16-foot lengths will save labor and make a stronger fence.

Strong fences are required for corrals, feedlots, and similar areas where livestock are closely confined and may subject the fence to considerable pressure. For such areas, planks 2 inches or more in thickness, 8 or more inches in width, and 10 to 16

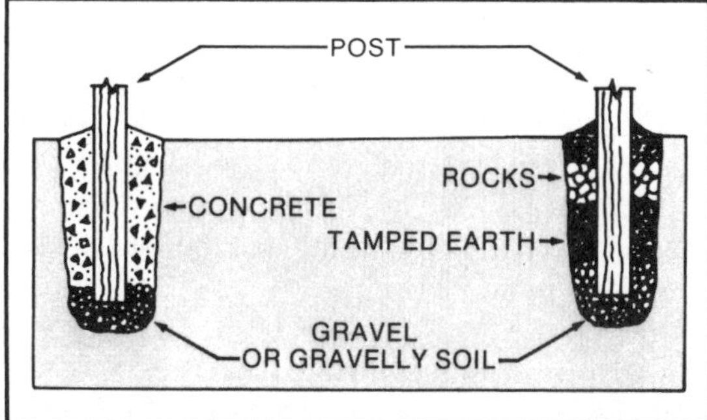


Fig. 4-10. Two common ways of filling rail fence postholes (courtesy Weyerhaeuser Co.).

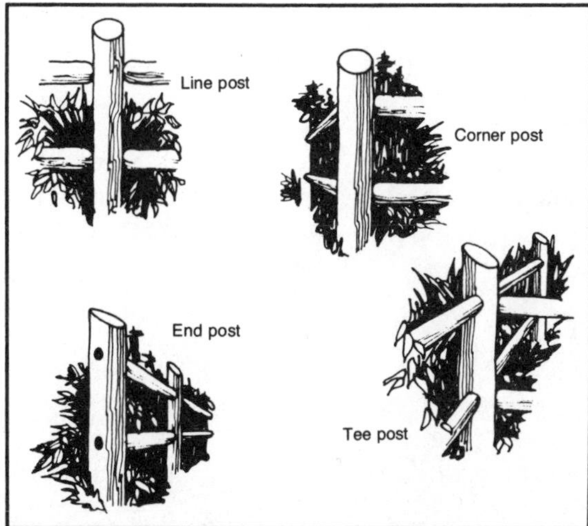


Fig. 4-11. Attaching rails to posts (courtesy Weyerhaeuser Co.).

feet in length are generally used. They should be spiked or bolted to substantial posts, spaced 5 or 6 feet apart.

Top and side fascia boards are used mainly for appearance. They afford some protection and strength to the fence.

## Lumber Quality

Minimum requirements in lumber for fences and gates are moderate bending strength, medium decay and weather resistance, high nail-holding power, and freedom from warp. Woods combining these properties to a high degree include cypress, Douglas fir, western larch, southern yellow pine,

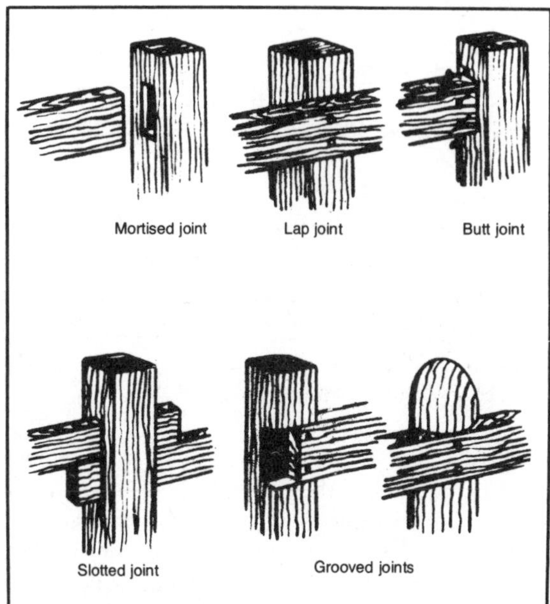


Fig. 4-12. Common post and rail joints.

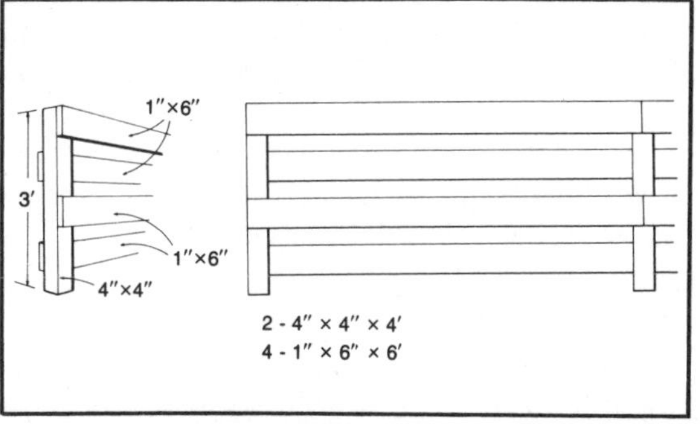


Fig. 4-13. Plans for a post and board fence (courtesy Georgia-Pacific Corp.).

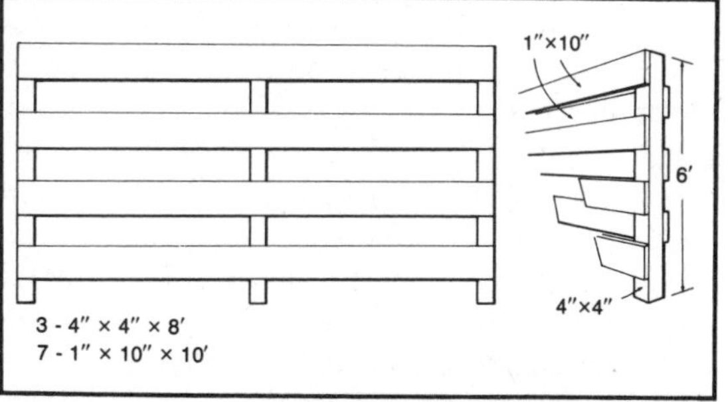


Fig. 4-14. Plans for a 6-foot post and board fence (courtesy Georgia-Pacific Corp.).

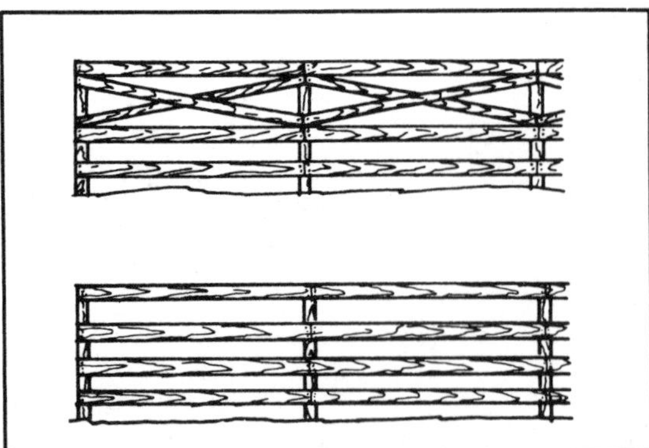

Fig. 4-15. Common post and board fences.

redwood, and white oak. The following woods weather well, but they have a small tendency to warp and are low in strength and nail-holding power: cedar, northern white pine, sugar pine, chestnut, and yellow poplar. The following woods are strong, hard, and high in nail-holding power, but they have a tendency to warp and do not weather as well as most: beech, birch, red gum, maple, red oak, and tupelo. Eastern hemlock, western hemlock, white fir, and spruce are intermediate in properties between the two groups just mentioned.

The No. 1 or No. 2 softwood or No. 2 Common hardwood grades of lumber should be used for stronger, more durable gates and fences.

### Preservative Treatment

Fences and gates will last years longer if the wood is treated with a good preservative. If not treated, the wood may soon start to decay at joints or any place where moisture is held (Fig. 4-16).

Commercially treated lumber may be available in most areas. Pressure-treated wood will last longer than that treated by other methods. You can treat the wood yourself by soaking it in a preservative solution. If you paint the fence, use a clear preservative that will not bleed through the paint, such as penta (pentachlorophenol) or copper naphthenate in light oil (mineral spirits or kerosene). If you will not paint the fence, you can use creosote, penta, or copper naphthenate in heavy (fuel) oil.

The lumber should be thoroughly seasoned before being treated with preservative. Green lumber will not absorb enough of the chemical for good protection against decay.

Cut the boards to the desired length before treating them. Soak them in the solution for at least 15 minutes but preferably for one hour for each inch of thickness. The longer the boards soak, the more preservative they will absorb and the longer they will resist decay.

While not the best method, you can apply preservative with a brush. Small quantities of ready-to-use wood preservative are available from building material centers, paint stores, and farm supply stores. The preservative should be flooded on, and the treatment should be repeated every few years for best results. Preservatives and their application are discussed in Chapter 13.

### Construction

Construction of post and board fences is essentially the same regardless of the design. Here

Fig. 4-16. This post is rotting out because it was not pretreated (photo by Val Ramos).

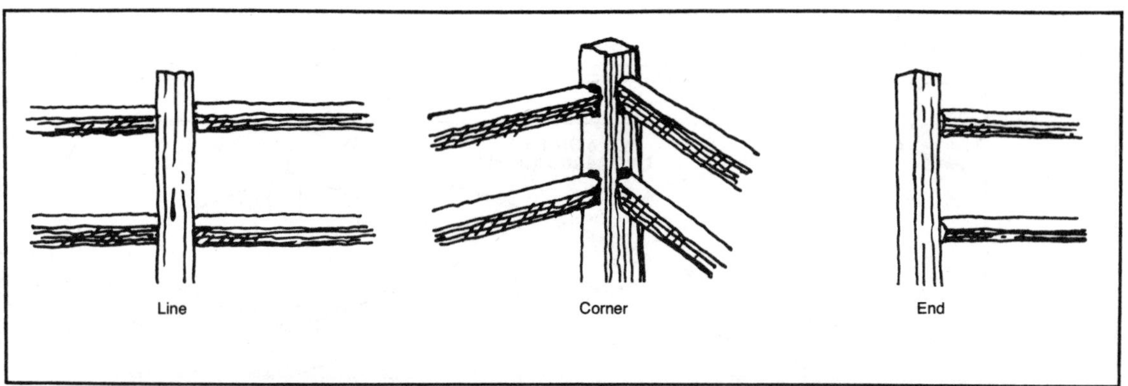


Fig. 4-17. Installing line, corner, and end posts (courtesy Weyerhaeuser Co.).

are the more important details of building a four-rail fence, using 4-inch posts, 16-foot boards, and top and side fascia boards.

Slope (saw) the tops of the posts slightly toward the side to which the boards will be fastened, so the top fascia boards will slope toward that side.

At the start of the fence and at corners, set the first line post 7 feet 10 inches from the gate or corner post, center to center (Fig. 4-17). Space the other line posts 8 feet apart, center to center. The first boards should extend across the face of the anchor post to the corner of the first or second line posts. Subsequent boards are nailed center to center on the posts.

You may have to shorten the spacing between posts near corners or the end of the fence, to make it come out even. For the best appearance, however, make the last panel as nearly full length as possible.

In the first or first two panels at the start of the fence and at corners, use 16-foot boards for the top and third rails and 8-foot boards for the second and fourth rails. Only two joints will fall on any one post with this arrangement, and you will have a stronger fence.

If you saw, trim, or bore preservative-treated boards, you may expose untreated or inadequately treated wood. Apply preservative if needed to prevent decay.

For the best appearance, fasten the boards to the "outside" of the posts. If the fence will be subject to pressure—from livestock, for example—attach the boards to the "inside" of the posts.

Nail the boards to the posts with three ring-shank or screw-shank nails staggered to avoid splitting the board. Hold the boards in place with cleats bolted to the posts for a stronger fence. This method makes it easier to remove the boards quickly if necessary.

In the first panel at the start of the fence and at the corners, use a 8-foot-long top fascia board. The top fascia board joints and the top fence board joints will fall on different posts. The top fascia should overlap both the top fence board and the vertical fascia board.

A variation of this construction is to install mortised rails. Posts are mortised to take rail tenons in one of two ways. A broad mortise lets the rails overlap side by side; a long narrow one lets them overlap one above the other. When rails

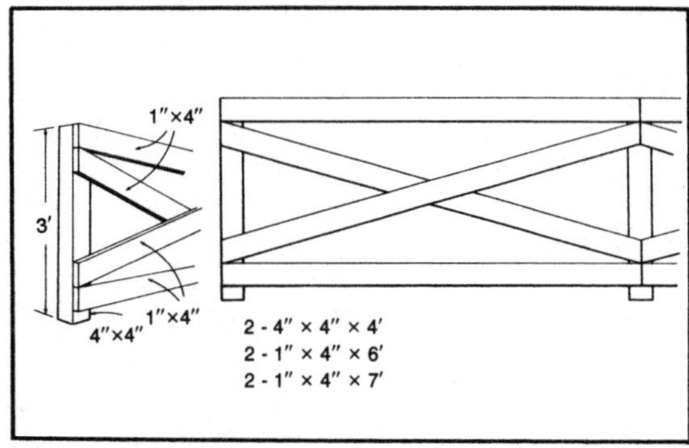


Fig. 4-18. Plans for a post and cross-rail fence (courtesy Georgia-Pacific Corp.).

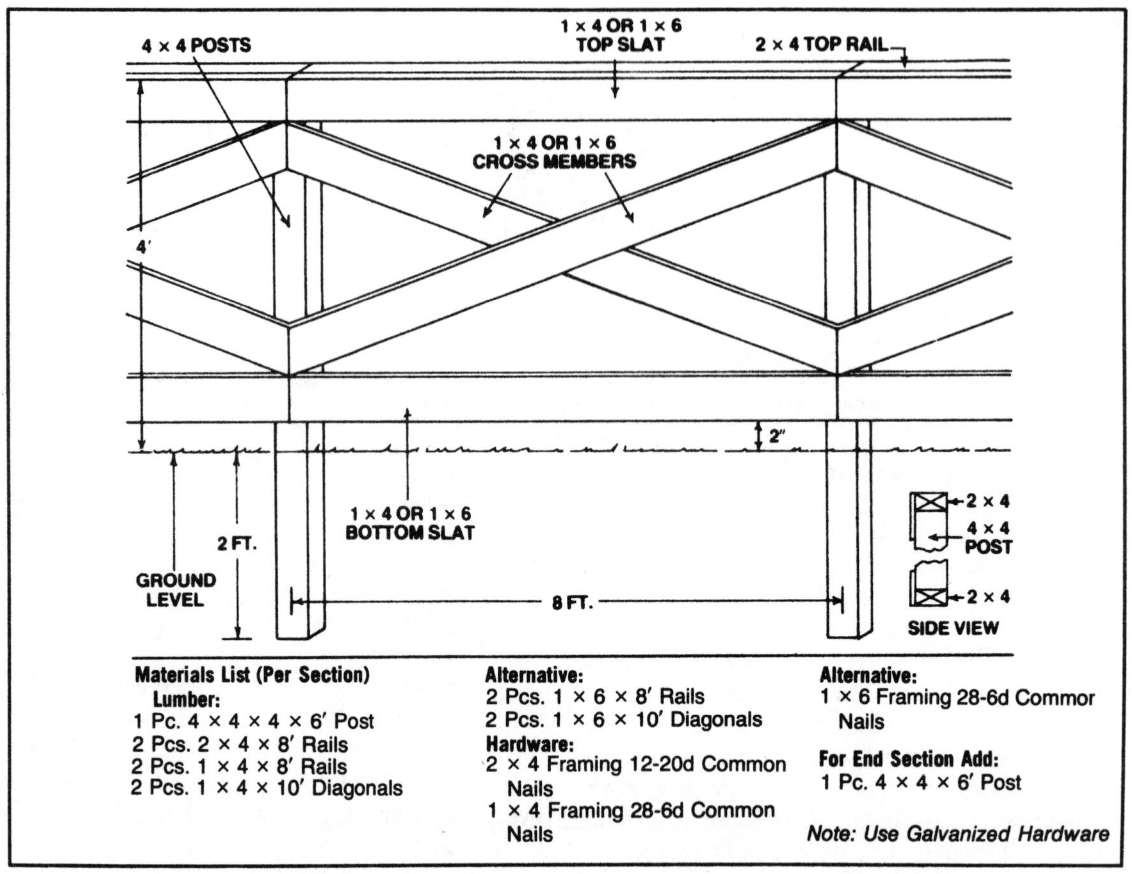


Fig. 4-19. Detailed plans for a post and cross-rail fence (courtesy Wolmanized pressure-treated lumber).

overlap at the side, a very wide and heavy post is needed. This joint adjusts more easily to sharp changes in grade than a joint with one rail above the other.

Rail fences are the easiest and least expensive fences to build. They offer the owner function, beauty, and pride of ownership (Figs. 4-18 and 4-19).

# Chapter 5

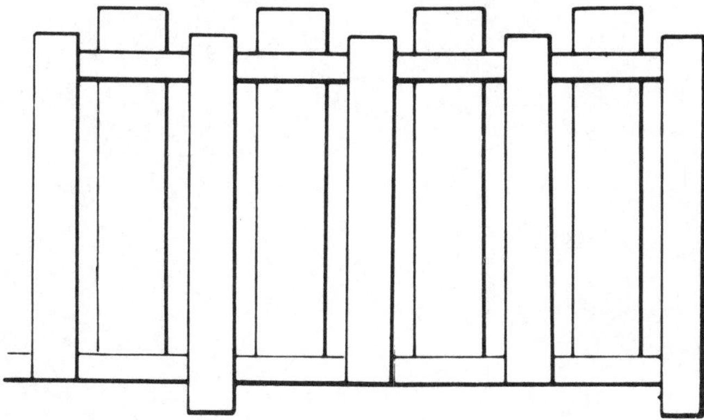

# Picket Fences

A "FENCE" MEANS A PICKET FENCE TO SOME people. The *picket* fence is traditional, decorative, and practical—especially for large, older homes on small lots. The picket fence has been modified to serve nearly every type of home imaginable. This is because of the inexhaustible range of picket designs and combinations that are available (Figs. 5-1 through 5-4). There are literally hundreds of patterns for picket tops, ranging from squared ends that produce a simple, straightforward fence to the intricate scroll-sawed patterns that make a formal design (Figs. 5-5 and 5-6). Post caps range from plain flat tops to fancy ornamental shapes such as the acorn, pineapple, turned goblet, and other designs (Fig. 5-7).

There are four considerations in selecting the overall design for your picket fence: fence height, picket width, ornamentation, and picket spacing. The typical picket fence is about 3 feet high. It has 3-inch pickets pointed like the prow of a ship and spaced 3 inches apart. Variations can be developed. Your fence may be 2 or 4 feet high. It may have narrow pickets widely spaced or broad pickets closely spaced. The tops of the pickets may be rounded, square, or dart-shaped.

The effectiveness of the picket fence design is due to its repetitive quality, but in a long stretch of fence this becomes monotonous. There are various ways of introducing some variety into the pattern:

- Alternate pickets of different heights.
- Mix different width pickets together.
- Use tapered pickets.
- Alternate groups of pickets (three broad, three narrow, etc.).

Picket fencing has some disadvantages. Some people feel that it's too commonplace and that there are fresher, more up-to-date fences from which to select. Picket fencing gives inadequate protection. It's an ineffective barrier to intruders, children can clamber over it, and an agile dog can leap it or tunnel underneath. Because most pickets are painted or whitewashed, they require periodic repainting as they lose their crisp, neat appearance quickly if allowed to weather too long.

Pickets don't provide privacy and are thus in-

Fig. 5-1. A well-built picket fence is a work of art (courtesy California Redwood Association).

adequate for fencing an outdoor living area unless it's also shielded by shrubs. This often compels the homeowner to install two types of fencing on his property.

## MATERIALS

Picket fences are available in three forms: fully-constructed sections, components with shaped pickets, and individual materials that can be shaped by the builder.

Prebuilt picket fences can be purchased through many mail-order catalog companies such as Sears and Montgomery Ward, or through local building material retailers. Wire-picket fences often come in rolls of 25 or 50 feet. Wood picket fences are sold in sections complete with a post, two rails, and pickets to a width of 4, 6, or 8 feet. You can even buy them prepainted.

If you're buying a component fence, standard picket fence posts are 4×4. Common rails are made of 1×3 or 2×4 lumber depending on the size and required strength of the fence. Pickets are usually 1×3, 4, or 6 inches and in lengths of 36, 42, or 48 inches.

## CONSTRUCTION

Picket fences are easy to build. Many are built by homeowners each year. Unless you're handy

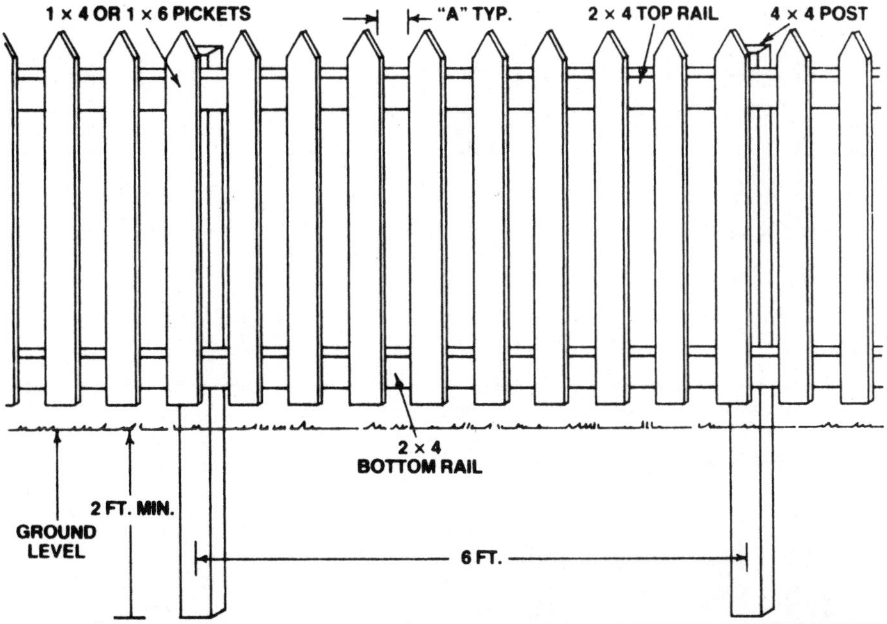

1 × 4 OR 1 × 6 PICKETS
"A" TYP.
2 × 4 TOP RAIL
4 × 4 POST
2 × 4
BOTTOM RAIL
2 FT. MIN.
GROUND
LEVEL
6 FT.

**Materials List (Per Section)**
**Lumber**
1 Pc. 4 × 4 × 8′ Post
2 Pcs. 2 × 4 × 6′ Rails
12 Pics. 1 × 4 × 5′ Pickets
**Alternate:**
8 Pcs. 1 × 6 × 5′ Pickets

**Note:** 1 × 4 Picket "A" = 2½″
1 × 6 Picket "A" = 3½″
**Hardware:**
Rails to Posts 8-20d Common Nails
Picket to Rails 96-6d Common Nails

**Alternate:**
1 × 6 Picket to Rails 64-6d Common Nails
**For End Section:**
1 Post, 1 Picket
8-6d Common Nails

Fig. 5-2. Detailed plans for a 5-foot-high picket fence (courtesy Wolmanized pressure-treated lumber).

2"x4"
1"x6"
1"x4"
3'
2"x4"
4"x4"

2 - 4″ × 4″ × 4′
2 - 2″ × 4″ × 6′
5 - 1″ × 6″ × 3′
4 - 1″ × 4″ × 3′

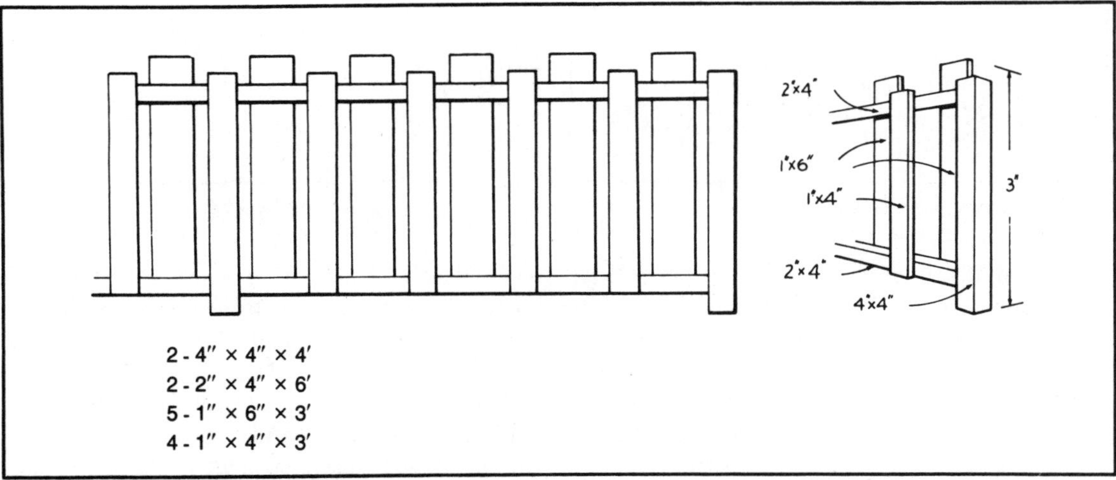

Fig. 5-3. Alternate board picket fence (courtesy Georgia-Pacific Corp.).

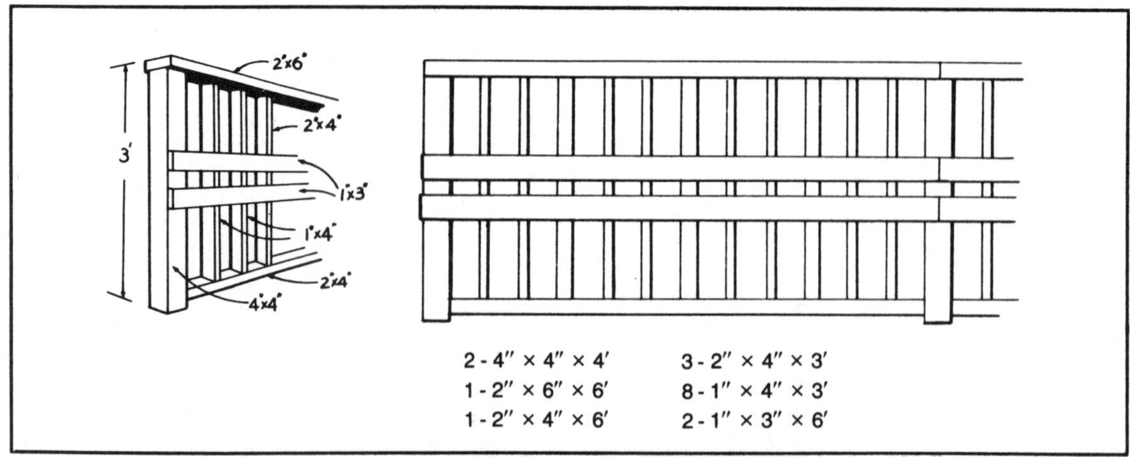


Fig. 5-4. Unique picket design for a 3-foot-high fence (courtesy Georgia-Pacific Corp.).

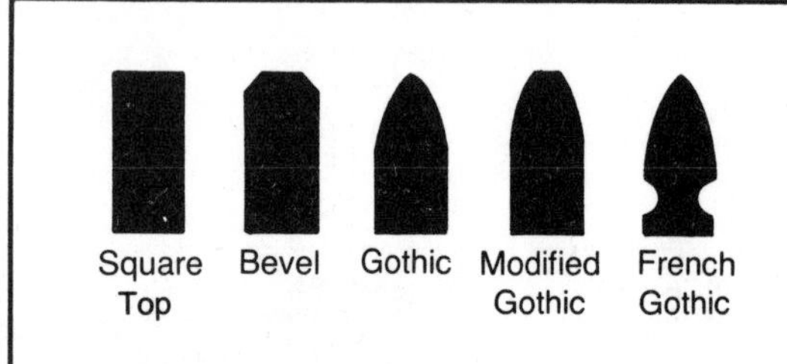


Fig. 5-5. Typical picket cap designs.

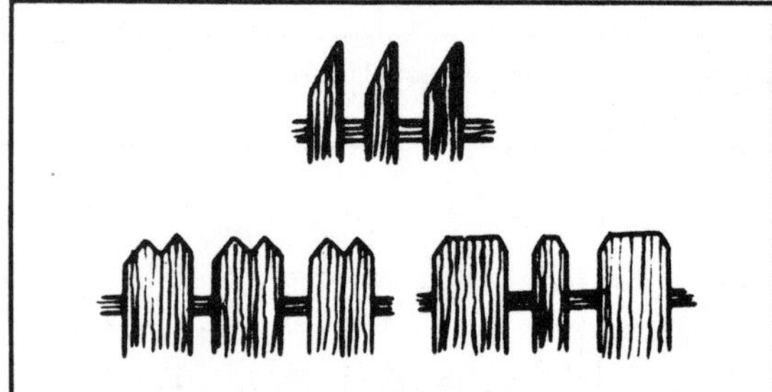

Fig. 5-6. Various picket patterns.

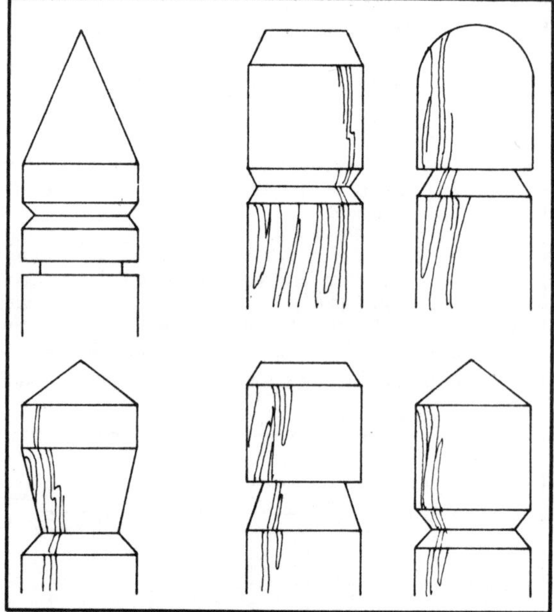

Fig. 5-7. Typical picket post designs.

with wood, it's often better to buy precut pickets rather than manufacture them yourself. You can do it, but a variety of power tools will be needed to help you cut and uniformly dress the vast number of pickets needed for the typical fence. If you decide to make your own, stay with standard-sized boards. For your picket tops you can copy a pattern that you may have noticed on a fence, or you can create your own. Make a cardboard template. Use the cardboard the way children make valentine hearts. Draw half the pattern, fold the cardboard, and cut out both sides simultaneously.

If you're planning to buy a prefabricated picket fence, make sure that it will fit your property. Some varieties that are made up in finished panels cannot be used on a slope. The panels will not fit the posts.

If dogs and other small animals persist in digging under your fence, install a baseboard that runs a few inches below the soil. Use a 1×6 or 1×8 and impregnate it with preservative, or it will rot away in a short time. You can also thwart the animals by nailing chicken wire to the bottom rail inside and burying it in the ground. It will not be noticed among the plantings.

A molding strip, nailed on the outside of the fence parallel to the top rail, will keep pickets from working loose and deter small boys from removing pickets.

If you select a picket with an unusual top design, you should order or make more than you need. Store them as replacements.

Refer to Chapter 3 for step-by-step instructions on how to dig postholes, set posts, attach rails, and install siding on wood fences (Figs. 5-8 through 5-11).

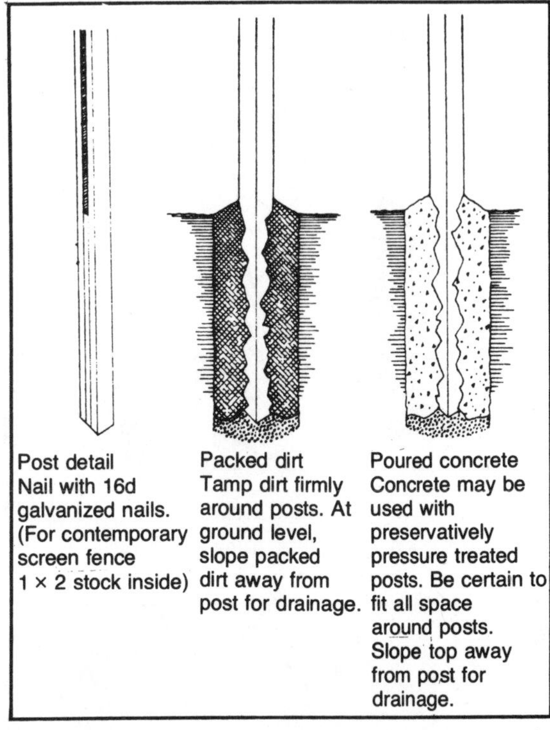


Fig. 5-9. Setting posts in dirt and concrete (courtesy Western Wood Products Association).

## GRAPE STAKE FENCES

The rustic cousin of the picket fence is the grape stake fence. A *grape stake* is simply a hand-split redwood stake about 2 inches square and anywhere from 3 to 6 feet in length. Grape stakes were first designed to support grape vines, but many years ago an enterprising fence builder began using them in fences. The grape stake fence can be seen today along both rural and suburban roads.

Grape stakes are usually split from redwood heartwood, although sapwood varieties are sometimes used. If they are straight grained and free of knots, they can be resplit to make 1×2s. A better method is to saw them in half lengthwise on a bench saw. This produces a 1×2 with one rustic side for display and one smooth side for nailing.

Fig. 5-8. Dig the posthole on the inside of your property line string.

Grape stake fences are decay-resistant and require no maintenance, except to drive home a loose nail now and then. The stakes are light in weight, easy to handle, and simple to install. The natural reddish tone that weathers to a soft gray blends smoothly with plantings and matches the warm tones of brick and stonework in the garden. Perhaps more than any other type of screen fence, grape stakes provide warmth to the barren lot when it's first fenced. Many types of fence merely accentuate the bleakness of an unplanted backyard.

Grape stakes are adaptable to many styles of construction. They may be driven into the soil. They may be nailed like pickets to a fence frame, pointed tip up for rustic effect, with the squared tip on top for a clean fence line. They may be fitted inside the frame to provide a two-sided fence. Also,

Fig. 5-10. Mound the posthole fill for proper runoff.

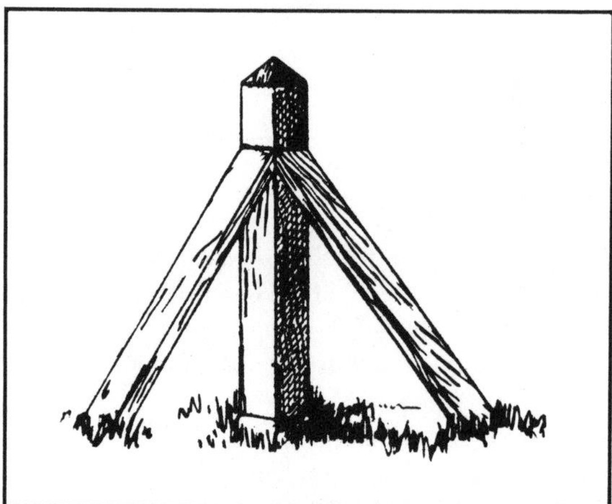

Fig. 5-11. Corner posts need extra bracing to withstand elements and pressures.

grape stakes may be attached either vertically or horizontally, or in alternating panels of both to produce a different fence design.

Grape stake fencing is not right for everyone. Many people feel that it's overused as a fencing material in some areas of the country, especially on the West Coast. Also, many installations have been made indiscriminately, without regard for the suitability of the fence to the house, garden, and neighborhood. Some people object to its splintery qualities—a hazard to pets and children. Others don't like the weathered gray look of aged grape stake.

Building a grape stake fence is much like building any other wood frame fence. Posts and rails are installed. The siding—grape stakes—in this case are nailed into place. You can split the stakes and nail them a short distance apart on the rail to save money.

Wear heavy gloves when handling grape stakes. Redwood splinters can easily enter your hand and give you problems trying to get them out.

## SLAT PICKETS

Somewhere between the picket fence and its rustic cousin, the grape stake, is a type of fencing put together with long, narrow slats. Like the picket it utilizes milled lumber, and like the grape stake it is a screen fence.

*Slat* fence materials include rough-finished redwood sawed into 1×1 or 1×2-inch strips. Because the redwood is cut from standard lumber, it's not limited to the 6-foot height of the grape stake. It can be built from 2 to 8 feet tall.

Even though the strips have to be cut on order at the lumberyard, they cost about the same as grape stakes. You may have the power tools to do the cutting yourself using larger, less expensive dimensional lumber as a starting point.

Slat fences are more formal than grape stakes, but they often look more truly at home in a city environment than their splintery relative. Their clean lines give a stronger vertical pattern than grape stakes with their irregular edges.

There are two basic ways of installing the slat picket fence. The first and probably most popular is to nail the slats over the standard post and rail fence frame, just as you would a grape stake. You can either nail them into place snugly against each other, or you can space them apart.

The second method of construction is to overlay the slats on a solid fence to bring interest to an otherwise dull design. Slats can be stained effectively, either the same color as the primary fence or a different shade, or even a different color for accent.

Slat fences are efficient in areas where wind is a problem. Wind tests indicate that an open slat fence provides more effective wind protection than any other type of fence. Closely-spaced slats break up and disperse the wind.

## WOVEN PICKETS

Here's another variation of the basic picket fence: *woven pickets*. Woven pickets are available in prefabricated form, either as panels or woven together in rolls. They are simply installed as siding on the basic post and rail wood fence frame. They make an effective windscreen and are durable.

Woven pickets are usually made of cedar and are available in many styles: peeled, machine finished or complete with bark; round or half-round; and wired together or strung on steel rods.

Check local building material stores and lumberyards for the cost and further instructions on woven picket installation.

## PICKET FENCE IDEAS

Here are a few unique ideas for designing and building your own picket fence:

**Lath and Picket.** By spacing your pickets about 5 inches apart and installing narrow wood lath in between, you can give your fence the necessary strength and security at a lower cost.

**Southern Picket.** Common in the South, the southern picket fence has pickets with one side slanted at the top and the other side straight. These can easily be modified from 1×2 dimensional lumber by most homeowners with a jig on a sawhorse.

**Split Pickets.** Rural fences where wood is plentiful can be sided with small timbers split lengthwise using a shake splitter and mallet or a bench saw.

**Ornamental Pickets.** By driving through the older parts of your town and neighboring communities, you can often find homes decorated with ornate pickets. With permission you can often copy the design by tracing it on paper or by asking to purchase a broken picket that has the design intact. You can offer to replace the broken pickets in exchange for a few.

**Sapling Pickets.** A short rustic fence can be built with sapling pickets gathered from near river and creek banks. As a variation, the saplings can be woven together as both rails and siding to form a unique fence or barrier.

**Wire and Pickets.** You can weave your own fence with pickets and wire and a few simple tools. Wrap your first picket a few turns with wire, then twist it a few times before wrapping the next picket. This wire picket fence can then be stretched between posts to make an inexpensive, yet practical and decorative fence.

## Chapter 6

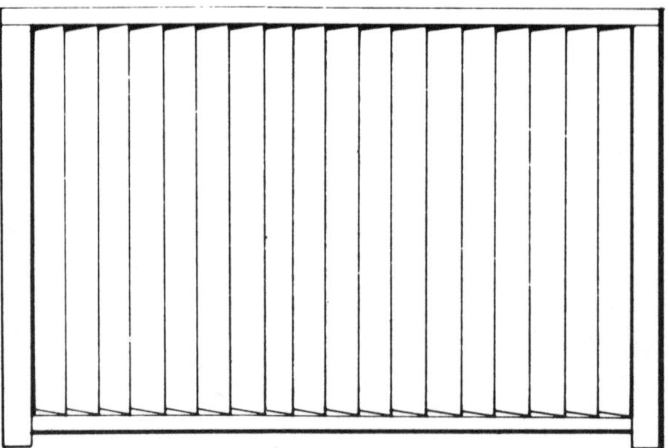

# Board Fences

AS THE SIZE OF THE HOMESTEAD HAS SHRUNK from measurement in sections to acres to feet, the fence has reflected the change. The short, open fence of the range has evolved into the tall, solid fence of the subdivision. The high wood fence has increased in popularity. There are two reasons for this increase: security and privacy.

The typical board fence offers security by becoming a solid barrier between the homeowner's world and the outside world (Figs. 6-1 through 6-3). The fence is designed to both keep the inside world—children and pets—from getting out and keep the outside world—often children and pets—from getting in.

The high board fence also offers privacy by blocking the view of passersby from private areas of the yard (Fig. 6-4). The homeowner has effectively enlarged his home by extending its walls to his property lines. The high board fence can also block undesired sights from view. For these and other reasons, the board fence is one of the most popular built today.

### VARIATIONS

There are dozens of styles and designs of board fences being built throughout the country. *Basic board* is often a series of 1×6 or 1×8-inch boards nailed side by side over a common post and rail fence frame. Height is usually 5 or 6 feet. Top designs can be flat, pointed, rounded, or framed.

*Alternate board* fences are "good neighbor" fences that are equally decorative on both sides (Fig. 6-5). The first board is placed on one side of the rail, and the next is staggered and nailed to the opposite side (Figs. 6-6 through 6-8).

*Alternate panel* fencing has every other fence section facing your property (Fig. 6-9). Alternate panel is both neighborly and more solid than alternate board (Fig. 6-10).

*Channeled* fences are constructed by cutting a channel for fence boards on the top of the bottom rail and the bottom of the top rail. Boards are then equally exposed to both sides (Fig. 6-11 through 6-14).

Fig. 6-1. Common board fence designs.

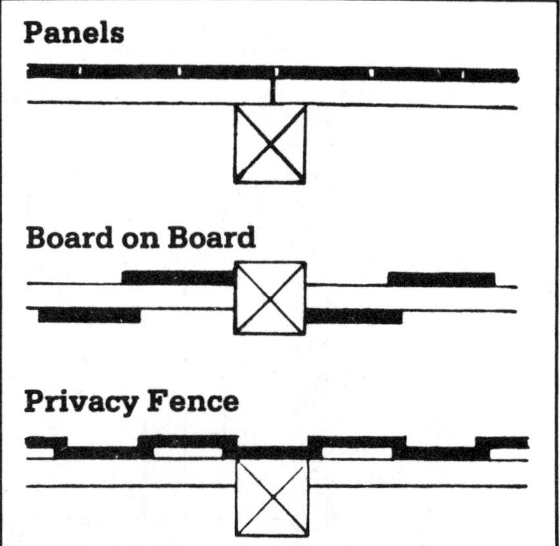

Fig. 6-2. Top view of common board fence designs.

*Siding* fences use the siding identical to that on the home to cover the fence (Figs. 6-15 and 6-16). Six-inch beveled siding is a common house siding that can also be used to cover your fence (Fig. 6-17).

*Horizontal* boards can be installed to make a unique and decorative board fence, especially in an area where everyone else has vertical board siding. Make sure your fence doesn't become a ladder for intruders.

*Diagonal* boards make a unique design offering security, privacy, and beauty (Fig. 6-18).

*Louver* board fences have boards installed at an angle to direct both the wind and the view. Boards may either be stationary or movable (Fig. 6-19).

*Basket weave* fences are both easy to construct and highly decorative. They are increasingly popular with the do-it-yourself fence builder (Fig. 6-20).

## BASIC BOARD FENCES

The common high board fence is a useful and easy-to-build fence (Fig. 6-21). The problem is that many of these fences offer a cheerless, boxed-in feeling to the yard and can easily become monotonous.

Try to come up with a more decorative design for your board fence. This can be done by reviewing

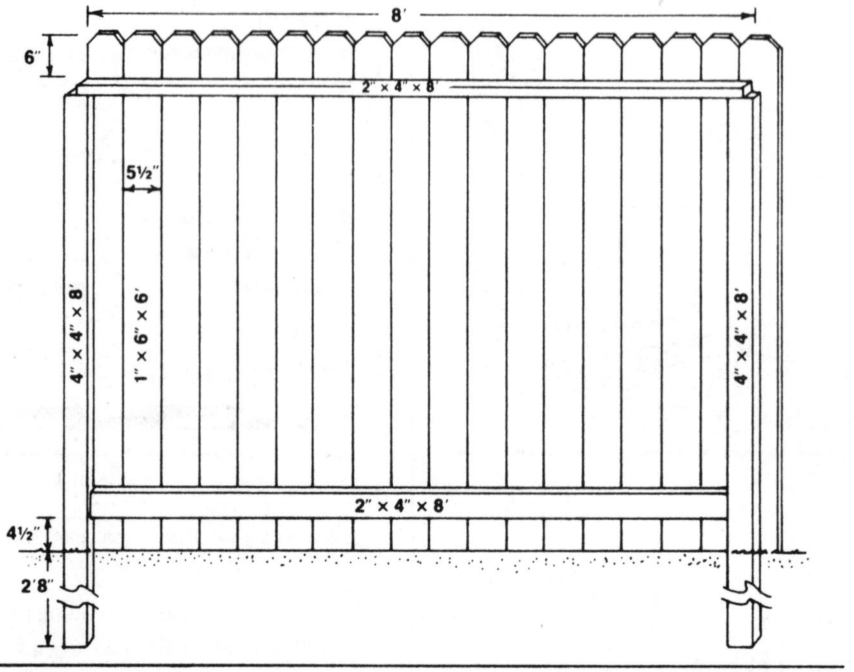

8′
6″
2″ × 4″ × 8′
5½″
4″ × 4″ × 8′
1″ × 6″ × 6′
4″ × 4″ × 8′
2″ × 4″ × 8′
4½″
2′8″

Material List
2 Pcx. 4 × 4 × 8′ Posts
2 Pcs. 2 × 4 × 8′ Braces
18 Pcs. 1 × 6 × 6′ Slats

*Note: Use Galvanized Hardware*

Boards should not be butted snugly together; allow space for wood swelling in humid weather.

Fig. 6-3. Detailed plans for a panel board fence.

ideas in this book and by studying unique designs in your area (Fig. 6-22). You may find the one that will complement your property while serving its primary purpose.

Solid board fences are expensive because they require a large amount of lumber and consequently should justify the cost. The solid fence does give absolute privacy, but often at the expense of making a person feel imprisoned behind it. Its blank surfaces are cool and impersonal, especially in a yard with little landscaping. Many solid board fences have an obvious "backside" that can make neighbors feel you're inhospitable.

These may seem like unsolvable problems for

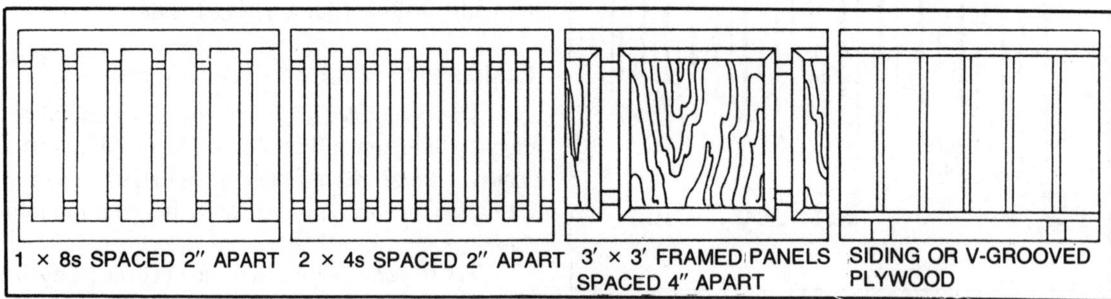


Fig. 6-4. Common board fence designs used as screening (courtesy Wolmanized pressure-treated lumber).

2"x4"
1"x10"
6'
2"x4"
4"x4"

2 - 4″ × 4″ × 8′
2 - 2″ × 4″ × 10′
13 - 1″ × 10″ × 6′

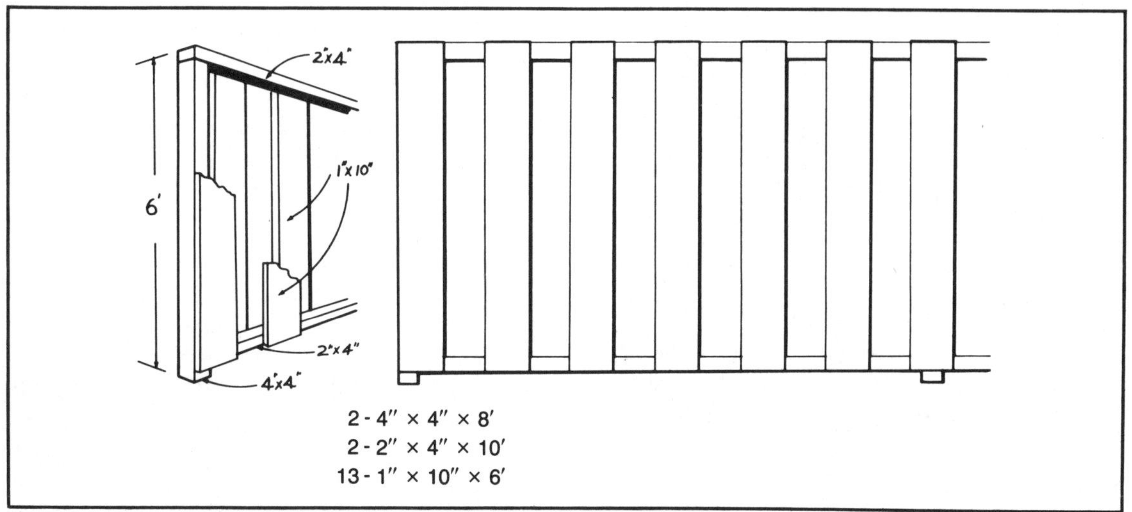

Fig. 6-5. Plans for an alternate board fence (courtesy Georgia-Pacific Corp.).

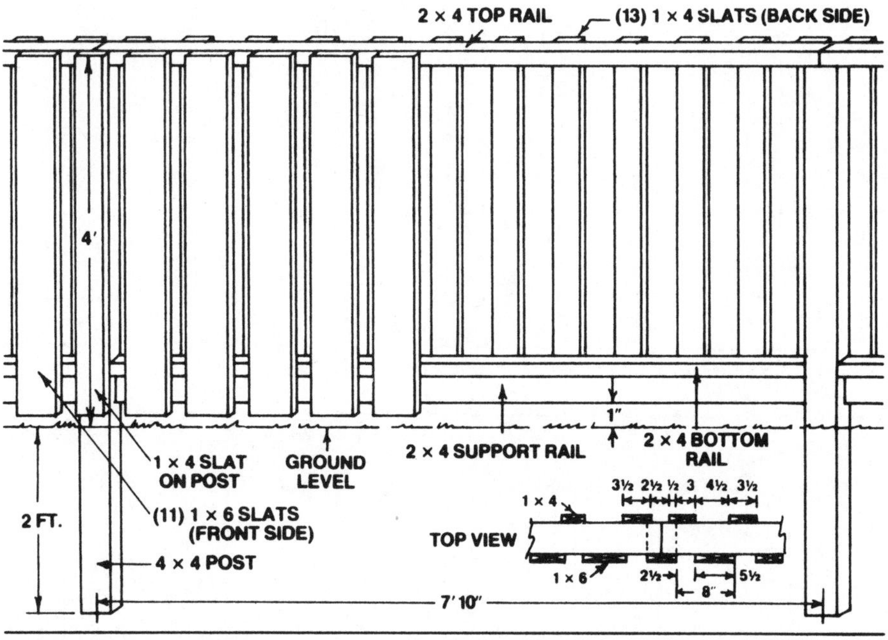

2 × 4 TOP RAIL
(13) 1 × 4 SLATS (BACK SIDE)
4′
1″
1 × 4 SLAT ON POST
GROUND LEVEL
2 × 4 SUPPORT RAIL
2 × 4 BOTTOM RAIL
3½ 2½ ½ 3 4½ 3½
1 × 4
(11) 1 × 6 SLATS (FRONT SIDE)
2 FT.
TOP VIEW
4 × 4 POST
1 × 6
2½
5½
8″
7′ 10″

**Materials List (Per Section)**
**Lumber:**
1 Pc. 4 × 4 × 6′ Post
3 Pcs. 2 × 4 × 8′ Rails
13 Pcs. 1 × 4 × 3′11″ Slats
11 Pcs. 1 × 6 × 3′11″

**Hardware:**
2 × 4 Framing 24-20d Common Nails
1 × 4 & 1 × 6 Framing 96-6d Common Nails

**For End Section Add:**
1 Pc. 4 × 4 × 6′ Post
1 Pc. 1 × 4 × 3′11″ Slat

*Note: Use Galvanized Hardware*

Fig. 6-6. Detailed plans for an alternate board fence (courtesy Wolmanized pressure-treated lumber).

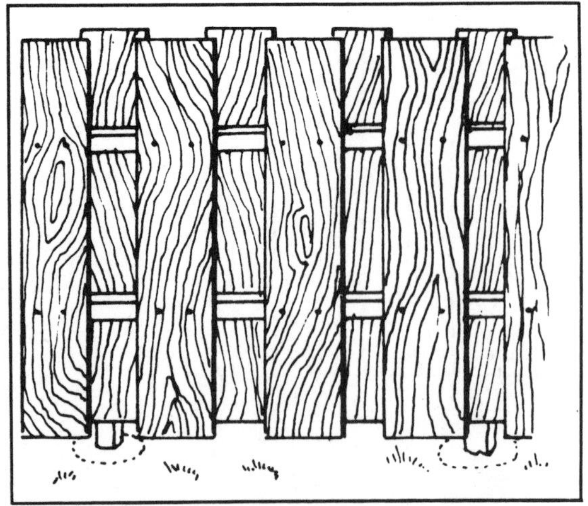
Fig. 6-7. Alternate board fence (courtesy Rollform, Inc.).

the do-it-yourself fence builder. Many homeowners have been discouraged by them and settled for fences that seem friendlier and are cheaper to build. Others have approached the problem head-on and have designed and built solid board fences that are both decorative and functional.

## Designing Tips

Board fences can be given interest and pattern by several methods. At the sacrifice of some privacy, a tall board fence may be opened up slightly to give a lighter feeling and a hint of the world outside. Boards may be set slightly separated like pickets, or they may be placed slantwise within the frame to form a louvered fence (discussed later). The upper quarter of the fence may be left open or fitted with

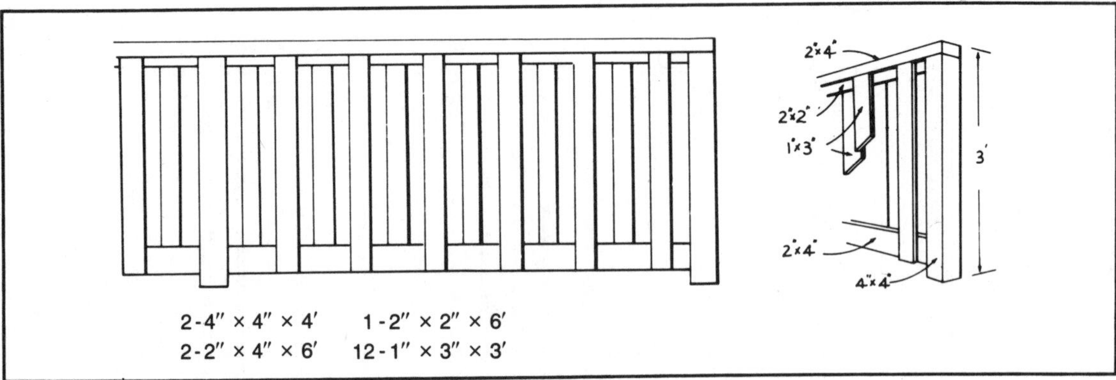

Fig. 6-8. Alternate board fence with cap and base rails (courtesy Georgia-Pacific Corp.).

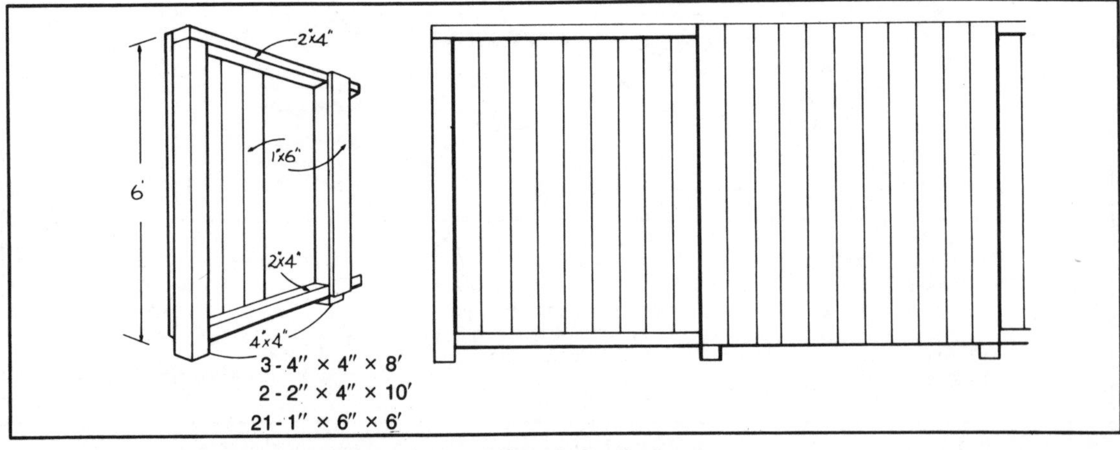

Fig. 6-9. Plans for an alternate panel fence (courtesy Georgia-Pacific Corp.).

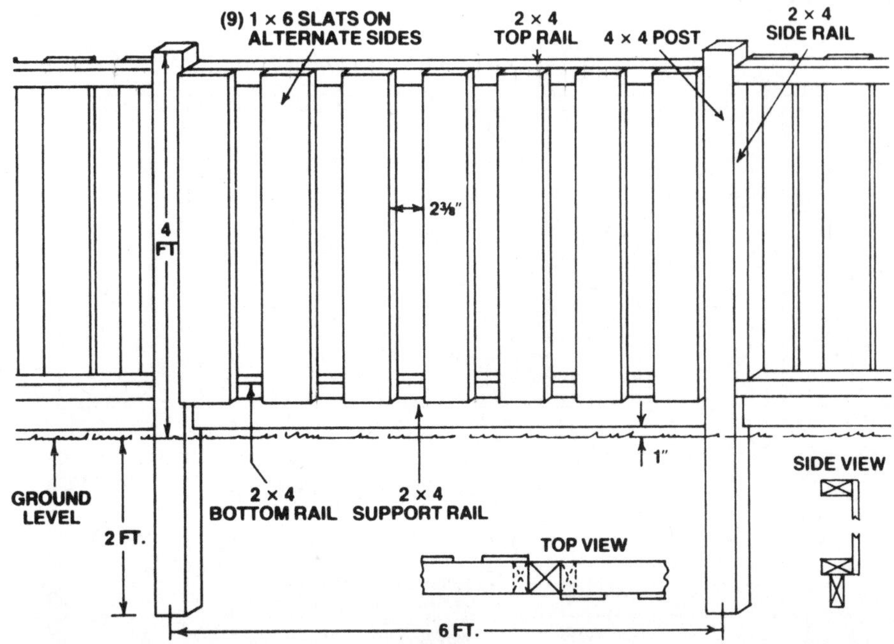

(9) 1 × 6 SLATS ON ALTERNATE SIDES
2 × 4 TOP RAIL
4 × 4 POST
2 × 4 SIDE RAIL
2⅜″
4 FT
1″
SIDE VIEW
GROUND LEVEL
2 × 4 BOTTOM RAIL
2 × 4 SUPPORT RAIL
2 FT.
TOP VIEW
6 FT.


**Materials List (Per Section)**
**Lumber:**
1 Pc. 4 × 4 × 6′ Post
3 Pcs. 2 × 4 × 6′ Rails
1 Pcs. 2 × 4 × 7′ Side Supports
9 Pcs. 2 × 6 × 3′8″ Slats

**Hardware:**
2 × 4 Framing 22-20d Common Nails
1 × 6 Slats 36-6d Common Nails

**For End Section Add:**
1 Post 4 × 4 × 6′

*Note: Use Galvanized Hardware*

Fig. 6-10. Detailed plans for an alternate panel fence (courtesy Wolmanized pressure-treated lumber).

2″x4″ CHANNELED
1″x10″ T&G
6′
2″x4″ CHANNELED
4″x4″


2 - 4″ × 4″ × 8′
2 - 2″ × 4″ × 10′
12 - 1″ × 10″ × 10′ T & G

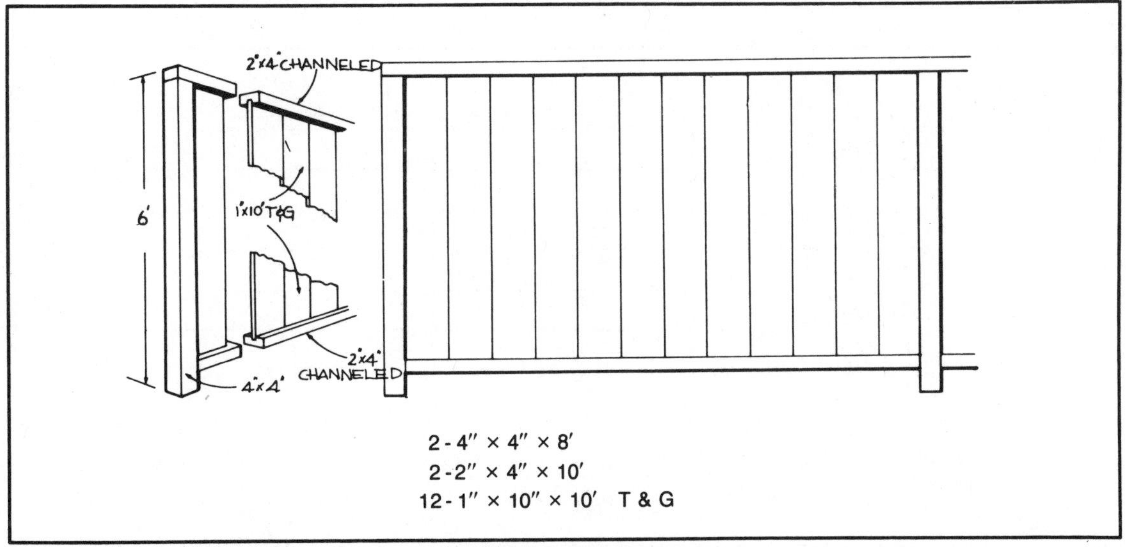

Fig. 6-11. Plans for a channeled board fence (courtesy Georgia-Pacific Corp.).

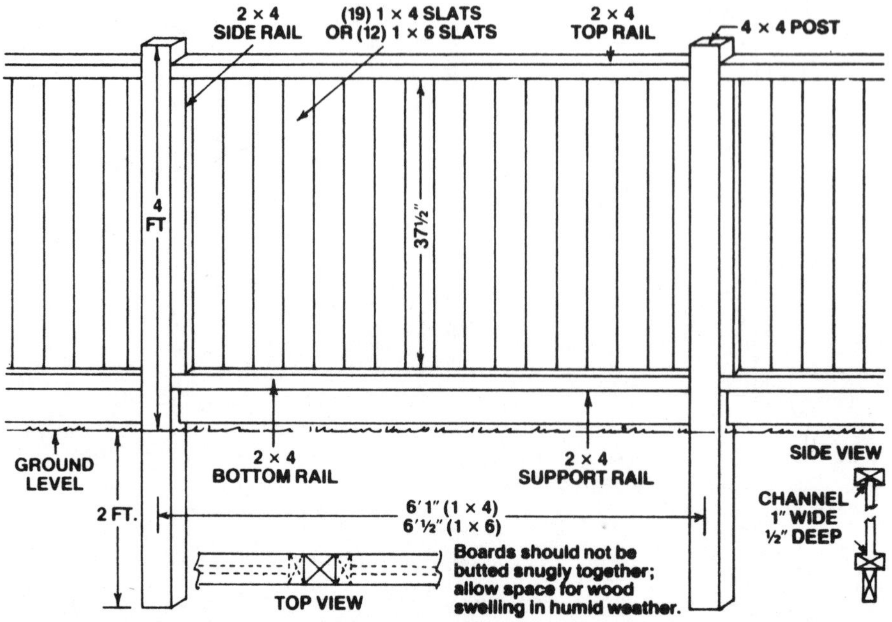

2 × 4
SIDE RAIL
(19) 1 × 4 SLATS
OR (12) 1 × 6 SLATS
2 × 4
TOP RAIL
4 × 4 POST
4
FT
37½"
GROUND
LEVEL
2 FT.
2 × 4
BOTTOM RAIL
2 × 4
SUPPORT RAIL
6′1″ (1 × 4)
6′½″ (1 × 6)
SIDE VIEW
CHANNEL
1″ WIDE
½″ DEEP
Boards should not be butted snugly together; allow space for wood swelling in humid weather.
TOP VIEW

**Materials List (Per Section)**
**Lumber:**
1 Pc. 4 × 4 × 6′ Post
3 Pcs. 2 × 4 × 6′ Rails
1 Pc. 2 × 4 × 7′ Side Supports
19 Pcs. 1 × 4 × 3′-2½″ Slats

**Alternate:**
12 Pcs. 1 × 6 × 3′2½″ Slats
**Hareware:**
2 × 4 Framing 22-20d Common Nails
1 × 4 Slats 38-6d Common Nails

**Alternate:**
1 × 6 Slats 24-6d Common Nails
**For End Section Add:**
1 Pc. 4 × 4 × 6′ Post

*Note: Use Galvanized Hardware*

Fig. 6-12. Detailed plans for a channeled board fence (courtesy Wolmanized pressure-treated lumber).

1″×4″
3′
1″×6″
4″×4″

3 - 4″ × 4″ × 4′
1 - 1″ × 4″ × 6′
12 - 1″ × 6″ × 3′

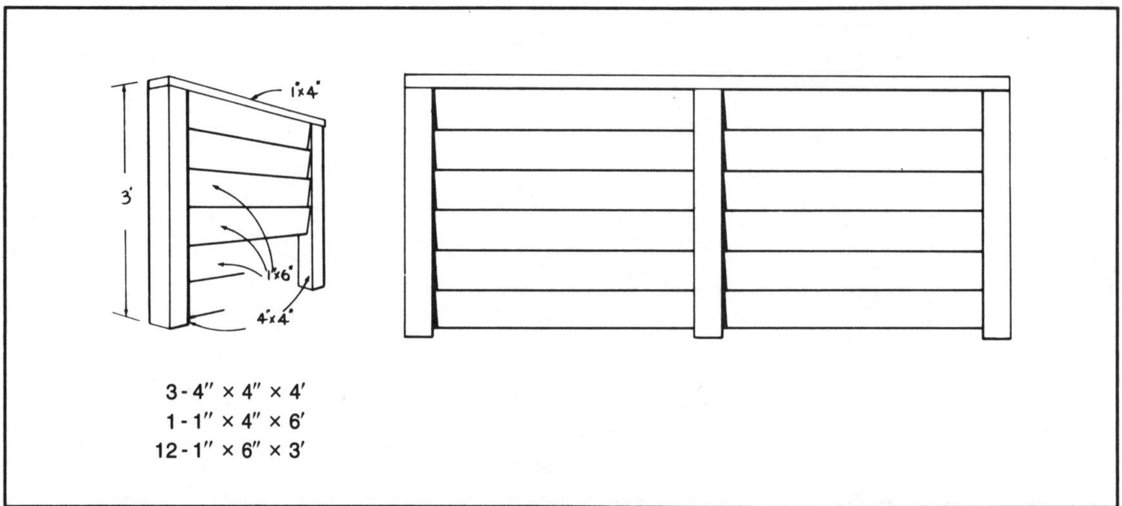

Fig. 6-13. Plans for a horizontal channeled board fence (courtesy Georgia-Pacific Corp.).

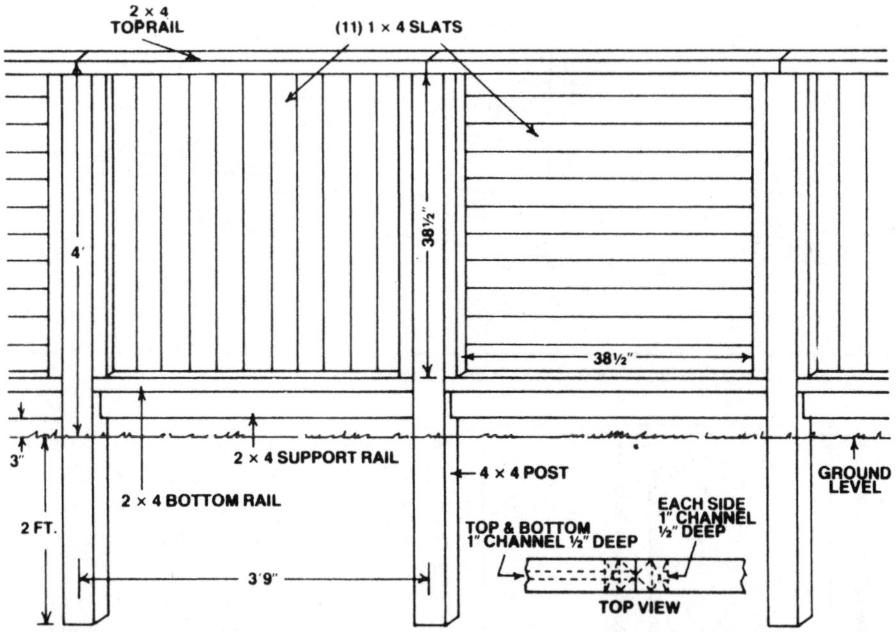

2 × 4
TOPRAIL
(11) 1 × 4 SLATS
4'
38½"
38½"
3"
2 × 4 SUPPORT RAIL
4 × 4 POST
GROUND
LEVEL
2 × 4 BOTTOM RAIL
2 FT.
3'9"
EACH SIDE
1" CHANNEL
½" DEEP
TOP & BOTTOM
1" CHANNEL ½" DEEP
TOP VIEW

**Materials List (Per Section)**

**Lumber:**

2 Pcs. 4 × 4 × 6′ Posts.
1 Pcs. 2 × 4 × 8′ Top Rail
2 Pcs. 2 × 4 × 14′ Framing
7-1/3 Pcs. 1 × 4 × 10′
(Cut 22-3′3½″) Slats

**Hardware:**

2 × 4 Framing 30-20d Common Nails
1 × 4 Slats 88-6d Common Nails

**For End Section Add:**

1 Pc. 4 × 4 × 6′ Post

*Note: Use Galvanized Hardware*

Boards should not be butted snugly together: allow space for wood swelling in humid weather

Fig. 6-14. Detailed plans for an alternate panel channeled fence (courtesy Wolmanized pressure-treated lumber).

1"x6"
3'
6"
BEVEL SIDING
4"x4"

2-4″ × 4″ × 4′
1-1″ × 6″ × 6′
6-1″ × 6″ × 6′ Bevel siding

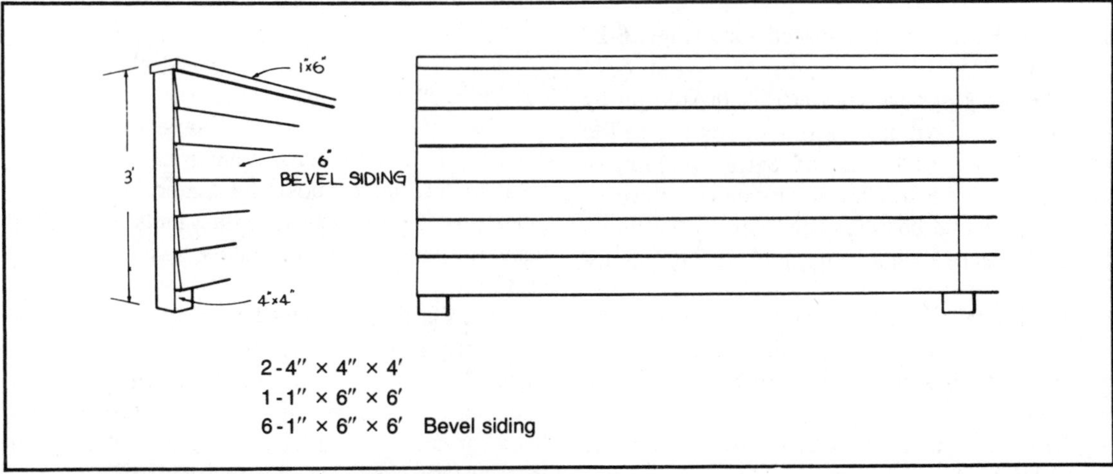

Fig. 6-15. Plans for a siding fence (courtesy Georgia-Pacific Corp.).

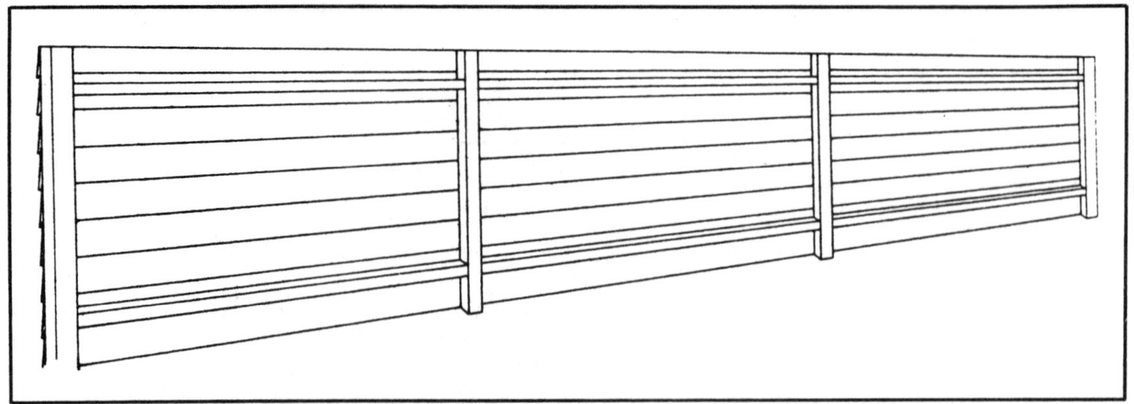

Fig. 6-16. Siding fence (courtesy Western Wood Products Association).

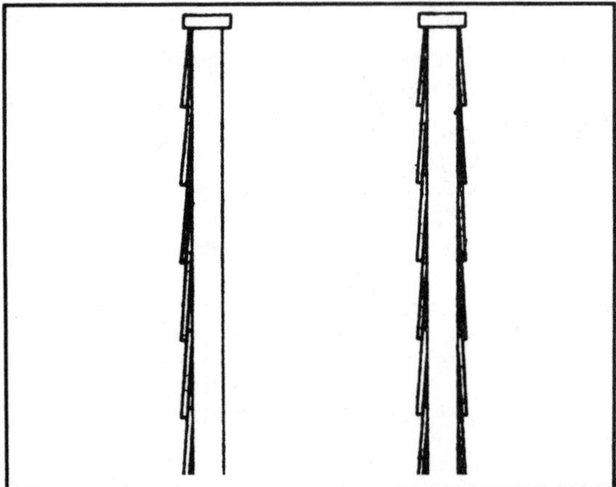

Fig. 6-17. Side view of single-siding and double-siding fence (courtesy Western Wood Products Association).

an inset of lattice or open-spaced slats (Figs. 6-23 and 6-24).

The blank surface area can be broken up by using materials that give pattern or texture to the structure, such as board and batten, siding, or tongue and groove; by alternating panels with vertical and horizontal boards; or by varying the direction of the fence, using a zigzag or serrated fence line.

Horizontal siding will give the fence a strong horizontal feeling and appear to stretch a small garden. Vertical siding will seem to compress a long fence.

The right-side, wrong-side problem can be solved by designing the frame side so that it has strong interest in itself, or by fitting the boards wholly within the frame so the fence appears the same from both sides. The frame side can also be improved with a simple trellis that will fill in with colorful vines.

A solid fence can be treated as an integral part of the house plan. Designed as an extension of the house wall to enclose the outdoor living area, it gives a feeling of continuity to outdoor-indoor living within its enclosure. Viewed through a glass wall, it becomes an outer wall of the house itself. The inner surface is therefore finished in materials that harmonize with the interior wall materials and color schemes. The public side of the fence is surfaced with the same materials as the house—siding, shakes, or board and batten. Your home is enlarged economically.

## Construction

Basic board fences are simple to construct. Tools you'll need include a hammer, shovel, tape measure, string, and posthole digger. Materials include posts, rails, boards, gates, nails, galvanized hangers, gate hardware, stakes, gravel, and concrete.

In locating your fence line, the fence should be built entirely on your property unless a common ownership agreement between you and your neighbor has been arranged. Go over the property lines carefully. If you have any doubts about their location, have your property surveyed.

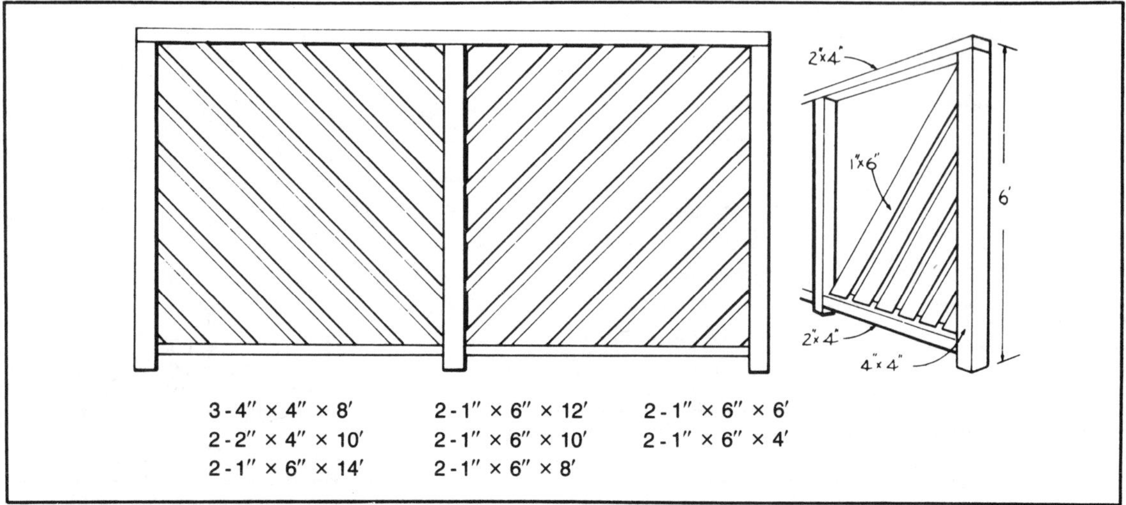


Fig. 6-18. Typical diagonal board fence plans (courtesy Georgia-Pacific Corp.).

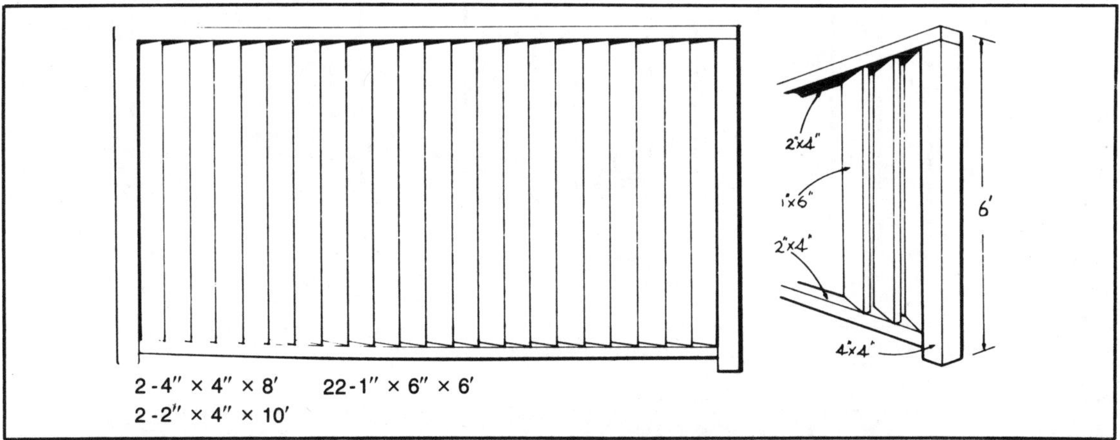


Fig. 6-19. Plans for a louver board fence (courtesy Georgia-Pacific Corp.).

The location and setting of the posts is the most important factor as to how attractive and long lasting your fence will be. Here are the steps for digging and setting postholes and posts:

- Stake out the property lines and stretch a string between the stakes.
- Locate the corner posts and where any gates should be.
- Mark off the post spacings not to exceed 8 feet on center.
- For pedestrian gates, locate the post a minimum of 3 feet apart.
- Start construction by setting corner and gate-posts first.
- When backfilling, compact gravel in the bottom of the hole for drainage followed by about 8 inches of concrete for stability. The remainder of the hole should be filled with more compacted gravel topped off with dirt. This type of installation allows the maximum drainage that will result in a longer post life and fewer costly repairs.

To assemble the fence, first locate the 2×4 rails about 12 inches from the tops and bottoms of posts (Fig. 6-25). The location of the rails on the

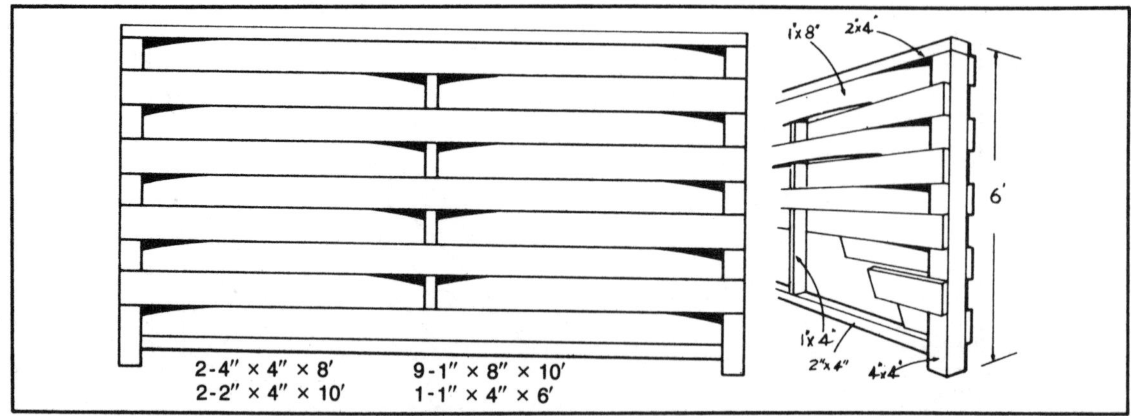


Fig. 6-20. Plans for a basket weave fence (courtesy Georgia-Pacific Corp.).

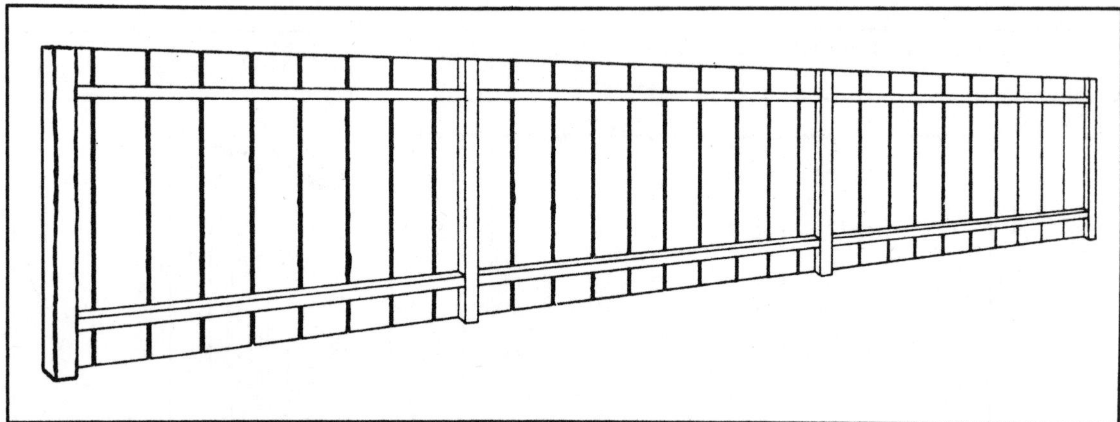

Fig. 6-21. Common board fence (courtesy Western Wood Products Association).

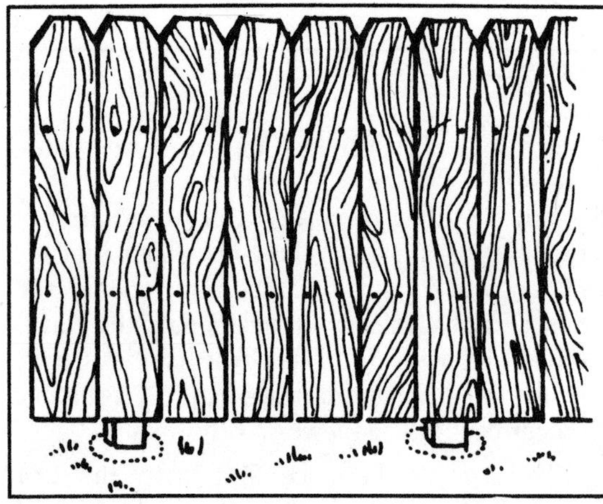

Fig. 6-22. Tightly-spaced dog-ear board fence (courtesy Rollform, Inc.).

posts depends on which style of fence you're building (Fig. 6-26). Always use galvanized nails or hangers when constructing a fence.

Locate the fence boards up to 1 inch off the ground. Plumb with a level as your assembly progresses.

If your materials are unseasoned, expect shrinkage as your fence dries out: 1×4 boards will shrink about 1/8 inch and 1×6 boards about 3/16 inch in width. Shrinkage of posts and rails is proportionate if unseasoned.

Dimensions are fairly standardized. Favored heights are 5, 5½, and 6 feet. Posts are usually 4×4 or 6×6 inches set 6 to 8 feet apart. Standard 2×4s serve as rails. A third rail is often recommended for fences taller than 5 feet.

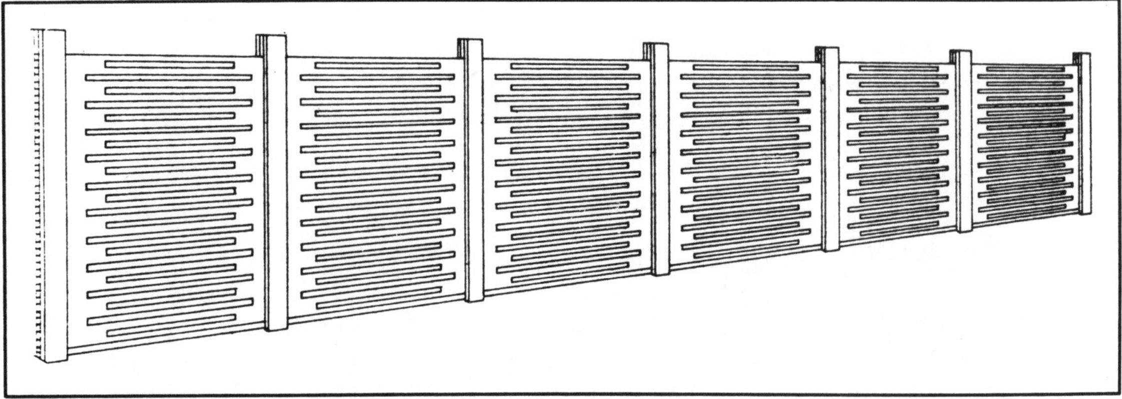

Fig. 6-23. Unique horizontal slat fence (courtesy Western Wood Products Association).

Basic board fences call for substantial foundations because they are heavy and subject to wind damage. Boards used should be of good quality. For a knotless surface, it's necessary to buy select grades of lumber. For crackless joints, use boards with interlocking edges such as shiplap or tongue and groove, or cover the joints between boards with battens.

## ALTERNATE BOARD FENCE

This type of fence goes by many names including board-and-board, alternate board, and shadow fence. It offers the advantages of the basic board fence, but it is a "good neighbor" fence. It also has many of the louver fence's advantages without having the high installation cost.

The fence is simple to build. Boards are nailed to the frame with an open space slightly narrower than the board left between them. Another set is then nailed to the other side, with the open spaces opposite the boards on the first side. The fence is the same on both sides.

The bafflelike arrangement of the boards breaks up strong wind currents but allows air to circulate freely. Like louvers, when the boards are placed vertically, they give filtered privacy and light. When the boards are set horizontally, they give absolute privacy but pass no direct sunlight.

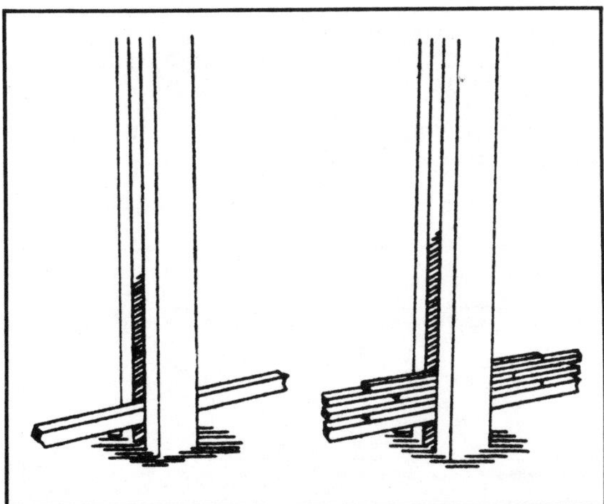

Fig. 6-24. Installing slats in the horizontal slat fence (courtesy Western Wood Products Association).

Fig. 6-25. Three ways to attach rails to posts on board fences.

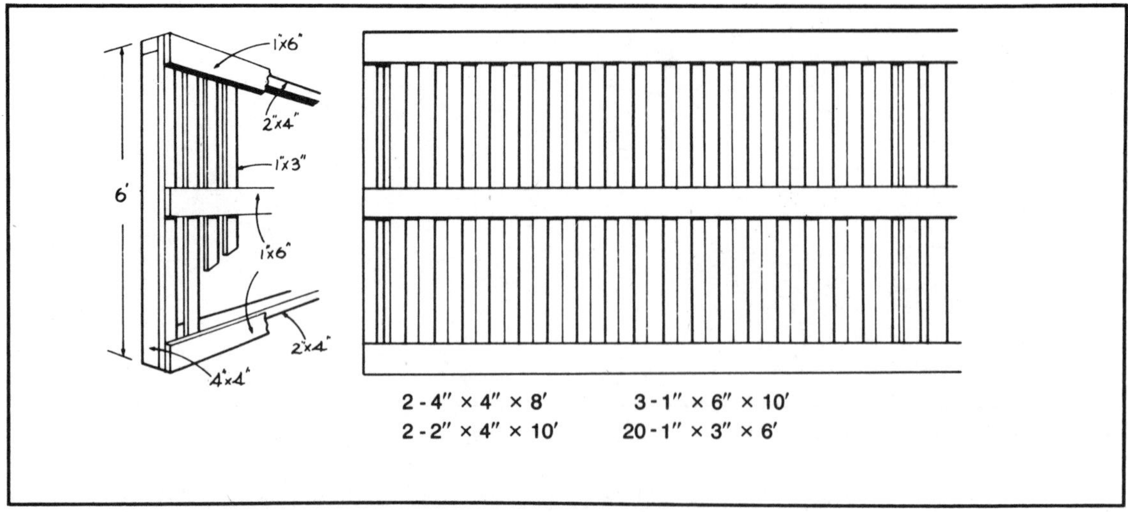


Fig. 6-26. Plans for an outside rail board fence (courtesy Georgia-Pacific Corp.).

This fence also takes on interesting shadow patterns as the sun advances in contrast to the basic board fence—hence the name shadow fence.

The alternate board fence can be assembled with mediocre lumber because a small amount of warping is not noticeable with this design. One disadvantage is that the fence is limited in value as a security fence. Small animals can wiggle their way through either vertical or horizontal panels, and the horizontal variety offers an attractive climbing surface for children and intruders.

Building an alternate board fence is quite similar to constructing the basic board fence (Fig. 6-27). The primary difference is that a spacer is needed so that placement of boards is uniform. The common board used is a 1×6. A spacer is made out of a 1×4 with a cleat nailed to one end so that it can rest on the rail. The first side is sided like this:

- Nail the fence board in place, checking plumb with a carpenter's level.
- Set the spacer on the rail against the previous board.
- Butt the next board up against the spacer and nail it into place.
- Lift the spacer out from between the two boards and lay it up against the second board. Repeat.

When you're done with one side of your alternate board fence, simply start the second side with the spacer rather than the board. Make sure that the alternate board is evenly spaced over the gap on the opposite side of the fence.

Although this is an exceptionally strong fence, it usually calls for extra bracing to prevent the boards from sagging. An extra rail, halfway between top and bottom, will keep the vertical boards from warping. An extra post or 2×4 halfway be-

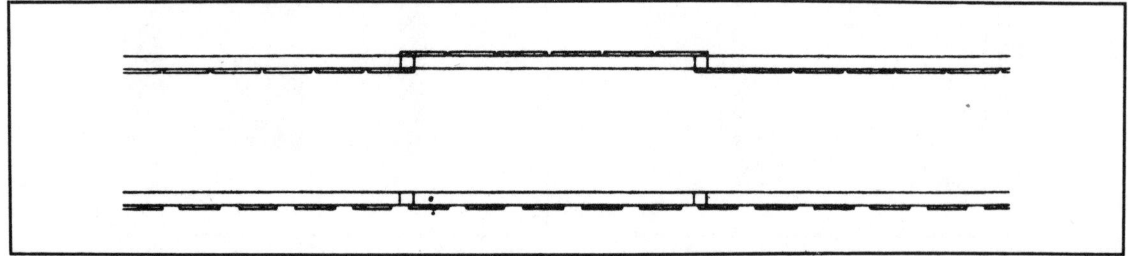

Fig. 6-27. Top view of common board and alternate panel board fence (courtesy Western Wood Products Association).

tween standard posts will keep horizontal boards from sagging.

## LOUVER FENCES

The louver fence is handsome, useful, and quite expensive to build (Fig. 6-28). Louvers give privacy without cutting off light and air or destroying the view. By adjusting the angle of the louvers, you can use the fence to control several factors. By orienting the louvers to the path of the sun, you can fix them so they furnish maximum light and shade for plants. You can temper the air circulation in your garden by facing them across the path of prevailing winds. If you set them with their "blind" side toward the public, you can use them to screen a service area or a drying yard without shutting off the flow of air needed to disperse rubbish odors or speed drying of clothes.

Narrow panels can also be placed near entryways or front windows to permit the householder to view the street or entry walk. A passerby will not be able to look into the home.

Vertically placed louvers provide only "progressive privacy." Some part of the garden is fully visible through the fence as a person moves along it. Horizontal louvers are needed to secure absolute privacy. These louvers will provide a more effective screen, but they are subject to structural weaknesses that discourage many builders from using them.

Louver fences are strong in design (Fig. 6-29). The pattern of alternating strips of shadow and

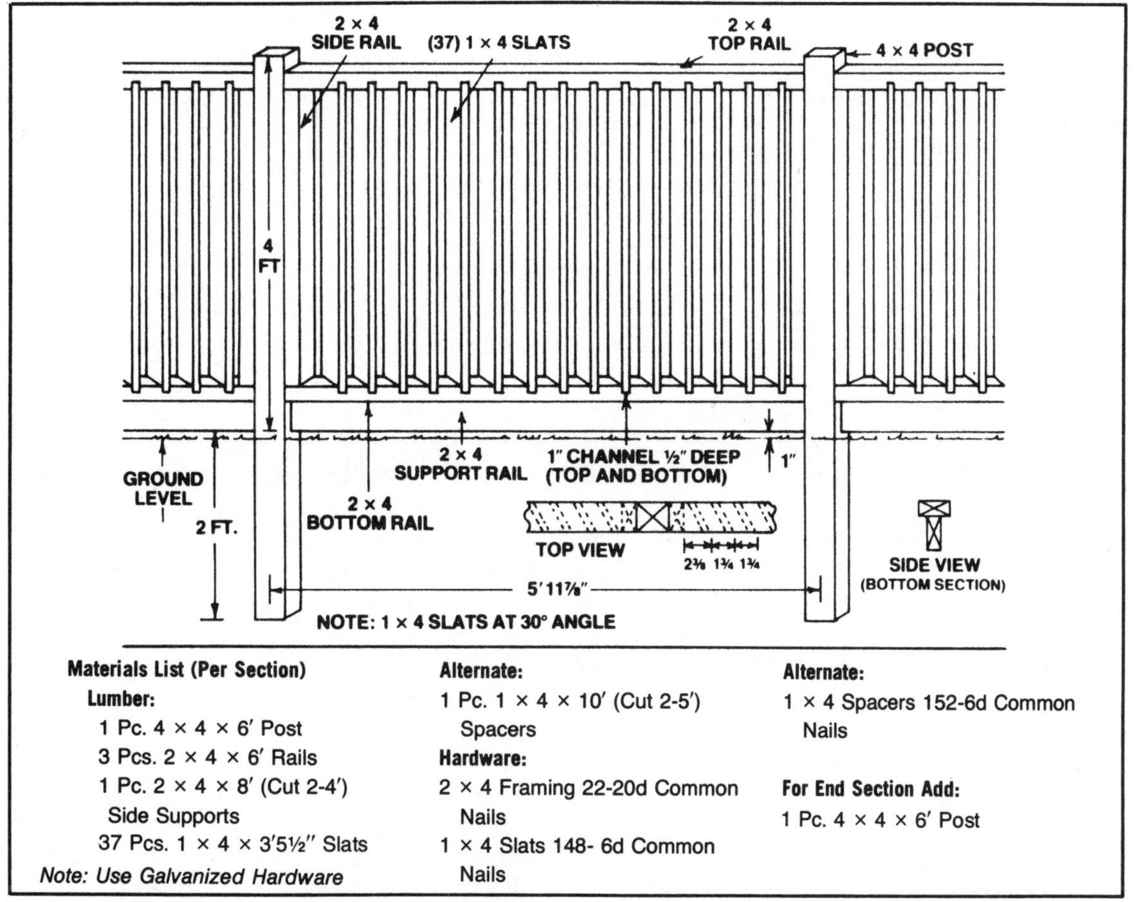


**Materials List (Per Section)**

**Lumber:**
1 Pc. 4 × 4 × 6′ Post
3 Pcs. 2 × 4 × 6′ Rails
1 Pc. 2 × 4 × 8′ (Cut 2-4′) Side Supports
37 Pcs. 1 × 4 × 3′5½" Slats

*Note: Use Galvanized Hardware*

**Alternate:**
1 Pc. 1 × 4 × 10′ (Cut 2-5′) Spacers

**Hardware:**
2 × 4 Framing 22-20d Common Nails
1 × 4 Slats 148- 6d Common Nails

**Alternate:**
1 × 4 Spacers 152-6d Common Nails

**For End Section Add:**
1 Pc. 4 × 4 × 6′ Post

Fig. 6-28. Detailed plans for a louvered board fence (courtesy Wolmanized pressure-treated lumber).

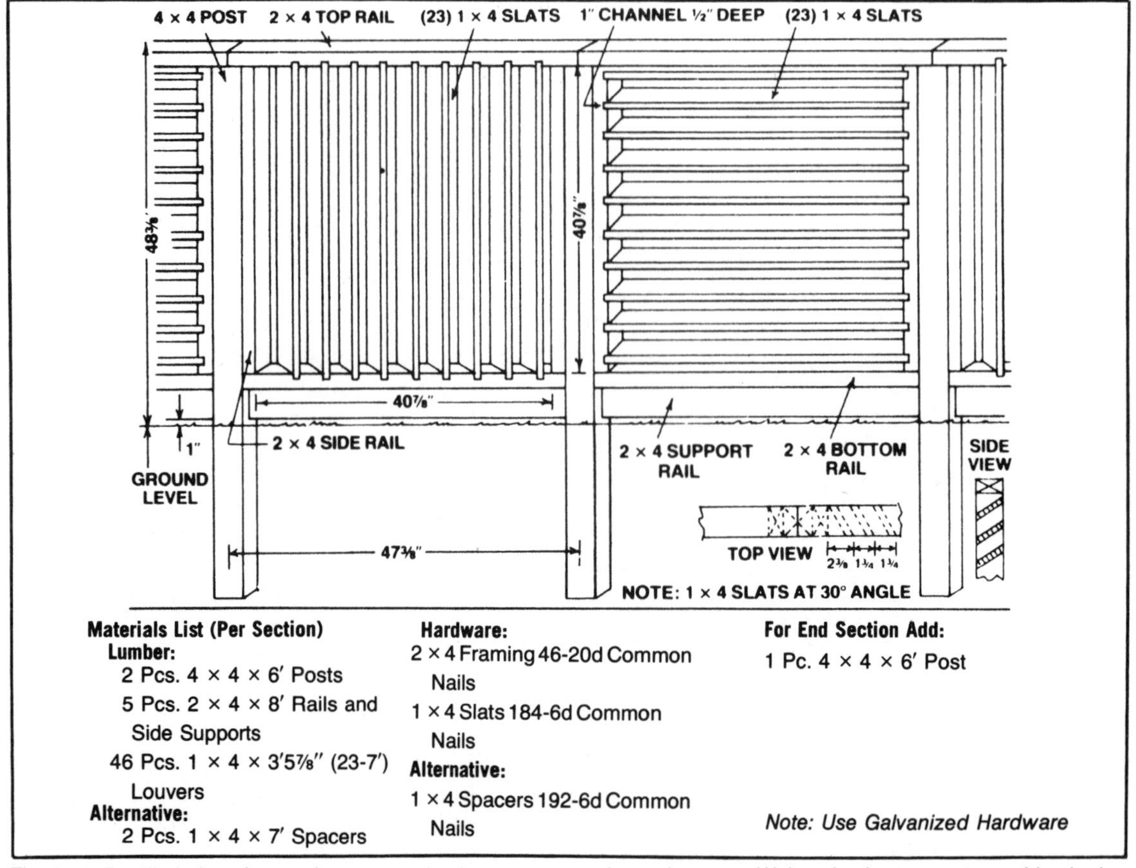


Fig. 6-29. Detailed plans for an alternate section louvered board fence (courtesy Wolmanized pressure-treated lumber).

highlight, varying through the day as the sun's angle changes, provides an interesting feature in the garden. Louver fences are meant to be seen and consequently have to be carefully worked into the landscape plan. They should not be concealed under vines or hidden behind shrubs. Overplanting along the fence line will close off the view and interfere with the free flow of air through the louvers.

Because of its architectural quality, louvered fencing should be matched to the design of the house. It's often treated as a part of the house, or as a means of tying to the house something such as a carport or an outdoor room. If painted or stained the same color as the house, the fencing's relationship can be further strengthened. Although louvered fencing can be used with most styles of residential architecture, it looks best with more modern structures that utilize simple planes, angles, and shadows to achieve their exterior lines and design.

Principal faults of the louver fence are its high construction costs and certain inborn weaknesses. The two are related, because much of the expense involved in erecting a louver fence is due to the extra costs in premium lumber and careful workmanship needed to prevent the fence from deteriorating.

Several factors force the costs upward. Louver fencing requires a larger amount of material than any other board fence. More vertical boards are required per running foot than for a solid board fence of comparable height. The louvers are supported only at the ends without center bracing. They tend to warp and twist after several months' exposure to sun and rain. To prevent this, many fence builders use top grade (and top price) kiln-dried lumber and apply some type of moisture seal. If the louvers are installed horizontally, they will develop a sag unless the span between the posts is fairly short or the boards are supported in the middle.

Another complication is due to the heavy weight of the fence structure. Much of the weight of the louvers is borne by the bottom rail, which may sag and throw the framing out of alignment. The whole structure requires staunch posts and substantial foundations.

Louver fences consume a surprising quantity of paint because of the unusually large surface area that must be covered. You rarely see louver fencing used for long, meandering boundary lines. It's usually found in fairly short installations and placed expertly where fullest advantages of its features can best be obtained.

There are basically two ways to build a louver fence. The first is to set the posts, attach the top and bottom rails, and nail the louvers in place. Toenail them to the bottom rail and drive through the top rail. This is most easily done by two persons. One person works at the top rail, and the other works the lower one.

The other system is to construct the fence in sections on the ground, then lift the completed panels into place and nail them to the posts. If you

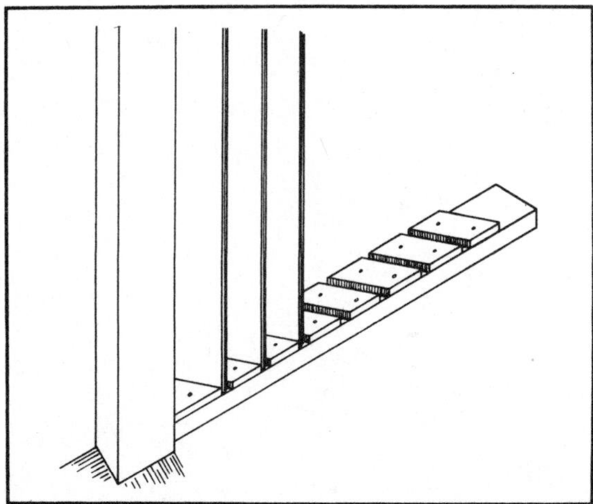

Fig. 6-30. Installation of louvers or baffles and spacers (courtesy Western Wood Products Association).

Fig. 6-31. Common basket weave fence.

have a flat surface on which to work, such as a driveway or garage floor, you may find this method easier.

Louvers can be set at almost any angle (Fig. 6-30). Some are installed at right angles to the fence line, but the accepted angle is 45 degrees. Use a template to make sure that the louvers are spaced properly for nailing. You won't have to measure each board's gap with it.

You should use boards heavy enough to resist warping. Many builders use 2×4s or 2×6s.

Attach a beveled or slanted cap along the top to shed rainwater. Keep it from seeping into the exposed grain of the wood.

You can sometimes reduce construction costs by eliminating posts and constructing the fence on concrete foundation pylons with nailing surfaces. Horizontal louver fencing can be effectively built in 4-foot-wide sections using spacers cut at a 45-degree angle and installed between each board along the posts.

## BASKET WEAVE FENCING

Basket weave fencing uses a minimum of material to get a solid screen, is attractive from both sides, and is surprisingly strong for its weight (Fig. 6-31). It's a favorite with contractors because they can use inexpensive ½-inch stock in construction. Some people, however, prefer the material in shorter fences as it is difficult to look at for very long—and even more difficult to paint.

The basket weave fence is built around the basic board fence frame: 4×4 posts and 2×4 rails.

Many basket weave fences, however, are built with 4 feet between posts rather than 8 feet.

The strips can be any standard width between 4 and 12 inches, with 8 and 10 inches being the most popular. The thickness should be ½ to 1 inch so that the stock can bend for the weave. Rough finish lumber is usually preferred, and redwood or cedar strips are the most common.

Start your fence at the bottom and nail the end of one strip horizontally to the post. Weave it across the fence around 1×2 stock that isn't nailed into place. Begin the next strip on the opposite side of the post, or at least alternate the direction of the strip around the 1×2 stock for a weave effect. Nails are only needed for attaching the strips to the posts.

Basket weave fences are the most difficult to paint, even with a spray gun. Plan to paint, stain, or preserve the fence before construction. For a true basket weave effect, use the strips as both horizontal and vertical boards.

# Chapter 7

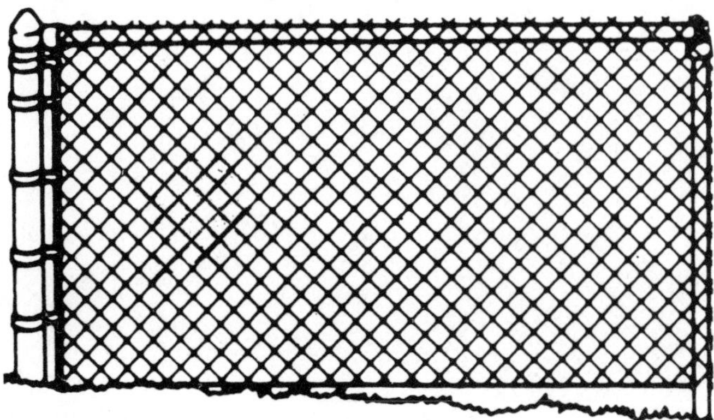

# Chain Link Fences

CHAIN LINK IS ONE OF THE MOST EFFICIENT fencing materials for many homes and commercial applications. It offers maximum visibility, adapts to irregular ground, keeps out most intruders, allows clear air passage, and needs little maintenance to insure a long life.

The biggest objection many people have to chain link fences is the lack of privacy. It's truly an "open fence." This objection can be overcome through landscaping; wood, metal, or plastic inserts; and with panels.

Chain link fencing is often less expensive to install and maintain than traditional wood fencing. You don't need a contractor to install it. You can do it yourself. Many fence supply companies will rent or loan you the special tools you need to install a chain link fence

## INSTALLING A CHAIN LINK FENCE

There are eight simple steps to installing a chain link fence:

- *Step one:* survey property lines.
- *Step two:* locate and set terminal posts.
- *Step three:* locate and set line posts.
- *Step four:* apply fittings to terminal posts.
- *Step five:* apply top rail.
- *Step six:* hang fabric.
- *Step seven:* stretch fabric.
- *Step eight:* hang gates.

You need a posthole digger, fence stretcher, wire grip and stretch bar, cutting pliers, an adjustable end wrench, tape measure, and a carpenter's level (Figs. 7-1 and 7-2).

### Step One: Survey Property Lines

Before you start to install your chain link fence, be sure your boundaries and property lines are legally established. Make sure that the location of your proposed fence lines does not exceed property lines. Place your fence line 2 to 4 inches *inside* your property line as insurance and to avoid encroaching on adjoining property with the concrete foundations.

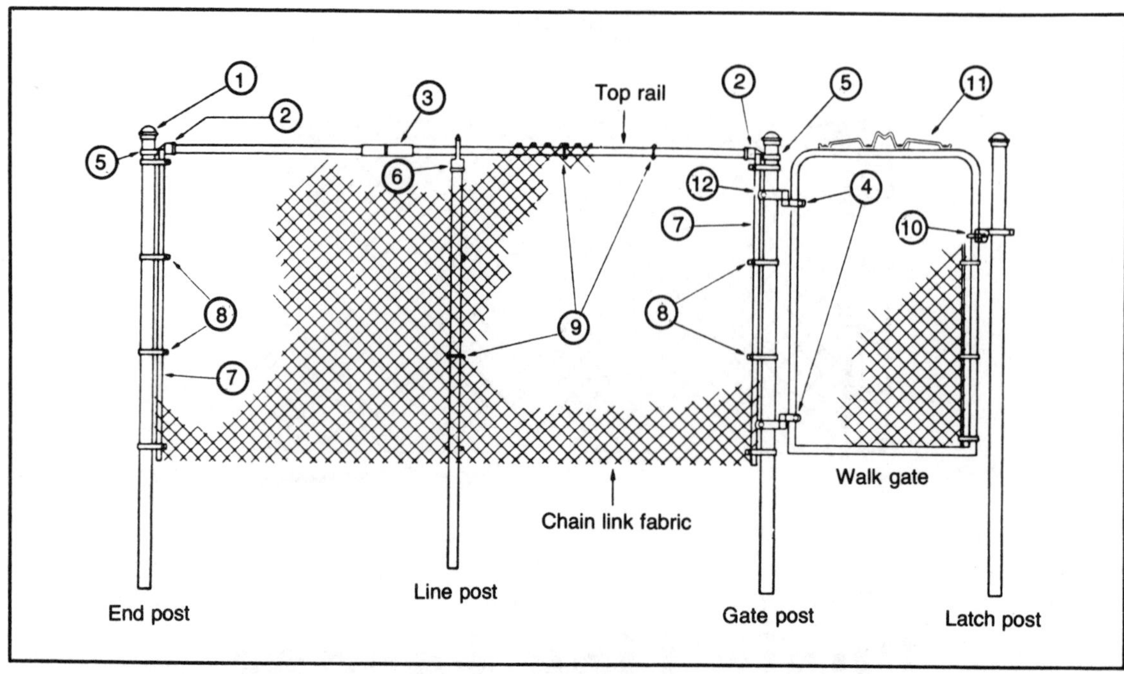


Fig. 7-1. Chain link fence components. Numbers refer to parts on the materials list in Fig. 7-2.

### Step Two: Locate and Set Terminal Posts

Determine the location of end, corner, and gate posts (which are referred to as terminal posts). See Fig. 7-3. Distance between gateposts is determined by adding the actual width of the gate to an allowance for hinges and latches. Single walk gates require 3¾ inches for hinges and latches. Double drive gates require 5½ inches. A 3-foot walk gate should measure 32¼ inches wide. Adding 3¾ inches to the width means that the distance between posts (inside face to inside face) should be 36 inches.

When digging postholes, watch for any underground cables or pipelines by contacting your local utilities. Figure 7-4 illustrates the right and wrong way to dig terminal and line postholes. Terminal postholes should be 10 inches wide at the top and 12 inches wide at the bottom. Line postholes should be 8 inches wide at the top and 10 inches at the bottom. If you're using a clamshell posthole digger, you can widen the bottom of the hole by simply angling the digger and scraping the sides or you can use a small shovel to finish out the hole.

Mark all posts with crayon or chalk for the correct height of fence you are installing (Fig. 7-5). Terminal posts should be set 2 inches higher than the fabric width. Line posts should be set 2 inches lower than the fabric width. Measurement C in Fig. 7-5 dictates the hole depth.

Set the terminal posts in concrete using a 1-2-4 concrete mix: 1 part cement, 2 parts sand and 4 parts gravel (Fig. 7-6). Mix a fairly heavy solution as too much water weakens concrete and may cause cracking. Use a carpenter's level to set posts plumb. Crown all post footings for water drainage by sloping concrete away from the post.

Because no two pieces of ground are alike or completely level, you must plan the contour of your installation in advance (Fig. 7-7). To make the top of your fence straight, you need to compensate for ground level variations by adjusting the amount of post above the ground to a level line of sight. In some cases it's necessary to trench the ground at a particular high ground level or, if the ground level is low, fill it with dirt. You can make a ground contour installation.

## MATERIALS NEEDED FOR RESIDENTIAL CHAIN LINK FENCE

| PIECES | ITEM–DESCRIPTION | QUANTITY TO USE | PRICE EACH |
|---|---|---|---|
| (1) | Fabric (50 feet per roll) | Divide total footage by 50 and round up | |
| (2) | Top Rail 21' x 1-3/8'' O.D. Swedged | Divide total footage by 21 and round up | |
| (3) | Line Post 1-5/8'' O.D. | Divide total footage by 10 and round up | |
| (4) | Loop Caps 1-5/8'' x 1-3/8'' | Use 1 per Line Post | |
| (5) | Terminal Post 2-1/2'' O.D. | — | |
| (6) | Tension Bar | Use 1 per end or gate post, 2 per corner post | |
| (7) | Brace Band | Use 1 per Tension Bar | |
| (8) | Rail Ends 1-3/8'' | Use 1 per Tension Bar | |
| (9) | Tension Band | Use 4 per tension bar or 1' per foot of fence height | |
| (10) | 5/16'' x 1¼'' Carriage Bolts | Use 1 per tension or brace band | |
| (11) | Post Caps (Acorn Style) 2½'' | Use 1 per terminal post | |
| (12) | Alum Cut Ties | Use 1 per foot of fence – Packaged 100 per bag | |
| (13) | Walk Gate (3' or 3½' wide) | — | |
| (14) | Double Drive Gate (10' or 12' wide) | — | |
| (15) | Male Hinge 2½'' | Use 2 per walk gate and 4 per double drive gate | |
| (16) | 3/8 x 3 Carriage Bolts | Used with the male hinge, 1 per hinge | |
| (17) | Female Hinge 1-3/8'' | Use 2 per walk gate and 4 per double drive gate | |
| (18) | 3/8 x 1-3/4 Carriage Bolts | Used with female hinge, 1 per hinge | |
| (19) | Fork Latch | Needed on walk gates only – 1 per gate | |

## TOOLS YOU WILL FIND USEFUL IN INSTALLING YOUR FENCE

1. Post Hole Digger
2. Wheelbarrow, shovel and hoe to mix and transport concrete
3. Tape Measure
4. Level
5. String and Stakes or Mason's Line
6. Pliers
7. Fence Stretcher (Block and tackle, ratchet type power pull, etc.
8. 1/2'' x 9/16'' Wrench or Crescent Wrench
9. Hacksaw or Pipe Cutter.

Fig. 7-2. Materials list for chain link fencing.

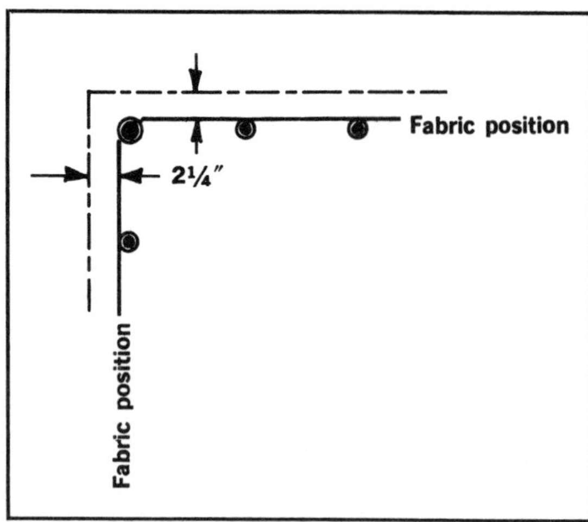


Fig. 7-3. Planning post positions (courtesy Builders Fence Co., Inc.).

### Step Three: Locate and Set Line Posts

Mark the grade line on all line posts measuring from the top down (Fig. 7-8). Then measure the distance between terminal posts and check the line post spacing chart (Table 7-1) for the exact distance to allow between line posts.

Stretch a mason's line from outside to outside of terminal posts once you're sure the concrete has set up sufficiently. The line postholes should be lined up so that when they are set in the center of their holes, their centers will line up with the terminal post centers. This means the outside faces of the line posts will be about ¼ inch inside of the line stretched between the outside of the terminal posts. Dig the line postholes and set the line posts.

Stretch your mason's line taut 4 inches below terminal post tops and use it as a guide to align the height of line posts (Fig. 7-9). If it's necessary to adjust the height of any post either up or down, simply raise or lower the post as illustrated before the concrete sets up. Use your level to keep the post plumb while adjusting the height. It's best to let the concrete set up for about a day before continuing the installation of your chain link fence.

### Step Four: Apply Fittings to Terminal Posts

After the posts are installed and the concrete has set, slip the tension and brace bands on to the terminal posts (Fig. 7-10). The tension bands should be spaced approximately 10 to 12 inches apart. Do not spread or distort the bands. All bolt heads for the bands should be on the outside of the fence, and the threaded ends should be on the inside. Apply all the terminal post caps.

### Step Five: Apply Top Rail

The loop caps are now attached (Fig. 7-11). They are set with the top rail hole offset toward the outside of the fence, making flush the outside face of the top rail through the loop caps.

Join the top rail with swaged end where required (Fig. 7-11). The end of the top rail fits into the rail end fittings on the terminal post.

### Step Six: Hang Fabric

After assembling the framework, unroll the fabric on the ground along the fence line starting at a terminal post. Slide the tension bar through the last

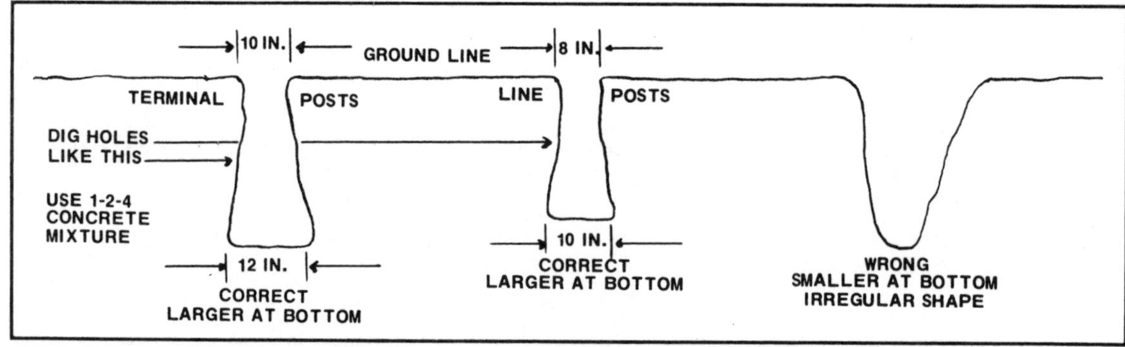


Fig. 7-4. The right and wrong way to dig fence posts (courtesy Builders Fence Co., Inc.).

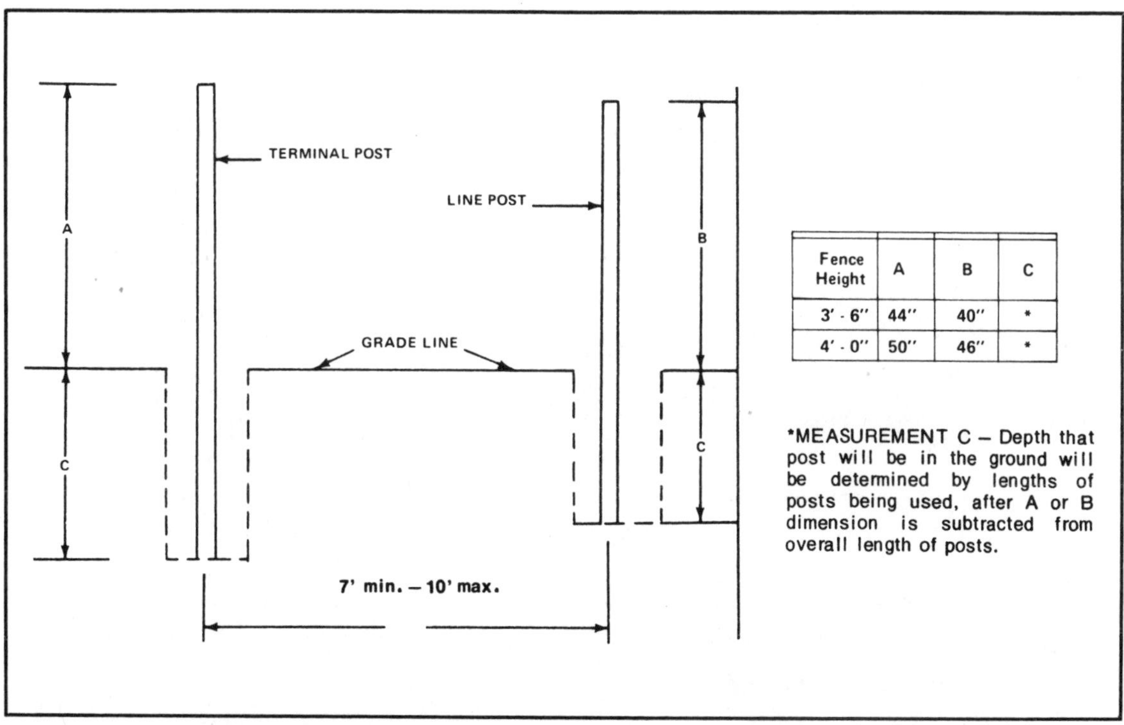


| Fence Height | A | B | C |
|---|---|---|---|
| 3' - 6" | 44" | 40" | * |
| 4' - 0" | 50" | 46" | * |

Fig. 7-5. Estimating posthole depth (courtesy Builders Fence Co., Inc.).

Fig. 7-6. Setting chain link fence posts (courtesy Builders Fence Co., Inc.).

link in your fabric. Attach this combination to the terminal post using the tension band and bolts provided (Fig. 7-12).

If more or less fabric is needed to span the opening, an additional amount can be connected or removed as shown in Fig. 7-13. The fabric should be on the outside face of all posts with either the knuckled or twisted edge at the top as desired. It should be loosely attached to the top rail by a tie wire (Fig. 7-14).

## Step Seven: Stretch Fabric

Fabric should be stretched from the terminal post already attached to the opposite terminal post. Insert the tension bar in the end of the fabric and attach the fence stretcher to the bar (Fig. 7-15). Ratchet type power pull, large carpenter's clamps, block and tackle, or a similar device may be used. Most wire stretching tools of this type can be rented or borrowed locally.

As you stretch the fabric, test it for tension. It's

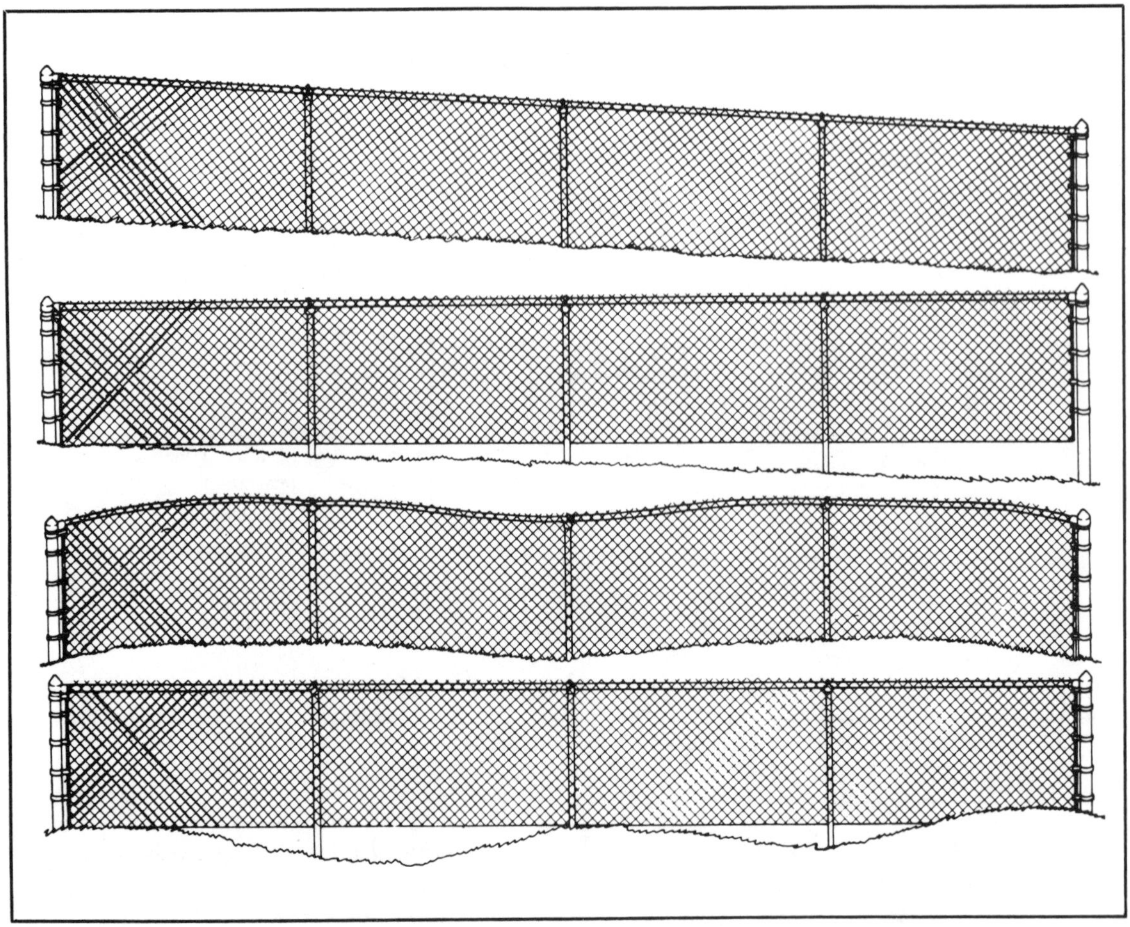

Fig. 7-7. Four ways of installing chain link fencing over uneven terrain (courtesy Builders Fence Co., Inc.).

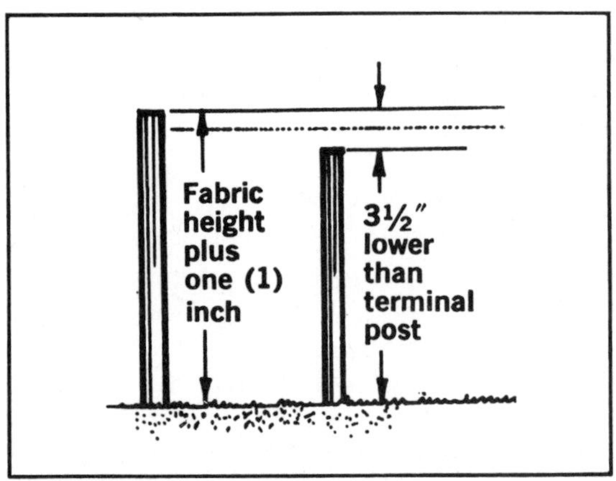


Fig. 7-8. Determining post height (courtesy Builders Fence Co., Inc.).

stretched enough when it gives slightly. The top of the fabric should be located approximately ½ inch above the top rail to insure proper height. After the fence fabric is sufficiently tight, remove the excess fabric as shown in Fig. 7-16 and connect the tension bar to the post with tension bands. Fasten the fabric to the top rail and line posts with tie wires spaced approximately 18 inches apart.

For most residential installations, the fabric should be installed with the smooth edge up. If added security is necessary, you can install the fabric with barbs up.

### Step Eight: Hang Gates

After the entire fence has been completed,

**Table 7-1. Line Post Spacing.**

| Space | Set Post Apart | Space | Set Post Apart | Space | Set Post Apart | Space | Set Post Apart | Space | Set Post Apart |
|---|---|---|---|---|---|---|---|---|---|
| 30 ft. | 10 ft. | 51 ft. | 8 ft. 6 in. | 71 ft. | 8 ft. 9 in. | 92 ft. | 9 ft. 2 in. | 112 ft. | 9 ft. 4 in. |
| 31 ft. | 7 ft. 9 in. | 52 ft. | 8 ft. 8 in. | 72 ft. | 9 ft. | 93 ft. | 9 ft. 3 in. | 113 ft. | 9 ft. 5 in. |
| 32 ft. | 8 ft. | 53 ft. | 8 ft. 10 in. | 73 ft. | 9 ft. 2 in. | 94 ft. | 9 ft. 5 in. | 114 ft. | 9 ft. 6 in. |
| 33 ft. | 8 ft. 3 in. | 54 ft. | 9 ft. | 74 ft. | 9 ft. 3 in. | 95 ft. | 9 ft. 6 in. | 115 ft. | 9 ft. 7 in. |
| 34 ft. | 8 ft. 6 in. | 55 ft. | 8 ft. 2 in. | 75 ft. | 9 ft. 4 in. | 96 ft. | 9 ft. 7 in. | 116 ft. | 9 ft. 8 in. |
| 35 ft. | 8 ft. 9 in. | 56 ft. | 9 ft. 4 in. | 76 ft. | 9 ft. 6 in. | 97 ft. | 9 ft. 7 in. | 117 ft. | 9 ft. 9 in. |
| 36 ft. | 9 ft. | 57 ft. | 9 ft. 6 in. | 77 ft. | 9 ft. 7 in. | 98 ft. | 9 ft. 8 in. | 118 ft. | 9 ft. 10 in. |
| 37 ft. | 9 ft. 3 in. | 58 ft. | 9 ft. 8 in. | 78 ft. | 9 ft. 9 in. | 99 ft. | 9 ft. 9 in. | 119 ft. | 9 ft. 10 in. |
| 38 ft. | 9 ft. 6 in. | 59 ft. | 9 ft. 10 in. | 79 ft. | 9 ft. 10 in. | 100 ft. | 10 ft. | 120 ft. | 10 ft. |
| 40 ft. | 10 ft. | 60 ft. | 10 ft. | 80 ft. | 10 ft. | 101 ft. | 9 ft. 2 in. | 121 ft. | 9 ft. 3 in. |
| 41 ft. | 8 ft. 2 in. | 61 ft. | 8 ft. 8 in. | 81 ft. | 9 ft. | 102 ft. | 9 ft. 3 in. | 122 ft. | 9 ft. 4 in. |
| 42 ft. | 8 ft. 5 in. | 62 ft. | 8 ft. 10 in. | 82 ft. | 9 ft. 1 in. | 103 ft. | 9 ft. 4 in. | 123 ft. | 9 ft. 5 in. |
| 43 ft. | 8 ft. 6 in. | 63 ft. | 9 ft. | 83 ft. | 9 ft. 3 in. | 104 ft. | 9 ft. 5 in. | 124 ft. | 9 ft. 6 in. |
| 44 ft. | 8 ft. 9 in. | 64 ft. | 9 ft. | 84 ft. | 9 ft. 4 in. | 105 ft. | 9 ft. 6 in. | 125 ft. | 9 ft. 7 in. |
| 45 ft. | 9 ft. | 65 ft. | 9 ft. 3 in. | 85 ft. | 9 ft. 6 in. | 106 ft. | 9 ft. 7 in. | 126 ft. | 9 ft. 8 in. |
| 46 ft. | 9 ft. 2 in. | 66 ft. | 9 ft. 5 in. | 86 ft. | 9 ft. 7 in. | 107 ft. | 9 ft. 8 in. | 127 ft. | 9 ft. 9 in. |
| 47 ft. | 9 ft. 5 in. | 67 ft. | 9 ft. 7 in. | 87 ft. | 9 ft. 8 in. | 108 ft. | 9 ft. 9 in. | 128 ft. | 9 ft. 10 in. |
| 48 ft. | 9 ft. 7 in. | 68 ft. | 9 ft. 8 in. | 88 ft. | 9 ft. 9 in. | 109 ft. | 9 ft. 10 in. | 129 ft. | 9 ft. 10 in. |
| 49 ft. | 9 ft. 9 in. | 69 ft. | 9 ft. 10 in. | 89 ft. | 9 ft. 10 in. | 110 ft. | 10 ft. | | |
| 50 ft. | 10 ft. | 70 ft. | 10 ft. | 91 ft. | 9 ft. 2 in. | 111 ft. | 9 ft. 3 in. | | |

apply male hinges to one of the gateposts, hanging the top hinge upside down to prevent the gate from being lifted off (Fig. 7-17). Loosely apply the female hinges on the gate frame and slip them onto the male hinges that have been installed on the gatepost (Fig. 7-18). Set the hinges to allow for full swing of the gate. Align the top of the gate with the top of the fence. Tighten all hinges securely. Install the gate latch for single gates (Fig. 7-19). Use the same procedure for double gates as on walk gates, but install a center latching device (fork latch) (Fig. 7-20).

## SHOPPING FOR A CHAIN LINK FENCE

Now that you see how simple installing a chain link fence can be, here's a closer look at the basic components of a chain link fence.

### Wire Size

The wire size is traditionally measured by gauge. Gauge designations can be and often are confusing for the consumer. Remember that the *smaller* the gauge number, the *bigger* (thus stronger) the wire.

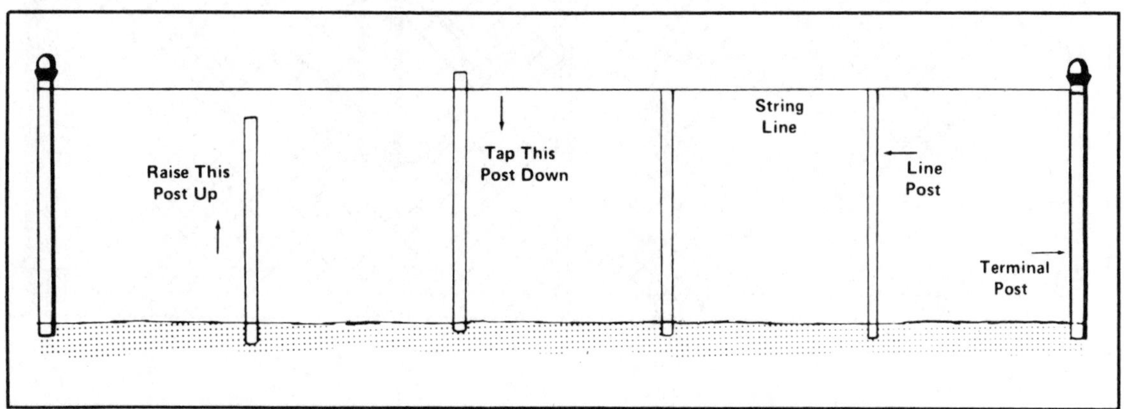


Fig. 7-9. Adjusting line posts to proper height.

Fig. 7-10. Sometimes the top rail must be dropped (photo by Val Ramos).

## Mesh Size

The size of the wire mesh is also important in determining the type of fence you ultimately have installed (Table 7-2). These two items—wire and mesh size—affect both price and durability.

The size of the mesh is determined by measuring the distance between the parallel sides of the mesh. Common sizes are 2⅛ inches and 2 inches (mesh size for tennis court fencing is usually 1¾ inches in diameter). Larger mesh takes less steel and is not as costly.

## Framework

The chain link fabric is supported by a framework consisting of line posts, terminal and corner posts, and top rail. They are held together by a set of specialized fence fittings (Fig. 7-21). This entire framework will be coated with either zinc or vinyl for long life and protection against the elements.

In residential fences the line posts are normally 1⅝ inches O.D. (outside diameter), with varying wall thicknesses depending on your individual desire for strength and rigidity. Terminal and corner posts may be 1⅞ or 2⅜ inches O.D.

Top rail is normally 1⅜ inch O.D. It comes in 21-foot lengths joined by sleeves or swaged ends that slide together.

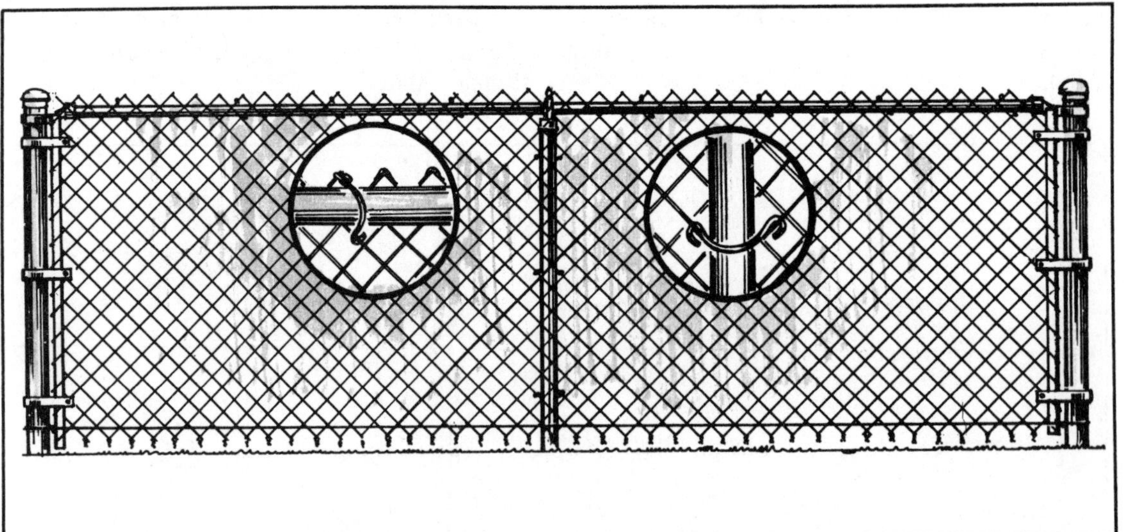

Fig. 7-11. Attaching fabric to posts and rails (courtesy Builders Fence Co., Inc.).

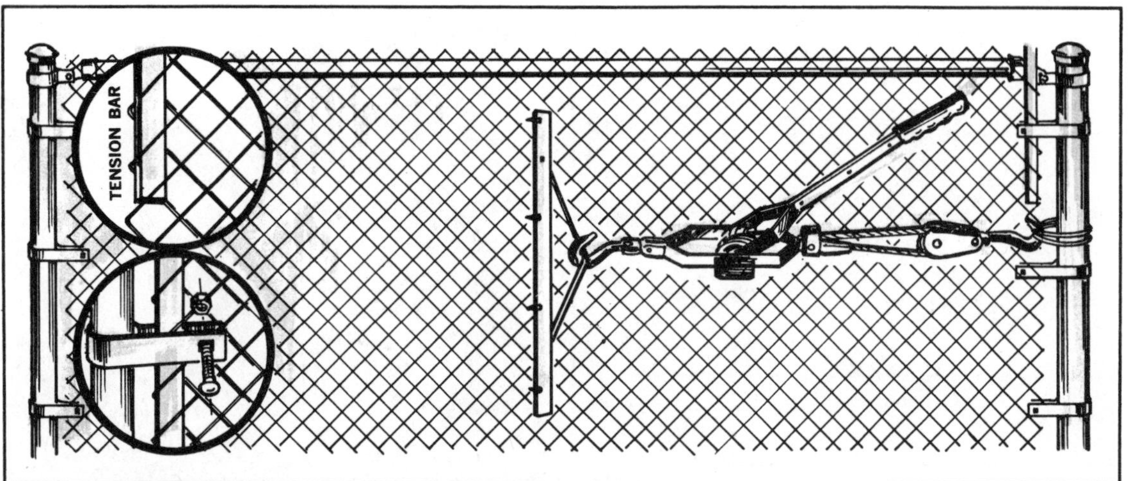


Fig. 7-12. Stretching fence fabric.

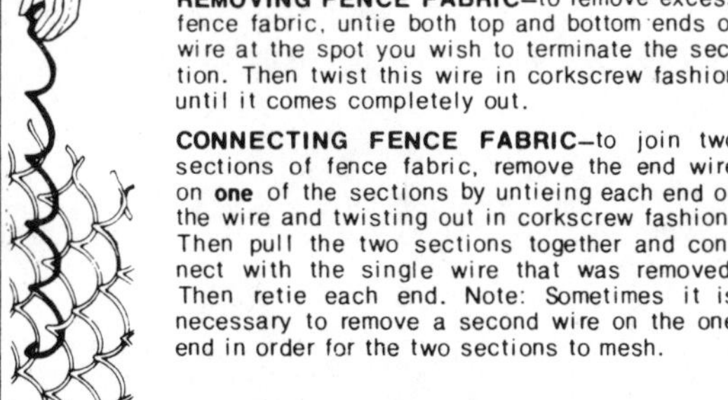


Fig. 7-13. How to remove or connect fence fabric.

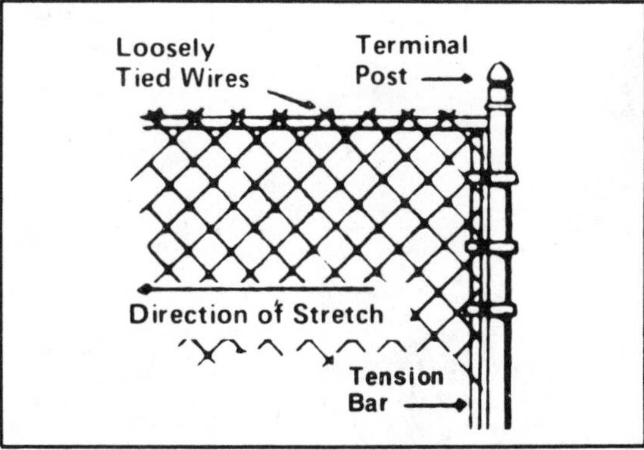


Fig. 7-14. Loosely tie wires in case additional stretching is necessary.

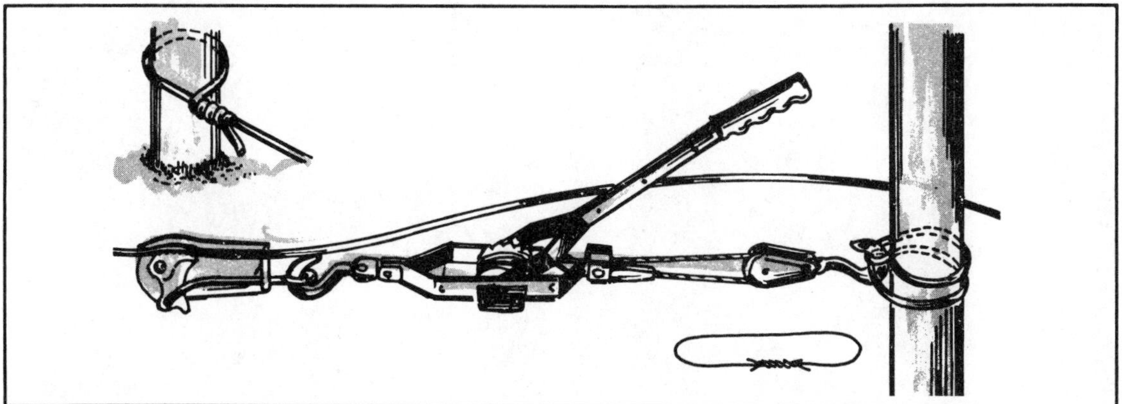

Fig. 7-15. Attaching the fabric stretcher (courtesy Builders Fence Co., Inc.).

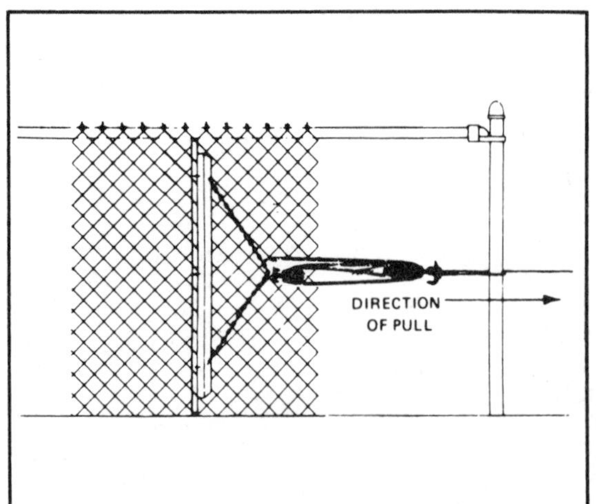


Fig. 7-16. Make sure the fabric is stretched evenly.

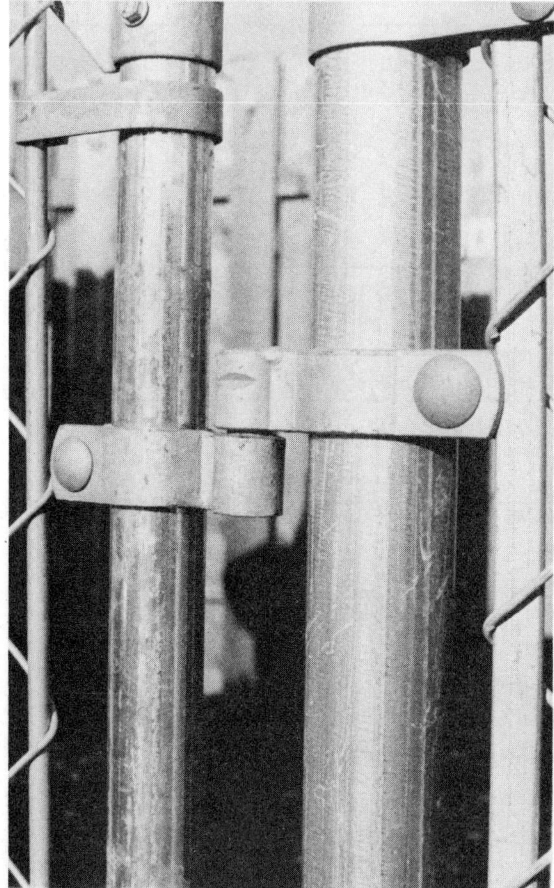

Fig. 7-17. Male and female hinge (photo by Val Ramos).

Fig. 7-18. Gate frame corner (photo by Val Ramos).

Fig. 7-19. Gate latch (photo by Val Ramos).

Fig. 7-20. Latch and chain for double drive gates (photo by Val Ramos).

**Table 7-2. Standard Diamond Count for Various Heights of Chain Link Fabric—2-Inch Mesh.**

| Fabric Height | Diamond Count | |
|---|---|---|
| | 11 Gauge | 9 Gauge |
| 36″ | 10½ | 10½ |
| 42″ | 12½ | 12½ |
| 48″ | 14½ | 13½ |
| 60″ | 17½ | 17½ |
| 72″ | 20½ | 20½ |
| 84″ | 24½ | 24½ |
| 96″ | 27½ | 27½ |
| 108″ | 31½ | 31½ |
| 120″ | 34½ | 34½ |
| 132″ | 37½ | 37½ |
| 144″ | 41½ | 41½ |

## Gates

Gates are the only moving part of a fence and should be of a sturdy construction with strong hinges, latches, and gateposts for long, trouble-free service (Figs. 7-22 and 7-23). Make certain that the gate you order provides a large enough opening to accommodate easily any items that you will be moving in or out of the enclosed area such as garden

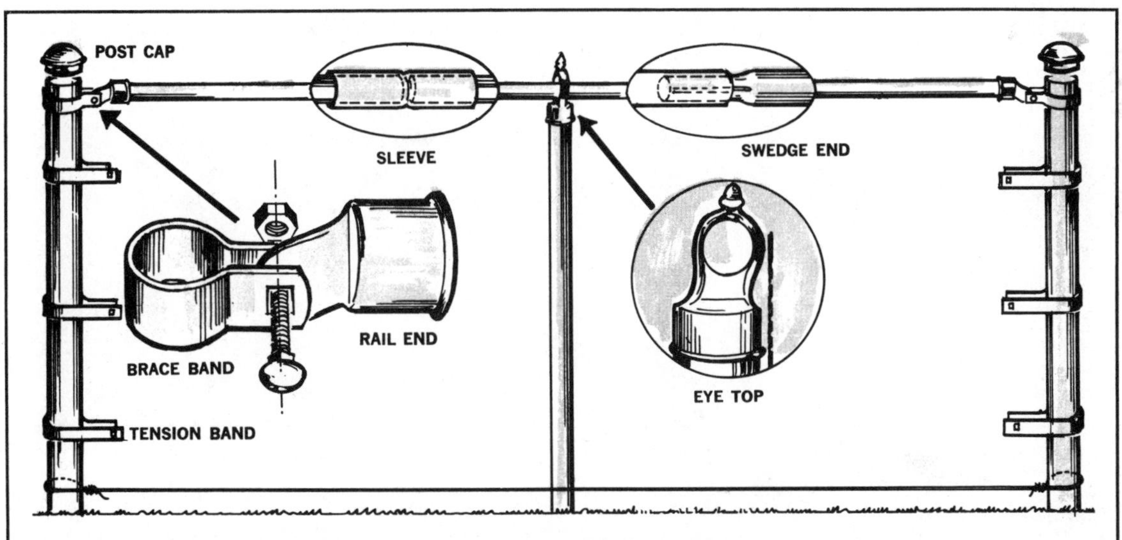


Fig. 7-21. Chain link fence posts, rails, and fittings (courtesy Builders Fence Co., Inc.).

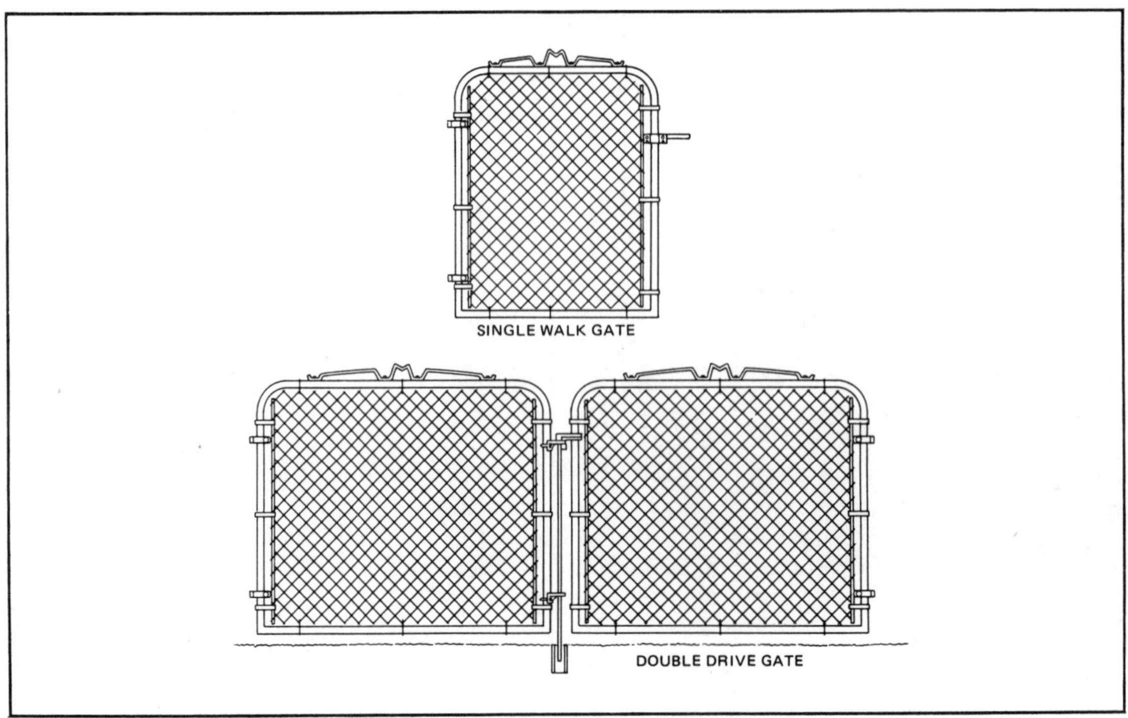


Fig. 7-22. Single walk and double drive gates.

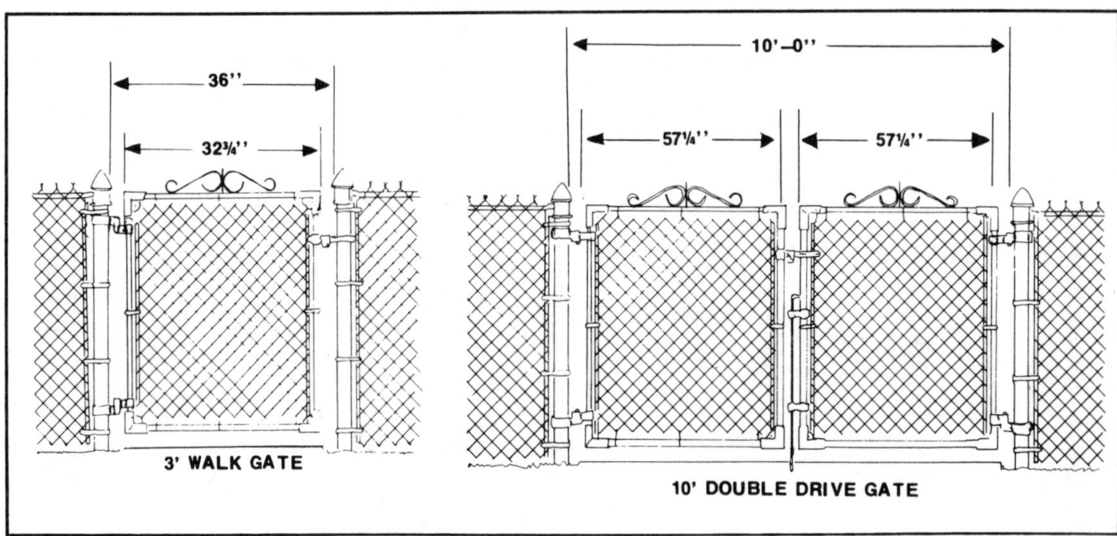


Fig. 7-23. Dimensions for single walk and double drive gates.

equipment, lawn furniture, a recreation vehicle, etc. You may want automatic closing and latching devices. These items and rolling gates are readily available. More detailed specifications for galvanized steel and aluminum chain link fences is included in Appendix C.

# Chapter 8

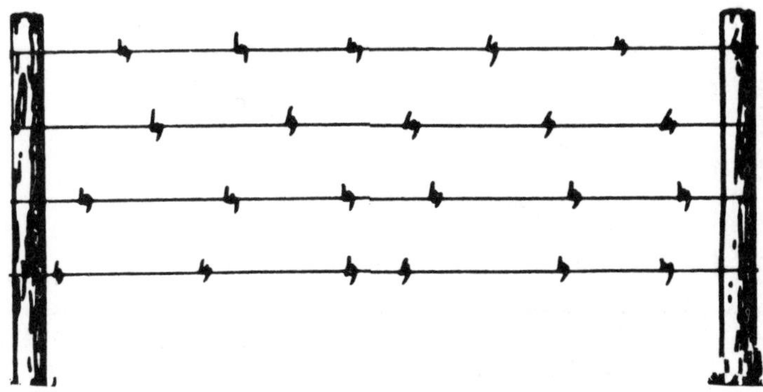

# Livestock Fences

FENCES ARE BUILT TO PROTECT OR DIVIDE property, to improve the appearance of property, or to confine animals. The fences should be planned carefully whatever their purpose. This is especially inportant on farms where the fences represent a large investment, and their location and arrangement may affect production efficiency.

Permanent fences should be constructed well and made of good materials. Temporary fences need not be so sturdily constructed and may be made of less expensive materials. The kinds of fences commonly used on farms include board, woven wire, barbed wire, combination woven wire and barbed wire, cable, and electric.

## PREPARATORY WORK

Before erecting a fence, you may have to lay out the fence line, clear it, or both.

### Laying Out a Fence Line

Figure 8-1 shows how to lay out a fence line on level ground. Set a stake at each end of the proposed fence line and station another person at one of the ends. Starting from that end, set a stake every 100 feet, with the other person verifying the alignment of the stakes with the two end stakes.

Figure 8-2 shows how to lay out a fence line over hills where you can't see the other end stake. Set two stakes on top of the hill where both can be seen from both end stakes. Line up the two stakes, first with one end stake, then with the other. You may have to move one or both stakes several times to obtain satisfactory alignment.

### Clearing a Fence Line

Fence lines should be cleared of trees, brush, stumps, rocks, old fencing, and other obstructions that might interfere with construction of the fence or detract from its appearance. The easiest and quickest way to clear a fence line is to use a bulldozer or a bulldozer blade mounted on a tractor. You can knock down small trees and old fencing, clear brush, level high spots, and fill in low spots with this equipment.

Large trees can be cut or pulled down with a

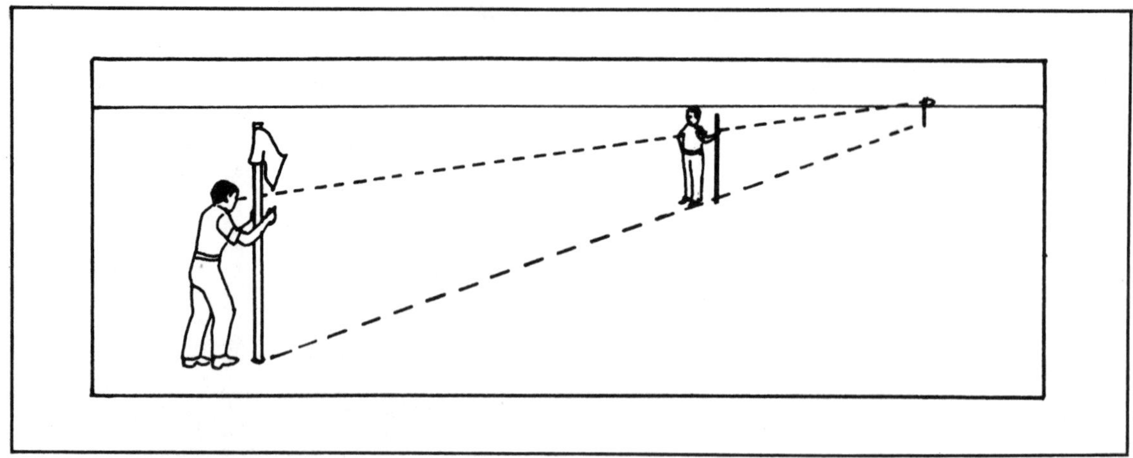

Fig. 8-1. Surveying the fence line.

tractor. If you pull them down, use a heavy rope, cable, or log chain long enough for you to be safe from the falling tree. Be careful of the dangerous recoil if the rope, cable, or chain should break. When trees, large brush, and old fencing have been removed, you can plow down or turn under small brush and grass with a disk harrow or field cultivator.

Figure 8-3 shows some of the hand tools available for clearing small growth. Always wear leather gloves to protect your hands.

If you clear a strip through woods or thicket, make it wide enough so you can distribute the posts and unroll the fence. A wide strip can later serve as a roadway or fire lane.

When replacing old fencing, you may want to use some of the old, sound posts. The easiest way to remove them from the ground is to use the hydraulic lift on a tractor or an A-frame.

Old wire usually is not worth saving. Never leave it in fence corners or other places where it may become a hazard to livestock. You can stake it in ditches to help prevent soil erosion.

## FENCE POSTS

Fence posts may be made of wood, steel, or concrete. Concrete posts are used mainly in farm fencing. Considerations in determining the kind, size, and number of posts to use include the availability and cost of the different kinds, the kind of

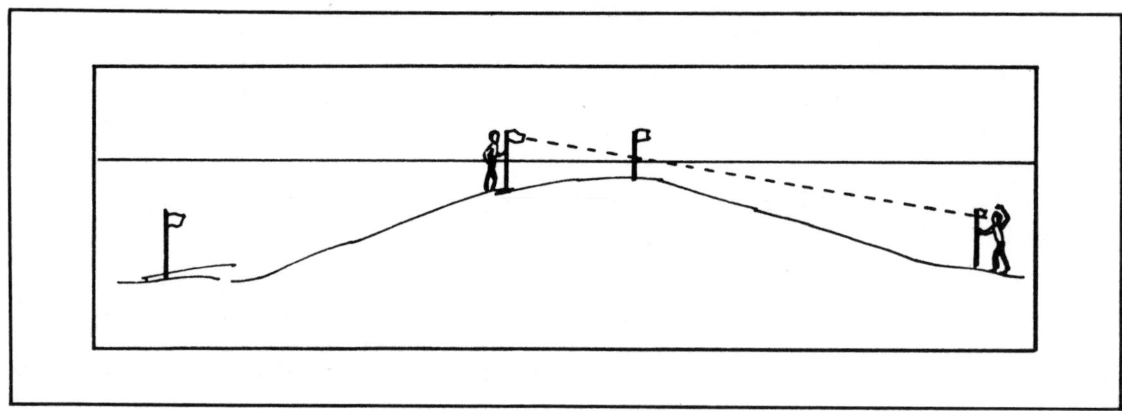

Fig. 8-2. Surveying the fence line over rough terrain.

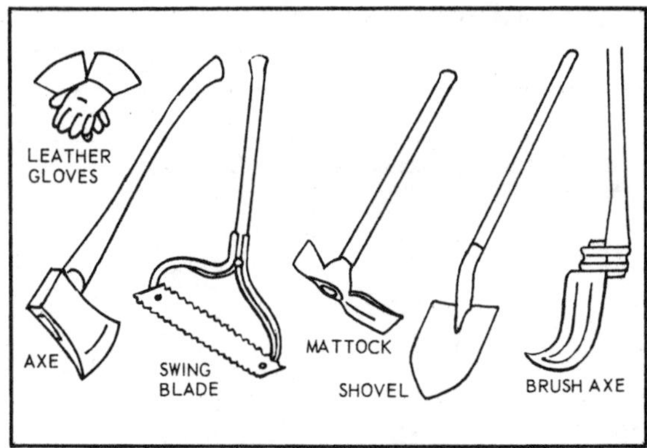


Fig. 8-3. Common fence building tools.

fence you plan to erect, how strong it needs to be, and how long you want it to last.

### Wood

Wood posts can be purchased in most areas and are comparatively low in cost. The farm woodland may be a good source of wood posts.

You should use the most durable wood posts available for permanent fencing or, better still, use pressure-preservative treated posts. The durability of untreated wood posts, even of the more decay-resistant kinds, depends largely on the heartwood content (Fig. 8-4). Whether bought or cut, untreated wood posts should be of mostly heartwood. Untreated sapwood of any species will usually rot in one to three years.

The probable life expectancy of untreated wood posts of mostly heartwood is: Osage orange, 25-30 years; red cedar and black locust, 15-25 years; sassafras, 10-15 years; white oak, blackjack oak, and cypress, 5-10 years; southern pine, sweet gum, hickory, red oak, sycamore, yellow poplar, cottonwood, and willow, 2-7 years. See Table 8-1.

Osage orange, red cedar, and black locust posts may no longer be available in some areas. If less durable posts are used, they should be treated with a good wood preservative to protect them against decay and insect damage. Depending on the kind of preservative used and the method of application, treated posts can extend their life 10 to 30 years.

Pressure-treated posts—posts treated with preservative by commercial process—are usually more durable than farm- or home-treated posts. Creosote or some other preservative is forced into the wood under pressure at a rate of 6 to 8 pounds per cubic foot. Such posts are available in most areas.

Farm or home methods of treating wood posts with preservative include: hot and cold bath, cold soak, end diffusion, and double diffusion. Brushing on wood preservative is not recommended for wood posts. The wood will not absorb enough of the chemical to give effective protection against decay.

Wood posts can usually be bought in lengths of 5½ to 8 feet and in diameters of 2½ to 6 inches or larger. Posts 5 inches or larger in diameter are generally used for anchor posts: gate, corner, end, and braced line posts. Line posts for straight, open-field woven wire fences are sometimes as small as 2½ inches in diameter, but a minimum diameter of 3½ inches is recommended. Four- or 5-inch posts should be used for barn lots, corrals, and in sandy and wet soils.

Height of the fence and the depth of post setting determine the length of posts required. Anchor posts are usually set 3 to 3½ feet in the ground, and line posts are usually set 2 to 2½ feet.

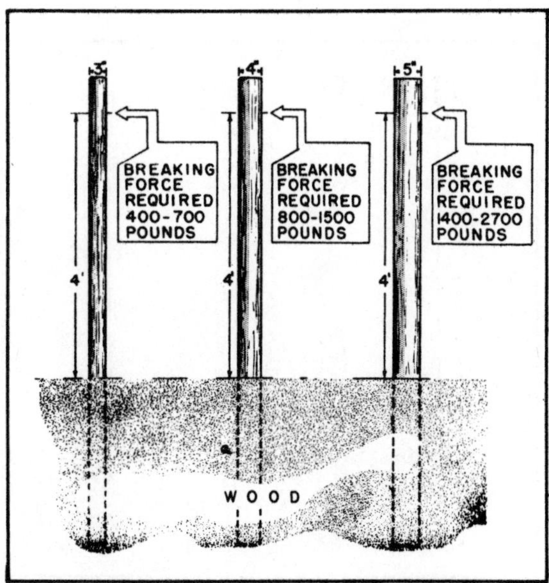


Fig. 8-4. Approximate strength of wooden posts.

Table 8-1. Life Expectancy in Years of Treated and Untreated Fence Posts.

| Kind of wood | Untreated | Treated | | |
|---|---|---|---|---|
| | | Pressure | Hot and cold bath | Cold soak |
| Osage orange | 25-30 | | | |
| Western red cedar | 12-15 | 20-25 | 20-25 | |
| Lodge pole pine | 2-4 | 20-25 | 15-20 | 10-20 |
| Ponderosa pine | 2-4 | 20-25 | 15-20 | 10-20 |
| Aspen, cottonwood | 1-3 | 15-20 | 10-15 | 5-10 |
| Juniper, western* | 20 | | | |
| Locust, black* | 20 | | | |
| Douglas fir | 3-6 | 20-35 | 15-25 | 10-20 |
| Western Hemlock | 3-6 | 20-35 | 15-25 | 10-20 |

*heartwood

### Steel

Steel posts offer a number of advantages (Fig. 8-5). They are lightweight, fireproof, extremely durable, and easily driven into most soils. Also, they will ground the fence against lightning when in contact with wet or moist soil.

Figure 8-6 shows the more common kinds of steel posts. The first three from the left are line posts, and the fourth is a corner post. Steel posts are usually sold in lengths of 5, 5½, 6, 6½, 7, 7½, and 8 feet.

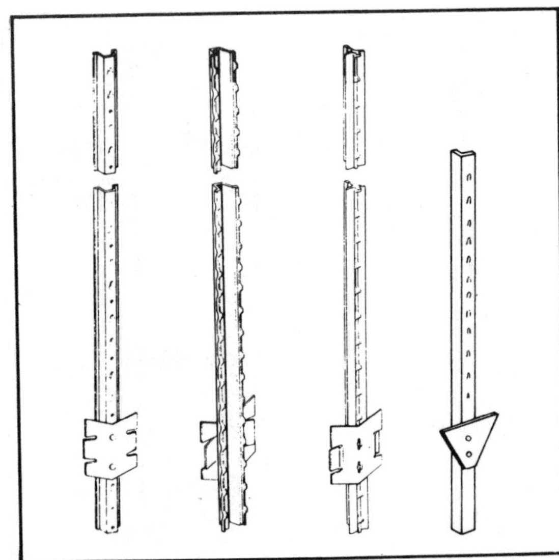

Fig. 8-5. Typical steel posts.

Animals crowding against the fence tend to force steel posts out of line. Anchor plates that are bolted, clamped, or riveted to the posts keep them firmly in the ground. See Fig. 8-7.

If you live near oil fields, boiler factories, or repair shops, you may be able to buy used pipe at reasonable cost for use as fence posts. The pipe should be at least 1¾ inches in diameter for line posts and larger for anchor posts. For heavy anchor posts, use pipe 6 to 8 inches in diameter that is filled with concrete.

### Concrete

Concrete posts are used mostly as anchor posts (gate, corner, and end posts) in farm fencing. Where a fence angles slightly, a concrete post will prevent the wire from pulling line posts out of line. Concrete posts can be extremely durable, lasting 30 years or longer, if they are well made. If not, they may start to crumble in a few years.

Concrete line posts are usually 4 inches square and are cast several at a time in forms of the desired length. Anchor posts are usually larger and are cast in place.

## WOVEN WIRE FENCES

Woven wire fencing is made in different classes (Fig. 8-8). Those for farm and general use include field or stock fencing, poultry garden fencing, chicken fencing, and wire netting. Chain link

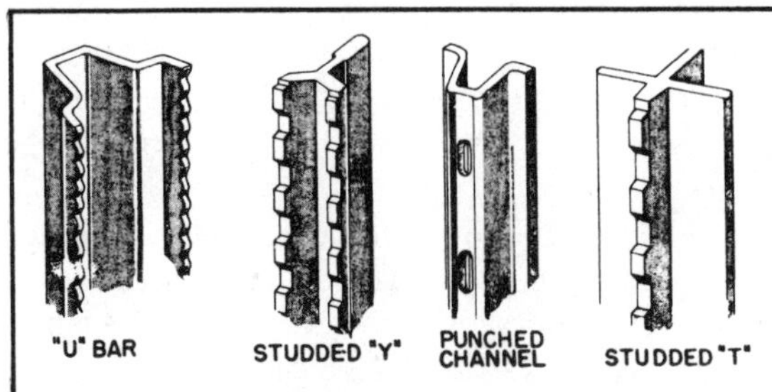


Fig. 8-6. Common shapes of steel posts.

fence, a more stylized form, is designed mainly for home lots (see Chapter 7). In most classes of woven wire fencing you have a choice of fencing weights, protective coatings on the wire, and styles or designs.

## Weight

The weight of woven wire fencing is determined by the gauge or size of the line or horizontal wires. The lower the gauge number, the larger the wire. The larger the wire, the stronger and more durable the fencing.

Field or stock fencing, for example, comes in four weights. See Table 8-2.

The stay (vertical) wires in the fencing are usually of the same gauge as the filler (intermediate) wires. They may be spaced 6 or 12 inches apart.

## Protective Coatings

Most woven wire fencing is either zinc-coated (galvanized) or aluminum-coated. Chain link fence also comes with a vinyl resin coating, which makes a more attractive fence.

The coating on zinc-coated fencing may be class 1, 2, or 3. The class number indicates that the fencing has at least the minimum amount of galvanizing per square foot of wire surface. Class 3 generally has at least twice as much zinc as class 1. The thicker the zinc coating, the more corrosion-resistant the fencing is. The class number will be indicated on the fencing roll's tag.

The coating on aluminum-coated fencing is usually about 0.25 ounce per square foot of wire

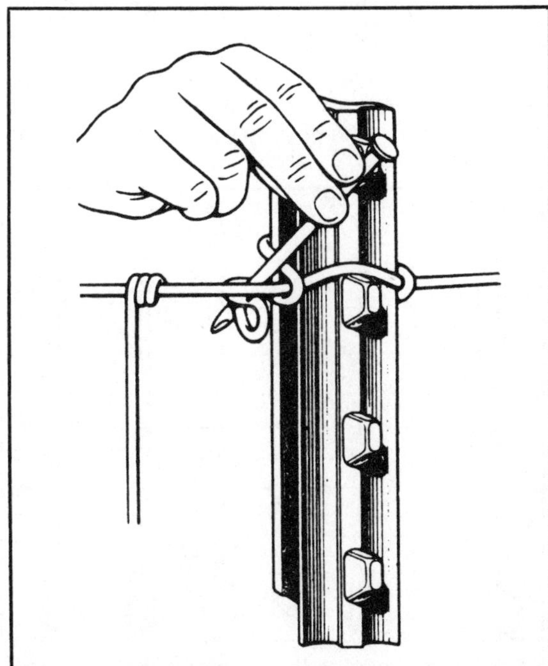

Fig. 8-7. Method of applying a steel post wire clip.

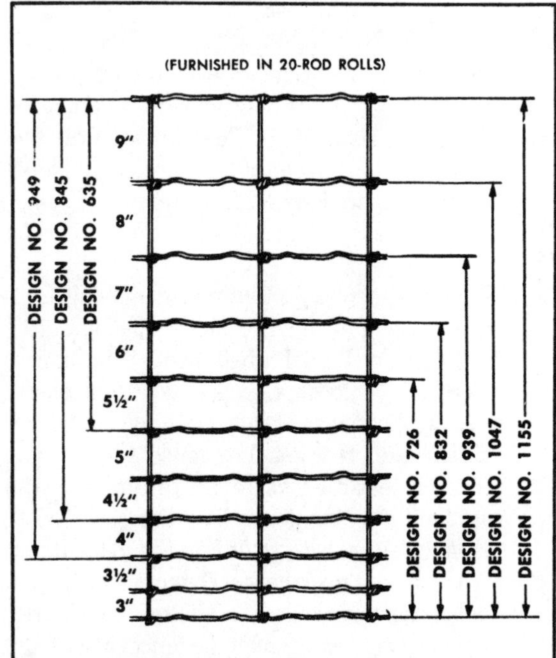


Fig. 8-8. Horizontal wire spacing for different designs of woven wire field fence.

**Table 8-2. Weights and Gauges of Stock Fencing.**

| | Gauge of Top and Bottom Line Wires | Gauge of Filler Line (Intermediate) Wires |
|---|---|---|
| Lightweight | 11 | 14½ |
| Medium weight | 10 | 12½ |
| Heavy weight | 9 | 11 |
| Extra heavy weight | 9 | 9 |

surface. This usually isn't indicated on the tag.

Under the same climatic conditions, aluminum-coated fencing could be expected to resist corrosion three to five times longer than zinc-coated fencing with the same thickness of coating. If the coating was broken in rural areas so that the wire was exposed to the air, the zinc would give better protection. While both metals act as "sacrificial agents"—they corrode instead of the wire—in rural atmospheres an oxide film tends to form on the aluminum coating and limits its ability to protect the wire. Any wire fencing will resist corrosion longer in a dry climate than in a humid area or in an industrial atmosphere.

## Styles or Designs

The styles or designs of woven wire fencing are designated by a three- or four-digit number—for example, 932 or 1155. The first or first two digits indicate the number of line wires in the fencing, and the last two indicate fence height in *inches*. Style 1155, for example, has 11 line wires and is 55 inches high.

Figure 8-9 shows the five most commonly used styles or designs of field or stock fencing: 1155, 1047, 939, 832, and 726. Barbed wire is also shown.

Here are suggested woven wire fences for livestock applications:

**Cattle and Horses.** Use fence A or B (Fig. 8-9). The single barbed wire at the top prevents the animals from mashing down the fence.

**Hogs.** Use fence C, D, or E in Fig. 8-9 without the barbed wires above the woven wire. The barbed wire below the woven wire discourages the animals from crawling or rooting under the fence. Styles 939 and 832 are available with a barbed bottom wire. Style 726 (fence E without barbed wire) is convenient for temporarily confining hogs while they eat corn.

**Sheep.** Use style 832 or 726—fence D or E in Fig. 8-9 without barbed wire. Barbs may tear the fleece on sheep.

Figure 8-10 shows a fence for protecting sheep from dogs and coyotes. The extended barbed wire at the top discourages dogs from jumping the fence. An apron of woven wire 18 inches wide along the ground will prevent predatory animals from burrowing beneath the fence (Fig.8-11).

**Cattle, Horses, Hogs, and Sheep All in the Same Field.** Use fence A, B, D, or E in Fig. 8-9.

**Poultry Garden and Chick Fencing.** Poultry garden fencing comes in two standard styles—2158 and 1948. Chick fencing comes in three styles—2672, 2360, and 2048.

Wire netting of 1- or 2-inch mesh is made in nine lengths ranging from 12 to 72 inches. The netting is commonly used for fencing small poultry yards, cages, poultry house windows, and tree guards. The 1-inch mesh wire is recommended for confining baby chicks, turkey poults, and goslings.

## Setting Posts

Setting untreated wood posts in concrete *is not* recommended. The post may shrink from the con-

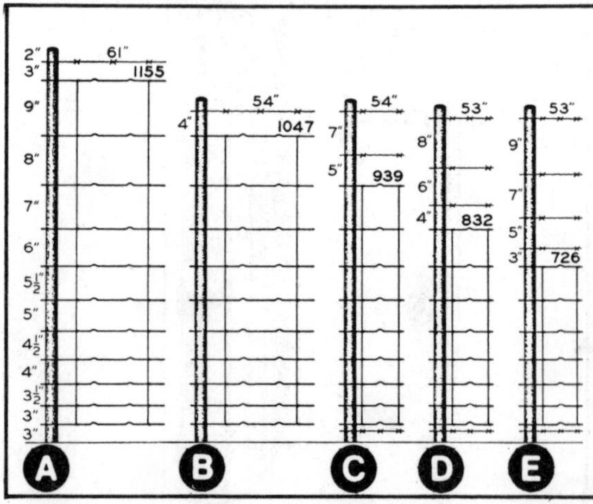

Fig. 8-9. Standard styles or designs of woven wire fencing combined with barbed wire. Stay (vertical) wires are spaced 12 inches in fences A and B and 6 inches in C, D, and E.

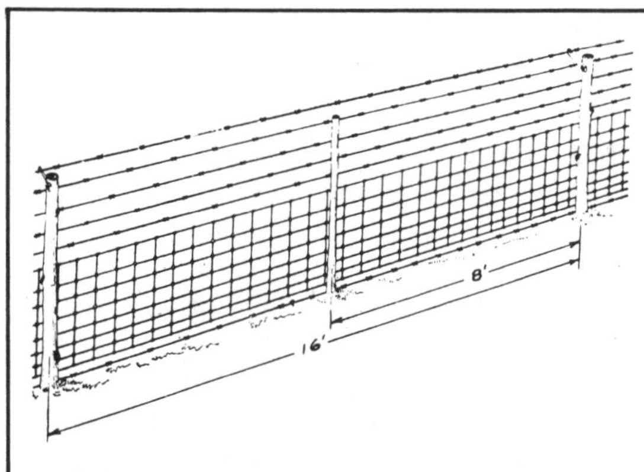


Fig. 8-10. Typical sheep fence.

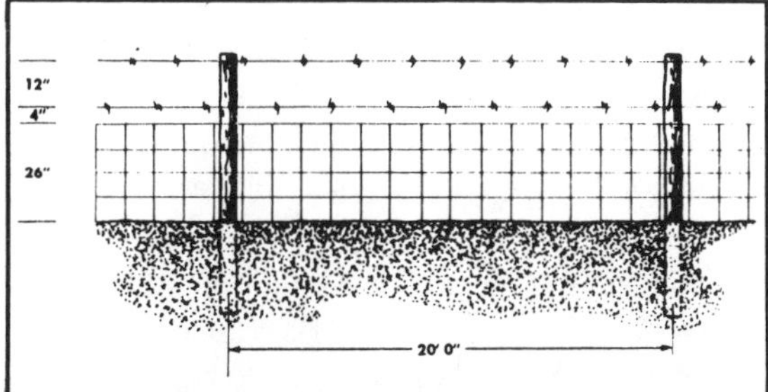


Fig. 8-11. Standard woven wire sheep-tight fence.

crete, leaving a crack for moisture to enter. With durable or treated posts, though, the stability and anchorage provided by the concrete may justify its use. Setting the treated posts in concrete is also recommended when the fences may be subject to heavy pressure or to wind strain.

Dirt-set wood posts may be set in predug holes or driven into the ground. Power posthole diggers or post drivers can save much time and labor in setting posts. Post drivers are available that can drive posts up to 8 inches in diameter.

For a stronger fence, set steel anchor posts (gate, corner, end, and braced line posts) in concrete. Dirt-set types of steel posts are available, but they will not provide quite so strong an assembly. Steel line posts should be driven directly into the ground and not set in concrete (Fig. 8-12).

### Corner- and End-Post Assemblies

Corner- and end-post assemblies are the foundation of a fence. If one fails, the whole fence or a section may fail.

Figure 8-13 shows different types of wood assemblies. The double-span assemblies have more than twice the strength of the single-span assemblies and only half the horizontal and vertical movement under heavy loads. Type C is superior to A and B, and B is superior to A. See Fig. 8-14.

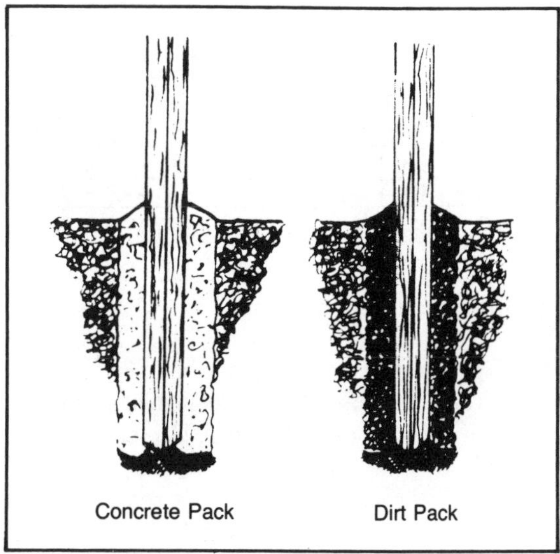


Fig. 8-12. Livestock fence postholes.

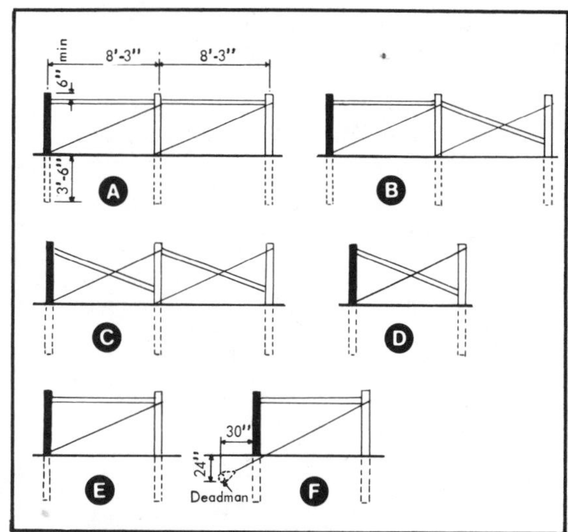


Fig. 8-13. Wood corner- and end-post assemblies. The corner or end posts are shaded.

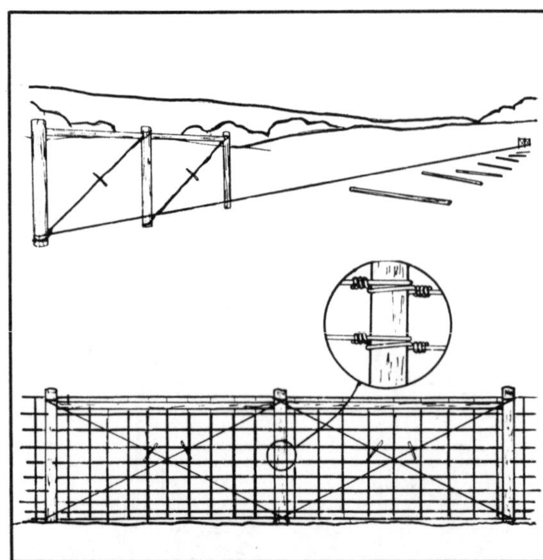

Fig. 8-14. Double-span end assembly for extra strength.

Single-span assemblies may be used for fence lengths up to 10 rods. Use double-span construction for fence lengths of 10 to 40 rods. Use double-span construction plus braced line posts for lengths of more than 40 rods. Minimum sizes recommended for the components of the assemblies are given in Table 8-3.

Height of the fence and the depth of post setting determine the length of posts needed. The posts should be set at least 3½ feet in the ground.

**Table 8-3. Minimum Sizes Recommended for Components of Single-Span and Double-Span Assemblies.**

| | |
|---|---|
| **Single Spans:** | |
| Corner post | 6-inch diameter |
| Brace post | 5-inch diameter |
| Brace | 4-inch diameter |
| Tie | two double strands of No. 9 gauge wire |
| **Double Spans:** | |
| Corner post | 5-inch diameter |
| Each brace post | 4-inch diameter |
| Each brace | 4-inch diameter |
| Each tie | two double strands of No. 9 gauge wire |

Here are the steps in constructing single-span assemblies. Repeat as necessary for double-span assemblies.

- Dig the holes for the anchor and brace posts. Space them 8 feet apart.
- Set the anchor post but not the brace post. Tamp the soil firmly as you replace it around the post. Lean the top of the post 1 inch away from the direction of the fence pull, so it will straighten to a plumb position when the fence is stretched.
- Stand the brace post in its hole and fasten the wood brace to both posts. Use dowel pin construction for a strong assembly (Fig. 8-15).
- Set the brace post. Tamp the soil firmly as you replace it around the post.
- Attach the brace wire as shown in Fig. 8-6 and splice the ends together. Tighten the wire by twisting it with a strong stick or rod. Leave the stick or rod in place so that you can adjust the tension when necessary.

Figure 8-7 shows construction of a steel corner- or end-post assembly. Both the post and the braces should be set in concrete. See Figs. 8-18 and 8-19.

- Dig a hole at least 3½ feet deep for the post. For a corner post, make the hole 20 inches square at the bottom and 18 inches square at the top. For an end post, make the hole 20 inches square at the bottom but 18 to 20 inches at the top with the

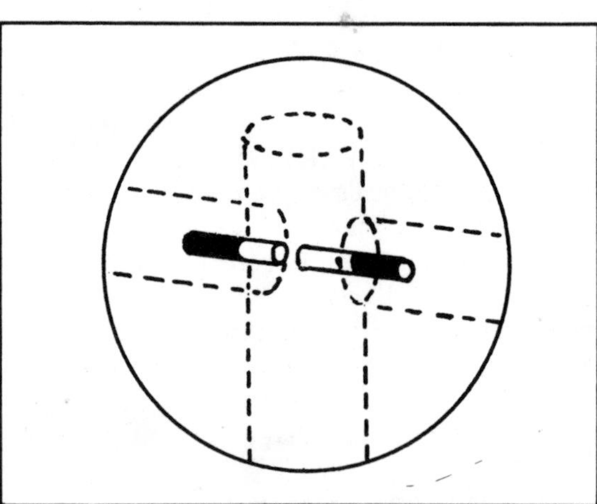

Fig. 8-15. Use dowel pins to connect a wood brace to a wood corner or end post or brace post.

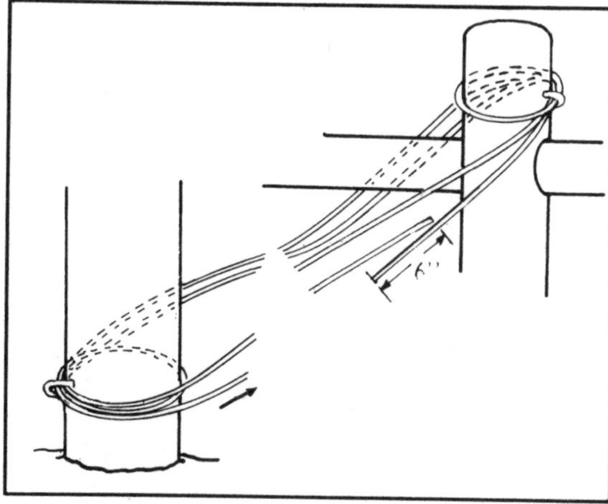

Fig. 8-16. Fastening wire brace or tie in wood corner- or end-post assembly.

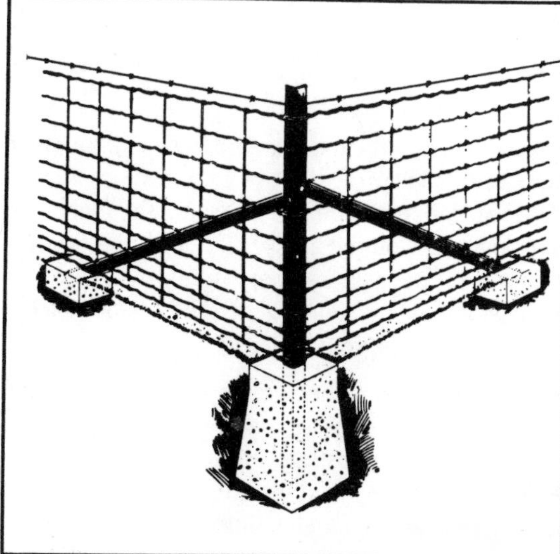

Fig. 8-17. Steel corner and braces set in concrete.

long dimension parallel with these hole dimensions.

- Attach the metal braces to the post.
- Holding the post plumb in its hole, mark the holes for the braces on the ground. The braces should enter the concrete pier 6 inches below the ground surface and extend 6 inches into the concrete. The center of the holes will be closer to the post than where the braces touch the ground.
- Dig the holes for the braces, making them at least 18 inches deep and 20 inches square at the top and bottom. At least 8 inches of the concrete pier should be below the frost line.

Fig. 8-18. Hand-driven diagonal brace for steel corners.

- Holding the post plumb in its hole, place the concrete around it and the braces. Tamp the concrete as you pour it. Slope it slightly away from the post and braces to drain water.

## Line Posts

Line posts are usually spaced 14, 16, or 20 feet apart for field fencing and 10 to 16 feet apart for home lot fencing. Closer spacing may be necessary if the ground is uneven or if you need a stronger fence. You may have to shorten the spacing between the posts to equalize it near the corner or end of the fence. Set wood line posts 2 to 2½ feet in the ground and steel line posts 1½ to 2 feet. Stretch a cord, rope, or wire between the two anchor posts to serve as a guide in aligning the posts.

When set in low places, line posts should be weighted down, set in concrete, or provided with subsoil cleats to help hold them in the ground. Don't set line posts in a gully or stream where they could be washed out by a heavy flow of water. If the fence line crosses a narrow gully or stream, stretch the

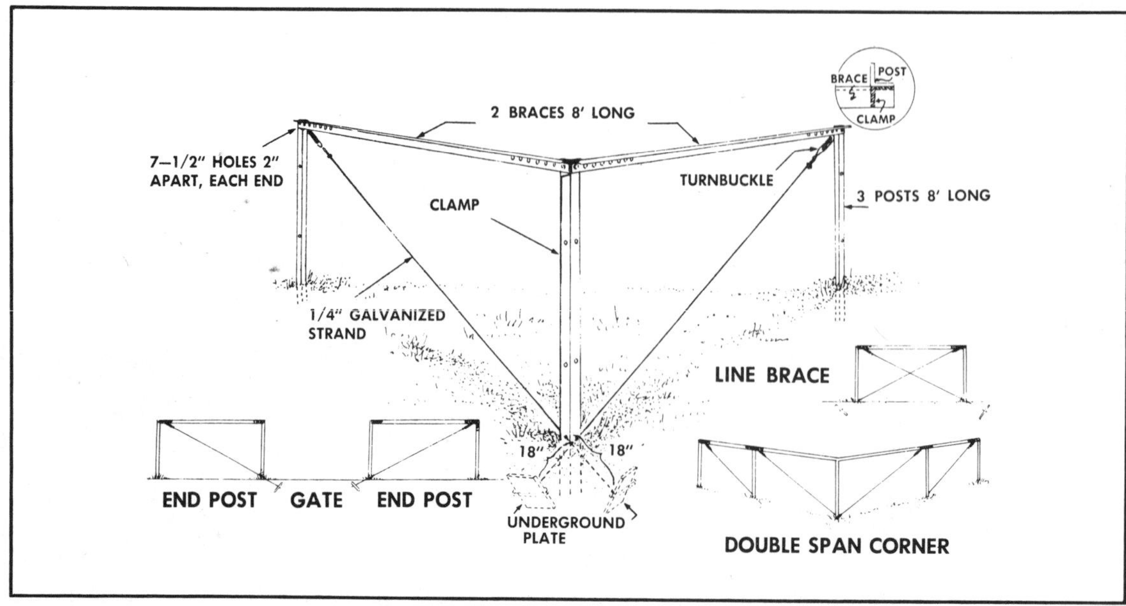


Fig. 8-19. Steps in attaching brace wire to a corner brace.

fence straight across from a well-secured post on each bank. Barbed wire can be stretched below the fence to prevent stock from crawling under it.

If the gully or stream is wide, terminate the fence section on the one bank with an end-post assembly and start a new section on the other bank. Install a floodgate across the gully or stream to restrain livestock.

## Braced Line Posts

In fences 40 rods or longer, braced line posts should be used every 20 yards. Construction is the same as for the corner or end-post assemblies, except that a second brace wire is used to take the fence pull in the opposite direction.

## Stretching and Attaching the Fencing

Woven wire fencing should be stretched and attached in sections running from one anchor post to the next. Anchor posts include gate, corner, end, and braced line posts. Don't attach the fencing to concrete-set posts until the concrete has thoroughly hardened.

In a combination woven wire and barbed wire fence, attach the woven wire first. Instructions for stretching and attaching barbed wire will be given later in this chapter.

For the best appearance, fasten the fencing to the "outside" of the posts. If the fence will be subject to pressure—from livestock, for example—fasten the fencing to the "inside" of the posts. The steps are:

- Starting about 2 feet ahead of the anchor post, unroll the fencing to the second line post and stand the fence roll on end.
- Remove one or two stay wires from the end of the fencing to free enough length of each line wire to wrap around the post and splice on itself (Fig. 8-20).
- With the next stay wire against the post, staple the fence to the post at the desired height.
- Starting with the middle wire, wrap each line wire around the post and back on itself. Make five wraps around the wire, using the splicing tool shown in Fig. 8-21. See Fig. 8-22.
- Unroll the fencing to the next anchor post.
- Four to 8 feet beyond the second anchor post, set a dummy post for attaching the stretcher unit. Brace the post as shown in Fig. 8-23.
- Prop the fencing against the line posts with

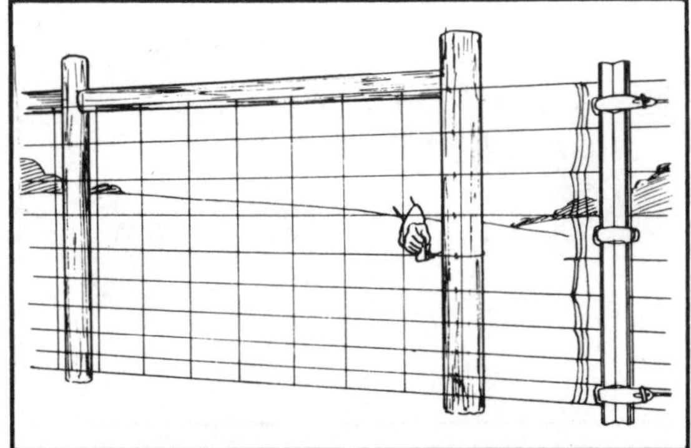

Fig. 8-20. Remove or drive back stay wire a sufficient distance to free working ends long enough to extend around the anchor post and wrap back on themselves.

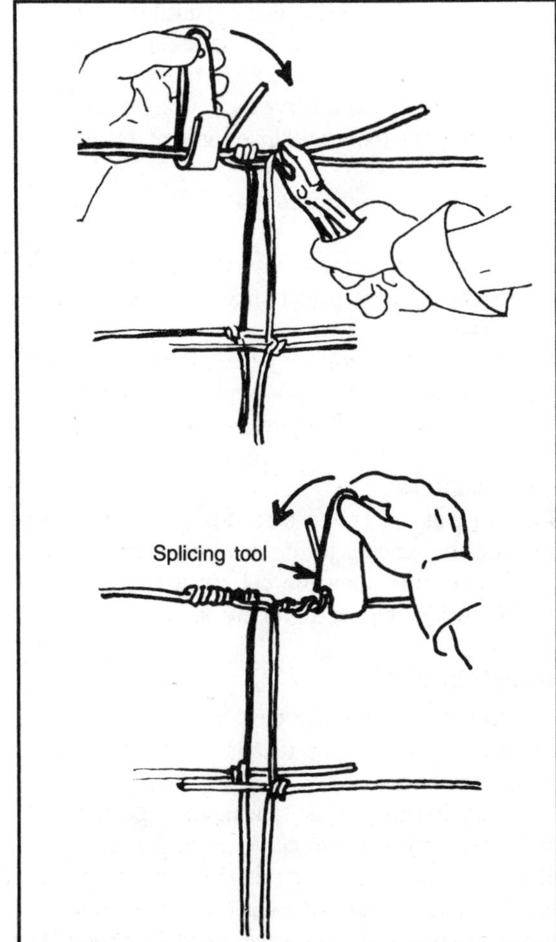


Fi.g 8-21. Method for splicing woven wire.

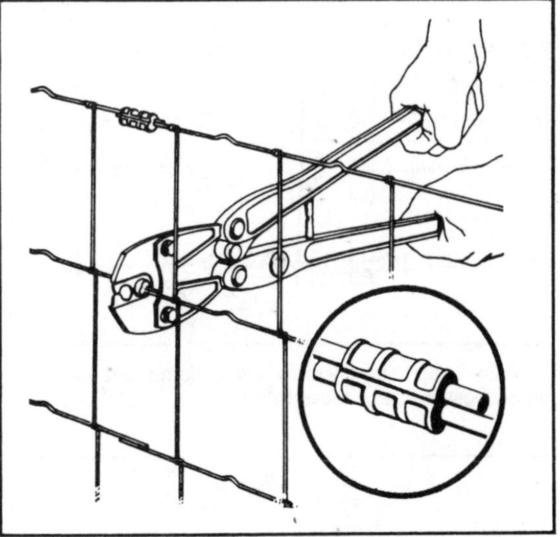

Fig. 8-22. Compression sleeve for splicing wire.

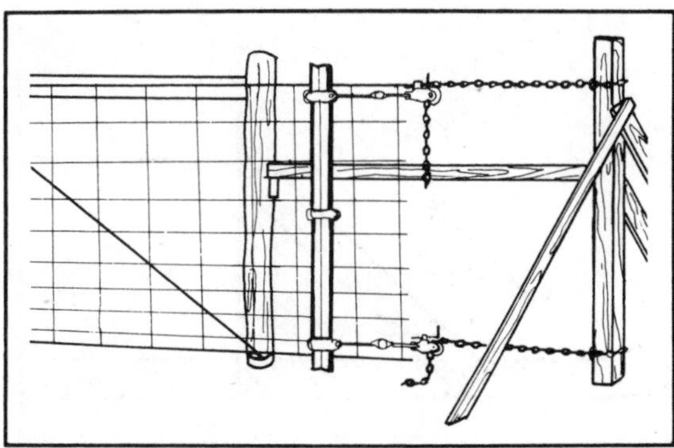

Fig. 8-23. Fence stretcher in position. Note braced "dummy" post at right.

stakes. Support it at the top, about a foot from every third or fourth post, and on the opposite side from the stretcher unit.

- Attach the stretcher unit to the fencing and to the dummy post (Fig.8-24). Use a single-jack unit for fencing up to 32 inches in height and a double-jack unit for higher fencing (Fig. 8-25). Attach the jack of a single-jack unit to the center of the bar and the jacks of a double-jack unit, so the wires are divided equally between the jacks.
- Stretch the fence slowly so that the tension will be evenly distributed over the entire length. Check the fencing during the stretching opera-

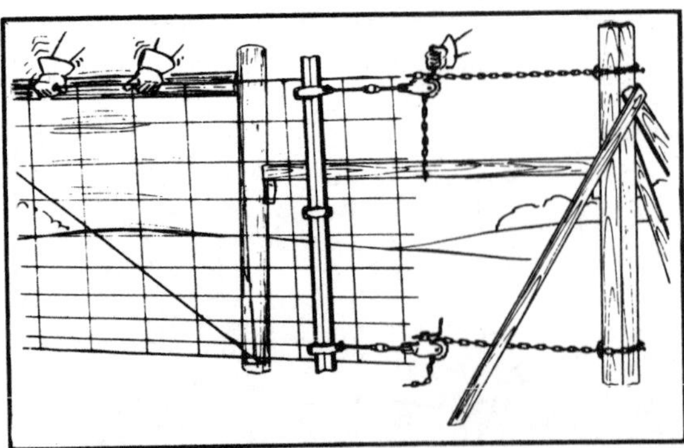

Fig. 8-24. Attach stretchers to a wire clamp and corner or dummy post to stretch woven wire.

Fig.8-26. Stretching fence with a tractor endangers the operator and may overstretch the wire.

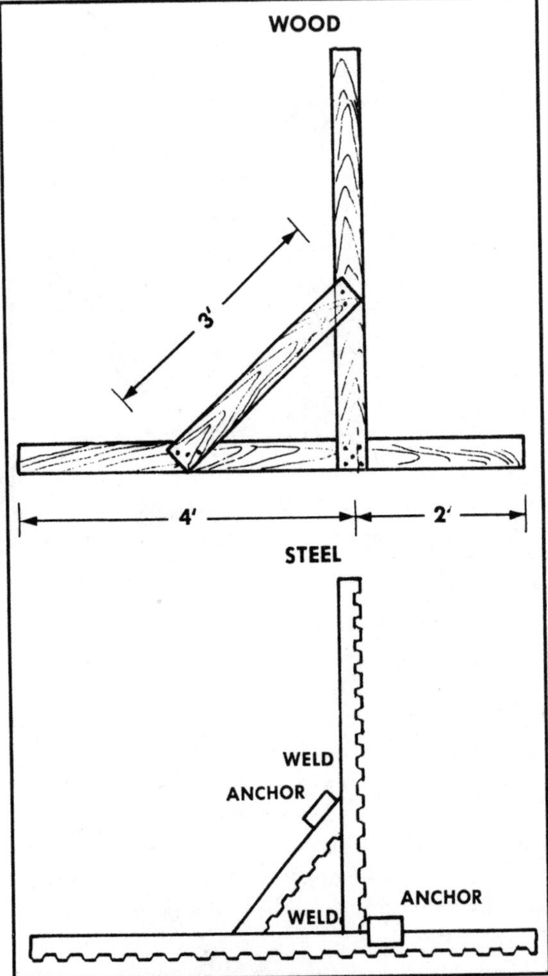


Fig. 8-25. Ways to construct fence jacks.

tion to make sure that it is riding free at all points. Continue the stretching until the tension curves in the wire are straightened out about one-third. Don't overstretch the fence (Fig. 8-26). If the tension curves are straightened out too much, the fence will lose some of its springiness.

- Staple the line wires to the anchor posts (Fig. 8-27).
- Loosen as many stay wires as necessary to complete the next step and slide them toward the stretcher.
- Starting with the middle wire, cut each line wire and wrap it around the post and back on itself four turns. Do every other wire, working toward the top and bottom, until all are done. Leave the top wire until last.
- Starting at the end farthest from the stretcher, fasten the fencing to the line posts. Fasten the top wire first, then the bottom wire, and then every other wire until all are fastened.

## Contour Fencing

Contour fencing may be required on terraced land or in strip-cropping. It calls for slightly different construction.

**Post Spacing.** Post spacing must be reduced whenever there is much curve in the fence line to keep the posts from overturning. To determine the proper spacing, stake out a smooth curve along the terrace or contour strip. Space the stakes about 14 feet apart.

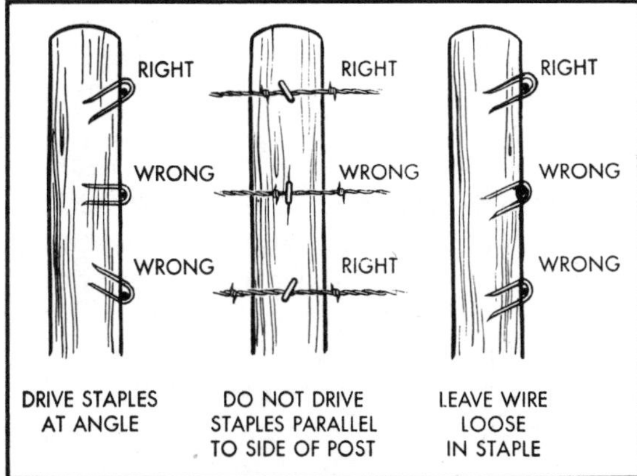


Fig. 8-27. Stapling wire to wooden posts.

At any one point of curvature, select three consecutive stakes and stretch a string between the first and third stakes. Measure the distance from the center stake to the string and space the posts as in Table 8-4.

- Repeat the above procedure whenever the curvature of the fence line appears to change noticeably.
- Check to see that no post is out of line of a smooth curve. With a smooth curve, the fencing will pull equally against each post.

**Setting Posts.** Lean the top of the post about 2 inches toward the side to which the fencing will be attached. When the fence is stretched, the post will straighten to a plumb position.

**Installation.** On curves, attach the fencing to the outside of the posts so that it will pull against the posts. This may mean that the fencing will first be on one side of the posts, then on the other.

Contour fencing can usually be stretched in 20 to 40-rod sections. It may be necessary to stretch it

**Table 8-4. Post Spacing for Contour Fencing.**

| Distance from Center Stake to String | Post Spacing |
|---|---|
| 4 inches or less | 14 feet |
| 5 to 6 inches | 12 feet |
| 7 to 8 inches | 10 feet |
| 9 to 14 inches | 8 feet |
| 15 to 20 inches | 7 feet |

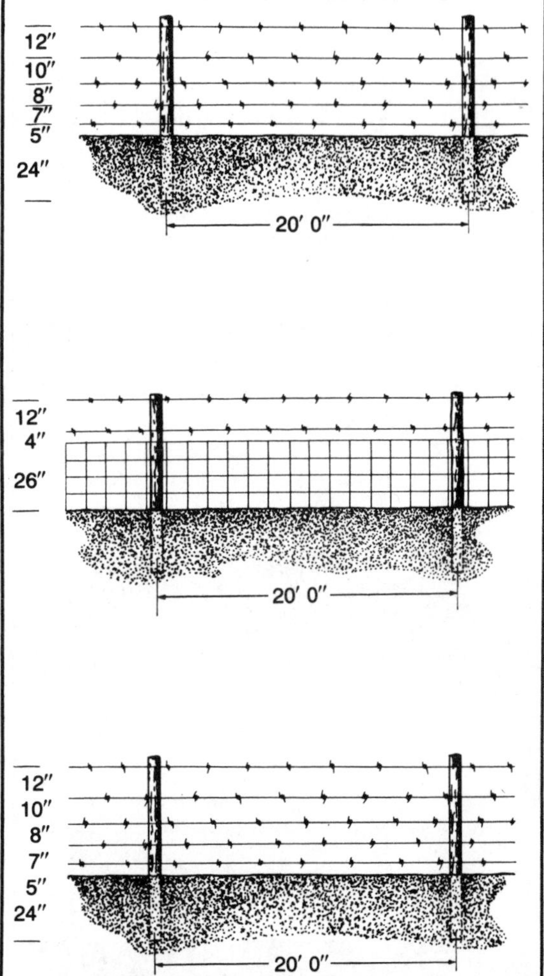


Fig. 8-28. Three common barbed wire sheep fences.

in 10-rod sections on sharp curves. Where the curvature of the fence line changes materially, you can start a new section at the sharpest point on the curve. Stretch a section of contour fencing from the end having the least curvature, so the end having the most curvature will have the least tension.

## BARBED WIRE FENCES

Barbed wire is used both in conjunction with other fencing and as fencing itself (Figs. 8-28 and 8-29). Its use in combination with woven wire fences and for electric fences is covered in this chapter. See Table 8-5.

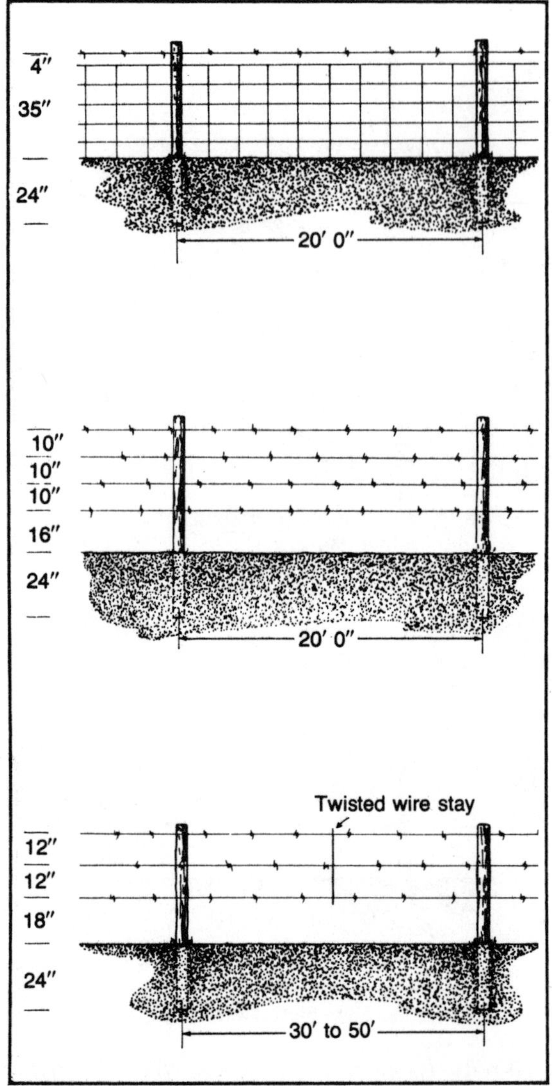


Fig. 8-29. Three common barbed wire cattle fences.

Figure 8-30 shows the usual wire spacing in three- to six-strand barbed wire fences. As few as two strands are sometimes used to fence large cattle ranges in the western states.

Barbed wire suspension fences (Fig. 8-31) are often used as cross fencing and boundary fencing on large cattle ranges. They consist of four to six strands of the wire supported by posts spaced 80 to 120 feet apart. Twisted wire stays, spaced about 16 feet apart, hold the wire apart.

When cattle come in contact with a suspension fence, it sways back and forth. The fence beats against the cattle and discourages them from trying to go through it.

Figure 8-32 shows the kinds of standard barbed wire commonly available. The 12½-gauge wire with two-point barbs is the most widely used for cattle ranges. For smaller fields where cattle may subject the fence to considerable pressure, four-point barbs may be more effective. The lighter 14-gauge wire is commonly used for temporary fencing. See Table 8-6.

You can also buy high-tensile barbed wire, which is stronger and more durable than the comparable sizes of standard wire. The 13½-gauge high-tensile wire has a breaking strength equal to that of the 12½-gauge standard wire.

Barbed wire, like woven wire, comes with a protective coating of either zinc or aluminum. Thickness of the coating is the same as on comparable sizes of woven wire. Under the same climatic conditions, aluminum-coated wire is more durable than zinc-coated wire.

Barbed wire is especially dangerous to work with because of the barbs. Follow these precautions;

—Wear heavy leather gloves, boots or high shoes, and tough, close-fitting clothing.

—Never use a tractor to stretch woven wire or barbed wire fencing. While on the tractor, you may not be able to tell when the fencing has been stretched to the breaking point. If the wire should break, you could be injured seriously by the recoil of the clamp bar, chain, or fencing.

—Carry staples, nails, or other fasteners in a metal container or in an apron—not on your person (Fig. 8-33). Never carry them in your mouth.

—When stretching barbed wire or woven wire, stand on the opposite side of the post from the wire and stretcher unit.

If you handle preservative-treated posts, don't rub your hands or gloves on your face or other parts of your body. Some people are allergic to the chemical.

Strong anchor post assemblies are essential if the barbed wire does not have tension curves. Any

Table 8-5. Barbed Wire Specifications.

| Line wire gauge | BARBS Shape | Points | Wire gauge | Spacing (inches) | Wraps on line wire | Approx. wt./80 rd. |
|---|---|---|---|---|---|---|
| 12½ | half round | 2 | 14 | 4 | 1 | 76 |
| 12½ | round | 2 | 14 | 4 | 2 | 80 |
| 13½ H.T.* | round | 2 | 14 | 4 | 2 | 64 |
| 14 | round | 2 | 16 | 4 | 2 | 52 |
| 12½ | flat | 2 | 12½ | 4 | 1 | 77 |
| 12½ | round | 4 | 14 | 5 | 2** | 88 |
| 12½ | half round | 4 | 14 | 5 | 1 | 83 |
| 13½ H.T.* | round | 4 | 14 | 5 | 2** | 71 |
| 15½ H.T.* | round | 4 | 16 | 5 | 2** | 41 |

*High tensile strength wire.

**Wrapped around both strands; interlocked with one barb projecting between the strands.

pressure on the fence will be transferred directly to the posts.

Installation is the same whether the wire is used in combination with another fencing or a separate fencing (Fig. 8-34). Unroll, stretch, and fasten one line at a time. In a combination fence attach the barbed wire below the woven wire first. Then attach the wires above the woven wire, starting with the lowest one and working upward.

- Fasten one end of the wire roll to the anchor post leaving enough wire free to wrap around the post and splice. If the anchor post is a gatepost, remove the barbs from the wire to be tightly wrapped around the post to prevent injury to persons or animals using the gate.
- Wrap the wire around the post and splice it onto itself, 3½ to 4 turns (Fig. 8-35).
- Unroll the wire along the ground to the next

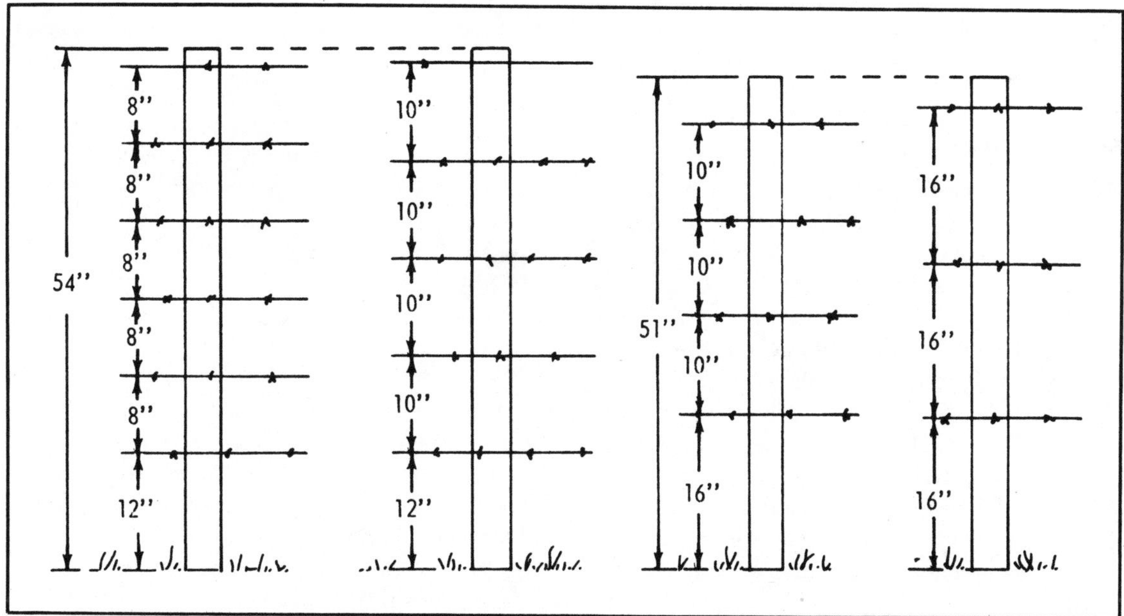


Fig. 8-30. Typical spacings of wires in barbed wire fences.

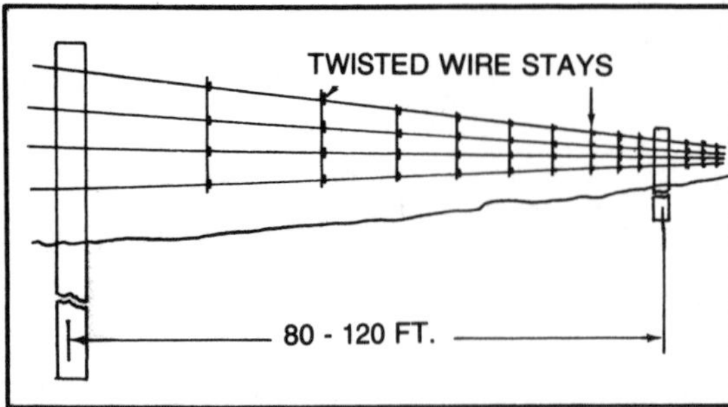

Fig. 8-31. Barbed wire suspension fence commonly used as cross or boundary fencing on cattle ranges.

Table 8-6. Decimal Equivalents of Steel Wire Gauge.

| Gauge number | Wire diameter (in.) |
|---|---|
| 9 | 0.1483 |
| 10 | .1350 |
| 11 | .1205 |
| 12½ | .0990 |
| 13 | .0915 |
| 14 | .0800 |
| 14½ | .0760 |
| 15½ | .0670 |
| 16 | .0625 |

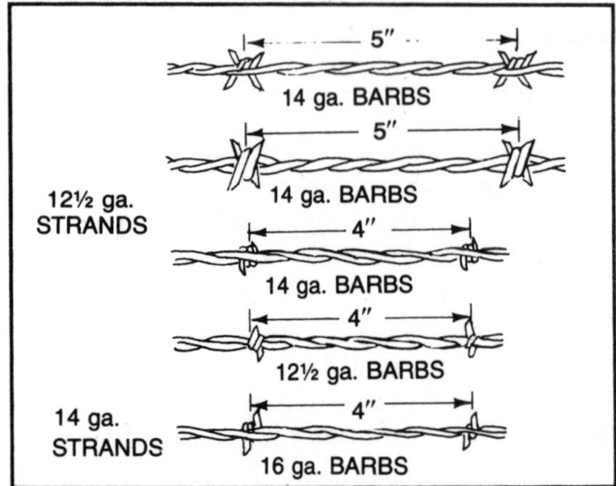

Fig. 8-32. Common barbed wire.

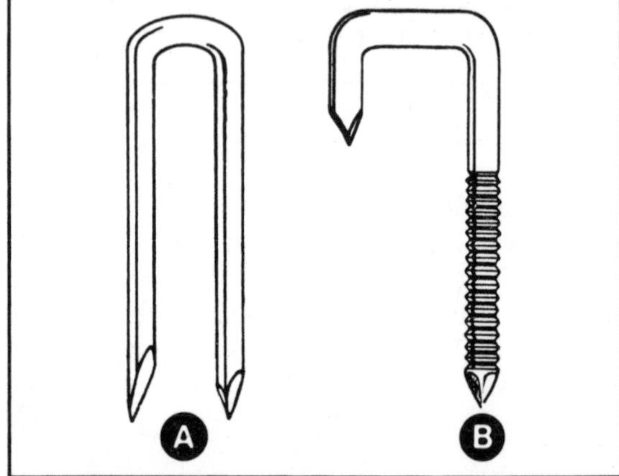

Fig. 8-33. (A) U-shaped staple. (B) L-shaped deformed shank staple.

anchor post. Unroll it straight off the roll—not off the side.

- Set up a dummy post about 8 feet beyond the second anchor post and brace it. If you're erecting a combination woven wire and barbed wire fence, you can use the dummy post set up to stretch the woven wire fencing. Attach a fence stretcher or a block and tackle unit to the dummy post. Attach the wire to the stretcher unit.
- Stretch the wire until it's fairly tight. Be careful not to stretch it so tightly that it breaks. You could be injured by the recoil.
- Fasten the wire to the anchor post.
- Remove the barbs from a sufficient length of wire to wrap around the anchor post and splice on itself.
- Cut and untwist one of the two strands of wire; the other strand will maintain the tension. Wrap the cut strand around the post and back on the wire 3½ to 4 turns. Leave enough space between each turn to interwrap the second strand. Cut the second strand, wrap it around the post, and splice it on the wire.
- Fasten the wire to the line posts (Fig. 8-36).

## CABLE FENCES

Cable fencing consists of heavy galvanized cables attached to metal posts or running through holes drilled through metal or wood posts. It makes strong, durable fencing when constructed of good materials.

The fencing is excellent for feedlots and similar areas where the cattle are closely confined. It allows unrestricted air circulation through the area,

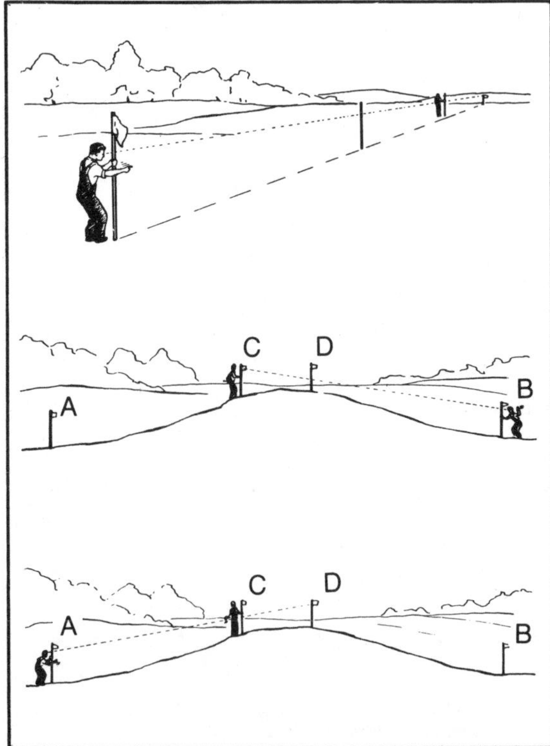


Fig. 8-34. Laying out a barbed wire fence line.

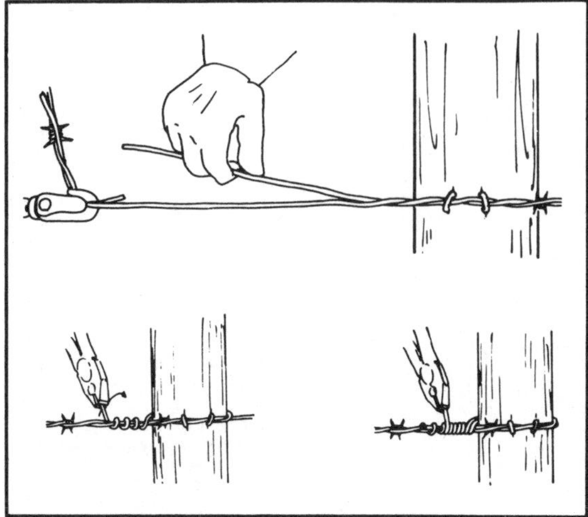

Fig. 8-36. Connecting barbed wire to a fence post.

resulting in maximum cooling of the animals in warm weather. Combined with woven wire fencing or barbed wire, the fencing can be used to confine hogs, sheep, and cattle. Detailed instructions for constructing the fencing should be obtained from fence manufacturers or dealers.

Figure 8-37 shows construction where the cables run through holes drilled through wood posts. Each cable is attached to the anchor post by a spring assembly. The cable is stretched with a block and tackle until the spring begins to open and is then clamped around the next anchor post. When necessary, the tension of the cable is adjusted by tightening or loosening the spring.

## ELECTRIC FENCES

An electric fence consists of one or more electrically charged wires supported by, but insulated from, wood or metal posts. Either smooth wire or barbed wire may be used. A *controller,* commonly called a fence charger, is required to regulate the amount and timing of the current through the wire (Fig. 8-38).

Electric fencing is commonly used to confine cattle and horses, but it also can be used to control hogs and sheep. A single charged wire along the top or side of a wood fence or other kind will deter stock from crowding the fence and breaking it down. This may make it possible for you to use an old permanent fence in poor condition.

Fig. 8-35. Wrap splice for splicing barbed wire.

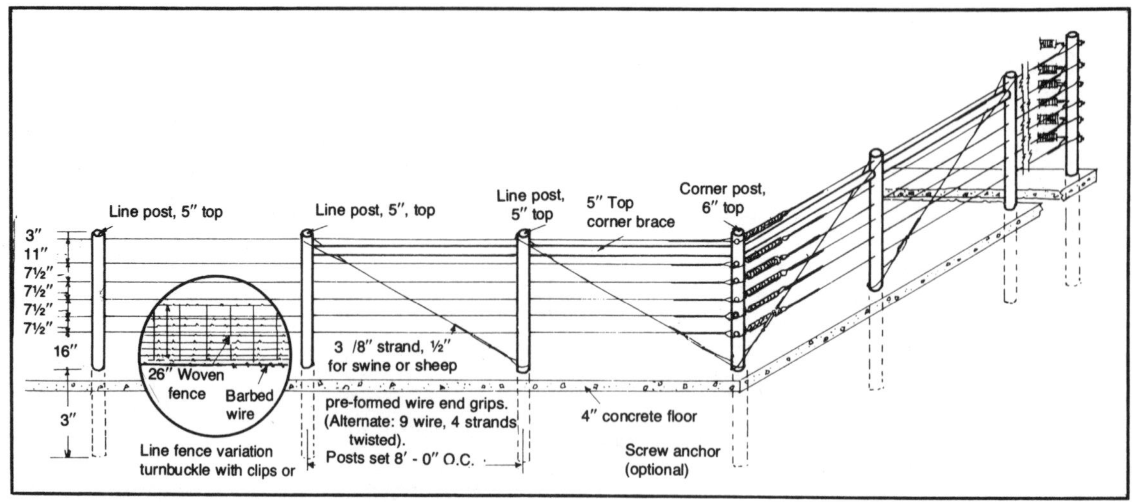


Fig. 8-37. Typical installation of cable fencing.

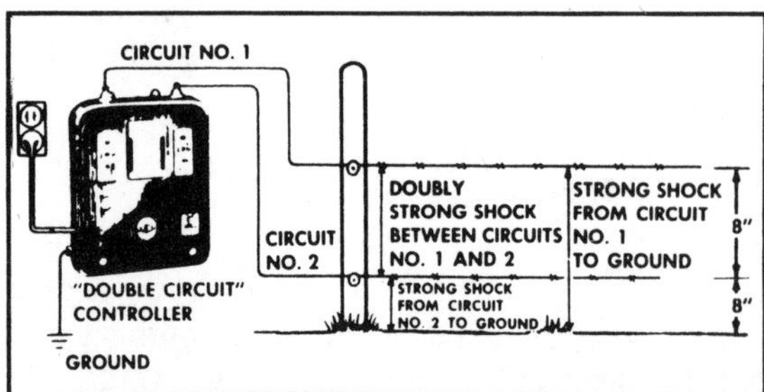


Fig. 8-38. Typical hookup of a double circuit electric fence controller.

Electric fencing is low in cost, economical to operate, and easy to erect and move around. The fence must be kept in continuous operation to be completely effective, and the livestock must be trained to respect it.

The fencing should be installed and operated according to the National Electrical Code, state and local regulations, and the manufacturer's directions. The fence charger and other equipment used should carry the label of Underwriter's Laboratories or the Industrial Commission of Wisconsin. Fence chargers not carrying these labels may cause injury and death to humans and livestock.

Fence chargers are usually designed to operate on 110-120 volts. Battery-operated units are available for use where electric power is not available.

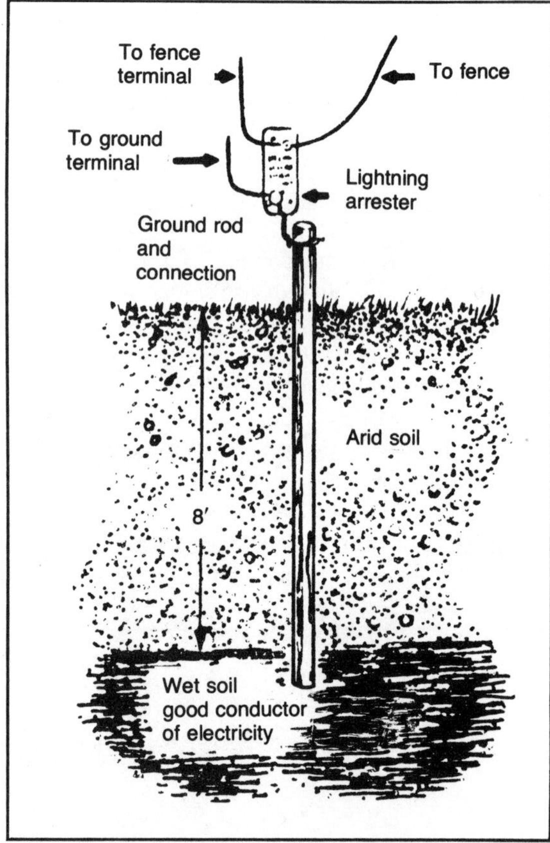


Fig. 8-39. Installation of lightning arrester on an electric fence.

Approved fence chargers emit the current intermittently and not continuously. The "on" time is usually 1/10 of a second 45 to 55 times a minute. The shock is sharp, but it is short and harmless.

Locate your fence charger in a building. It must be protected from the weather. Figure 8-39 shows the installation of a lightning arrester on an electric fence.

# Chapter 9

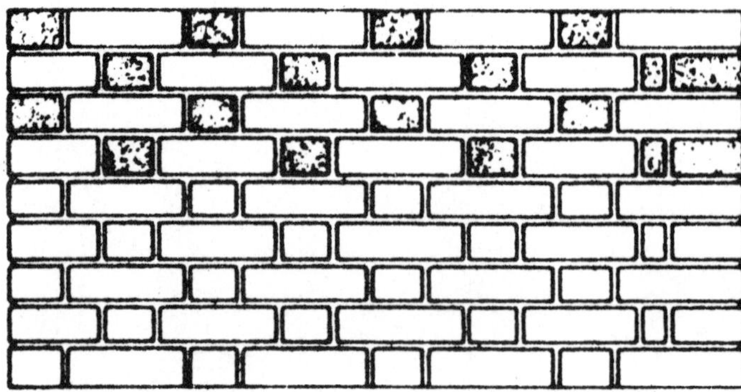

# Masonry Fences and Walls

MASONRY FENCES AND WALLS ARE EXCELLENT long-term investments in your property. They can be both functional and decorative (Figs. 9-1 and 9-2).

Brick, stone, and concrete walls can mark boundaries, keep people in or out, control privacy and the elements, retain soil, and inprove the visual effect of your property. Masonry walls and fences can be constructed by most patient do-it-yourselfers, once they have the right tools and understand the basis of building with masonry (Fig. 9-3).

## MASONRY TOOLS

Figure 9-4 illustrates the most common mason's tools. They can be purchased, rented, or borrowed at minimal cost.

**Trowels.** The trowel is usually triangular. The largest size is from 9 to 11 inches long and from 4 to 8 inches wide. The height and weight of the trowel used depends on you, the mason. You should select the one that you can handle the best. Generally, the short wide trowels are best because the weight is nearer the wrist and doesn't put as much strain on it. Trowels used for pointing and striking joints are smaller in size: 3 to 6 inches long and 2 to 3 inches wide. the trowel is used to mix and pick up mortar from the board, throw mortar on the block, spread mortar, and tap the block down into its bed when necessary.

**Chisel or Bolster.** This tool is used to cut concrete block. It's 2½ to 4½ inches wide.

**Hammer.** The mason's hammer has a square face on one end and a long chisel peen on the other. It weighs from 1½ to 3½ pounds and is used for splitting and rough-breaking blocks.

**Jointer.** This tool is used for making various types of joints. There are several different types: rounded, flat, or pointed, depending on the shape of the mortar joint desired. Figure 9-5 illustrates other mason's tools.

**Square.** The square is used to measure right angles and lay out corners.

**Mason's Level.** The level enables the mason to plumb and level walls. It's from 36 to 48 inches long and is made of wood or metal. When the level is placed horizontally on the masonry and the bubble

Fig. 9-1. Masonry walls and fences are both functional and decorative (courtesy Brick Institute of America).

in the center tube is in the center of the tube, the masonry is level. When the level is placed vertically against the masonry and the bubble in the end tube is in the center of the tube, the masonry is plumb. An offset line from the face of the work should be established for long, high walls or tall columns. To assure straightness and plumbness, offset checks between this line and the face should be made often.

**Straightedge.** The straightedge can be of any length up to 16 feet and should be 1⅛ inches thick and 6 to 10 inches wide. The top and bottom edges must be parallel. The straightedge can be used as an extension of the level to cover distances longer than the length of the level.

**Miscellaneous Tools.** Additional equipment required includes shovels, mortar hoes, wheelbarrows, chalk, plumb bobs, and a 200-foot ball of No. 18 to 21 hard-twisted cotton cord.

## EQUIPMENT

You'll also need a couple pieces of equipment that you can build yourself (Fig. 9-6). The *mortar box* is used to mix mortar by hand. It should be as watertight as possible.

The *mortar board* is usually from 3 to 4 feet square. The board should be thoroughly wetted down before any mortar is placed on it to prevent the wood from absorbing moisture and causing the mortar to dry out. The mortar should be kept rounded up in the center of the board, and the outer edges should be kept clean. If spread in a thin layer, the mortar will dry out quickly. Lumps will often form.

## MORTAR

Good mortar is necessary to excellent workmanship and a fine wall. The strength of the bond is affected by various factors including the type and quality of the cementing material, the workability or plasticity of the mortar, the surface texture of the mortar bedding areas, the water retentivity of the mortar, and the quality of workmanship in laying the

Fig. 9-2. This brick fence is purely decorative (courtesy Brick Institute of America).

Fig. 9-3. Concrete block fences can be built by nearly anyone (photo by Val Ramos).

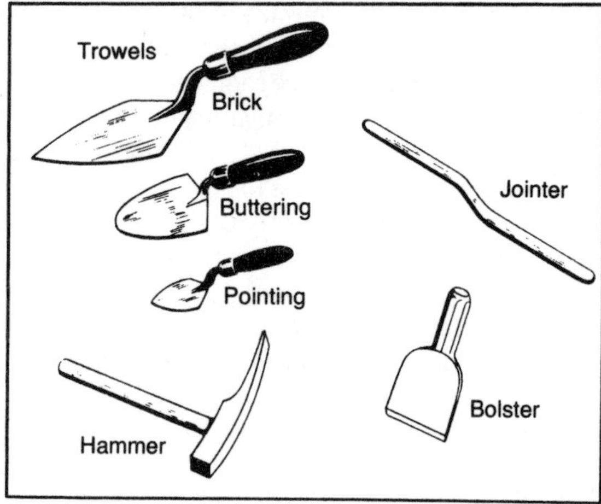

Fig. 9-4. Mason's tools.

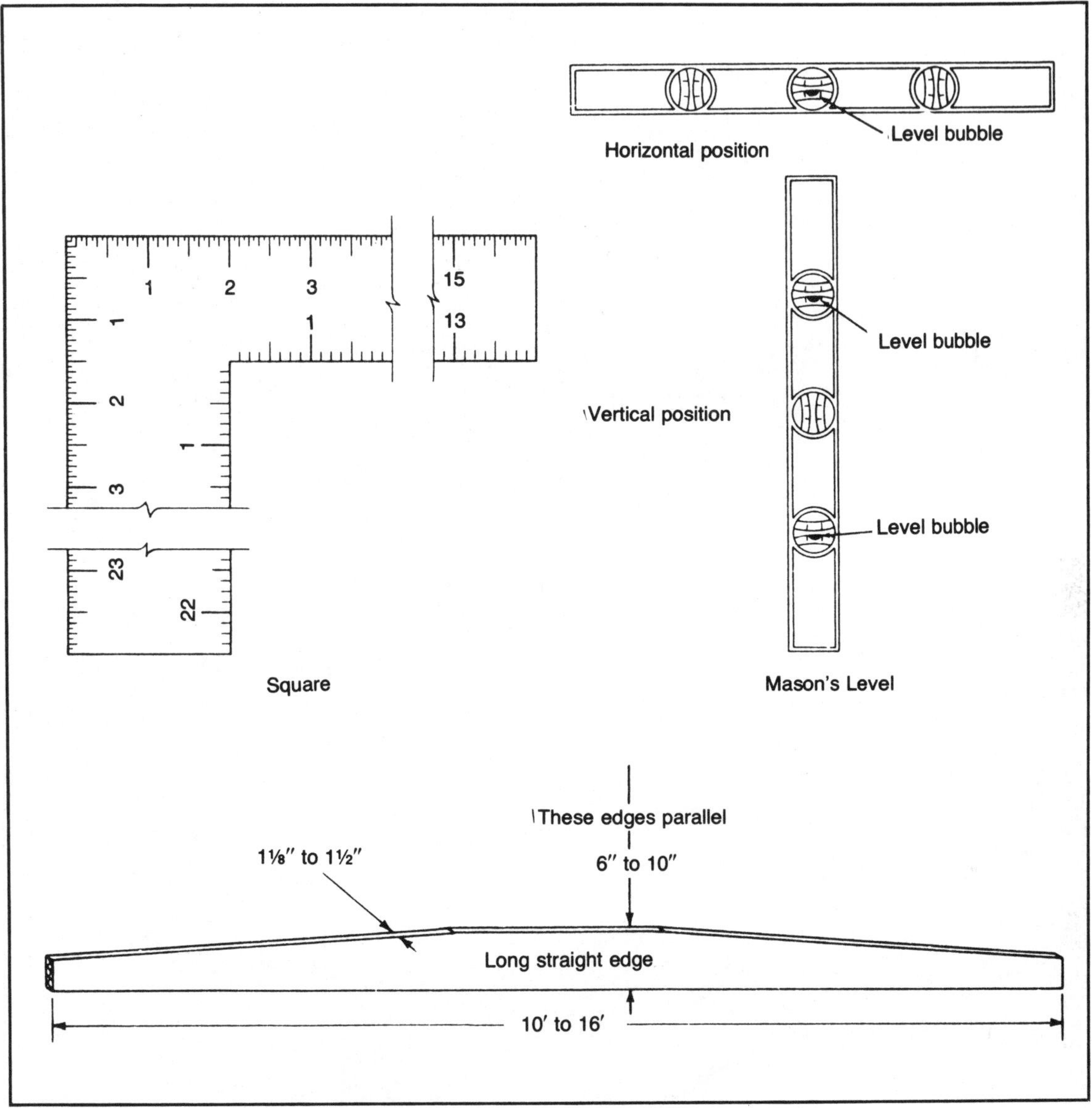


Fig. 9-5. Square, mason's level, and straightedge.

units. Mortar used to bond brick together will be the weakest part of brick masonry unless properly mixed and applied.

Both the strength and resistance to rain penetration of brick masonry walls are dependent on the strength of the mortar's bond. Water in the mortar is essential to the development of the bond. If the mortar contains insufficient water, the bond will be weak and spotty. When brick walls leak, it is usually through the mortar joints.

The most common mortar mixture is made with 1 part portland cement, ¼ part hydrated lime or lime putty, and 3 parts sand. A similar mixture is 1 part portland cement, 1 part type II masonry cement, and 6 parts sand.

This mortar is suitable for general use. It is

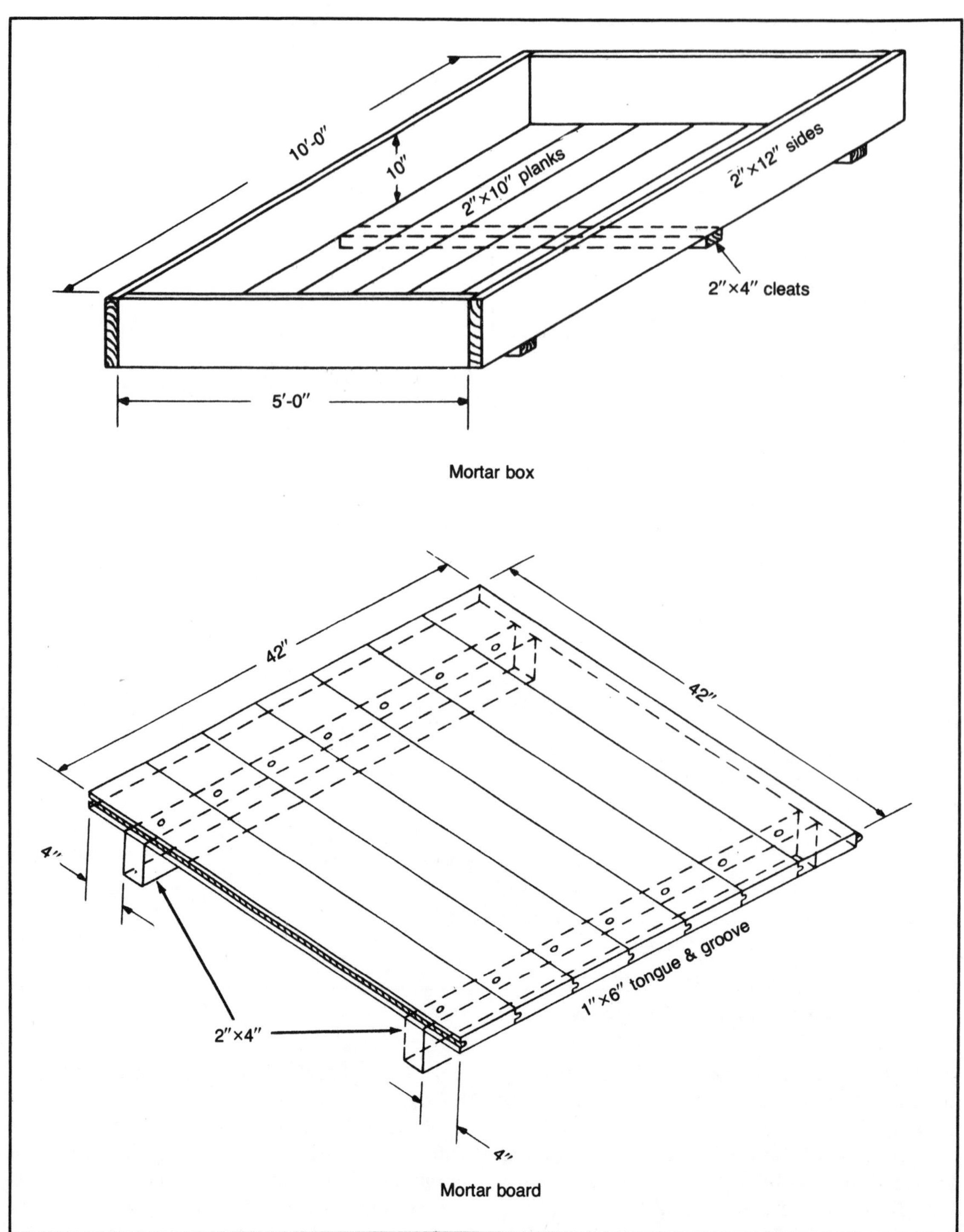


Fig. 9-6. Mortar board and mortar box.

recommended specifically for masonry below grade and in contact with earth such as foundations, retaining walls, and walks. All mortar materials except sand and slaked quicklime must be stored in a dry place.

If a large quantity of mortar is required, it should be mixed in a drum-type mixer similar to those used for mixing concrete. Mixing time should not be less than three minutes. All dry ingredients should be placed in the mixer first and mixed for one minute before adding water.

Unless large amounts of mortar are required, the mortar is mixed by hand using a mortar box. Mix all the ingredients thoroughly to obtain a uniform mixture. All dry materials should be mixed first. A steel drum full of water should be kept close to the mortar box for the water supply. A second steel drum of water should be available for shovels and hoes when not in use.

Calcium chloride is sometimes added to mortar to accelerate the rate of hardening and to increase early strengths. Not more than 2 percent calcium chloride by weight of the portland cement should be used for this purpose. Not more than 1 percent of calcium chloride should be used with masonry cements.

## BUILDING CONCRETE BLOCK WALLS

Concrete masonry has become increasingly important as a construction material. Concrete block walls and fences can be efficient, economical, and practical. Concrete masonry building units include hollow load-bearing concrete block, solid load-bearing concrete block, hollow non-load-bearing concrete block, concrete building tile, and concrete brick.

The different units or blocks are made with heavyweight or lightweight aggregates and are referred to as heavyweight and lightweight units respectively. A hollow load-bearing concrete block of 8×8×16 inches nominal size will weigh from 40 to 50 pounds when made with heavyweight aggregate such as sand, gravel, crushed stone, or air-cooled slag. Concrete blocks mde with lightweight aggregate will weigh from 25 to 35 pounds each and are made with coal cinders expanded shale, clay, slag, or natural lightweight materials such as volcanic cinders and pumice.

A solid concrete block is defined in ASTM (American Society for Testing and Materials) specifications as a unit in which the core area is not more than 25 percent of the gross cross-sectional area. Concrete blocks are generally solid and are sometimes available with a recessed pocket called a "frog." A hollow concrete block is a unit having a core area greater than 25 percent of its gross cross-sectional area. The core area of hollow units is generally 40 to 50 percent of the gross area.

Concrete building units are made in sizes and shapes to fit different construction needs. Units are made in full and half-length sizes as shown in Fig. 9-7. Concrete unit sizes are usually referred to by their nominal dimensions. A unit measuring 7⅝ inches wide, 7⅝ inches high, and 15⅝ inches long is referred to as an 8×8×16-inch unit. When the unit is laid in a wall with ⅜-inch mortar joints, it will occupy a space exactly 16 inches long and 8 inches high.

### Construction

Concrete masonry walls should be laid out to make maximum use of full- and half-length units to minimize cutting and fitting blocks on the job. Length and height of the wall and the width and height of openings for gates should be planned to use full-size and half-size units.

Table 9-1 lists the nominal length of concrete masonry walls by stretchers. Table 9-2 lists nominal height of block walls by courses.

Masonry wall footings should be placed on firm, undisturbed soil of adequate load-bearing capacity to carry the design load. They should be below frost penetration. Unless local requirements read otherwise, the general practice is to make footings for walls and masonry fences 1½ to 2 times as wide as the thickness of the wall they support (Fig. 9-8).

When the ground water level in the wet season can be expected to be higher than the footing, a line of drain tile should be placed in the outer side of the footing. The tile line should have a fall of at least ½ inch in 12 feet and should drain to a suitable outlet.

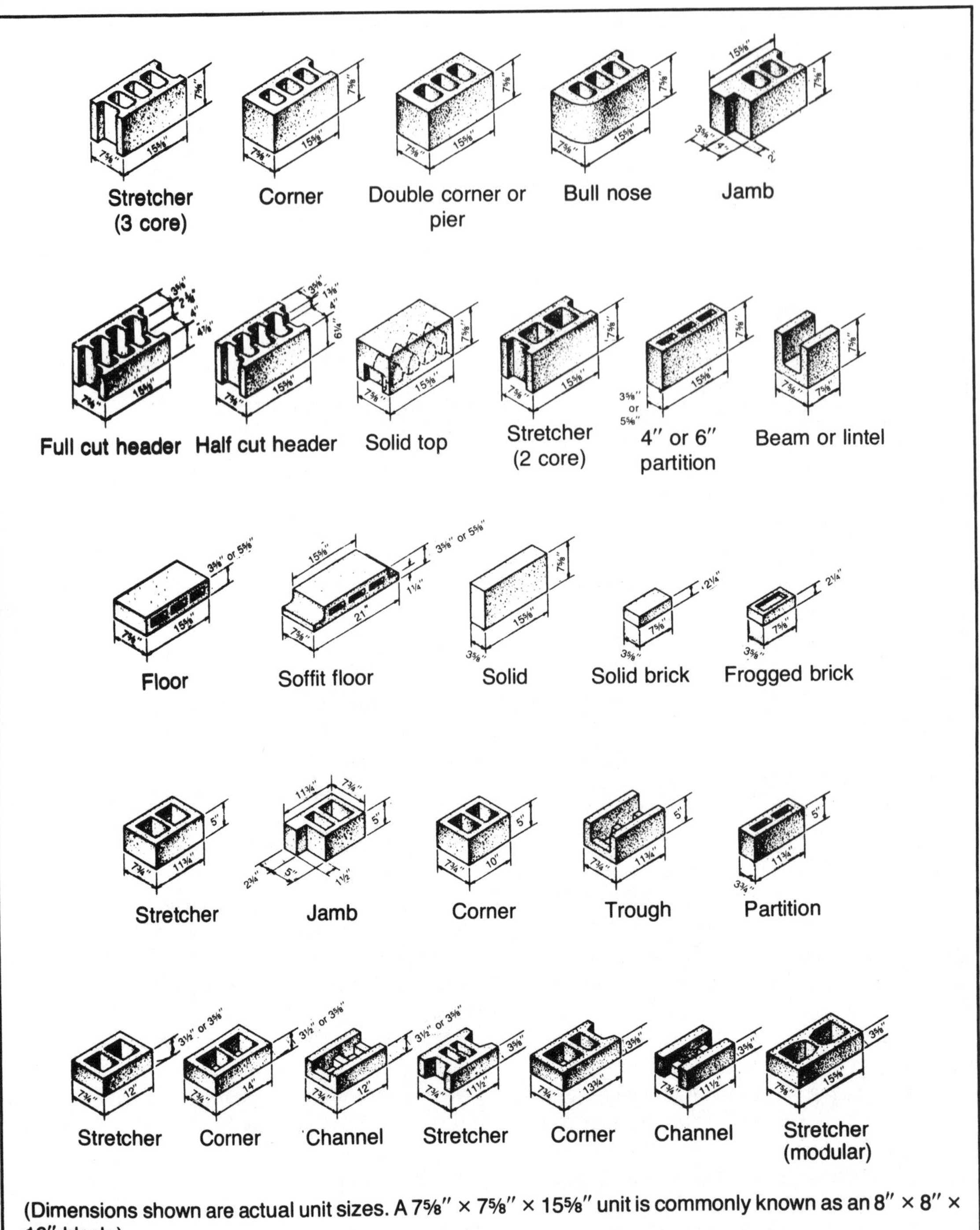


Fig. 9-7. Typical sizes and shapes of concrete masonry units.

**Table 9-1. Nominal Length of Concrete Masonry Walls by Stretchers.**

| No. of Stretchers | Nominal Length of Concrete Masonry Walls | |
|---|---|---|
| | Units 15⅝" Long and Half Units 7⅝" Long with ⅜" Thick Head Joints. | Units 11⅝" Long and Half Units 5⅝" Long with ⅜" Thick Head Joints. |
| 1 | 1'4" | 1'0". |
| 1½ | 2'0" | 1'6" |
| 2 | 2'8" | 2'0". |
| 2½ | 3'4" | 2'6". |
| 3 | 4'0" | 3'0". |
| 3½ | 4'8" | 3'6". |
| 4 | 5'4" | 4'0". |
| 4½ | 6'0" | 4'6". |
| 5 | 6'8" | 5'0". |
| 5½ | 7'4" | 5'6". |
| 6 | 8'0" | 6'0". |
| 6½ | 8'8" | 6'6". |
| 7 | 9'4" | 7'0". |
| 7½ | 10'0" | 7'6". |
| 8 | 10'8" | 8'0" |
| 8½ | 11'4" | 8'6" |
| 9 | 12'0" | 9'0". |
| 9½ | 12'8" | 9'6". |
| 10 | 13'4" | 10'0". |
| 10½ | 14'0" | 10'6". |
| 11 | 14'8" | 11'0". |
| 11½ | 15'4" | 11'6". |
| 12 | 16'0" | 12'0". |
| 12½ | 16'8" | 12'6". |
| 13 | 17'4" | 13'0". |
| 13½ | 18'0" | 13'6". |
| 14 | 18'8" | 14'0". |
| 14½ | 19'4" | 14'6". |
| 15 | 20'0" | 15'0". |
| 20 | 26'8" | 20'0". |

(Actual length of wall is measured from outside edge to outside edge of units and is equal to the nominal length minus ⅜" (one mortar joint).

**Table 9-2. Nominal Height of Concrete Masonry Walls by Courses.**

| No. of Courses | Nominal Height of Concrete Masonry Walls | |
|---|---|---|
| | Units 7⅝" High and ⅜" Thick Bed Joint | Units 3⅝" High and ⅜" Thick Bed Joint |
| 1 | 8" | 4" |
| 2 | 1'4" | 8". |
| 3 | 2'0" | 1'0". |
| 4 | 2'8" | 1'4". |
| 5 | 3'4" | 1'8". |
| 6 | 4'0" | 2'0". |
| 7 | 4'8" | 2'4". |
| 8 | 5'4" | 2'8". |
| 9 | 6'0" | 3'0". |
| 10 | 6'8" | 3'4". |
| 15 | 10'0" | 5'0" |
| 20 | 13'4" | 6'8". |
| 25 | 16'8" | 8'4". |
| 30 | 20'0" | 10'0". |
| 35 | 23'4" | 11'8". |
| 40 | 26'8" | 13'4". |
| 45 | 30'0" | 15'0". |
| 50 | 33'4" | 16'8". |

(For concrete masonry units 7⅝" and 3⅝' in height laid with ⅜" mortar joints. Height is measured from center to center of mortar joints.)

Good workmanship is always an important factor in building weathertight walls. Each masonry unit should be laid plumb and true. Both horizontal and vertical joints should be filled well and compacted by tooling when the mortar is partly stiffened.

## First Course

After locating the corners of the wall, the mason usually checks the layout by stringing out the blocks for the first course without mortar. A chalked snap line can be used to mark the footing and align the block accurately. A full bed of mortar is then spread and furrowed with the trowel to insure plenty of mortar along the bottom edges of the face shells of the block for the first course. The corner block should be laid first and carefully positioned. All blocks should be laid with the thicker end of the face shell up to provide a larger mortar-bedding area. Mortar is applied only to the ends of the face shells for vertical joints. Several blocks can be placed on end. The mortar is then applied to the vertical face shells in one operation. Each block is then brought over its final position and pushed downward into the mortar bed and against the previously laid block to obtain a well-filled vertical mortar joint.

After three or four blocks have been laid, the mason's level is used as a straightedge to assure correct alignment of the blocks. The blocks are carefully checked with the level, brought to proper grade, and made plumb by tapping with the trowel handle.

The first course of concrete masonry should be laid carefully so it's properly aligned, leveled, and plumbed, and to assure that succeeding courses are straight and true.

## Laying Up the Corners

After the first course is laid, mortar is applied only to the horizontal face shells of the block. Mortar for the vertical joints may be applied to the vertical face shells of the block to be placed, to the previously laid block, or to both to insure well-filled joints.

The corners of the wall are built first, usually

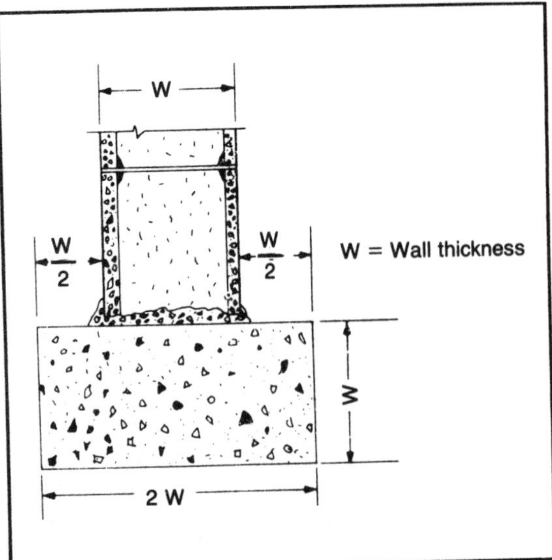


Fig. 9-8. Dimensions of masonry wall footings.

four or five courses higher than the wall's center. As each course is laid at the corner, it's checked with a level for alignment, for level, and for plumb. Each block is carefully checked with a level or straightedge so that the faces of the block are all in the same plane to insure true, straight walls.

A course pole is handy to have. It's simply a board with markings 8 inches apart designed to provide an accurate method of determining the top of the masonry for each course.

## Laying Blocks Between Corners

When filling in the wall between the corners, a mason's line is stretched from corner to corner for each course. The top outside edge of each block is laid to this line. The manner of gripping the block is important. It should be tipped slightly toward you, the mason, so that you can see the edge of the course below. You can then place the lower edge of the block directly over the course below.

To assure good bond, mortar should not be spread too far ahead of the actual laying of the block, or it will stiffen and lose its plasticity. As each block is laid, excess mortar extruding from the joints is cut off with the trowel and thrown back on the mortar board to be reworked into the fresh mortar. Dead mortar that has been picked up from the scaffold or from the floor should not be used.

When installing the closure block, all edges of the opening and all four vertical edges are buttered with mortar. The block is carefully lowered into place. If any of the mortar falls out, leaving an open joint, remove the block and repeat the procedure.

## Tooling

Weathertight joints and neat appearance of concrete block walls are dependent on proper tooling. The mortar joints should be tooled after a section of the wall has been laid, and the mortar has become "thumbprint" hard. Tooling compacts the mortar and forces it tightly against the masonry on each side of the joint.

All joints should be tooled either concave or V-shaped (Fig. 9-9). Horizontal joints should be tooled first, followed by striking the vertical joints with a small S-shaped jointer. Mortar burrs remaining after tooling is completed should be trimmed off with a trowel flush with the face of the wall or removed by rubbing with a burlap bag.

## Control Joints

Control joints are continuous vertical joints built into concrete masonry walls and fences to control cracking resulting from unusual stresses. The joints are intended to permit slight wall movement without cracking. Control joints should be laid up in mortar just as any other joint. Full- and half-length blocks are used to form a continuous vertical joint.

## Intersecting Bearing Walls

Intersecting concrete block bearing walls should not be tied together in a masonry bond except at the corners. Instead, one wall should terminate at the face of the other wall with a control joint at the point. Bearing walls are tied together with a metal tie bar $\frac{1}{4} \times 1\frac{1}{4} \times 28$ inches, with 2-inch right angle bends on each end. Tie bars are spaced not over 4 feet apart vertically. Bends at the ends of the tie bars are embedded in cores filled with mortar or concrete. Pieces of metal lath placed under the cores support the concrete or mortar filling.

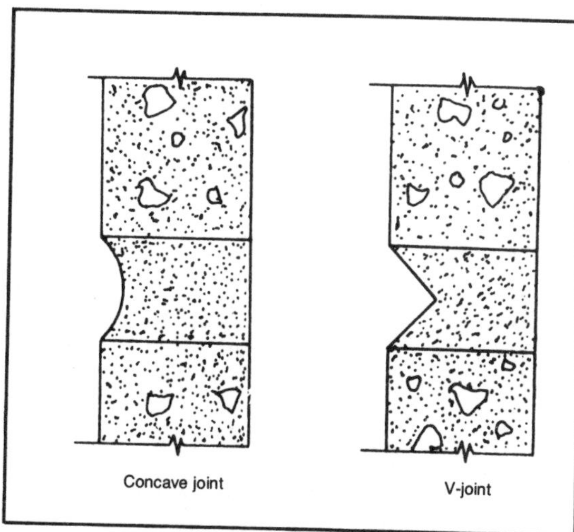

Fig. 9-9. Tooled joints for weathertight construction.

## BUILDING BRICK WALLS AND FENCES

Brick masonry uses units of baked clay or shale of uniform size, small enough to be placed with one hand, and laid in courses with mortar joints. Bricks are kiln-baked from various clay and shale mixtures. The chemical and physical characteristics of the ingredients vary considerably; these and the kiln temperatures combine to produce brick in many colors and hardnesses. In some regions pits are opened and found to yield clay or shale which, when ground and moistened, can be formed and baked into durable brick. In other regions clays or shales from several pits must be mixed.

### Bricks

Standard bricks manufactured in the United States are 2¼ by 3¾ by 8 inches. English bricks are 3 by 4½ by 9 inches. Roman bricks are 1½ by 4 by 12 inches. Norman bricks are 2¾ by 4 by 12 inches. The actual dimensions vary slightly because of shrinkage during burning.

The bricklayer frequently cuts the brick into various shapes. The more common of these are shown in Fig. 9-10. They are called half or bat, three-quarter closure, quarter closure, king closure, queen closure, and split. They are used to fill in the spaces at corners and such other places where a full brick will not fit.

The six surfaces of a brick are called the face, side, cull, end, and the beds (Fig. 9-11).

There are three general types of structural clay masonry units: solid masonry, hollow masonry, and architectural terra-cotta. These units may serve a structural function only, as a decorative finish, or a combination of both. Structural clay products include brick, hollow tile of all types, and architectural terra-cotta. They do not include thin wall tile, sewer pipe, flue linings, drain tile, and the like.

There are many types of brick. Some are different in formation and composition while others vary according to their use.

**Building Brick.** The term building brick, formerly called common brick, is applied to brick made of ordinary clays or shales and burned in kilns in the usual manner. These bricks do not have special scorings or markings and are not produced in any special color or surface texture. Building brick is also known as hard and kiln run brick. It is used generally for the backing courses in solid or cavity brick walls. The harder and more durable kinds are preferred for this purpose.

**Face Brick.** Face brick are used in the exposed face of a wall and are higher quality units than backup brick. They have better durability and appearance. The most common colors of face brick are various shades of brown, red, gray, yellow, and white.

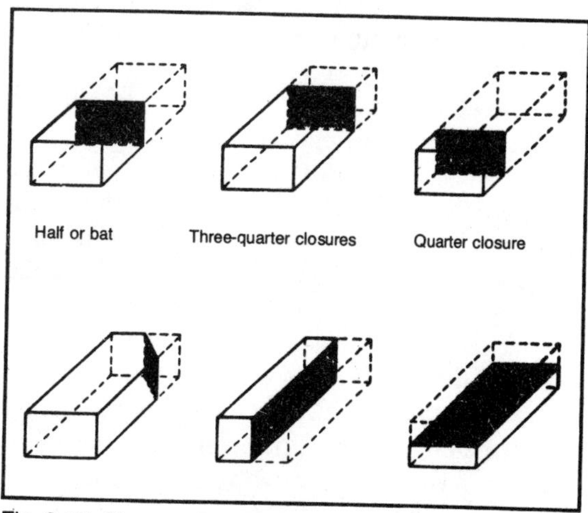

Fig. 9-10. Shapes of cut brick.

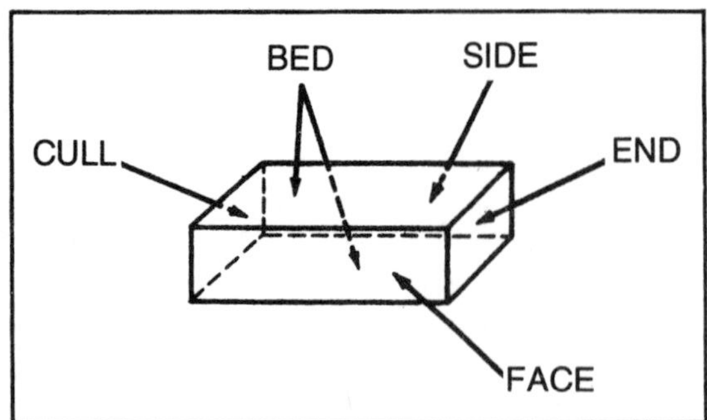

Fig. 9-11. Names of brick surfaces.

**Clinker Brick.** When bricks are overburned in the kilns, they are called clinker brick. This type of brick is usually hard and durable and may be irregular in shape.

**Pressed Brick.** The dry press process is used to make this brick that has regular smooth faces, sharp edges, and perfectly square corners. Ordinarily, all press brick is used as face brick.

**Glazed Brick.** This type of brick has one surface of each brick glazed in white or other color. The ceramic glazing consists of mineral ingredients that fuse together in a glasslike coating during burning. It's particularly suited for walls or partitions in hospitals, dairies, laboratories, or other buildings where cleanliness and ease of cleaning is necessary. It is also sometimes used as a decorative brick for designs in outdoor walls and fences.

**Firebrick.** This type of brick is made of a special type of fireclay that will withstand the high temperatures of fireplaces and boilers without cracking or decomposing.

**Cored Brick.** Cored brick are made with two rows of five holes extending through their beds to reduce weight. There is no significant difference between the strength of walls constructed with cored brick and those constructed with solid brick. Resistance to moisture penetration is about the same for both types of walls. The most easily available brick that will meet requirements should be used whether the brick is cored or solid.

**European Brick.** The strength and durability of most European clay brick, particularly English and Dutch, compares favorably with the clay brick made in the United States.

**Sand-Lime Brick.** Sand-lime bricks are made from a lean mixture under mechanical pressure and hardened under steam pressure. They are used extensively in Germany and are available in many parts of the United States.

Good bricklaying depends on good workmanship and efficiency. The work must be arranged in such a way that the bricklayer is continually supplied with brick and mortar. Mason's tools and equipment needed for bricklaying are the same as those for concrete block construction.

## Bonds

The term *bond,* when applied to masonry, has three different meanings: structural bond, mortar bond, and pattern bond. *Structural bond* is the method by which individual bricks are tied together to cause the entire assembly to act as a single structural unit. Structural bonding is done by overlapping or interlocking bricks with metal ties in the joint and by the adhesion of grout. *Mortar bond* is the adhesion of the joint mortar to bricks or to the reinforcing steel. *Pattern bond* is the pattern formed by the brick and the mortar joints on the face of the wall.

There are five basic pattern bonds in common use today: running bond, common or American bond, Flemish bond, English bond, and stack or block bond (Fig. 9-12).

**Running Bond.** This is the simplest of the basic pattern bonds. The running bond consists of all stretchers. Because there are no headers used in this bond, metal ties are usually used. Running bond is used largely in cavity wall construction and veneered brick walls.

**Common or American Bond.** Common bond is a variation of running bond with a course of full length headers at regular intervals. These headers provide structural bonding and pattern. Header courses usually appear at every fifth, sixth, or seventh course depending on the structural bonding requirements.

**Flemish Bond.** Each course of brick is made up of alternate stretchers and headers. The headers in alternate courses are centered over the stretchers in the intervening courses. Where the headers

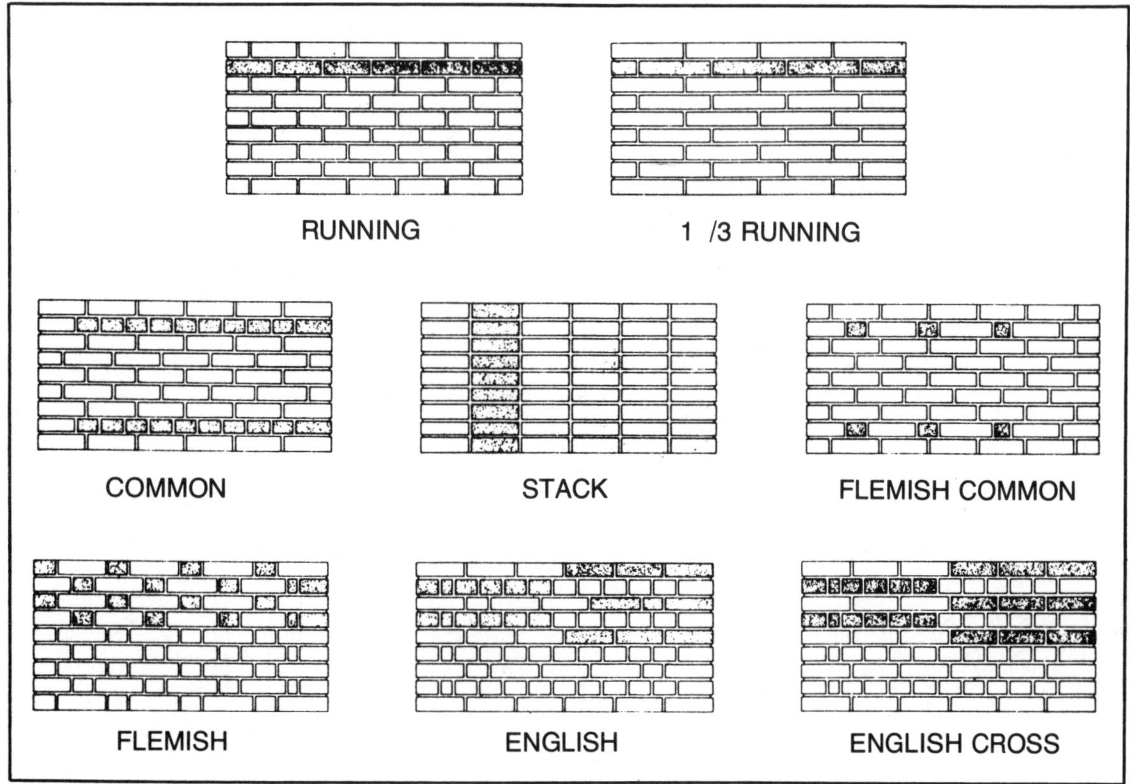


Fig. 9-12. Some types of brick masonry bond.

are not used for the structural bonding, they may be obtained by using half brick called blind headers.

**English Bond.** English bond is composed of alternate courses of headers and stretchers. The headers are centered on the stretchers, and joints between stretchers in all courses line up vertically. Blind headers are used in courses that are not structural bonding courses.

**Stack or Block Bond.** Stack bond is purely a pattern bond. There is no overlapping of the units. All vertical joints are aligned. This pattern is usually bonded to the backing with rigid steel ties. In large wall areas and in load-bearing construction, it's best to reinforce the wall with steel pencil rods placed in the horizontal mortar joints. The vertical alignment requires dimensionally accurate units.

**English Cross or Dutch Bond.** This bond is a variation of English bond and differs only in that vertical joints between the stretchers in alternate courses do not line up vertically. These joints center on the stretchers themselves in the course above and below.

Figure 9-13 shows a course, stretcher, and header. Figure 9-14 illustrates a bull header, bull stretcher, soldier, and wythe.

## Bricklaying

The trowel should be held firmly in the position shown in Fig. 9-15. The thumb should rest on top of the handle and should not encircle it.

If you are a right-handed bricklayer, pick up mortar with the left edge of the trowel from the outside of the pile (Fig. 9-16). Pick up the correct amount of spread for one to five bricks, according to the wall space and your skill. A pickup for one brick forms a small windrow along the left edge of the trowel. A pickup for five bricks is a full load for a large trowel (Fig. 9-17).

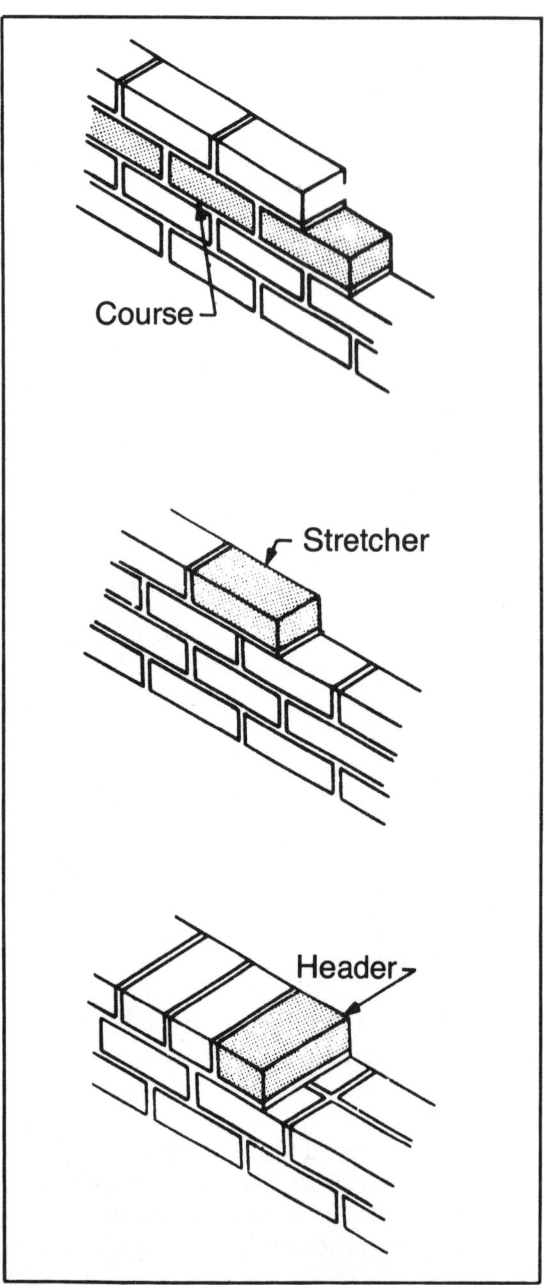


Fig. 9-13. A course is one of the continuous horizontal layers (or rows) of masonry that form the masonry structure when bonded together. A stretcher is a masonry unit laid flat with its longest dimension parallel to the face of the wall. A header is a masonry unit laid flat with its longest dimension perpendicular to the face of the wall. It is generally used to tie two wythes of masonry together.

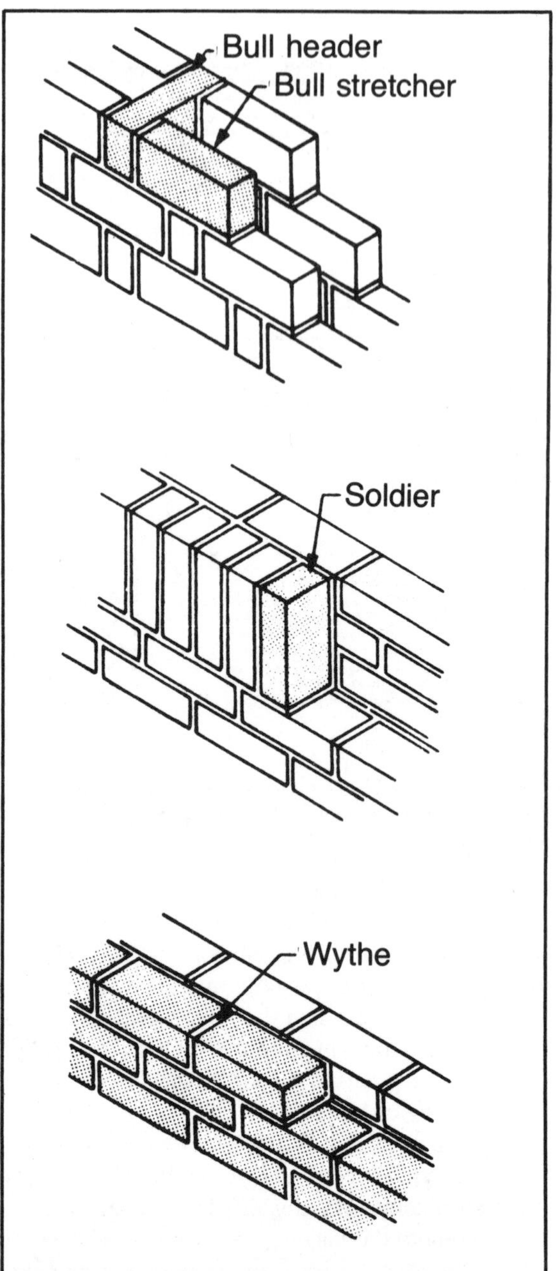


Fig. 9-14. A bull header is a rowlock brick laid with its longest dimension perpendicular to the face of the wall. A bull stretcher is a rowlock brick laid with its longest dimension parallel to the face of the wall. A soldier is a brick laid on its end so that its longest dimension is parallel to the vertical axis of the face of the wall. A wythe is a continuous vertical 4-inch or greater section or thickness of masonry that separates flues in a chimney.

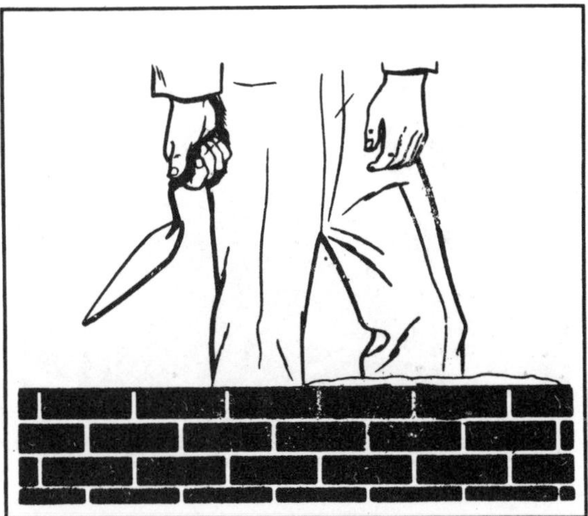

Fig. 9-15. Correct way to hold a trowel.

Fig. 9-17. Trowel full of mortar.

Fig. 9-16. Proper way to pick up mortar.

Fig. 9-18. Mortar thrown on brick.

Holding the trowel with its left edge directly over the center line of the previous course, tilt the trowel slightly and move it to the right. Drop a windrow of mortar along the wall unit until the trowel is empty (Fig. 9-18). In some instances mortar will be left on the trowel when the spreading of mortar on the course below has been completed. When this occurs, the remaining mortar is returned to the board. Work from left to right along the wall if you are right-handed.

Mortar projecting beyond the wall line is cut off with the trowel edge (Fig. 9-19) and thrown back on the mortar board. Enough is retained to "butter" the left end of the first brick to be laid in the fresh mortar.

With the mortar spread about 1 inch thick for the bed joint as shown in Fig. 9-20, a shallow furrow is made (Fig. 9-21). The brick is pushed into the mortar (Fig. 9-22). If the furrow is too deep, there will be a gap left between the mortar and the brick bedded in the mortar. This gap will reduce the resistance of the wall to water penetration. The mortar for a bed joint should not be spread out too far in advance of the laying. A distance of four or five

Fig. 9-19. Mortar spread for a distance of three to five bricks.

Fig. 9-21. Making the shallow furrow.

Fig. 9-20. Cutting off mortar.

Fig. 9-22. Placing the brick on the mortar bed.

bricks is advisable. Mortar that has been spread out too far will dry out before the brick is bedded in it. This results in a poor bond (Fig. 9-23). The mortar must be soft and plastic so that the brick can be easily bedded in it.

The next step after the bed joint mortar has been spread is the laying of the brick. The brick to be laid is picked up as shown in Fig. 9-24 with the thumb on one side of the brick and the fingers on the other. Place as much mortar on the end of the brick as will stick. The brick should then be pushed into place so excess mortar squeezes out at the head joint and at the sides of the wall (Fig. 9-25). The head joint must be completely filled with mortar. This can only be done by placing plenty of mortar on the end of the brick. After the brick is bedded, excess mortar is cut off and used for the next end joint. Surplus mortar should be thrown to the back of the mortar board for retempering if necessary. The proper position of the brick is determined by the use of a cord (Fig. 9-26).

The method of inserting a brick in a space left

in a wall is shown in Fig. 9-27. A thick bed of mortar is spread (step 1). The brick is shoved into this deep bed of mortar (step 2) until it squeezes out at the top of the joint at the face tier and at the header joint (step 3), so that the joints are full of mortar at every point.

Figure 9-28 illustrates how to make cross joints in header courses. These joints must be completely filled with mortar. The mortar for the bed joint should be spread several brick widths in advance. The mortar is spread over the entire side of the header brick before it is placed in the wall (step 1). The brick is then shoved into place so that mortar is forced out at the top of the joint, and the excess mortar is cut off (step 2).

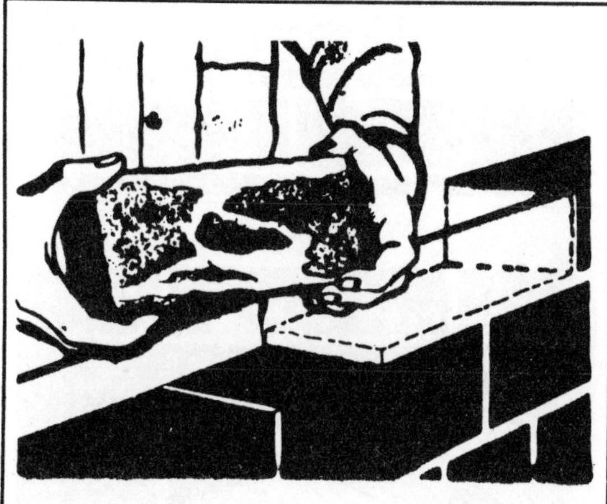

Fig. 9-23. A poorly bonded brick.

Fig. 9-24. Proper way to hold a brick.

Figure 9-26 shows the method of laying a closure brick in a header course. Before laying the closure brick, plenty of mortar should be placed on the sides of the brick already in place (step 1). Mortar should also be spread on both sides of the closure brick to a thickness of about 1 inch (step 2). The closure brick should then be laid in position without disturbing the brick already in place (step 3).

Figure 9-29 gives a step-by-step procedure for making closure joints in stretcher courses. Before laying the closure brick, the ends of the brick on each side of the opening to be filled should be covered well with mortar (step 1). Plenty of mortar should then be thrown on both ends of the closure of brick (step 2). The brick laid without cracks will form between the brick and mortar, allowing moisture into the wall.

There is no hard and fast rule regarding the thickness of the mortar joint. Brick that is irregular in shape may require mortar joints up to ½ inch thick. All brick irregularities are taken up in the mortar joint. Mortar joints ¼ inch thick are the

Fig. 9-25. Head joint in a stretcher course.

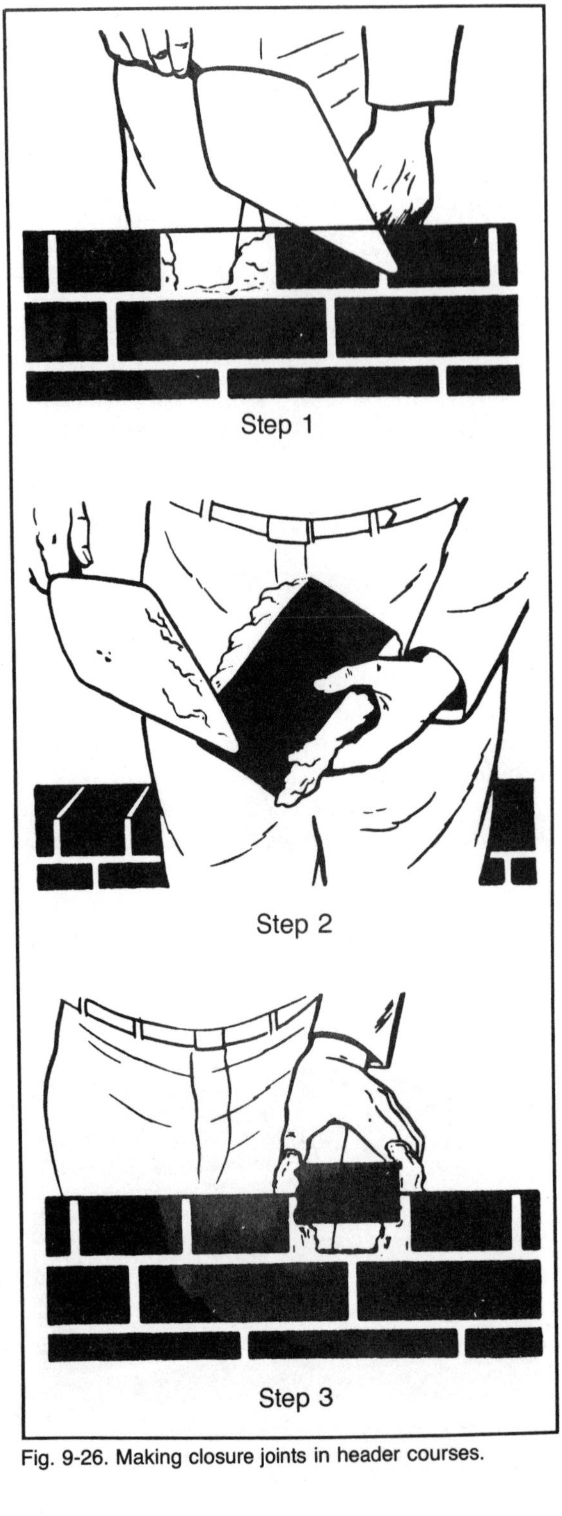

Step 1
Step 2
Step 3

Fig. 9-26. Making closure joints in header courses.

Step 1
Step 2
Step 3

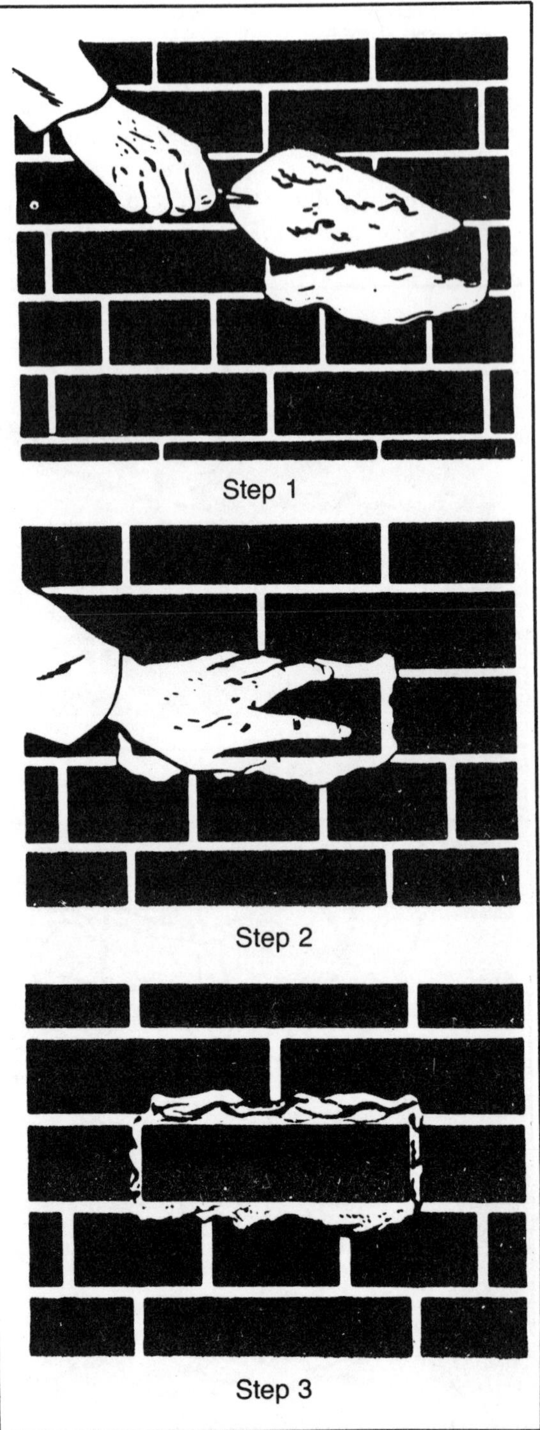

Fig. 9-27. Laying inside brick.

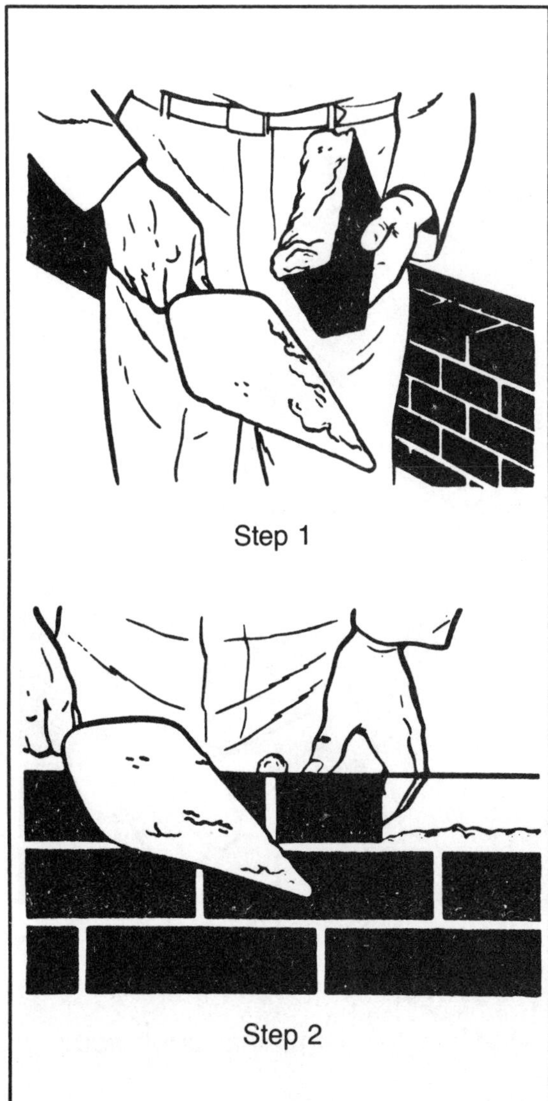

Fig. 9-28. Making cross joints in header courses.

strongest. They should be used when the bricks are regular enough to permit it.

Slushed joints are those made by depositing the mortar on the head joints so that the mortar will run down between the brick to form a solid joint. This isn't good practice. Even when the space between the brick is completely filled, there's no way to compact the mortar against the faces of the brick. A poor bond results.

Fig. 9-29. Making closure joints in stretcher courses.

## CUTTING BRICK

If a brick is to be cut to exact line, the bolster or brick set should be used. When using these tools, the straight side of the cutting edge should face the part of the brick to be saved and also face the bricklayer. One blow of the hammer on the brick set should be enough to break the brick. Extremely hard brick will need to be cut roughly with the hammerhead so there is enough brick left to be cut accurately with the brick set (Fig. 9-30).

For normal cutting work, such as for making closures and bats required around openings in walls and for the completion of corners, the brick hammer should be used. The first step is to cut a line all the way around the brick with light blows of the hammerhead (Fig. 9-31). When the line is complete, a sharp blow to one side of the cutting line will split the brick at the cutting line. Rough places are trimmed using the blade of the hammer (Fig. 9-31). The brick can be held in the hand while being cut.

Fig. 9-31. Cutting brick with a hammer.

## JOINT FINISHES

Exterior surfaces of mortar joints are finished to make the brickwork more waterproof and to improve the appearance. There are several types of joint finishes (Fig. 9-32). The more important types are discussed below. When joints are cut flush with the brick and not finished, cracks are immediately apparent between the brick and the mortar. Although these cracks are not deep, they are undesirable and can be eliminated by finishing or tooling the joint. In every case the mortar joint should be finished before the mortar is hardened to any appreciable extent. The jointing tool is shown in Fig. 9-4.

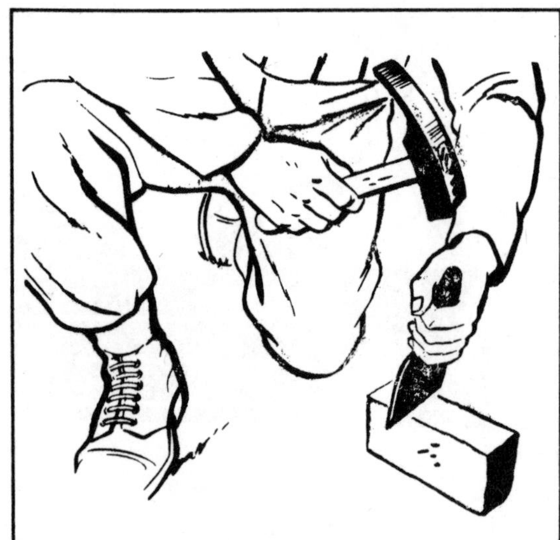

Fig. 9-30. Cutting brick with a bolster.

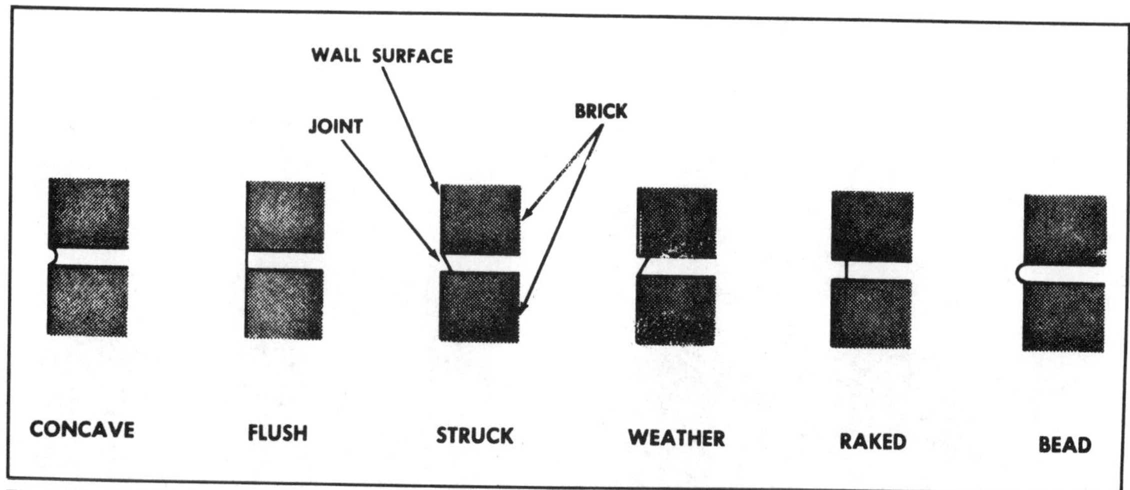

Fig. 9-32. Joint finishes.

**Concave Joint.** The best weathertight joint is the concave joint. This joint is made with a special tool after the excess mortar has been removed with the trowel. The tool should be slightly larger than the joint. Force is used to press the mortar right against the brick on both sides of the mortar joint.

**Flush Joint.** The flush joint (Fig. 9-32) is made by keeping the trowel almost parallel to the face of the wall while drawing the point of the trowel along the joint.

**Weather Joint.** A weather joint sheds water more easily from the surface of the wall. It is formed by pushing downward on the mortar with the top edge of the trowel.

## BUILDING SPECIAL TYPES OF WALLS

Many walls may be built of brick. The solid 8- and 12-inch walls in common bond are the ones usually used for solid wall construction in the United States. The most important of the hollow walls are the cavity wall and the rowlock wall.

### Cavity Walls

Cavity walls provide a means of obtaining a watertight wall that may be plastered without the use of furring or lathing. They appear the same as solid walls without header courses from the outside (Fig. 9-33). No headers are required because the two tiers of brick are held together by metal ties installed every sixth course and on 24-inch centers. To prevent waterflow to the inside tier, ties must be angled in a downward direction from the inside tier to the outside tier.

The 2-inch cavity between the two brick tiers provides a space down which water that penetrates the outside tier may flow without passing through to the inside of the wall. The bottom of the cavity is above ground level. It is drained by weep holes placed in the vertical joints between two bricks in the first course of the outer tier. These holes may be formed by leaving the mortar out of some vertical joints in the first course. The holes should be spaced at about 24-inch intervals. The air space also gives the wall better heat and sound insulation properties.

### Rowlock-Back Walls

One type of rowlock wall is shown in Fig. 9-34. The face tier of this wall has the same appearance as a common bond wall with a full header course every seventh course. The backing tier is laid with the brick on edge. The face tier and backing tier are tied together by a header course as shown. A 2-inch space is provided between the two tiers of brick, as for a cavity wall.

An all-rowlock wall is constructed with brick in the face and backing tier both laid on edge. The header course would be installed at every fourth

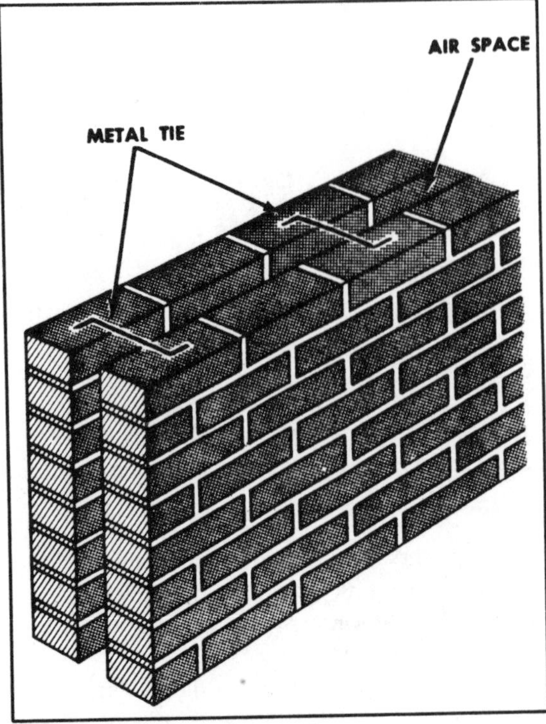

Fig. 9-33. Details for a cavity wall.

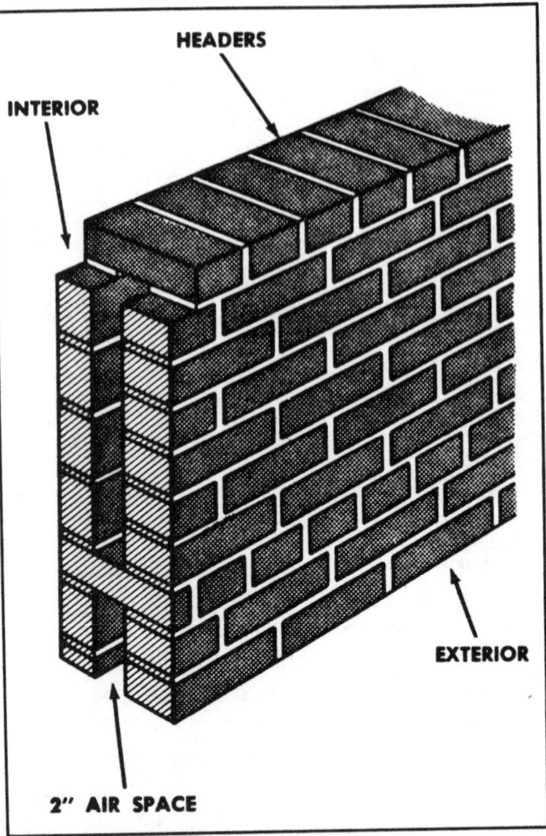

Fig. 9-34. Details for a rowlock-back wall.

course: three rowlock courses to every header course.

A rowlock wall is not as watertight as the cavity wall. Water is able to follow any crack present in the header course and pass through the wall to the outside surface.

### Partition Walls

Partition walls that carry very little load can be made using one tier of brick only. This produces a wall 4 inches thick. A wall of this thickness is laid up without headers.

Bricks are laid in partition walls and cavity walls according to the procedure given earlier for making bed joints, head joints, cross joints, and closures. The line is used the same as for a common bond wall. Corner leads for these walls are erected first. The wall between is built up afterward.

## BUILDING BRICK ARCHES

A brick arch can be an attractive addition to a garden gate opening. It can often be constructed by the patient novice bricklayer.

A brick arch can support a heavy load if properly constructed. The ability to support loads is derived primarily from its curved shape. Several arch shapes can be used; the circular and elliptical shapes are the most common (Figs. 9-35 and 9-36). The width of the mortar joint is less at the bottom of the brick than it is at the top, and it should not be thinner than ¼ inch at any point. Arches made of brick must be constructed with full mortar joints. As laying progresses, make sure the arch doesn't bulge out of position.

A brick arch is constructed on a temporary support that is left in position until the mortar is set. The temporary support is made of wood (Fig. 9-37). The dimensions required are obtained from drawings. For arches up to 6 feet in span, ¾-inch

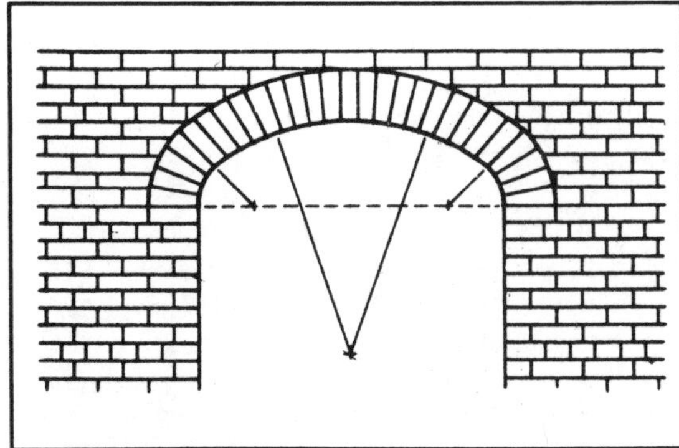

Fig. 9-35. Elliptical arch.

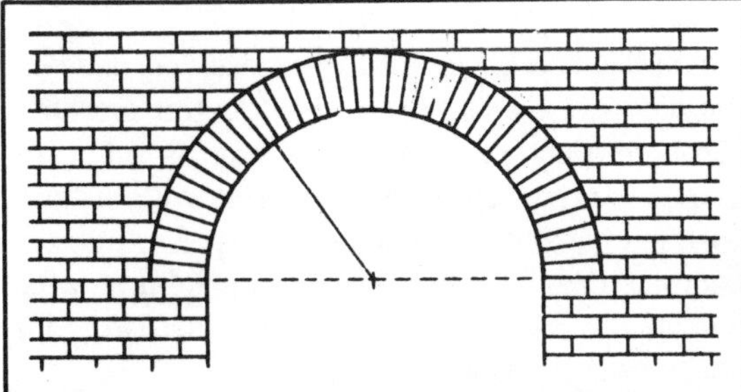

Fig. 9-36. Circular arch.

plywood should be used for temporary supports. Two pieces cut to the proper curved shape are made and nailed to 2 by 4s placed between them. This will provide a wide enough surface to support the brick adequately. The temporary support should be held in position with wedges that can be driven out when the mortar is hardened enough for the arch to be self-supporting.

Construction of an arch is begun at its two ends or abutments. The brick is laid from each end toward the center or crown. The key or middle brick is the last to be placed. There should be an odd number of brick in order for the key or middle brick to come at the arch's center. The arch should be laid out in such a way that no brick need be cut.

The best way to determine the number of brick required for an arch is to lay a temporary support on its side on level ground and set brick around it. Adjust the spacing until the key brick comes at the exact center of the arch. When this has been done, the position of the brick can be marked on the temporary support to be used as a guide when the arch is actually built.

## BUILDING STONE WALLS

Stone walls and fences make a decorative addition to most yards. Many do-it-yourselfers shy away from stone masonry because it looks complicated. It isn't.

There are two basic types of stone walls you can build. Either can be laid up with or without mortar. If strength and stability are desired, mortar should be used.

*Random rubble* is the crudest of all types of stonework. Little attention is paid to laying the stone in courses (Fig. 9-38). Each layer must contain bonding stones that extend through the wall (Fig. 9-39). This produces a wall that is well-tied together. The bed joints should be horizontal for stability, but the "builds" or head joints may run in any direction.

*Coursed rubble* is assembled of roughly squared stones in such a manner as to produce approximately continuous horizontal bed joints (Fig. 9-40).

### Stone

The stone for use in random rubble stone masonry should be strong, durable, and cheap. Durability and strength depend on the chemical composition and physical structure of the stone. Some more commonly found suitable stones are limestone, sandstone, granite, and slate. Un-

Fig. 9-37. Use of a template in arch construction.

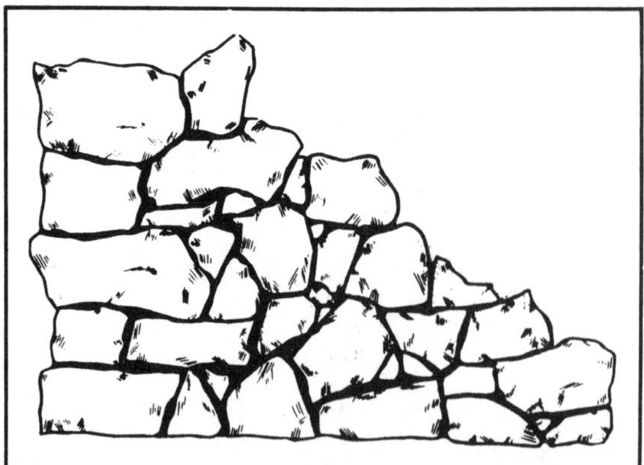

Fig. 9-38. Random rubble masonry.

squared stones obtained from nearby ledges or quarries and fieldstones may be used. The size of the stone should be such that two men can easily handle it. A variety of sizes is necessary to avoid using large quantities of mortar.

### Mortar

The mortar for use in random rubble masonry may be composed of portland cement and sand in the proportions of 1 part cement to 3 parts sand by

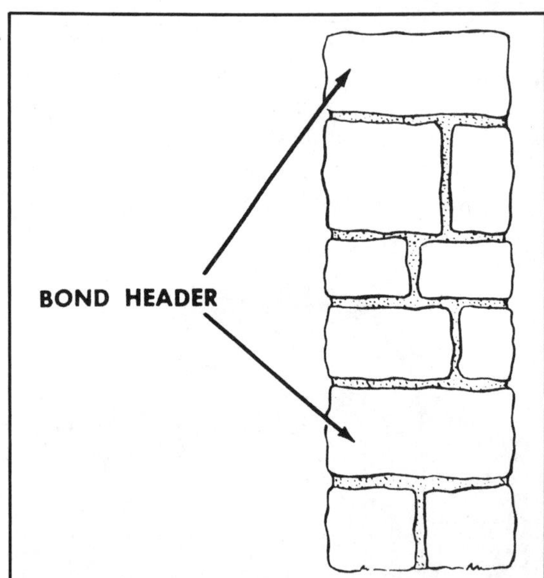


Fig. 9-39. Rubble stone masonry wall showing bonding stone.

Fig. 9-40. Coursed rubble masonry.

volume. Such mortar shrinks excessively and does not work well with the trowel. A better mortar to use is portland cement/lime mortar as suggested earlier in this chapter. Mortar made with ordinary portland cement will stain most types of stone. If staining must be prevented, nonstaining white portland cement should be used instead. Lime doesn't usually stain the stone.

### Laying Rubble Stone Masonry

Workmanship in laying stone masonry affects the economy, durability, and strength of the wall more than any other factor. Here are the basic rules for laying rubble stone masonry:

- Each stone should be laid on its broadest face.
- If appearance is to be considered, the larger stones should be placed in the lower courses. The size of the stones should gradually diminish toward the top of the wall.
- Porous stones should be moistened before being placed in mortar to prevent the stone from absorbing water from the mortar, thereby weakening the bond between the stone and the mortar.
- The spaces between adjoining stones should be as small as practical. These spaces should be completely filled with mortar and smaller stones.
- If you must remove a stone after it has been placed on the mortar bed, it should be lifted clear and reset.

The footing is larger than the wall itself. The largest stones should be used in it to give the greatest strength and lessen the danger of unequal settlement. The footing stones should be as long as the footing is wide, if possible. The footing stones should be laid in a mortar bed about 2 inches deep. All space between the stones should be filled with mortar and smaller stones.

The thickness of the bed joint will vary depending on the stone used. When making the bed joint, enough mortar should be spread on the stone below the one being placed to fill the space between the two stones completely. Care must be taken not to spread the mortar too far ahead of stone-laying.

Bond stones should occur at least once in every 6 to 10 square feet of wall. These stones pass all the way through the wall (Fig. 9-39). Each head joint should be offset from adjacent head joints above and below it as much as possible (Fig. 9-38) to bond the wall together and make it stronger.

If the wall need not be exactly plumb and true to line, the level and line will not be used. The wall will be laid by eye. Frequent sighting is necessary. If the wall must be exactly plumb and erected to line, corner posts of wood should be erected to act as corner leads. The stone is laid with a line. No particular attention is paid to laying the stone in level courses. Some parts of the stone will be farther away from the line than other parts.

# Chapter 10

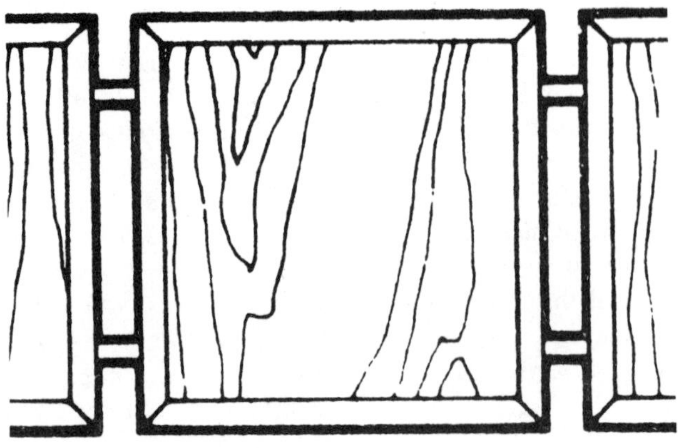

# Other Fence Materials

FENCING MATERIALS ARE ONLY LIMITED BY THE fence builder's imagination. Successful barriers have been built from dimensional lumber, logs, twigs, living plants, clay, adobe, stones, concrete, bricks, wire, glass, plastic, iron, steel, aluminum, tin cans, bottles, railroad ties, wagon wheels, canvas, and hundreds of other natural and man-made materials (Figs. 10-1 through 10-4).

## SOLID PANEL FENCING

One of the simplest and least expensive types of fence or screen to erect is the solid panel fence. The solid panel fence goes up quickly. There's a wide range of materials and textures from which to choose. The panel makes a good display surface, and it insures complete privacy. The solid panel fence or screen has a few drawbacks. The panels need strong structural support, especially in windy areas. A long panel fence seems confining. Some of the materials need periodic painting or treatment to prevent weathering.

### Plywood

Softwood plywood is one of the most versatile building materials available. Plywood is a flat panel made of a number of thin sheets of wood (veneer) glued under pressure. The grain of each sheet is perpendicular to the grain of the adjacent sheets. This cross bonding produces great strength in both directions, and the glue line forms a bond stronger than the wood itself.

Plywood comes in many species and thicknesses. The most common size is 4 by 8 feet and from ¼ to ¾ inch thick. Plywood comes in two basic types: interior and exterior. The principal differences are that more of the lower veneer grades are permitted in the interior type. Also, the interior glue line does not have to waterproof. The rule is simple; interior plywood should not be exposed to the weather and should not be used in building fences. Specify "exterior" grade only.

Both interior and exterior grades of plywood are available in several appearance grades (A, B, C,

Fig. 10-1. Fences can be constructed of nearly any material, including plastic pipe and chain (photo by Val Ramos).

Fig. 10-3. Wood 4×4 posts make good fences and walls (photo by Val Ramos).

Fig. 10-2. Wood and chain link fence (photo by Val Ramos).

Fig. 10-4. Another treated-post retaining wall (photo by Val Ramos).

and D). The veneer used for the face of each panel determines the grade of the product. Unsanded engineered grades are also available for other uses.

Plywood is also classified by group based on the strength of the species used to make it. Group I is the strongest, made up largely of Douglas fir and southern pine plywood.

Here's a rough guide to exterior plywood grades. *A-C* is for applications where the appearance of only one side is important, such as in siding, soffits, and some fencing (Fig. 10-5). *B-C* is an outdoor utility panel with one smooth paintable side.

You'll also see these grades as you shop for plywood. *Standard C-D* means the interior is unsanded. It's a sheathing grade. *CDX* is also available (exterior glue).

*Shop* is a nongrade stamp plywood panel. This economical grade may be used for various projects around the home where appearance or structural considerations are not significant.

A plywood product called T-111 is being used for siding on many new homes. It has recently become a popular product for fencing designed to blend in with the home. T-111 is an exterior rough-finished plywood grooved to look like individual boards. The name comes from T for textured, 1 for the 1-inch groove, and 11 for the 11 inches between grooves.

Again, for outdoor use in fencing, specify *exterior* grade. Plan on painting it regularly—as regularly as you paint your home. Use a high gloss paint.

## Hardboard

Hardboard is a smooth panel without knots or grain. It's almost entirely natural wood—cellulose

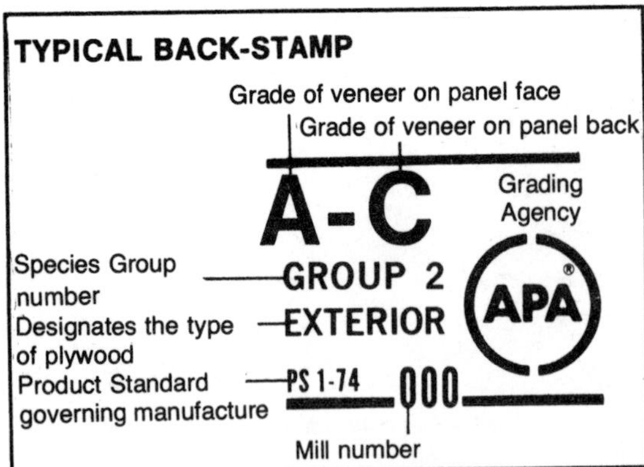

Fig. 10-5. Plywood grade stamp (courtesy Georgia-Pacific Corp.).

for strength and lining for bonding power, as in the tree itself. The difference is that the fibers are rearranged to provide special properties. Hardboard is tough and dense. Under most conditions it won't crack, splinter, check, craze, or flake in outdoor environments. It's generally available in panel sizes up to 4×8 feet and in thicknesses from ⅛ to ¼ inch.

There are *three* basic types of hardboard. *Service* hardboard is for miscellaneous interior uses such as storage areas, closet liners, shelving, cabinet backs, and drawer bottoms.

*Standard* hardboard is for interior paneling, underlayment, screens, and wardrobe doors. It is available perforated for storage areas, such as a garage liner where items can be hung from small hooks and brackets inserted in the holes.

*Tempered* is a manufacturing process that introduces oil into the board and is permanently "set" with a heat process. This gives the board greater abrasion resistance, strength, and moisture resistance. It's used for exterior applications such as fencing, soffits, shutters, flower boxes, windbreakers, and garden sheds. Other specially treated hardboards are available in exterior siding patterns, both lap and panel.

Tempered hardboard comes in several textures: smooth, striated, corrugated, or perforated. Remember that both plywood and hardboard need a solid frame of posts and rails to stand up to wind and weather. Plan on painting hardboard even more frequently than plywood. If possible, build your fence in 4 by 8-foot sections to get the greatest use of each sheet of hardboard.

### Corrugated Aluminum

Corrugated aluminum provides a bright surface that is useful for reflecting warmth into dark corners of the garden. It's also good in a patio around a barbecue. Corrugated aluminum comes in sheets 26 inches wide and 7, 8, 10, and 12 feet long. Corrugated aluminum doesn't rust, but it will corrode if allowed to touch the ground.

### Asbestos Board

Asbestos board is a very durable fencing material that isn't very popular. It's made from cement and asbestos fiber and comes in 4 by 8-foot sheets ¼ inch thick. A 4 by 8 panel weighs 75 pounds or more. You'll need heavier posts and rails for framing.

### Fiberglass Panels

Fiberglass panels are inexpensive, yet decorative fencing materials that are enjoying increased popularity—especially for enclosing pool areas. The panels stop foot traffic while allowing sunlight. They are also easy to build and maintain.

Fiberglass panels have a fiberglass core sealed between layers of polyester resin. The panels are available in many colors and even designs. They are easy to install. Because the panels are quite flexible, you'll need to build your frames smaller for extra support. They are installed on a basic wood fence frame of post and rails. Corrugated fiberglass panels can be overlapped and nailed into place with aluminum nails with neoprene washers.

### Plastic Screen

Plastic screen fencing consists of regular window screen sealed in translucent plastic. Plastic screen fencing diffuses sunlight to a soft radiance. It also diffuses images so that people within a few feet of the screen cannot see through it. Plastic screen fencing is inexpensive to install and maintain.

Install plastic screen the same as you would install porch screen. Attach it to your frame with battens or molding strips, so it can be removed easily when it's damaged or needs replacement.

### Glass

There are many places in the United States where the difference between comfort and discomfort outdoors is determined by the wind rather than temperatures. The windchill factor is at work. One of the greatest windbreak fences is the glass fence that offers a view without the wind.

The way you build your glass fence will depend on the local velocity of the wind and the stability of the soil. Your frame must be substantial. Many glass windscreens are built on top of low masonry walls or anchored to heavy concrete foundations.

Double-weight window glass or ⅛-inch plate is adequate for installations with panes 2 by 3 feet or smaller. Use ¼-inch plate or crystal glass for larger panes. If glare is a problem, get glare-resistant glass. Always try to buy your glass in standard pane sizes in case you have to replace it someday.

Fig. 10-6. Unique fences can be built by combining wood and masonry (photo by Val Ramos).

Fig. 10-7. Another wood-and-masonry fence (photo by Val Ramos).

### Canvas

Canvas fencing offers many advantages in low wind areas. It is easy to install. Canvas fencing is also available in many colors and can be painted. It also makes a good privacy screen. The canvas panel is installed on the basic fence frame with metal eyes and either screws or rope attaching it.

### Bamboo

Bamboo can be gathered in many semiarid locations and cut into strips for fencing. Most people purchase bamboo strips already woven together with wire and stretch them over the basic wood fence frame for the same effect. Bamboo fences are most popular around swimming pools and combined with tropical landscaping.

## OPEN PANEL FENCES

There are many types and styles of open panel fences constructed from materials other than wood or masonry (Figs. 10-6 and 10-7). The most common are wrought iron, ornamental iron, and aluminum.

## Wrought Iron

Wrought iron fences offer both security and beauty (Figs. 10-8 and 10-9). The problem is that they are expensive to construct and install, and they need repeated maintenance. A typical wrought iron fence may cost twice as much as a wood fence of the same length and height (Fig. 10-10).

Wrought iron posts are usually 1-inch tubular steel and are set 4 feet apart in most applications. The posts can either be sunk 2 feet into the ground or built on floor flanges. Most wrought iron fences are simple to design and painted black.

## Ornamental Iron

Ornamental iron fences are more ornate, including cast iron figures and scrolls. Because of the increasing costs, few ornamental iron fences are constructed today. Some are salvaged by fence builders and reinstalled at new locations.

## Aluminum

Aluminum is used in panels, tubing, caps, ornaments, siding, etc. Aluminum is replacing steel in the construction of many so-called wrought iron fences because of the lower cost and its ability to withstand weather. Aluminum can also be easier to maintain.

Fig. 10-9. Wrought iron railing (photo by Val Ramos).

Fig. 10-8. Wrought iron and masonry fence (photo by Val Ramos).

Fig. 10-10. Wrought iron can be used to decorate a wood fence (photo by Val Ramos).

Fig. 10-11. Used railroad ties can become the foundation of a sturdy wood fence (photo by Val Ramos).

Fig. 10-12. Railroad ties form a landscape barrier (photo by Val Ramos).

## MISCELLANEOUS FENCING MATERIALS

Fence builders are creative. Here are some materials that have been used to build barriers.

### Railroad Ties

Railroad ties are large timbers specially treated with creosote to withstand the elements and support railroad tracks across the nation. Large machines now replace old railroad ties in sections miles long. The better ties are sold to wholesalers or directly to the general public for gardening and fence building (Figs. 10-11 and 10-12).

Railroad ties are turned into short fences by simply stacking the ties either tiered or in zigzag fashion. They can be attached, or anchored, to the ground by drilling a hole, driving a pipe through the hole and into the ground, and then spiking succeeding layers.

### Junk

Many fences are literally made of "junk": spare parts, bottles, cans, salvaged doors, and even trash. The bonding used can either be a frame of chicken wire into which the junk is poured and compacted, a mortar such as that suggested in Chapter 9, or an adobe mix. Fences and even homes in old mining towns of the West were woven together with discarded liquor bottles or bean cans from miners.

# Chapter 11

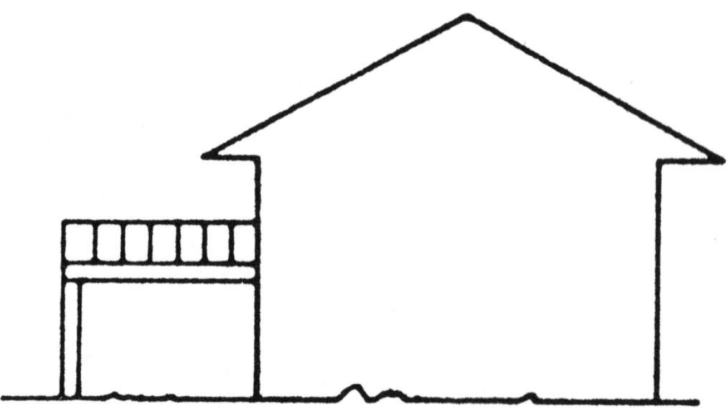

# Outdoor Structures

MANY OUTDOOR STRUCTURES ARE COMplementary to the fence and can easily be built by the do-it-yourselfer. These include decks, railings, benches, swings, walks, engawas, screens, pool enclosures, treillage, arbors, gazebos, pavilions, aeries, sun traps, tree houses, storage sheds, greenhouses, and other practical outdoor structures.

## DECKS

Few home improvements can match a wood *deck* for usefulness, beauty, and enhanced value to a home. For adults, decks offer outdoor living space for entertaining, sunbathing, and dining. They provide an excellent outdoor play area for children. No advanced carpentry skills or sophisticated tools are needed. If you can hammer a nail, saw on a straight line, and read a level, building a deck should present no major problems.

Figure 11-1 illustrates a popular 12×12 sun deck, complete with construction details and materials list.

### Planning

The location and design of your deck should be influenced by several factors (Fig. 11-2).

- *Anticipated use:* private sunbathing, large parties, family recreation, outdoor cooking, etc.
- *Air currents:* allow the flow of gentle breezes and block out prevailing winds.
- *Sunlight:* sun or shade.
- *Privacy:* screen certain areas, avoid street noise, landscaping.
- *View:* emphasize a good view or mask a poor one.
- *Safety:* children, grandchildren, and senior citizens.
- *Access to home:* adjoin kitchen, living room, or bedroom.
- *Terrain:* elevated deck, ground level, split level.
- *Other personal needs and preferences.*

Decks originally gained popularity as a way of adding outdoor living space on hillside lots. Many decks today are built on level ground where they offer firm, dry footing close to the home.

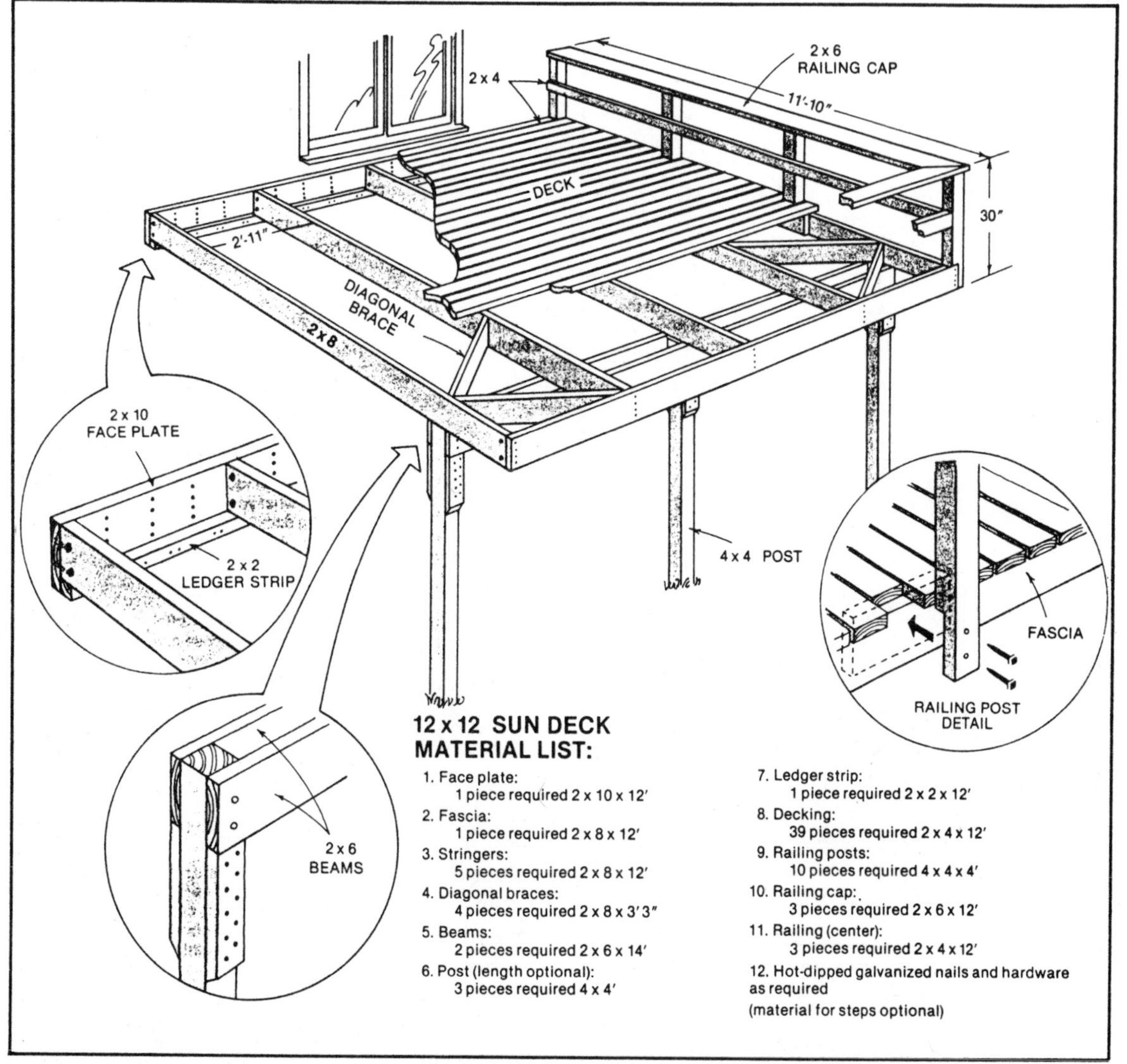


Fig. 11-1. Detailed plans for a 12×12-foot sun deck (courtesy Wolmanized pressure-treated lumber).

Decks can be built just inches high or elevated well above the ground (Fig. 11-3). They may be freestanding or attached to the home or other building. They can even be built in a second story above a garage, carport, or other roofed structure.

Make certain the deck does not seal access to any utility or drainage lines. If you aren't sure of the location or depth of buried electric, telephone, gas, water, or sewer lines, ask your utility companies.

Keep in mind how you intend to use your deck. Will it accommodate benches, lounge chairs, or perhaps a table for outdoor dining? See Figs. 11-4 and 11-5. How many people will be using the deck at any given time? These are elements that must be considered in planning for proper size and design.

When you've decided on the basic size, shape, and location of your deck, check local building codes. You may find there are restrictions as to height and size within your subdivision or community. A construction permit will probably be

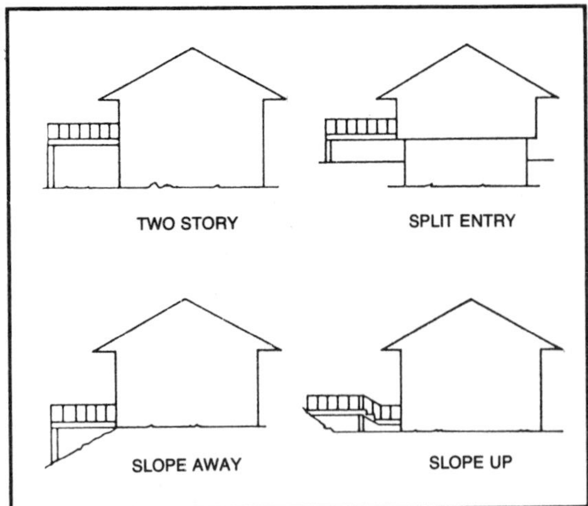

Fig. 11-2. Locating your deck (courtesy Wolmanized pressure-treated lumber).

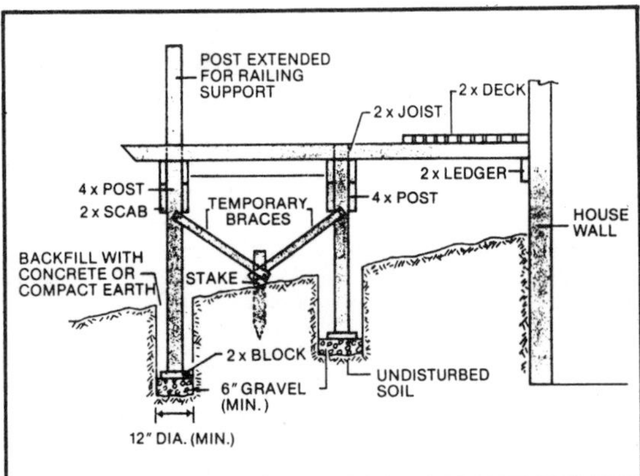

Fig. 11-3. Planning decks over a slope (courtesy Wolmanized pressure-treated lumber).

needed, but don't apply for one until you've finalized your plans.

## Design

Decks consist of six parts: footings, posts, beams, joists, decking, and railings (Fig. 11-6). In planning for these you have three basic considerations: function, structural stability, and appearance.

The aesthetics of your deck will probably be most noticeable in your choice of railing and decking. The location of posts and beams can have a major effect on the appearance of a raised deck.

In almost every instance your choice lies be-

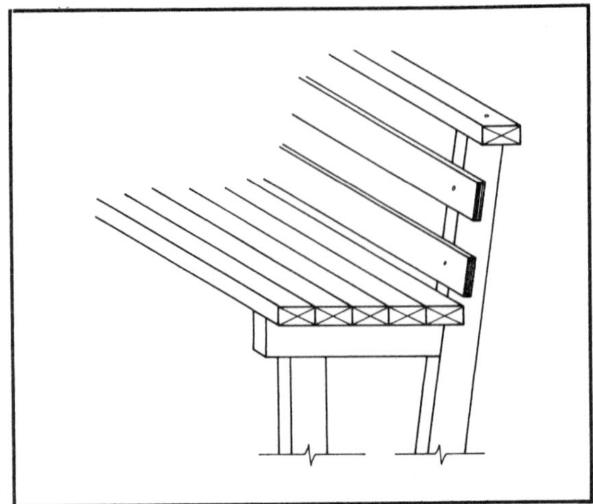
Fig. 11-4. Typical wooden bench construction (courtesy Western Wood Products Association).

tween several small pieces of lumber or comparatively fewer large ones. A railing may be held by 2×4 posts spaced every 16 inches or less, or it may have 4×4 posts capped by a 2×6 spaced as far apart as 8 feet.

Look at various deck plans. Inspect decks completed by friends and neighbors to help you decide what you like best.

Choosing decking presents similar alternatives. A popular choice is 2-inch thick lumber in widths of 4 or 6 inches. (Wider boards may present warping problems.) These can be alternated to make more interesting patterns. You'll want to use pressure-treated wood and rustproof galvanized fasteners.

Tables 11-1 through 11-4 will help you in designing your own deck, using lumber with 1200 psi (pounds per square inch) bending stress rating and a live load of 40 psf (pounds per square foot). The design and construction information is for normal usage. If special loading conditions are anticipated or unusual circumstances exist, consult a competent designer.

Let's say that your deck will extend 8 feet from the house and be 14 feet long. If it's to be just above ground level, there's little need for a railing. Higher decks call for a sturdy railing using 4×4 posts or something comparable. One of the best ways is to extend the posts supporting the deck so they also

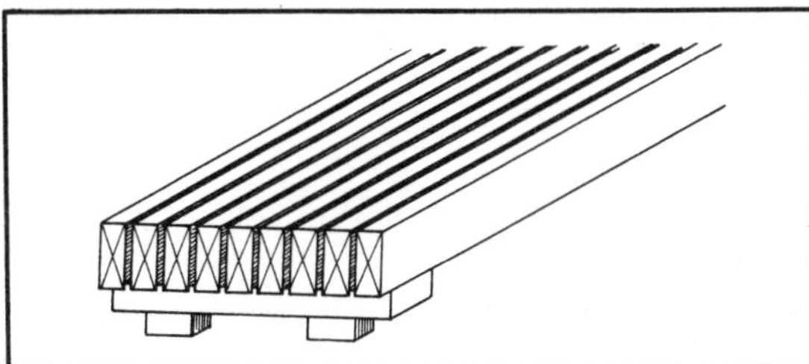

Fig. 11-5. Simple seating (courtesy Western Wood Products Association).

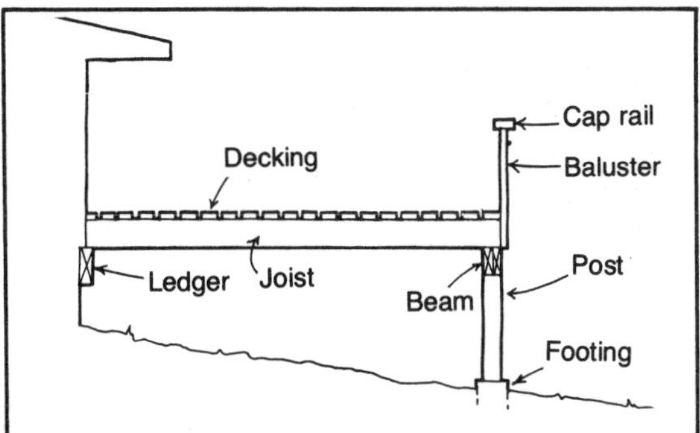


Fig. 11-6. Typical deck components (courtesy Georgia-Pacific Corp.).

support the railing, but this isn't always possible.

Figure 11-4 shows that 4×4 posts can be up to 6 feet apart if capped by a 2×6. Rail height should be between 30 and 40 inches. Side rails can be made of nominal 2-inch lumber. The fastening system used will depend on desired rigidity, especially when anchoring to stub cantilevered posts.

Table 11-1 shows the appropriate beam size. The distance between the house and the beam is 8 feet. A 4×8 beam allows a span of 7 feet between posts, which is a convenient figure for a deck 14 feet long. A beam can be a single piece of the dimension specified or built up from two smaller pieces, either nailed together or placed a few inches apart on either side of a post. Note, however, that two 2×8s are not equivalent to a 4×8 in *actual* dimensions.

To calculate the size post needed, multiply the beam spacing (8 feet) by the post spacing (7 feet). This gives you the load area: 56 feet. Table 11-2 shows that a 4×4 post is adequate for a load area less than 72 square feet and a post height under 6 feet.

Decking in this example will be 2×6 boards

**Table 11-1. Minimum Beam Sizes.**

| Length of Span (ft.) | Spacing between beams (ft.) | | | | | | |
|---|---|---|---|---|---|---|---|
| | 4 | 5 | 6 | 7 | 8 | 9 | 10 |
| 6 | 4 × 6 | 4 × 6 | 4 × 6 | 4 × 8 | 4 × 8 | 4 × 8 | 4 × 10 |
| 7 | 4 × 8 | 4 × 8 | 4 × 8 | 4 × 8 | 4 × 8 | 4 × 10 | 4 × 10 |
| 8 | 4 × 8 | 4 × 8 | 4 × 8 | 4 × 10 | 4 × 10 | 4 × 10 | 4 × 12 |
| 9 | 4 × 8 | 4 × 8 | 4 × 10 | 4 × 10 | 4 × 10 | 4 × 12 | * |
| 10 | 4 × 8 | 4 × 10 | 4 × 10 | 4 × 12 | 4 × 12 | * | * |
| 11 | 4 × 10 | 4 × 10 | 4 × 12 | 4 × 12 | * | * | * |
| 12 | 4 × 10 | 4 × 12 | 4 × 12 | 4 × 12 | * | * | * |

*Beams larger than 4 × 12 recommended. Consult a designer for appropriate sizes..

**Table 11-2. Minimum Post Sizes.**

| Height (ft.) | Load area (sq. ft.) = beam spacing × post spacing | | | | |
|---|---|---|---|---|---|
| | 48 | 72 | 96 | 120 | 144 |
| Up to 6 | 4 × 4 | 4 × 4 | 6 × 6 | 6 × 6 | 6 × 6 |
| Up to 9 | 6 × 6 | 6 × 6 | 6 × 6 | 6 × 6 | 6 × 6 |

Vertical loads figured as concentric along post axis. No lateral loads considered.

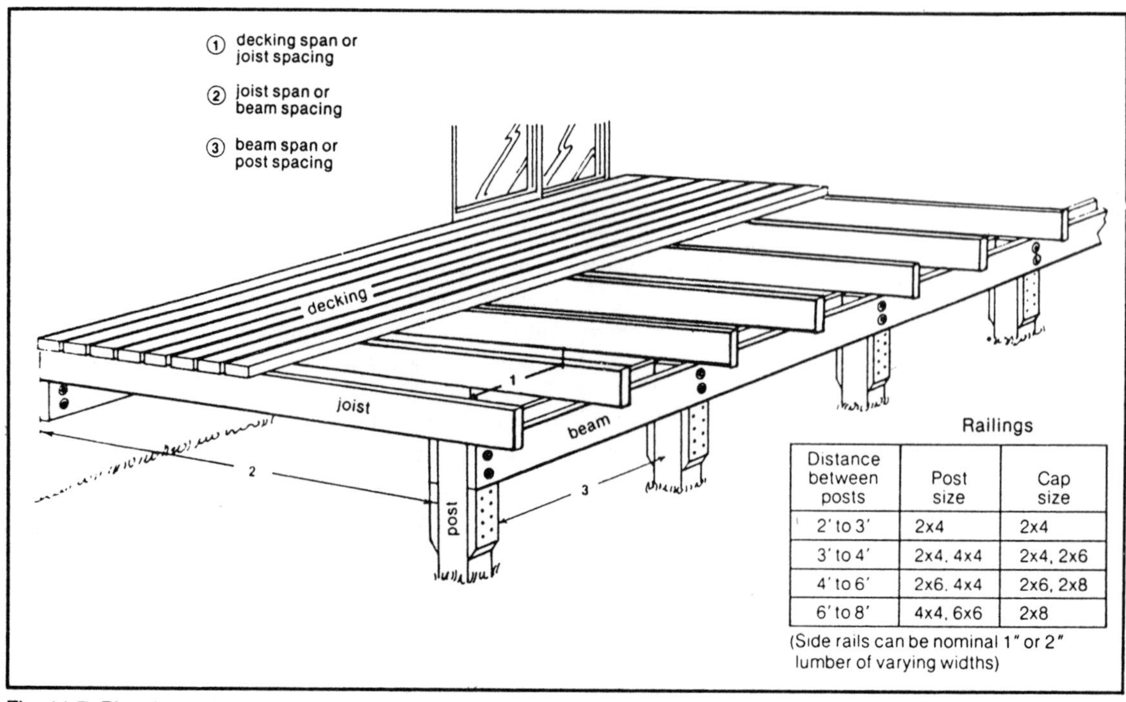


Railings

| Distance between posts | Post size | Cap size |
|---|---|---|
| 2' to 3' | 2x4 | 2x4 |
| 3' to 4' | 2x4, 4x4 | 2x4, 2x6 |
| 4' to 6' | 2x6, 4x4 | 2x6, 2x8 |
| 6' to 8' | 4x4, 6x6 | 2x8 |

(Side rails can be nominal 1" or 2" lumber of varying widths)

Fig. 11-7. Planning a deck (courtesy Wolmanized pressure-treated lumber).

laid flat. Table 11-3 shows the safe spans for the decking.

Refer to Table 11-4. As in our example, your joists must span the 8 feet between the house and the outer beam. That can be achieved with 2×8 joists spaced 32 inches apart. The 32-inch spacing is within the maximum span of 48 inches allowable for the 2×6 decking.

**Table 11-3. Maximum Allowable Spans for Spaced Deck Boards.**

| Maximum allowable span (inches) | | |
|---|---|---|
| Laid flat | | Laid on edge |
| 2 x 4 | 2 x 6 | 2 x 4 |
| 32 | 48 | 96 |

Though able to support greater spans, the maximum spans will result in undesirable deflection or springiness in a deck.

**Table 11-4. Maximum Allowable Spans for Deck Joists.**

| Joist size (inches) | Joist spacing (inches) | | |
|---|---|---|---|
| | 16 | 24 | 32 |
| 2x6 | 9'-9" | 7'-11" | 6'-2" |
| 2x8 | 12'-10" | 10'-6" | 8'-1" |
| 2x10 | 16'-5" | 13'-4" | 10'-4" |

## Estimating

After deciding the type, space, and size of deck you'll build, the next step is to estimate the materials you'll need. If you use a ready-made design with a materials list, this work is already done for you. If you design your own deck or use a variation from a standard plan, you'll have to estimate material requirements. It's better to overestimate because you can always use any excess material in other projects, such as benches or planter boxes.

Draw a simple sketch of the deck—decking, rails, footings, posts, and beams. The best scale is ¼ inch per foot. To save money, stick to standard lumber sizes and lengths to the fullest extent possible. Deck boards are usually stocked 2×4, 2×6, or 2×10-inch and 8, 10, 12, 14, and 16-foot lengths. Allow ¼ to ½-inch spacing between boards.

Prepare your materials list by dimensions and lengths for posts, beams, decking, stairs, and railings. Although lumber is sold at retail on a unit basis—so much for a 12-foot 2×4, etc.—you may also want to calculate your requirements in terms of total board feet. To determine the board footage in a piece of lumber, multiply the *thickness* in inches by the *width* in inches by the *length* in feet. Divide the total by 12. The formula is expressed as follows:

$$\frac{T \times W \times L}{12} = \text{Board feet}$$

The board-feet measure for various standard sizes and lengths of lumber can also be calculated by using Table 11-5.

After estimating your lumber requirements, review your design sketch and compile a list of the hardware you'll need: nails, bolts, joist hangers, and other fasteners, as well as the quantity of gravel and concrete needed. It's better to overestimate so you won't have to interrupt work for a trip for additional supplies.

### Accessories and Connectors

Some special connectors and accessories that you should be familiar with are shown in Fig. 11-8. These connectors are easy to use and yet give a strong, long lasting connection. Make sure all connectors, nails, screws, bolts, and related hardware are hot-dipped galvanized or otherwise rustproof.

### Construction Steps

The first step in building your deck is to mark off the deck area using string and batter boards (Fig. 11-9). Make sure that it is level and square. The string will help you visualize the size and appearance of the finished deck and will also serve as a guide for excavating and post placement (Fig. 11-10).

**Table 11-5. Lumber Scale of Board Feet per Timber.**

| Length of Timber | 8 | 10 | 12 | 14 | 16 | 18 | 20 | 22 | 24 |
|---|---|---|---|---|---|---|---|---|---|
| 1 × 4 | 2⅔ | 3⅓ | 4 | 4⅔ | 5⅓ | — | — | — | — |
| 1 × 6 | 4 | 5 | 6 | 7 | 8 | — | — | — | — |
| 1 × 8 | 5⅓ | 6⅔ | 8 | 9⅓ | 10⅔ | — | — | — | — |
| 2 × 4 | 5⅓ | 6⅔ | 8 | 9⅓ | 10⅔ | 12 | 13⅓ | — | — |
| 2 × 6 | 8 | 10 | 12 | 14 | 16 | 18 | 20 | — | — |
| 2 × 8 | 10⅔ | 13⅓ | 16 | 18⅔ | 21⅓ | 24 | 26⅔ | — | — |
| 2 × 10 | 13⅓ | 16⅔ | 20 | 23⅓ | 26⅔ | 30 | 33⅓ | — | — |
| 2 × 12 | 16 | 20 | 24 | 28 | 32 | 36 | 40 | | |
| 4 × 4 | 10⅔ | 13⅓ | 16 | 18⅔ | 21⅓ | 24 | 26⅔ | — | — |
| 4 ×6 | 16 | 20 | 24 | 28 | 32 | 36 | 40 | — | — |
| 6 × 6 | 24 | 30 | 36 | 42 | 48 | 54 | 60 | 66 | 72 |

To square the site with a string, first attach the string to the house and/or batter boards. Make sure it's level. Then use a felt tip marker to mark the string 3 feet from the corner in one direction and 4 feet from the corner in the other direction. When the diagonal connecting these two points is 5 feet, you have a right triangle. The angle at the corner will be 90 degrees.

The second step is to prepare the site. With a spade or sod cutter, remove sod to a depth of 2 or 3 inches. Uncover an area about 2 feet larger than the planned deck. It's unlikely that grass will be able to grow in the shadow of your deck, so you might transfer the sod to a bare spot in your yard where it will be useful. To prevent weeds and unwanted vegetation from growing up through the deck, spread a sheet of polyethylene film over the area. You'll have to slit this to embed posts in the ground. After the posts have been installed, cover the sheet with gravel, pebbles, or bark chips.

Locate and dig holes for footings. In normal soil the holes should be a minimum of 24 inches deep, although the actual depth will depend on the height of the column and the depth of the frost line. Posts should go deeper than the frost line to avoid heaving during freeze and thaw cycles. In the bottom of the holes place a 6-inch layer of gravel and tamp firm, or pour a 3-inch concrete footing and top it with gravel to allow for drainage. You can also use a Wolmanized wood footer plate. Upright posts can then be positioned on this base (Fig. 11-11).

If concrete collars are used, taper the tops downward and away from the posts for drainage. When setting the posts, make sure they are plumb and in alignment with one another. Use a carpenter's level to check for vertical alignment.

The fourth step is to secure beams to the posts (Fig. 11-12). Using a string and level, find the desired deck height on the posts. By subtracting the thickness of the deck board, joist, and beam (use the actual dimensions and not the nominal one), you'll have determined the correct spot for the bottom side of the beam. Cut the post at that point and

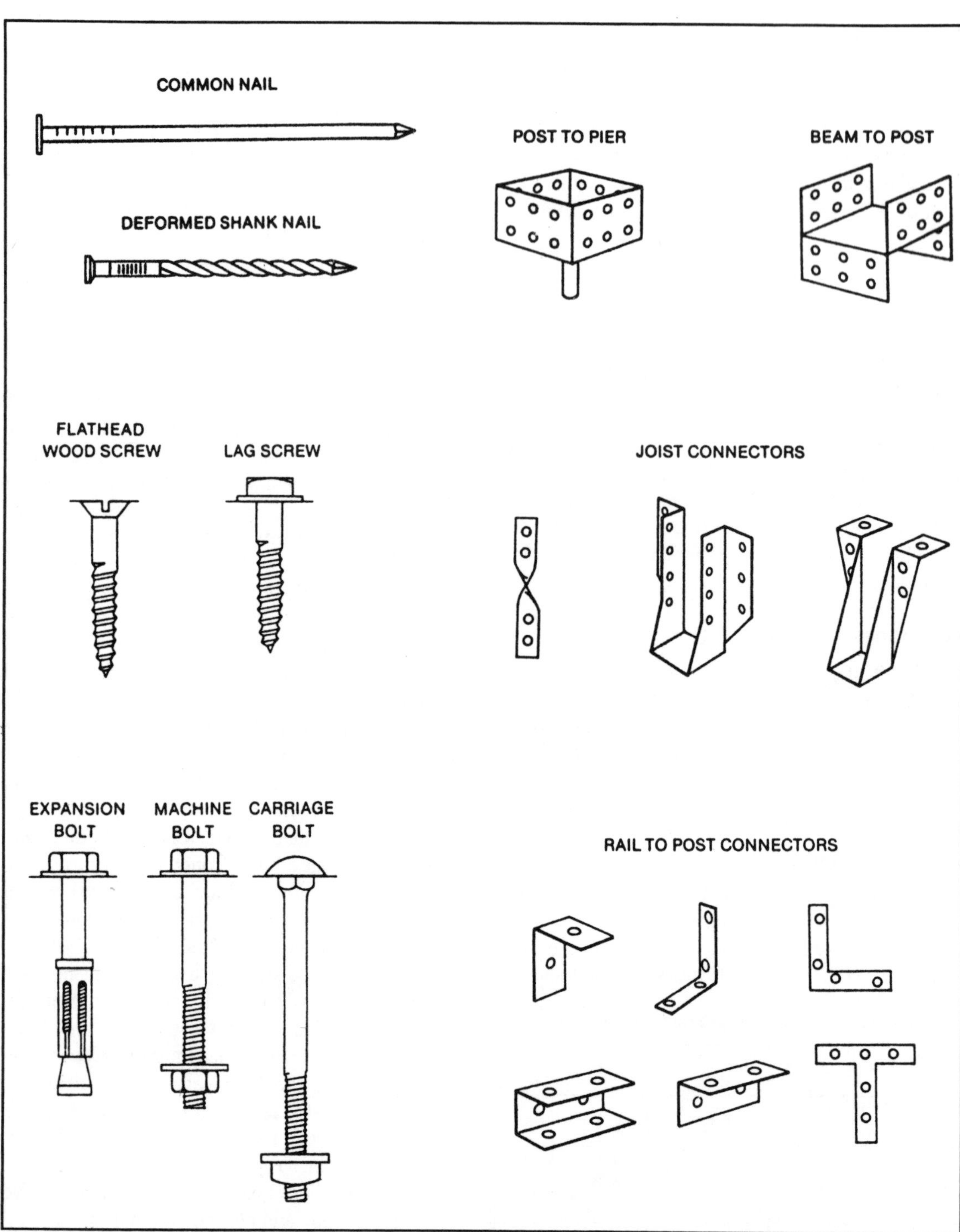


Fig. 11-8. Accessories and connectors used in constructing decks and fences (courtesy Wolmanized pressure-treated lumber).

Fig. 11-9. Remove grass under your deck before installation (courtesy Wolmanized pressure-treated lumber).

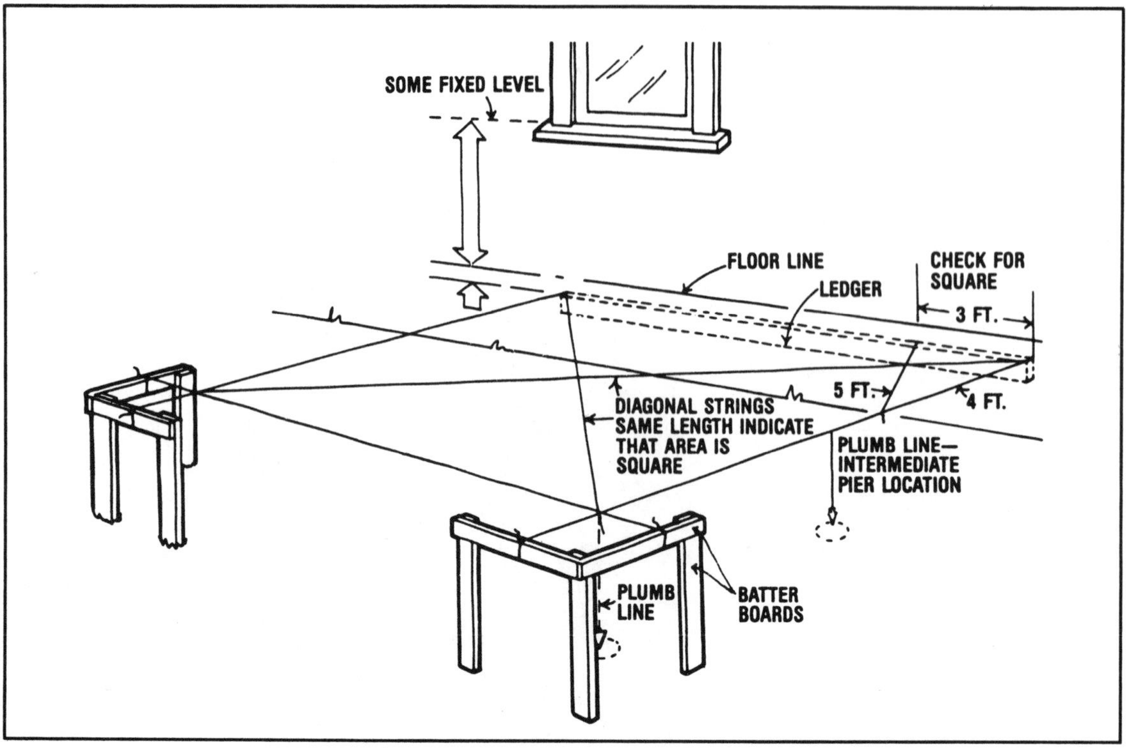

Fig. 11-10. How to measure and lay out your deck (courtesy Georgia-Pacific Corp.).

fasten the beam on top by one of the methods in Fig. 11-13. If the posts are also serving as railing supports, they can not be sawed off. Beams should be fastened to their sides. Double beams equaling a single beam of their combined thickness, can be installed instead of single beam supports.

Fig. 11-11. Position and level upright posts (courtesy Wolmanized pressure-treated lumber).

Step five involves attaching the joists to the house and beams (Fig. 11-14). Joists are attached to the house with joist hangers or supported by a ledger strip—a board secured to the house (Fig. 11-15). The placement of the ledger determines the level of the deck floor, so position it at the correct height and make sure it's horizontal (Fig. 11-16).

When fastening to wood, ledgers can be held securely with lag screws. Predrill a pilot hole first before driving the screws. If you have lap siding, a strip of the siding can be inverted and used as a shim to hold the ledger perpendicular. Expansion shields and lag bolts are needed for masonry construction.

Install posts for the railing. This can be a continuation of the posts that support the deck, or railing posts may be bolted to the outside joist or joist extension (Fig. 11-17).

When using posts, they support the deck as in Fig. 11-17. Notice how the main posts continue up

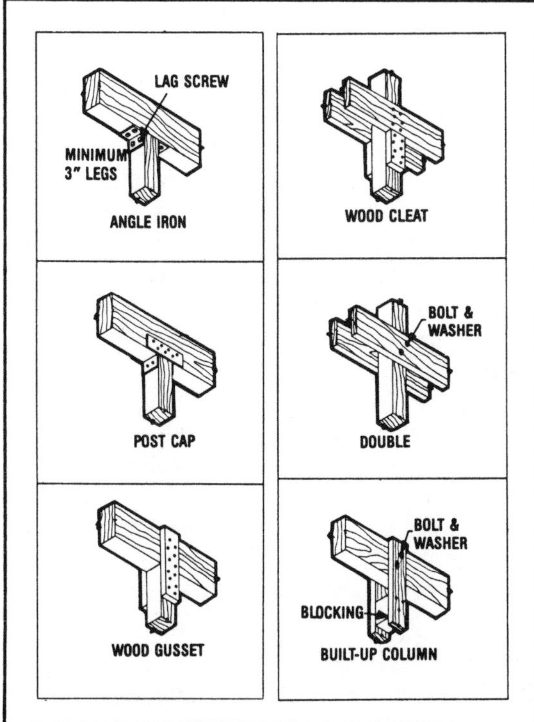


Fig. 11-12. Six ways to attach beams to posts (courtesy Georgia-Pacific Corp.).

from the actual deck floor level and provide a sturdy railing post. Intermittent posts or spacer posts can be used between the main support posts. The top railing member can be easily nailed to the side of the main posts at the desired height. Posts can then be cut off. The height of spacer posts can be determined and added for additional support and appearance. Railing caps of suitable size can now be added along with additional side rails.

Step seven is to install deck boards using hot-dipped galvanized coated 12-penny nails. You may want to consider various nailheads and choose one with the appearance you like best.

Separate boards ¼ to ½ inch to allow for expansion and contraction. This can be quickly done using a spacer (Fig. 11-18) of the desired thickness.

Make your deck surface simple with boards of equal width set on joists, or experiment by alternating plants of different widths, making parquet patterns, diagonal or herringbone designs, or using 2×4s set on edge (Fig. 11-19). Whatever pattern you choose, lay the deck board side up. Make sure you measure as you go. If you discover that your spacing is off, adjust between the next three or four boards (Fig. 11-20). When you get near the end, start adjusting your space to avoid a gap at the end of your deck.

If you install decking using straight planking, you can trim your deck after nailing to assure a straight line (Fig. 11-21). Don't allow any overhang

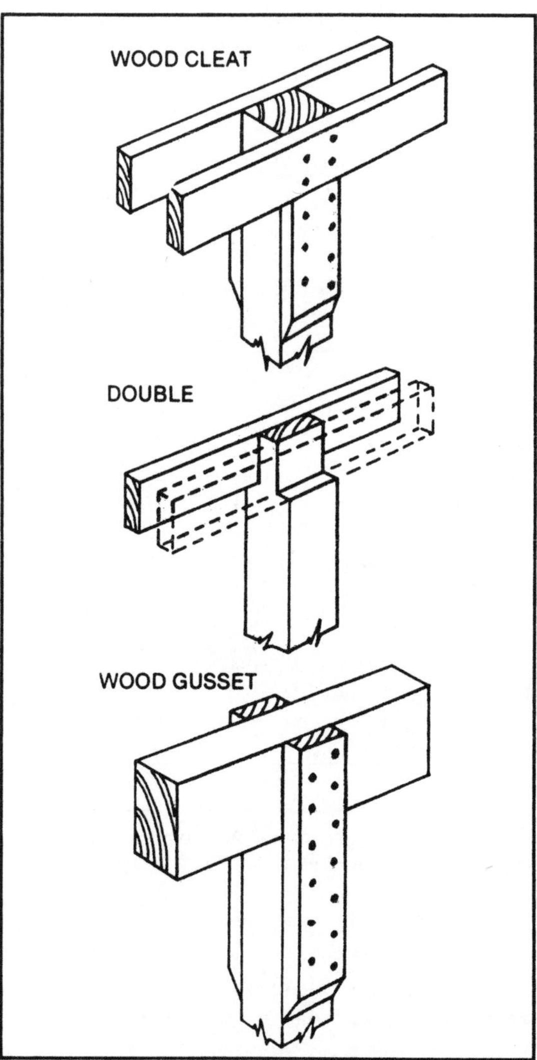


Fig. 11-13. Methods of fastening beams and posts (courtesy Wolmanized pressure-treated lumber).

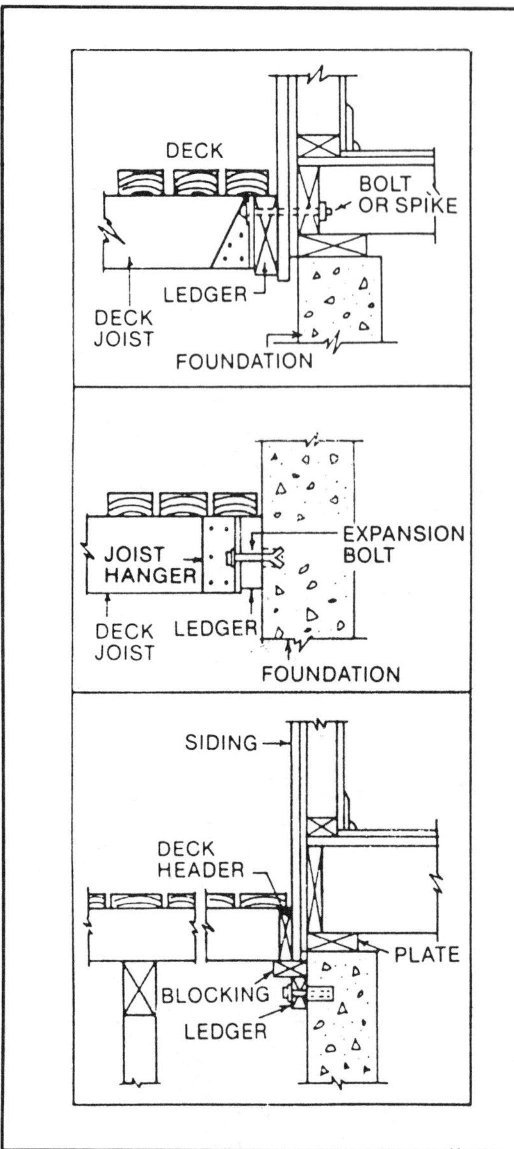


Fig. 11-14. Various ledgers and deck components (courtesy Wolmanized pressure-treated lumber).

exceeding 1½ inches, or cut boards flush to the joist and add a fascia board.

The next step is to finish the railing. The safety and beauty of your deck are enhanced by its railings. They can be plain or very elaborate.

Benches can be integrated into the railing on one or all sides (Figs. 11-22 through 11-25). Bench seats should be at least 15 inches wide and 15 to 18 inches above the deck floor.

Privacy screens can enhance the beauty of your deck and offer you privacy. They can also be used effectively under an elevated deck to create a storage facility or hide an unsightly hillside.

The final step is to install steps. Measure the vertical rise and decide on the best riser size for each step. This will determine the number of steps needed. Figure 11-26 shows some recommended ratios of tread length to find the overall run of the stairs. See Fig. 11-27.

Figure 11-28 illustrates two types of stairway stringers: open, in which the treads are placed on sawed cuts; or closed, where concealed cleats support each tread. See Fig. 11-29.

You can purchase precut steps at many lumberyards. A call ahead might eliminate some of the more difficult angle cutting you need to do.

### Additional Construction Tips

- Always nail a thinner member to a thicker member.
- Drive nails at a slight angle toward each other for greater holding power.
- When toenailing, stagger opposing nails so they pass each other.
- Use annular- or spiral-shank nails for maximum holding power.
- To reduce splitting, drill a pilot hole about three quarters of the nail's diameter. For dense or brittle wood, grind sharpness from nails or blunt the points by striking them carefully with a hammer. Blunt nails cut through; sharp ones pry apart.
- Place nails no closer to the edge than about half the board thickness and no closer to the end than the board's thickness. When nailing closer to an edge, use predrilled holes.
- Use 12d nails on nominal 2-inch decking. Use two at each joist with 2×4s laid flat; use three for 2×6s laid flat and just one for nominal 2-inch lumber on edge.
- Use a flat washer under the head with lag screws.
- Use washers under the nut and head of machine bolts and just under the nut of carriage bolts.

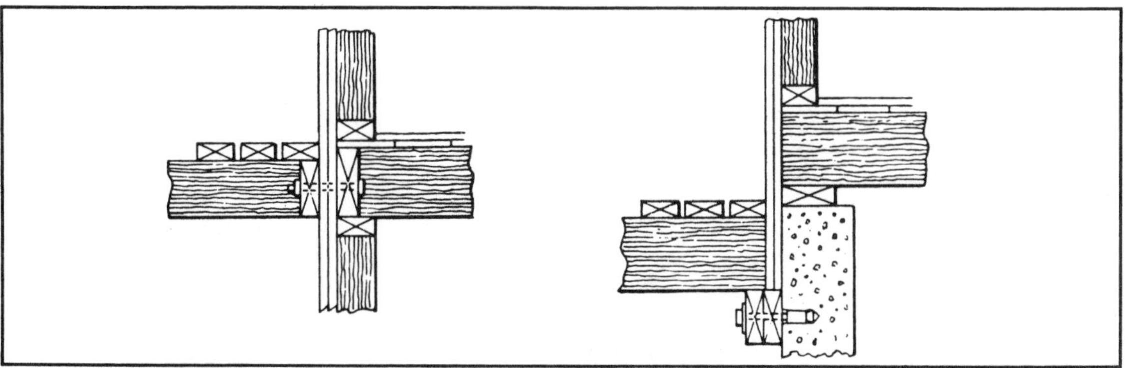

Fig. 11-15. Installing ledgers (courtesy California Redwood Association).

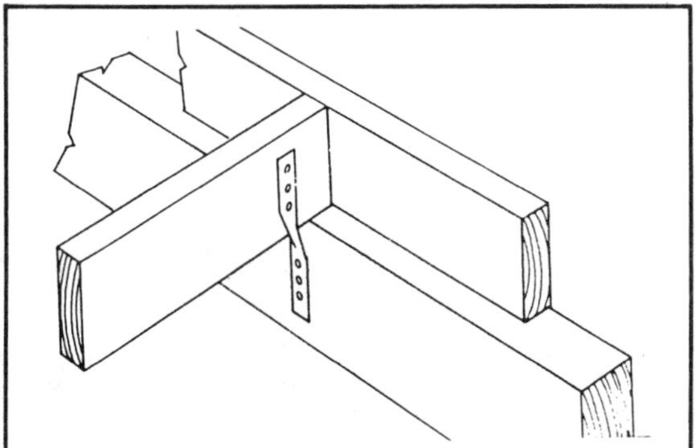

Fig. 11-16. Attaching the deck to the ledger (courtesy Wolmanized pressure-treated lumber).

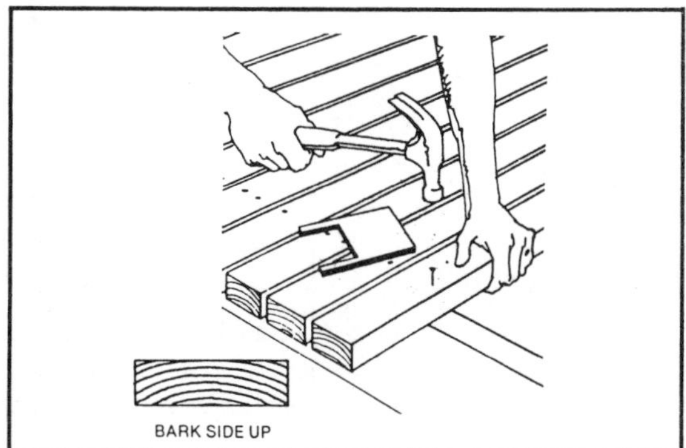


Fig. 11-18. Installing deck boards (courtesy Wolmanized pressure-treated lumber).

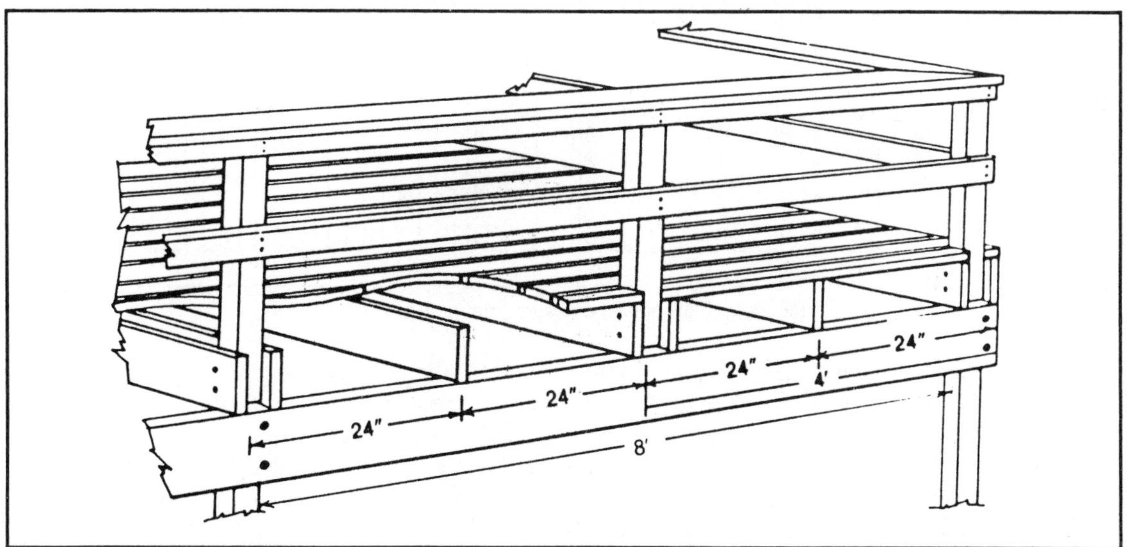


Fig. 11-17. Outside joists (courtesy Wolmanized pressure-treated lumber).

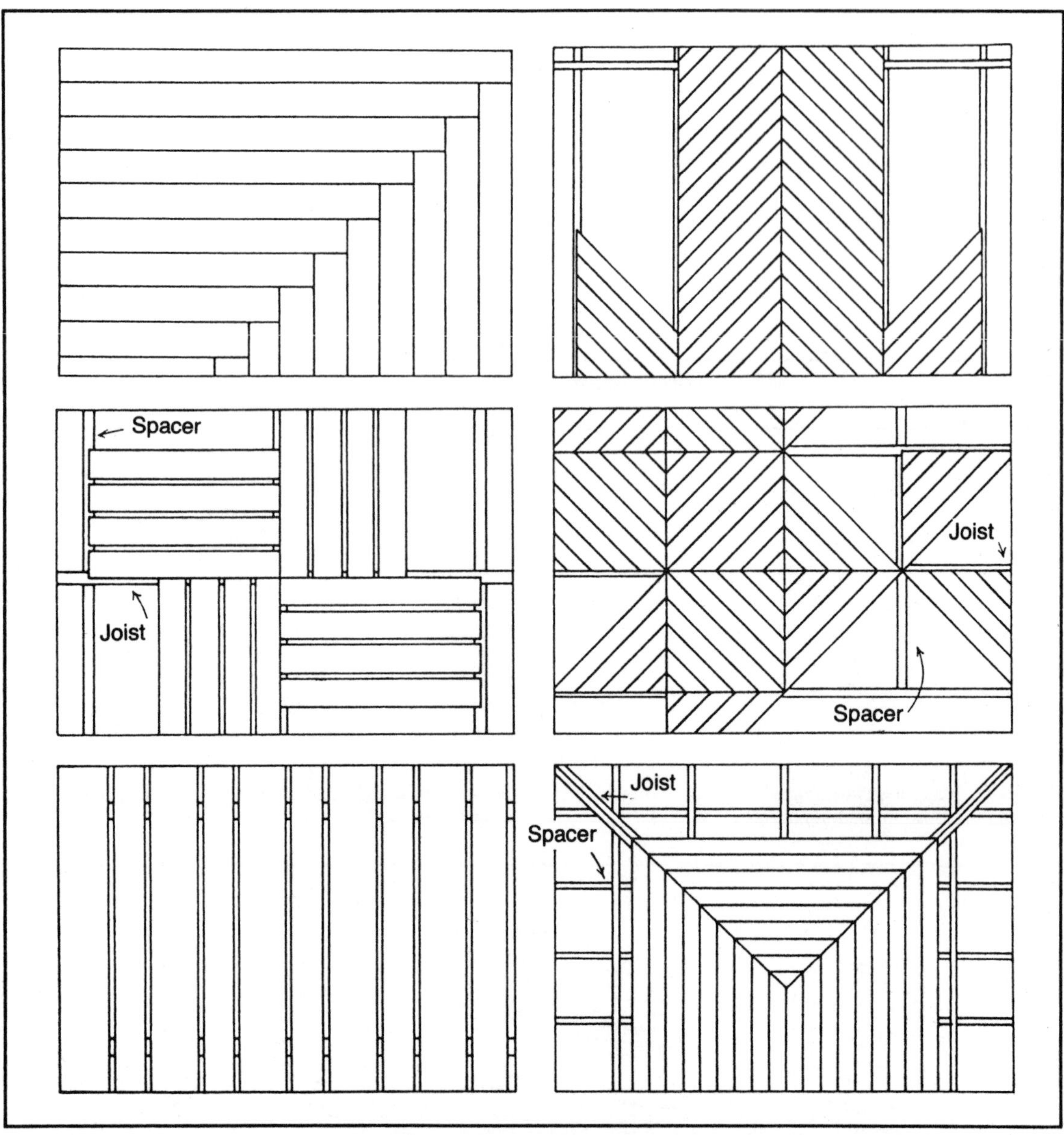


Fig. 11-19. Popular deck patterns (courtesy Wolmanized pressure-treated lumber).

- When sanding or sawing treated or untreated wood, avoid inhaling dust. The fine dust particles are air pollutants and could cause nose and throat irritation. Avoid getting dust or wood chips in your eye. Eyes are extremely sensitive, and any type of foreign matter can cause irritation. Pounding nails should be done cautiously; small flying particles of metal can cause serious eye damage. Ask your dealer about dust masks and eye protection devices.
- Wear gloves to help avoid splinters.
- Maintain a clean shop. Don't leave sawdust or scrap lumber lying around, as they pose fire and accident hazards. Pressure-treated wood should

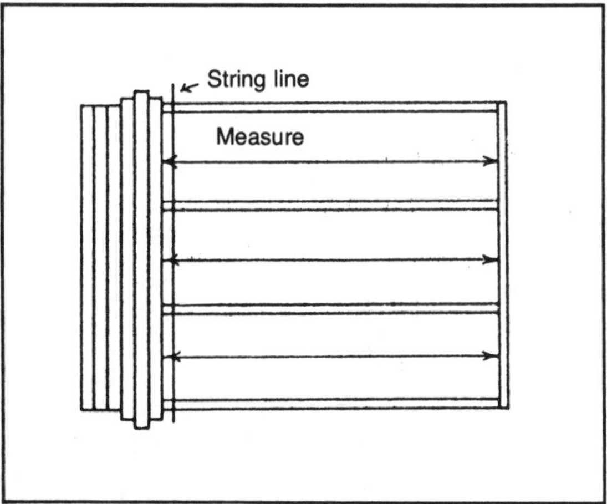


Fig. 11-20. Measure after installing every third or fourth board to make sure your deck will be square (courtesy Wolmanized pressure-treated lumber).

Fig. 11-21. Once boards are installed, you can lay a straightedge and trim the edge of your deck (courtesy Wolmanized pressure-treated lumber).

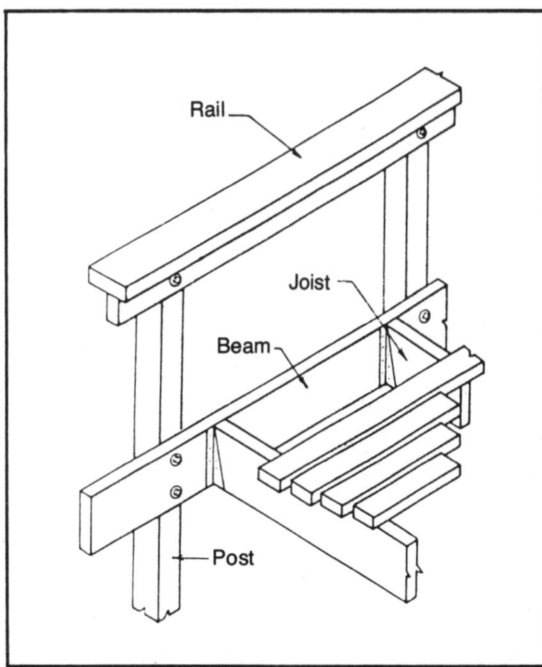


Fig. 11-22. Typical post railing (courtesy Wolmanized pressure-treated lumber).

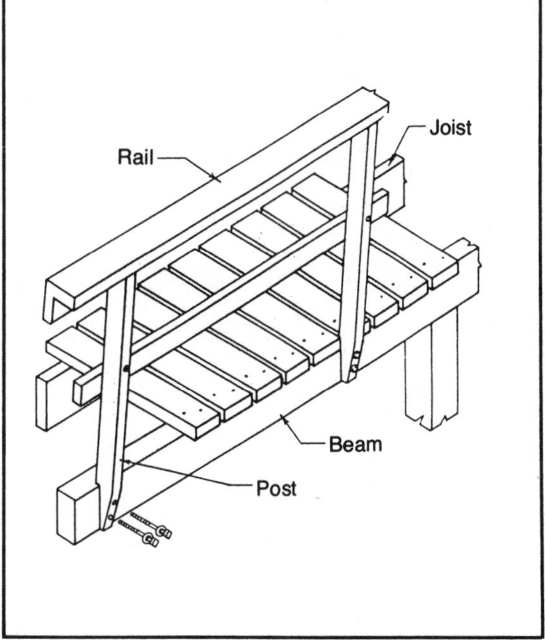


Fig. 11-23. Typical slant railing (courtesy Wolmanized pressure-treated lumber).

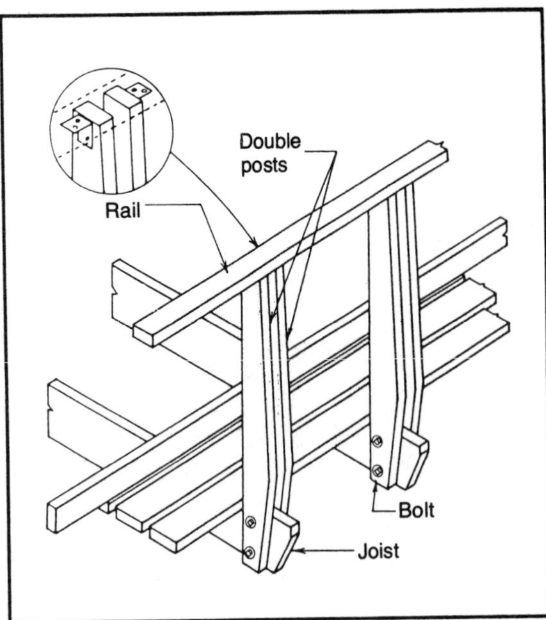


Fig. 11-24. Typical double post railing (courtesy Wolmanized pressure-treated lumber).

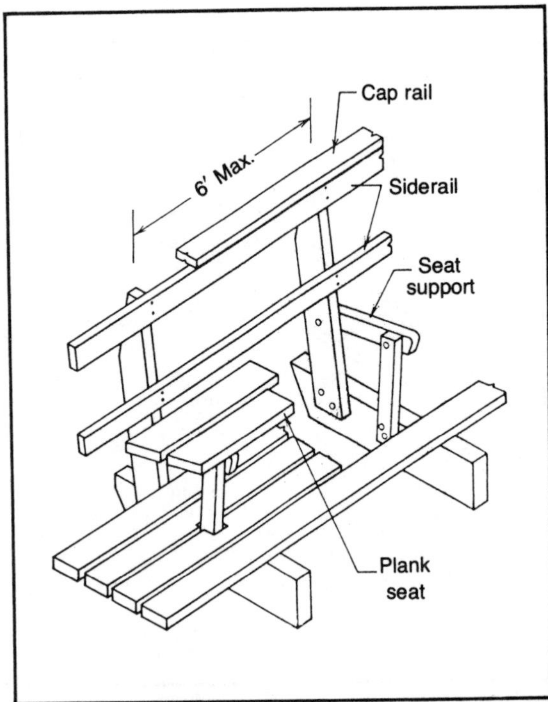


Fig. 11-25. Bench rail plans (courtesy Wolmanized pressure-treated lumber).

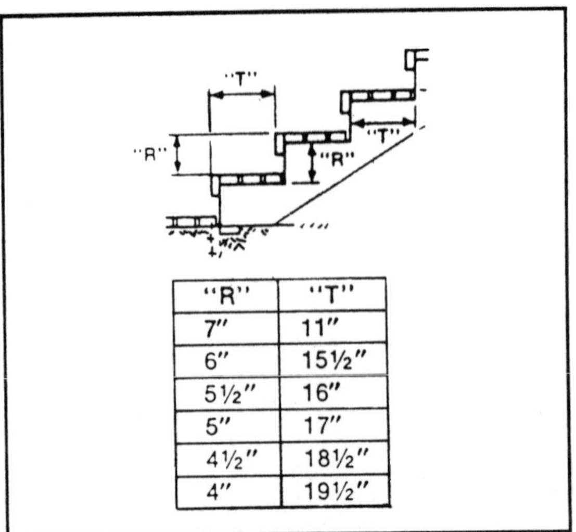


| "R" | "T" |
|---|---|
| 7" | 11" |
| 6" | 15½" |
| 5½" | 16" |
| 5" | 17" |
| 4½" | 18½" |
| 4" | 19½" |

Fig. 11-26. Suggested ratios for risers and treads (courtesy Wolmanized pressure-treated lumber).

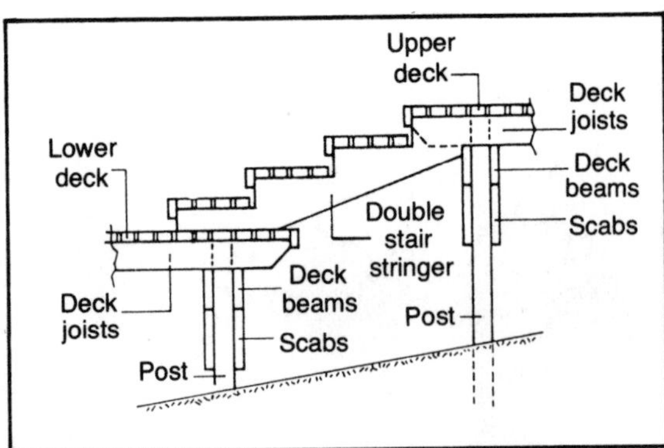


Fig. 11-27. Typical stair construction for deck to deck and ground to deck (courtesy Wolmanized pressure-treated lumber).

not be burned either indoors or outdoors. Any scrap should be disposed of in a government-approved landfill or buried.

■ Tops of upright structurals and joist ends should be beveled to a 30 to 45-degree angle for drainage to minimize moisture absorption (Fig. 11-30). Figures 11-31 through 11-33 show more plans for decks.

## CONVERSATION PIT

An outdoor *conversation pit* is shown in Fig. 11-34. The central table can be a cover for a sunken

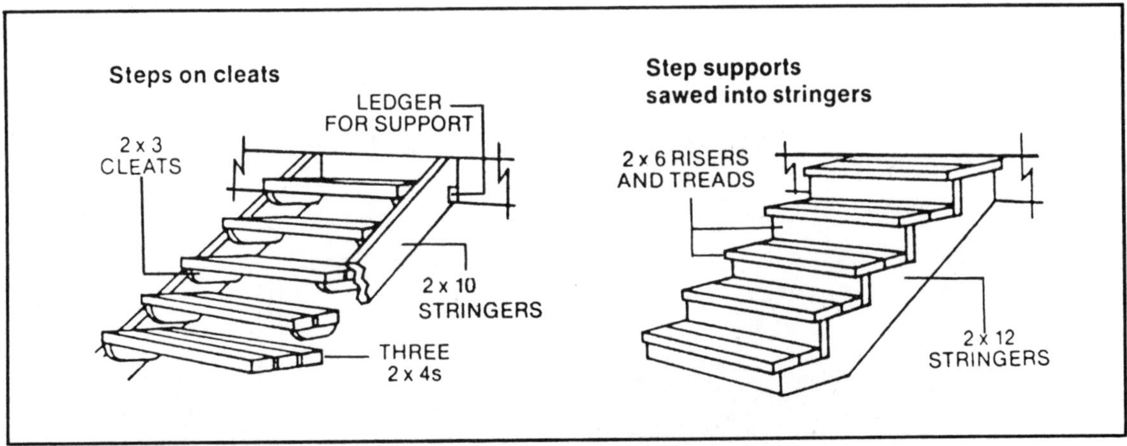

Fig. 11-28. Two types of stairway stringers (courtesy Wolmanized pressure-treated lumber).

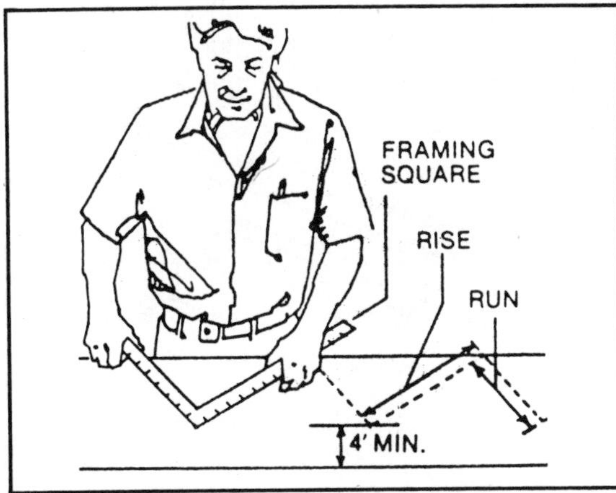

Fig. 11-29. Designing your stair stringer (courtesy Wolmanized pressure-treated lumber).

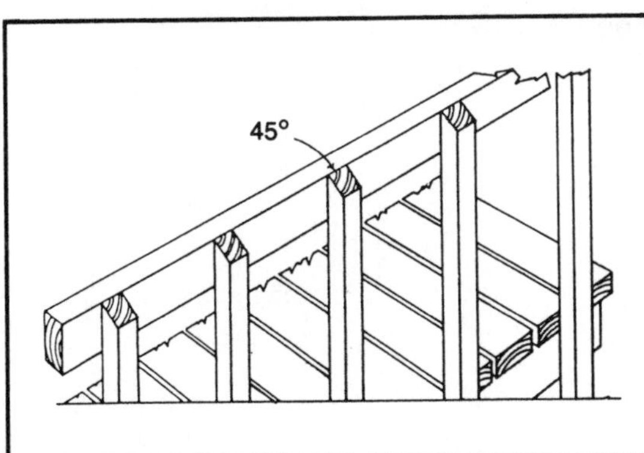

Fig. 11-30. Angle-cut rail post tops to improve moisture runoff (courtesy Wolmanized pressure treated lumber).

fire pit for cooking or for warmth on chilly evenings. The main platform is a lumber deck constructed in conventional fashion but with vertical 2×6s nailed to joists to serve as supports for the bench tops. Use ⅜-inch nuts and bolts to attach 2×6 rails to uprights and then span across with 2×4s placed on edge. Frame the opening with 2×12s and then make a cover to fit. If you include a fire pit, it must be fireproof. One way is to build a double-brick wall on four sides and then add a veneer of firebrick bonded with fireclay.

You can also do a deck on the ground if you nail deck boards to 2×4 pressure-treated lumber cleats placed flat on a 3 to 4-inch bed of tamped sand. This lends itself to prefabrication of decking squares (about 4×4 inches) that you place uniformly or in a parquet pattern.

Another idea is to make a grid frame with 2×6 pressure-treated lumber. This may be placed on a sand bed and then covered with deck boards placed parallel.

## ENGAWA

An *engawa* is simply an outdoor corridor or passageway made up of lumber (Fig. 11-35). The idea came over from Japan and is very popular in Oriental garden landscaping, where it serves as a link between rooms that open onto a court or garden. A rail may also be part of this floor-level platform. Once the frame is built on short posts, 2×4s

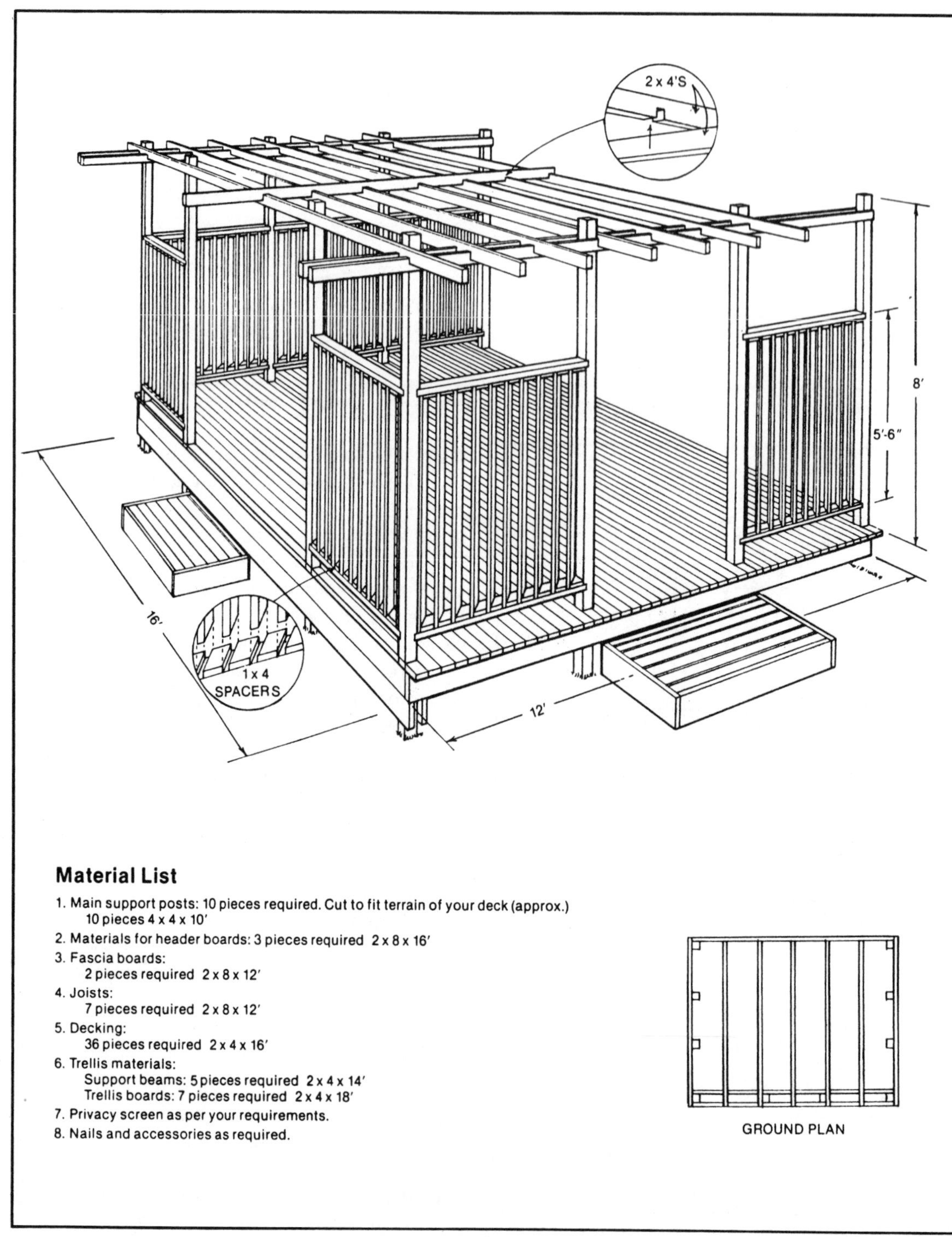


Fig. 11-31. Detailed plans for a 12×16-foot trellis-covered privacy deck (courtesy Wolmanized pressure-treated lumber).

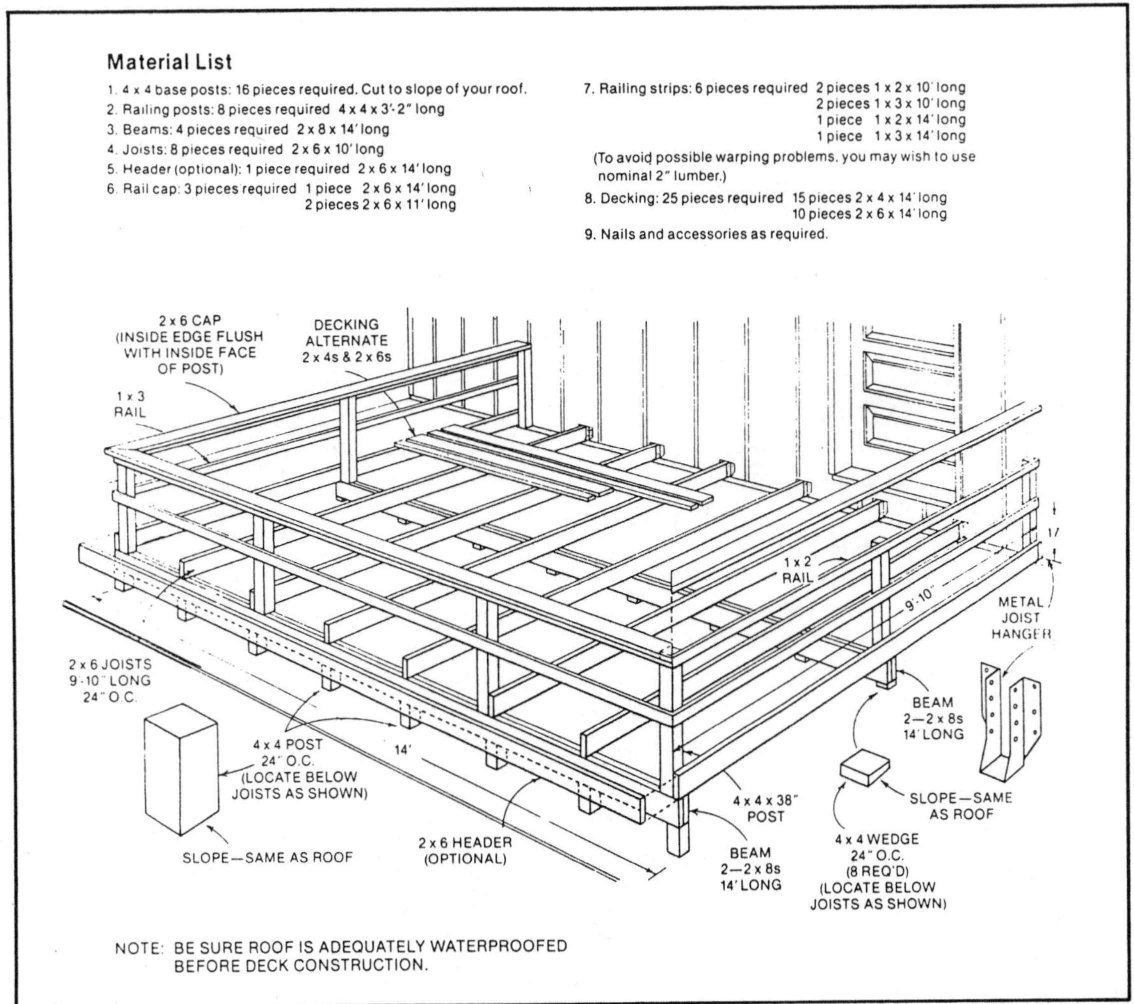


Fig. 11-32. Detailed plans for a 10×14 roof deck (courtesy Wolmanized pressure-treated lumber).

are turned on their edges and evenly spaced to make the decking. Then 2×6 fascia boards are often used as trim.

## GAZEBO

*Gazebo* comes from the Latin *videbo*, probably not etymologically correct, but it conveys the idea. A gazebo is a freestanding structure, sometimes with a touch of wall (like wainscoting) or an attractive railing, sometimes with full walls on two or three sides built by fancy latticework, but always sturdy, light, and airy (Fig. 11-36).

Here are the basic parts for planning your gazebo (see Fig. 11-37).

- The *base* can be simple like small concrete pads supporting concrete blocks that hold beams for the floor. You can pour a concrete slab or erect a small deck.
- The *floor* can be wood, concrete, brick, or tile. You may have an in-place floor or deck on which you can build.
- *Structural supports* must both look good and do the job. A type of post-and-beam design makes sense because it has the necessary strength and

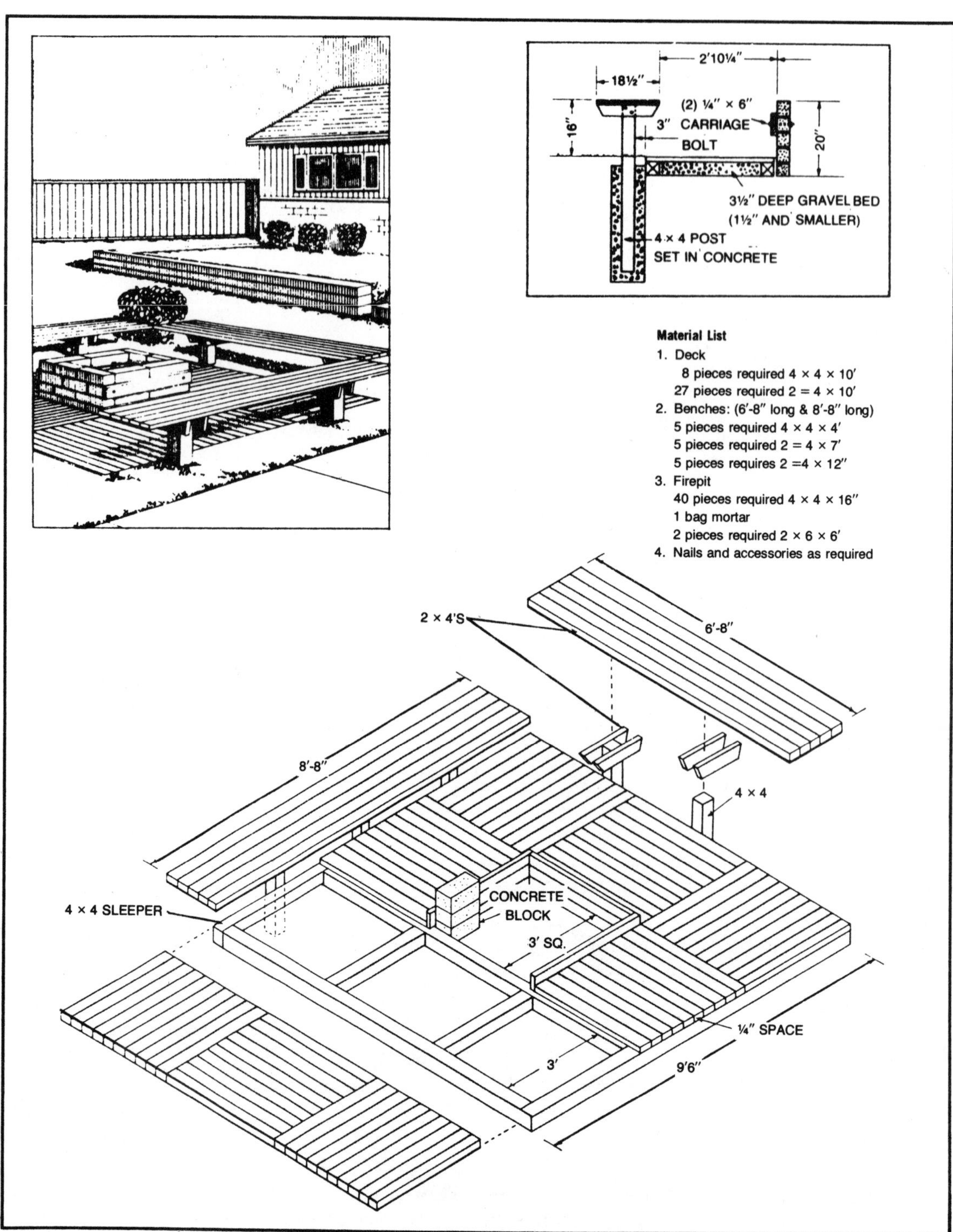


Fig. 11-33. Detailed plans for a 10×10-foot fire pit deck (courtesy Wolmanized pressure-treated lumber).

Fig. 11-34. Conversation pit (courtesy Georgia-Pacific Corp.).

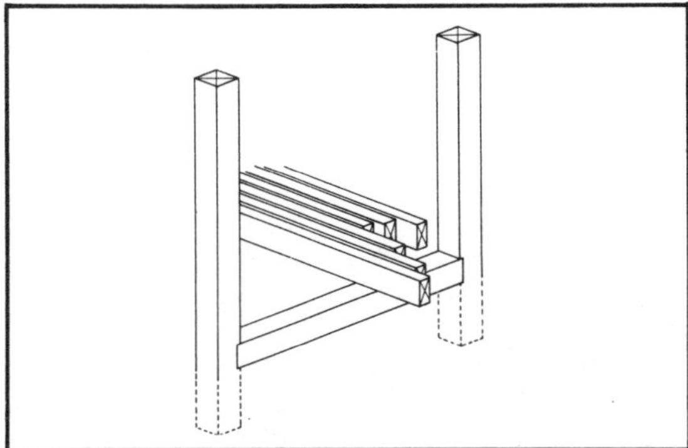

Fig. 11-35. Details of an engawa or elevated walkway (courtesy Western Wood Products Association).

few components to obstruct the view.

- The *cover* can be closed or open. It can be tight for sun protection or loose for mixed shade.
- *Decorative touches* are optional, but they can add plenty of character to the design at little cost.
- The *cupola* is added for appearance or for increased ventilation if your gazebo is covered with a solid roof.

## SUNSHADES

*Sunshades* are often called trellises. They can be light and airy and frequently are used as *espaliers* for vines. Essentially they are overhead constructions whose purpose is to filter the sun's rays, creating a pleasant, open atmosphere that contributes much to outdoor relaxation. The use of a deciduous vine as a cover makes sense because the plant affords maximum protection during summer

Fig. 11-36. Unique gazebo design (courtesy Georgia-Pacific Corp.).

Fig. 11-37. Typical gazebo (courtesy Georgia-Pacific Corp.).

Fig. 11-38. Easy-to-build sunshade (courtesy Georgia-Pacific Corp.).

months. After dropping its leaves, the plant allows more of the sun to come through when the weather turns cold.

A sunshade can project from a house wall and be situated over an existing patio or deck, or it can be a freestanding unit, isolated a bit so it serves as a private retreat. Location and placement affect how it should be erected. Figure 11-38 offers basic considerations for planning and building a sunshade.

**Floor.** The sunshade can go over your existing patio or can be built together with it.

**Main Supports.** Supports or posts depend on the size, weight, and framing of the shading top. The most common are 2×4 posts for light frame shades and 4×4 posts for heavy frame shades.

Fig. 11-39. Covered deck (courtesy Georgia-Pacific Corp.).

Fig. 11-40. Structures for greater outdoor living: sunshade with benches, work area with enclosed trash cabinets, wood storage, and wooden planters (courtesy Western Wood Products Association).

**Joists.** Joists for a sunshade are chosen and attached much like those for a deck, except the sunshade doesn't need as much structural stability. The joists can be of smaller materials and farther apart because they won't carry any weight.

**Ledger.** Consider how you will attach the sunshade to your house. You may be able to lock it to the roof rafters with bolts or spike a ledger into wall studs.

**Cover.** How much filtration do you want? Your decision affects what you should use: 2×4s, lath strips, fiberglass panels, etc.

**Sidewalls.** Not all sunscreens have sidewalls, but they should be considered for a windbreak or privacy. They can either be open or solid. See Figs. 11-39 and 11-40.

## LATTICE WALLS

*Lattice* can be used for several purposes. A tightly woven lattice can be used to screen out an objectionable view, or to shield a service yard or garden work center. With its spaces open wide, a lattice will let in a view, serve as a traffic director, or double as a display tier for potted plants.

Lattices may be used to support climbing roses and other vines. Such plantings must be kept pruned, or they will run away with the wall. They also have to be removed to permit periodic repainting. As some vines damage wood by keeping it too damp, check with your nurseryman before planting alongside a lattice wall or screen.

The only construction tip is to use a basic post and rail frame. Space evenly the thin lattice slats either horizontally and vertically or diagonally.

## PAVILION

A pavilion is simply a large gazebo that is often square or rectangular in shape rather than round. Pavilions can be used for shade in the garden, as an outdoor eating area, or as a cover for outdoor activities. Construction consists of setting posts and joists as you would with a sunscreen or deck and covering with an appropriate cover.

## AERIE

An *aerie* is a small gazebo that usually contains two or four benches and a small table for eating. Aerie literally means a "nest." Construct as you would a gazebo. Aeries are often built just outside the kitchen door, so breakfast or lunch can be served in the outdoors during better weather.

## TREE HOUSE

A *tree house* is simply a deck built around a tree (Fig. 11-41). Support for the structure comes from the tree itself with a frame that girds the trunk, then joins the joists for the flooring.

The railing on a tree house is especially important. It must be strong and tall enough to contain children and discourage exit other than down the ladder or rope. Many tree houses have slanted top rails and lower bottom rails to help solve this problem.

Don't secure the tree house to the tree with too many nails. The nails open the trunk to infection. If possible, paint over any nails with tree paint.

Fig. 11-41. Ahoy! It's a tree house without a tree (courtesy Georgia-Pacific Corp.).

## GREENHOUSE

A *greenhouse* is a fun project that can be a source of year-round vegetables (Fig. 11-42). Whether you build a freestanding unit or a lean-to, a good construction technique is to prefabricate frames using 2×4 fir or pine with joints reinforced with ⅜-inch exterior grade plywood gussets attached with glue and nails. Space frames 16 to 24 inches on centers and run 2×4s horizontally inside, at the ridge line, frame corners, and along the base. Covering can be polyethylene sheet, corrugated fiberglass, smooth rigid plastic, or double-strength glass. Polyethylene can be attached with staples, but a better way is to use lath strips as battens so the material won't tear as easily. Corrugated or rigid plastic can be secured directly to framing, but lay down a bead or two of caulking over the frame members first.

## BACKYARD STORAGE SHED

Build the shed on a concrete pad as you would a small house or make a foundation of precast con-

Fig. 11-42. Solar greenhouse (courtesy Georgia-Pacific Corp.).

Fig. 11-43. Storage shed (courtesy Georgia-Pacific Corp.).

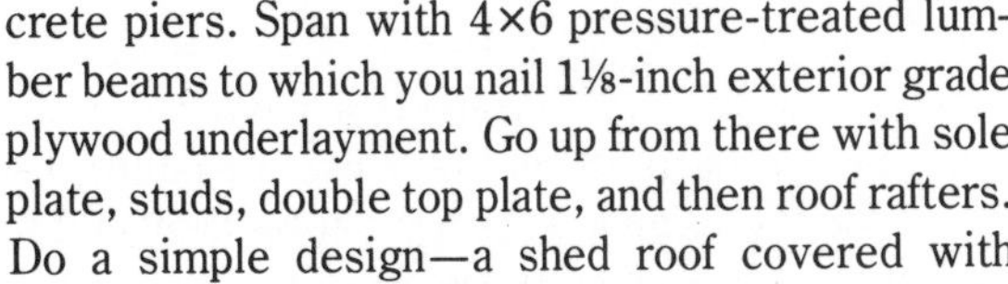

crete piers. Span with 4×6 pressure-treated lumber beams to which you nail 1⅛-inch exterior grade plywood underlayment. Go up from there with sole plate, studs, double top plate, and then roof rafters. Do a simple design—a shed roof covered with mineral-surfaced roll roofing—or a gable covered with cedar shakes. Cover the exterior walls with plywood siding—textured, channel-grooved, or smooth. You can match it to the house or make the project look different (Fig. 11-43).

# Chapter 12

# Gates

THE GATE IS A VERY IMPORTANT PART OF ANY fence (Fig. 12-1). It's the "door" to your yard and is functional and decorative. The gate is also the place where the workmanship of your fence shows up.

The purpose of the gate is to allow passage in and out of the fenced area: a field, backyard, or patio. The design and purpose of the fence somewhat dictates the design of the gate (Fig. 12-2). You can make the gate blend right into the fence by using the same materials. You can accent it, such as a wrought iron gate with a masonry fence. There are dozens of possibilities (Fig. 12-3).

The size of your gate will be determined by the height of the fence it serves and the amount of security you're requiring. The gate should be on a scale with its surroundings. A low, inadequate front gate is an annoyance to adults and a temptation to children. Oversized gates may be ostentatious or institutional.

Some gates come preassembled and don't leave you much originality in design, such as gates for chain link fences. The ones that seem to look the best are the basic gates that close a pasture, orchard, or the barnyard. Gates can be designed to accent your yard and provide controlled access to a fenced area (Figs. 12-4 through 12-10).

## PLANNING

Gates get more wear and abuse than any other part of the fence. Gates must be built solidly and be attached with top quality, heavy-duty hardware. If a post isn't exactly plumb or a board is not quite perfect, only you will know the difference. A few miscalculations or a little sloppy workmanship will result in a gate that doesn't open or close properly and soon must be replaced.

A good first step, particularly if the project is complex, is to make a sketch of your proposed gate and show it to your lumber dealer. He can usually tell you whether your plan is feasible, how much it will cost, and whether there's some way to make the job easier by slightly modifying the design. Before you make a sketch, however, you'll have to

Fig. 12-1. No fence is complete without a gate (courtesy Western Red Cedar Lumber Association).

Fig. 12-2. Gate design reflects the mood of the home (photo by Val Ramos).

know something about gate construction. There are three considerations: the latch, hinges, and the gate itself.

## LATCHES

Sometimes you have to build the gate around the *latch*, unless it's a simple hasp or hook. A sliding bolt action latch may be too difficult to install on a gate with grape stake siding. Check hardware and lumber supply stores for latch ideas. Latches are commonly made of aluminum, steel or iron, and woods (Figs. 12-11 through 12-15).

The latch must take rough treatment. A flimsy one put on with small nails or screws won't last long. If you want to keep children from opening the gate, get a latch that you can set up high or on top of the fence.

## HINGES

The main reason why gates fail is inadequate hinges. The best advice is to spend a couple extra dollars and buy heavier-duty hinges than you need for your gate (Figs. 12-16 through 12-18).

Like latches, hinges have to be considered in terms of the gate siding. It would be impossible, for example, to mount heavy strap hinges on a gate paneled in translucent plastic. Sometimes you'll want to buy hinges that match your latch, which may call for a revision in your gate design. When your fence is used to confine small children, self-closing hinges are a worthwhile investment. Springs in the hinge mechanism automatically close one gate that

Fig. 12-3. Your gate should be easily recognized (photo by Val Ramos).

Fig. 12-4. Even a minor design change will make the gate stand out from the rest of your fence (photo by Val Ramos).

Fig. 12-5. This gate is quite different than the surrounding fence (photo by Val Ramos).

Fig. 12-6. A gate can also be a simple opening in a fence (photo by Val Ramos).

might otherwise be left ajar by visitors or deliverymen.

Here are a few hints on buying hinges for your gate:

- Many packaged hinges include screws that are too short for a heavy gate. Buy extra screws that go as far into the wood as possible without coming out the other side.
- Always use three hinges on gates more than 5 feet tall.
- Make sure your hinges have a weather-resistant coating such as cadmium, zinc, or galvanized unless you plan to paint them.
- Ask your building materials retailer which type of hinge you should have for your gate: butt hinge, T hinge, strap hinge, or common gate hinge.

Fig. 12-7. Your gate reflects both the fence design and the design of nearby structures (photo by Val Ramos).

Fig. 12-9. A wrought iron gate can enclose a courtyard (photo by Val Ramos).

Fig. 12-8. The vertical fence lines are broken by the horizontal lines of the gate (photo by Val Ramos).

Fig. 12-10. A wrought iron gate can also enclose an entryway (photo by Val Ramos).

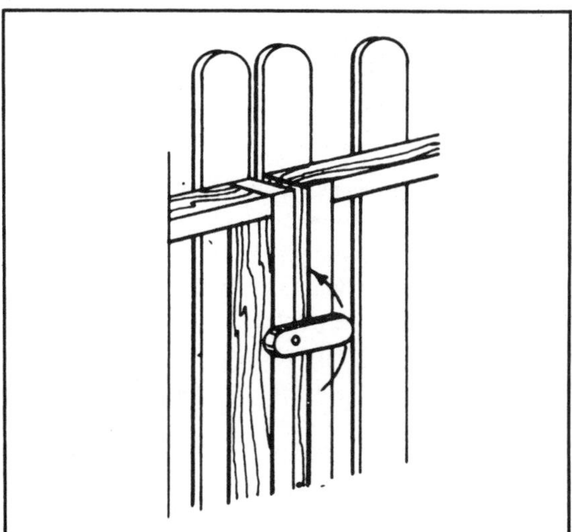

Fig. 12-11. Simple gate latch (courtesy Wolmanized pressure-treated lumber).

Fig. 12-12. The latch should blend with the gate design (photo by Val Ramos).

Fig. 12-13. A closer look at a simple wooden latch (photo by Val Ramos).

Fig. 12-14. Common metal gate handle (photo by Val Ramos).

## MATERIALS

There are many types of gate siding from which you can choose. Most wood gates have 2×4-inch frames covered with fencing material (Fig. 12-19). You can use lighter frames if the siding is exterior plywood or some other light material. These won't sag, but they usually need support on the flat sides to keep them from bowing and to give you a place to fasten hinges and latches. Don't buy warped lumber. It doesn't take much of a curve to throw the whole gate out of line. Sometimes you may have to go through half a dozen pieces before you get a straight one. If you have to buy green

Fig. 12-15. Simple metal latch used on many wood fences (photo by Val Ramos).

lumber, let it dry out for at least a week before you use it. Lay the boards on blocks to let the air circulate around the wood.

## CONSTRUCTION

Standard gates run from 3 to 5 feet wide. Anything less than 3 feet wide doesn't allow for the passage of wheelbarrows and larger outdoor furniture. Gates much wider than 5 feet need extra bracing to make sure they don't sag. Gate openings wider than 5 feet are best split into two gates: one that's commonly stationary and one that's easy to swing.

If you have a chain link or masonry fence, your gate is probably preassembled. Your own problem is how to hang it.

Your fence posts should be firmly embedded to withstand the gate's pull and weight. When possible, attach the hinge post to the house wall for added support. To measure the opening, take your measurements at the top and bottom. If there's a considerable difference, you'll have to make the posts plumb before you can hang a gate between them.

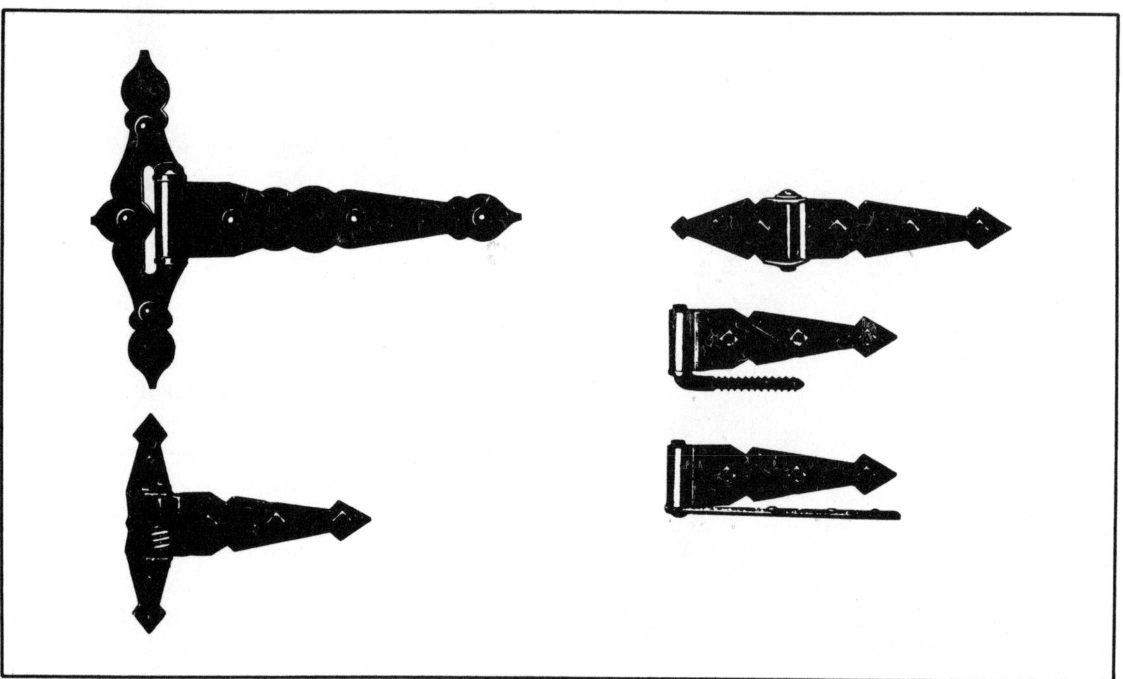

Fig. 12-16. Typical metal gate hinges (courtesy Arrowsmith).

Fig. 12-17. Assorted gate hardware is available at most lumber and hardware stores (photo by Val Ramos).

## Building the Frame

The first step is to nail a temporary 1×1 stake onto the inside of the latch post. This will serve as the spacer to standardize the gap between the gate frame and the latch post so that, once the gate is installed and the spacer is removed, the gate will swing without binding. The 1-inch nominal width of the spacer is actually about ¾ inch.

Measure the distance between the latch post and gatepost. Hold the measuring tape as level as possible. Cut the 2×4s to that length. They will act as rails for the gate frame. Make sure you cut square corners on all frame members, as they are not always sawed square at the mill. Cut lap joints for all corners for strength. Redrill your nail and screw holes with a bit that's slightly smaller in diameter than the fasteners. Use galvanized or other treated hardware that won't corrode and discolor the face of your fence.

## Installing the Bracing

Brace your gate frame to prevent sagging. The most common brace is a 2×4 set diagonally from the bottom corner of the frame on the hinge post side to the top corner of the latch side (Fig. 12-20). This actually pushes up the frame from the bottom of the hinge post. You can't run a wood brace the opposite way and not have the gate sag. The amateur gate builder has a hard time getting this brace in place. The solution is to hold the 2×4 in place and mark the angle with a pencil. A mistake of ⅛ inch will produce a loose fitting brace. If the brace doesn't fit snugly, tighten it up with a wedge.

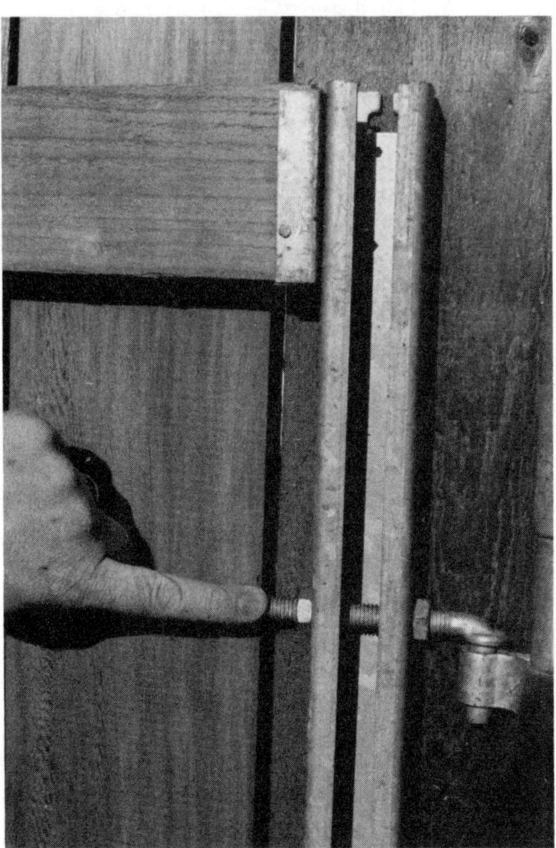

Fig. 12-18. Hinge for metal-framed wood fences (photo by Val Ramos).

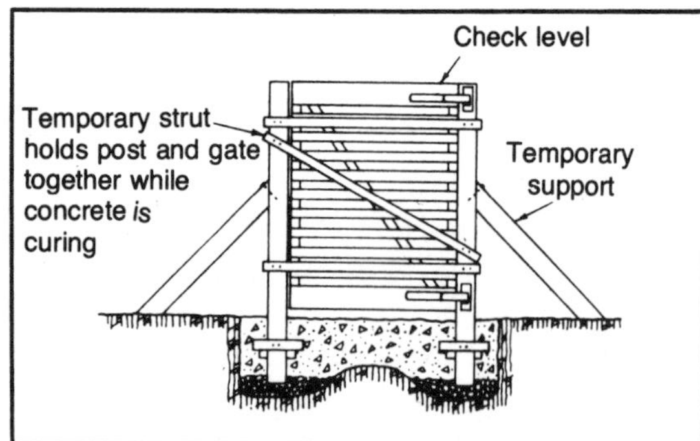


Fig. 12-19. Supporting your gate frame (courtesy Wolmanized pressure-treated lumber).

Fig. 12-20. Note the cross brace (courtesy Wolmanized pressure-treated lumber).

Another popular way of bracing a gate is to install a turnbuckle and wire or metal rod from the top of the frame on the hinge side to the bottom on the latch side—just the opposite of the wood brace (Fig. 12-21). The turnbuckle brace pulls up the frame to the top of the hinge post. You can buy sets containing wire, a turnbuckle, and two metal angle plates that fit over the edges of the gate frame. You can attach the wire to screw eyes set in the frame.

Wire or rod bracing has three advantages. It's easier and faster to install, easier to adjust if the gate sags, and is not as bulky or heavy as a wood brace. The cost is comparable (Fig. 12-22).

## Adding the Siding

The gate siding can be identical or vastly different from the siding used on your fence. A solid board fence can be accented with a short picket gate or by a diagonal board gate.

Lay the siding on the gate frame as it lies on the ground. If the gate requires a partial board, you may be able to loosen or tighten the gapping to allow for it and reduce cutting. You can place the partial board in the center of the gate for a decorative effect. Install the siding from the hinge side of the frame. Make sure you also nail the siding into any diagonal wood bracing.

Fig. 12-21. Turnbuckle cross bracing (photo by Val Ramos).

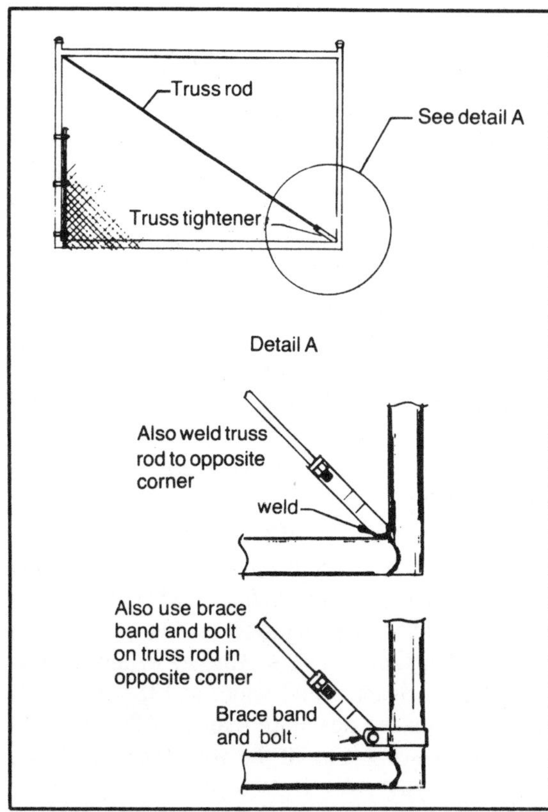


Fig. 12-22. Typical truss rod and tightener installation (courtesy International Fence Industry Association).

### Hanging the Gate

The simplest method of installing a wood gate is to have someone help you hold it in place while you temporarily nail it to the gate and latch posts. Check for fit and levelness. Then install the hinges.

It's best to predrill hinge screw holes with a bit that's slightly smaller than the screw you'll be using. Use the longest screws that won't come out the other side of the wood.

### Installing the Latch

Each latch will have its own method of installation (Figs. 12-23 and 12-24). Install the female part first, then the male, for the best fit (Fig. 12-25).

## INSTALLING CHAIN LINK GATES

Preassembled chain link gates are the simplest to install. After the entire fence has been completed, apply the male hinges to one of the gateposts. Position the top hinge with the pintle in a down position and the lower hinge with the pintle in an up position. This prevents the gate from being lifted off. Install the female hinges on the gate frame, insert the bolts and nuts, and slide the female hinges over the male hinges attached to the gate's post. Set the hinges to allow for the gate's full swing (Fig. 12-26).

The gate should be set so that the top of the gate frame is even with the top rail. Tighten all hinges securely. This helps prevent sagging.

Position the fork latch on the frame. Install the center drop rod if required. See Figs. 12-27 and 12-28.

## INSTALLING GATES ON MASONRY FENCES

To install a gate on a masonry fence, first make sure that the masonry is solid and not hollow (Fig.

Fig. 12-23. Two types of fence latches (photo by Val Ramos).

Fig. 12-24. Simple metal gate latch (photo by Val Ramos).

12-29). If the masonry is hollow, fill it with concrete and let it cure before trying to hang the gate. You may be able to embed the anchors for the gate into the setting concrete (Fig. 12-30).

Mark the locations of bolt holes and drill them out with a masonry drill larger than the bolt. Fill the hole with mortar and install the fastener. Let it set (Fig. 12-31). Go ahead and install the metal or wooden gate as with other fences.

## VARIATIONS

There are as many variations of gates as there are purposes for fences. Most are used on farms and ranches (Fig. 12-32).

### Cattle Guards

*Cattle guards* (Fig. 12-33) permit the passage of vehicles through the fence line while restraining livestock. A guard strong enough for heavy vehicles may be built of heavy plants set on edge, steel rails, small I-beams, or pipes 2 to 3 inches in diameter. It should be at least 8 feet wide, and the members should be spaced not more than 3 inches apart to prevent severe jolting of the vehicles as they are driven across.

If the guard is intended to restrain sheep or

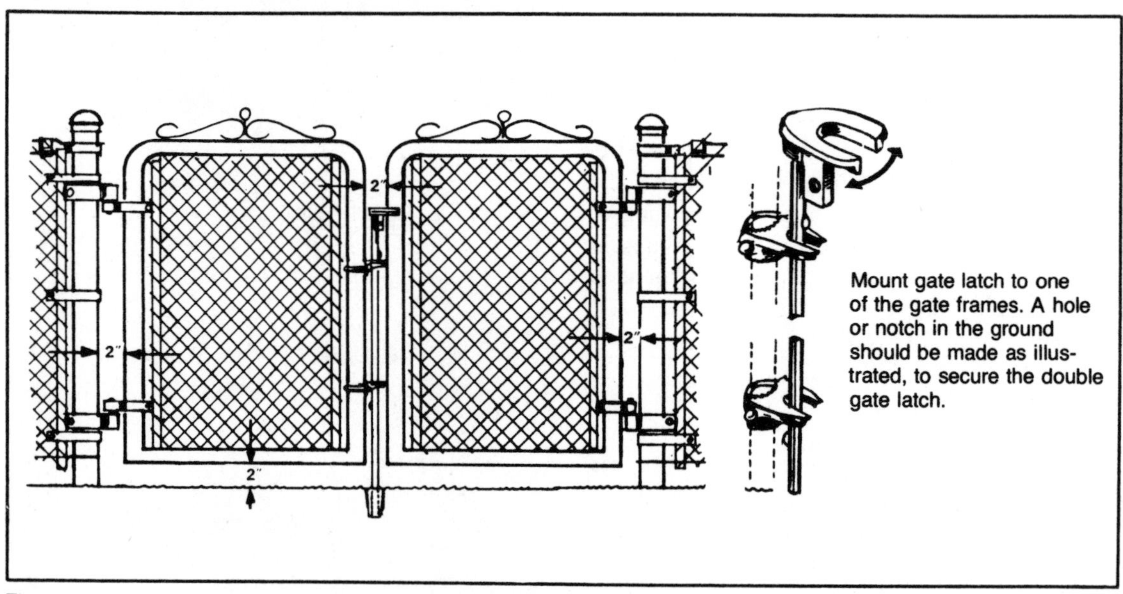

Fig. 12-25. Hinges and latch for driveway double gate (courtesy Builders Fence Co., Inc.).

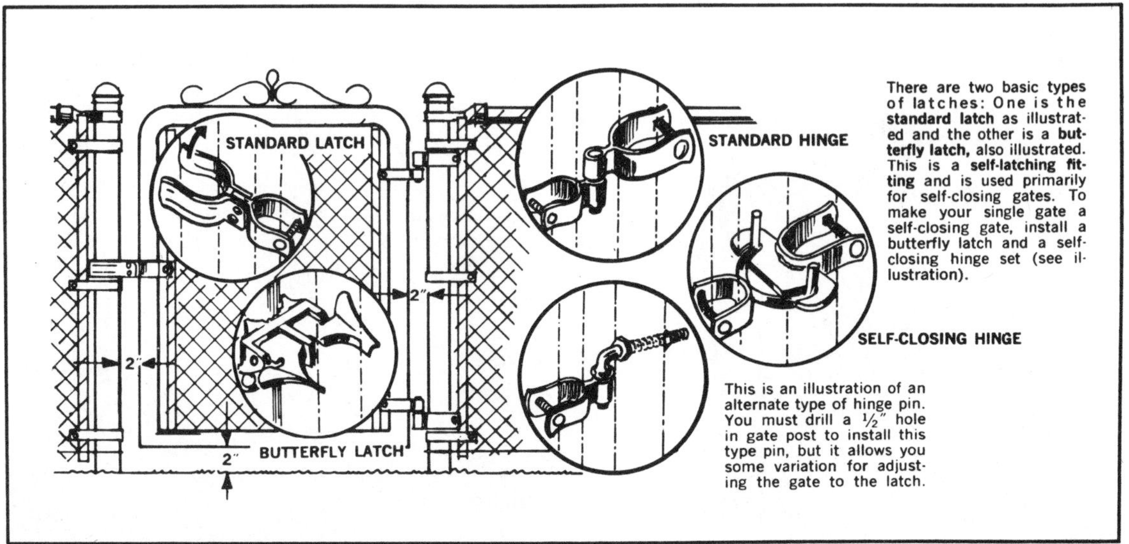


Fig. 12-26. Hinges and latches for chain link fencing (courtesy Builders Fence Co., Inc.).

Fig. 12-27. Larger gates can be installed on wheels (photo by Val Ramos).

Fig. 12-28. Rails and rollers are also used for moving large gates (photo by Val Ramos).

Fig. 12-29. Wrought iron gates can be installed on masonry fences (photo by Val Ramos).

Fig. 12-30. Typical metal-to-masonry installation (photo by Val Ramos).

Fig. 12-31. Gate hinges can be attached to masonry fences with an intermediate member of wood or metal (photo by Val Ramos).

goats, there should be no smooth strip across its top. Sheep and goats will walk across a strip as narrow as 2 inches.

The pit beneath the cattle guard should be 12 to 18 inches deep. Use crankcase oil to control weeds and mosquitoes in the pit.

## Floodgates

A *floodgate* may be used to restrain livestock where the fence line crosses a wide stream or gully. Figure 12-34 shows one kind of floodgate. Strong, well-secured end-post assemblies are required on each bank. Take precautions to prevent soil erosion around the posts. Keep floodgates free of debris to prevent the water from backing up and flooding the adjacent land.

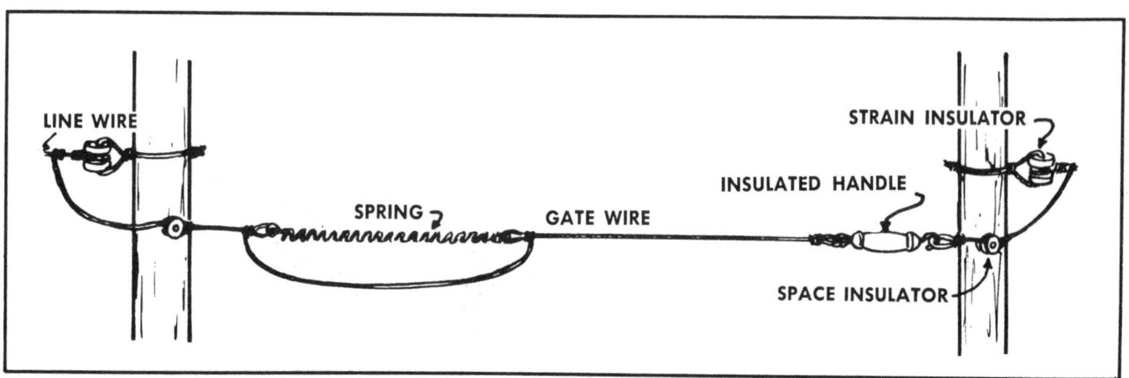


Fig. 12-32. Simple gate for electric fences.

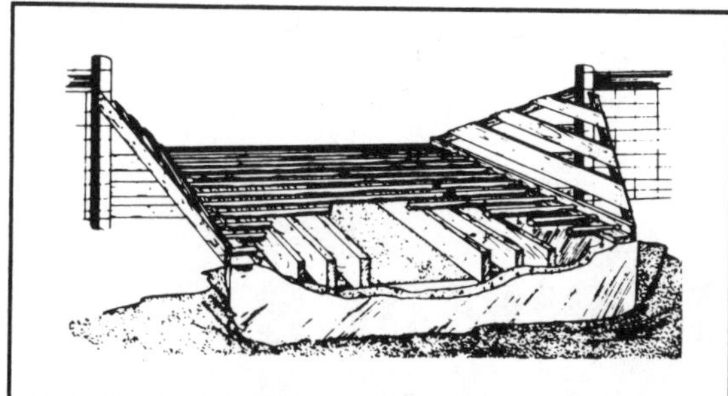

Fig. 12-33. Cattle guards allow vehicles to pass while restraining cattle.

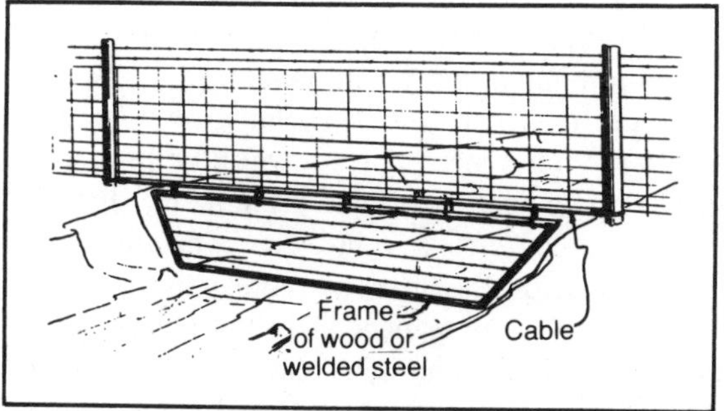


Fig. 12-34. Top hinged, wire, self-cleaning floodgate for narrow waterways.

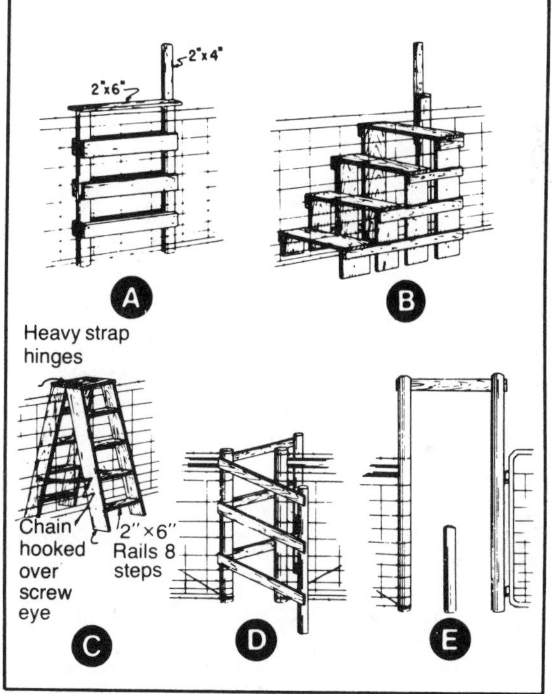


Fig. 12-35. Passageways for humans to eliminate some gates.

## Stiles and Walk-Throughs

A *stile* or a *walk-through* can easily be built where people cross a fence frequently. Figures 12-35A, 12-35B, and 12-35C illustrate common stiles that allow pedestrians to safely climb over a short fence. Figures 12-35D and 12-35E are walk-throughs for narrow foot traffic. Stiles will turn all kinds and sizes of livestock, while a walk-through will turn only large animals.

# Chapter 13

# Fence Maintenance

FENCING IS A MAJOR INVESTMENT FOR THE property owner. A wood fence built with preservative-treated posts will cost more to construct than one with nontreated posts, but the life of the fence can be extended 20 years or more. This is especially true if the fence is maintained properly. This chapter covers the preservation and maintenance of wood, masonry, wire, and other fences (Fig. 13-1).

## CAUSES OF DECAY IN POSTS

Virtually all decay in wooden fence posts is caused by certain types of fungi (Fig. 13-2). *Fungi* are forms of plant life that lack chlorophyll and are unable to produce their own food. They can utilize food already prepared such as that occurring in wooden fence posts.

Water is essential for decay to occur. Wood that can be maintained at a moisture content below its fiber saturation point—24 to 32 percent of the dry weight of the wood—will never rot. This is not possible with fence posts in service because they are being constantly wetted by rain and surface water.

The amount of oxygen present in the air and soil surrounding the wood is also critical. If oxygen is too low, then decay will be slowed.

The optimum conditions for growth of wood decay fungi in fence posts are within a zone a foot above and a foot below the groundline. Here the moisture content is relatively constant, never dropping below the fiber saturation point, and sufficient oxygen is present to allow optimal growth of the fungus. It is in this zone that most decay occurs and where most wooden fence posts fail in service.

## TREATABILITY OF POSTS

Almost any wood can be treated with a preservative to make it last longer. The sapwood of a tree is easier to penetrate with preservatives than is the heartwood. It usually retains a higher concentration of preservative. Home treatments should be limited primarily to sapwood, although even slight penetration of preservative into heartwood posts will in-

Fig. 13-1. Semiannual inspection of your fence may reveal minor repairs that may save major repairs later (photo by Val Ramos).

crease their life. Round posts, split wood, or dimensional lumber can be treated equally well.

## CHOOSING A PRESERVATIVE

The most generally used oil-soluble wood preservative for home and farm use is *pentachlorophenol* or penta. It is relatively low in cost, easy and comparatively safe to apply, and is effective in preventing decay in posts. It is sold under several trade names and is available in either a dry, flaky powder or as a concentrated solution. The latter is preferred because the dust in the flakes is very irritating to mucous membranes of the eyes, nose, and throat.

The concentrated solution is usually mixed with a petroleum solvent such as diesel oil to give a final proportion of 5 percent penta (by weight). The 10 to 1 penta concentrate should be mixed using 1 gallon of penta to 10 gallons of oil.

Coal-tar creosote gives superior results, but its proper application requires equipment not readily available. It is an oily, brownish black, smelly liquid of indefinite composition and is obtained from the distillation of coal tar. It usually comes as a 97 to 100 percent formulation and should not be diluted. Some formulations are especially designed for open-tank soak treatments, but for most effective penetration all creosotes should be heated during the application period. A cold soak is often used.

Copper naphthenate is formulated as a solution usually containing 1 to 8 percent metallic copper

Fig. 13-2. Heavy winds can put additional stress on decay-weakened posts to topple a wooden fence (photo by Val Ramos).

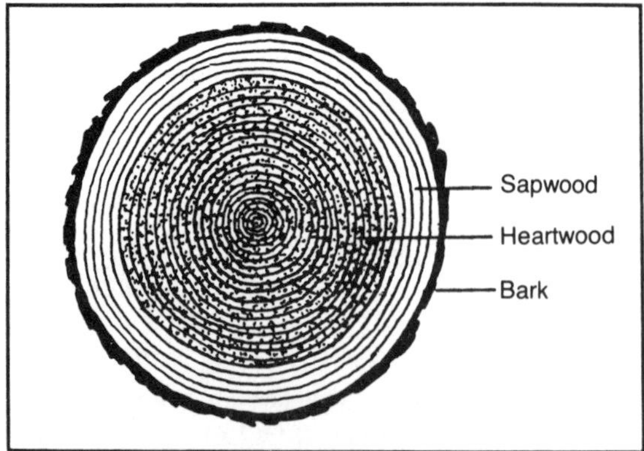


Fig. 13-3. Cross section of a typical tree showing the light-colored sapwood and dark-colored heartwood.

content. It could be diluted in mineral spirits or naphtha to a concentrate of 1 to 2 percent metallic copper content for treating fence posts. See Appendix B for more information on these and other wood preservatives.

## PREPARING POSTS

Here are the steps to preparing posts for wood fences from logs and dimensional lumber.

### Peeling

Remove bark from all wood for most treating methods. Bark resists penetration by preservative solutions and favors decay and insect attack by keeping wood moist. Trees peel most easily during the spring and early summer. A barking spud, tire iron, or shovel with a flat or concave cutting edge will remove bark. A drawknife or other sharp cutting tool may be necessary to "clean peel" wood during the fall and winter when the bark is "tight." Remove as little sapwood as possible (Fig. 13-3).

### Seasoning

Wood should be thoroughly air-dried before treating with oily preservatives. "Green" dimensional lumber doesn't absorb the preservative as well. Material to be seasoned should be loosely cross-piled on decay-free supports to permit air circulation (Fig. 13-4). Supports should be at least 18 inches high. The rate of drying can be speeded up by increasing the spacing between pieces. Although warm summer months are best for seasoning, wet wood will continue to dry slowly during winter months if stored under cover with good air circulation.

Posts and small poles can be dried in one to three summer months. Some woods, such as lodgepole pine, form a resinous glaze after peeling. Eliminating this surface condition may require either incising or seasoning through one winter exposed to the weather.

### Incising

Incisions aid penetration of preservative solution into the side grain of timbers. Many small

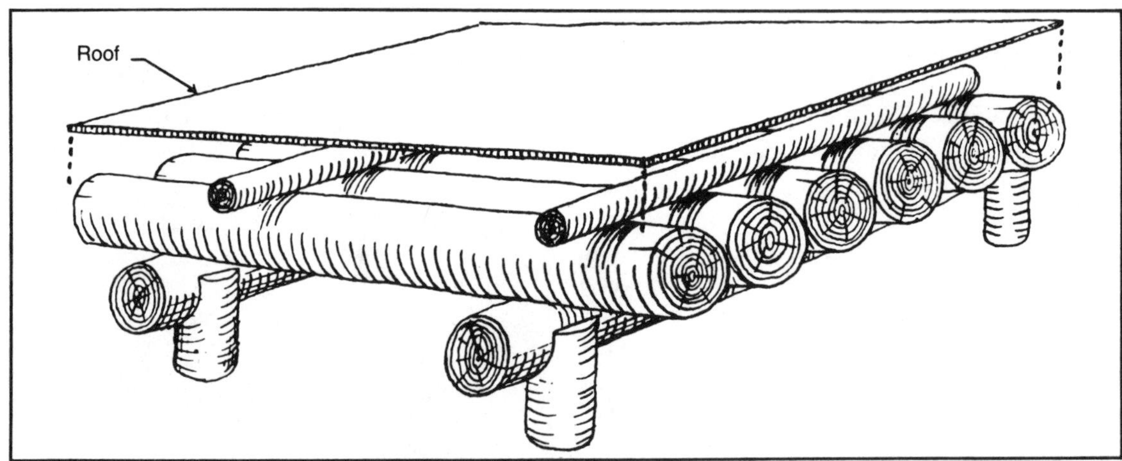


Fig. 13-4. A stack of peeled posts piled for seasoning prior to treatment.

incisions, staggered to prevent serious loss of strength, usually provide more uniform penetration than do a few large incisions. They can be made with a drill, ax, or saw, but more evenly spaced incisions can be made more quickly with an incising hammer. It should have sharp teeth capable of making incisions about ½ inch deep and less than 1 inch apart. An incising hammer can sometimes be rented or borrowed.

### Framing

All cuts or holes for fitting or fastenings should be made before treatment to prevent exposure of unprotected wood after treatment. Openings made through treated wood should be flooded with preservative.

## TREATING POSTS

The most convenient way to treat fence posts is to begin by embedding a 55-gallon drum into the soil—about a third to a half of its length (Fig. 13-5). Only one drum is needed unless you're building a long fence on a farm. The top end or lid of the barrel should be removed.

The seasoned posts are placed upright in the drums. Enough preservative is added to cover the lower end of the drum to about ground level, and the posts are allowed to soak for 48 to 72 hours. Preservative may need to be added at intervals to replace that absorbed by the wood. Short soak periods are adequate for softer, easier-to-penetrate woods such as pine. Longer soak periods are needed for woods such as Douglas fir that are more difficult to penetrate.

The drum should have a removable roof to prevent excessive contamination of the preservative mix by rainwater. Several inches of water in the drum may be desirable if easy-to-penetrate woods are being treated with pentachlorophenol. The water, being heavier than the oil, sinks to the bottom of the drum. It is absorbed by the lower end of the post, thereby reducing excessive uptake and waste of the preservative by a portion of the post that very seldom decays in service.

Horizontal drums can also be used. Cut out about one-third of the circumference, lengthwise, of a 55-gallon metal drum. The ends are cut out. Drums are welded together with a bunghole kept in each end for draining the preservative (Fig. 13-6). Two drums would be long enough for posts, although three or four may be welded together if long poles or lumber are to be treated. The top horizontal sections cut from the drums can be hinged to the lower portions and used as a lid to keep foreign matter out of the treating solution.

Other horizontal tanks can be made from old service station gasoline storage tanks or other suitable containers. Horizontal tanks can also be built with tongue and groove lumber and properly caulked.

## COSTS

Table 13-1 will give you a rough estimate of the number of 6-foot posts that 50 gallons of ready-to-use penta will treat. Fifty gallons of ready-to-use Penta comprise about 4.5 gallons of penta concentrate and 45 gallons of solvent. Add the costs and

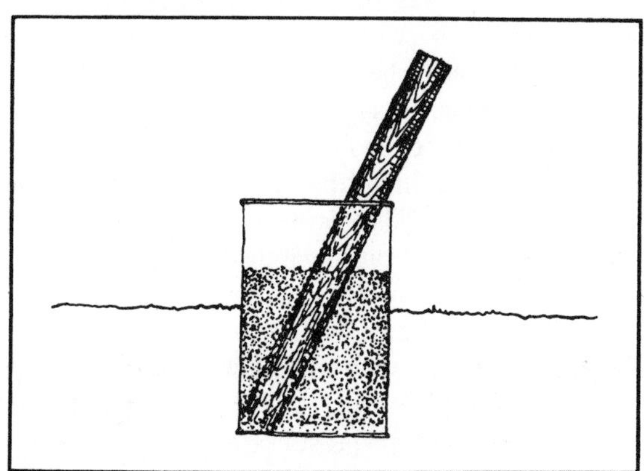

Fig. 13-5. Oil drum being used for butt treatment of fence posts.

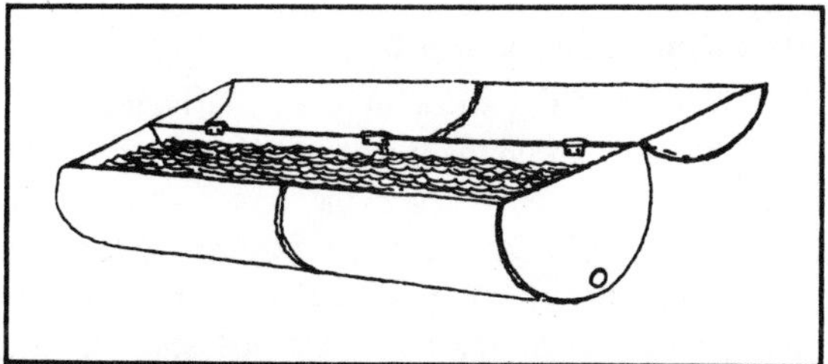

Fig. 13-6. Treatment of posts using horizontal drums.

**Table 13-1. Number of 6-foot Posts 50 Gallons of Ready-to-Use Penta Will Treat.**

| Post Diameter-Inches | Number of Posts |
|---|---|
| 3 | 200 |
| 4 | 100 |
| 6 | 50 |
| 7 | 33 |
| 10 | 17 |

divide by the number of posts you can treat to determine the cost of preservative per post.

Creosote absorption rates will be given on the side of the creosote can. Coal-tar creosote is usually ready to use and should not be diluted.

Regardless of the preservative used, when the posts are removed from the drums, especially when the upright drum method is used, each should be inverted and placed in the preservative solution for several minutes. Tops are less subject to decay, but dipping the tops will provide added protection. After final removal, the posts should be stacked so that excess preservative solution dripping from the posts will be absorbed by the posts beneath them. The treated posts may be used immediately or may be stored until needed.

Anyone handling freshly treated wood should wear gloves and other protective clothing to prevent preservative from touching the skin. Preservative on the skin should be washed off at once.

Children, pets, and livestock are not normally harmed by contact with treated wood once it's dry. Although new plants may be damaged by touching or being near oil-type preservatives, plants are not likely to suffer from treated wood that has weathered for a few years unless the preservative has continued to bleed from the wood.

## PRESSURE-TREATED WOOD

While soaking wood in preservatives can be effective and extend the life of your fence, the most efficient method of preserving wood is *pressure treating* (Fig. 13-7). Pressure-treated wood has been impregnated with a preservative in a process that forces the chemicals under pressure deeply into the wood. The preservatives are locked permanently into the wood and are present in sufficient quantities to deter attack by insects and decay.

Most pressure-treating plants use chromated copper arsenate (CCA) and ammoniacal copper arsenate (ACA). These preservatives are dissolved in water and other solvents. Preservatives such as creosote and pentachlorophenol are also available from pressure-treating plants, but generally they are used for industrial projects such as telephone poles.

How long will pressure-treated lumber last? The U.S. Department of Agriculture's Forest Products Laboratory has concluded that properly pressure-treated wood will last more than 50 years.

Pressure-treated lumber is available at most lumberyards and building supply centers. Most species (fir, pine, spruce, hemlock, etc.) and grades of lumber (No. 1, No. 2, Construction, Standard, etc.) are available as pressure-treated lumber.

There are different depths of penetration and variations in the amount of preservatives injected into the wood, depending on the wood's intended use. Two levels of treatment are available for outdoor home projects. LP-2 wood is treated to a minimum retention of .25 pounds per cubic foot. This is recommended for above-ground use and definitely should not be used for portions of a fence in contact with the ground. LP-22 wood is treated to a minimum retention of .40 pounds per cubic foot and can be used in ground contact applications. LP-22 is recommended for all fences and outdoor home projects. Minimum penetration depth for both levels of treatment is .4 inch. Marks on the surface of some pressure-treated lumber are made by in-

| Methods of Treating Wood and Their Effectiveness in Ground Contact Applications | Brush Treatment | Dip Treatment | Pressure Treatment |
|---|---|---|---|
| Protection | Surface with Slight Penetration | 1/16" to 1/8" Penetration | Sapwood Treated |
| Average amount solution required to treat 80-foot fence, made from 4 × 4 posts and 1" × 6" × 6' boards | 6 Gal. | 23 Gal. | 120 Gal. |
| Service life in ground contact | Unsatisfactory | Unsatisfactory | Long-lasting Protection |

Fig. 13-7. Methods of treating wood and their effectiveness.

cisors (or teeth) permitting more complete penetration of preservative.

Pressure-treated wood can be painted or stained if dry. Many people allow the wood to weather to natural tones because it won't deteriorate.

Pressure-treated wood is recommended for the fence posts. It is preferred also for other wood in contact with the ground.

## FINISHES

Many finishes are available to enhance your fence. Bleaches are used to gain a weathered appearance quickly. Paints and stains are used for overall effect or for accent in combination with natural wood. Water repellent treatment is used to retain the wood's natural appearance. Table 13-2 has basic information on various paints, stains, weathering agents, and repellents.

### Paints and Painting

White is the traditional color for fences, especially picket fences. It gives the appearance of neatness, complements floral display, calls attention to the fence in dim light, and sets a positive boundary line. Colored fences are also popular.

For long fence life and infrequent repainting, use the best quality paints that you can obtain.Apply a base coat for a superior finish and, after it dries, brush on two coats of outdoor paint. You will find the application easier if you paint the pieces before they are assembled. It's difficult to reach all parts and crevices with the brush after the fence is completed. When the fence is assembled, you can touch up hammer marks, handprints, and nailheads.

Fences that resemble house siding or those with large flat surfaces can be painted with an exterior type paint roller. There are rollers designed to paint in V-grooved siding and for corner work,

**Table 13-2. Common Wood Finishes and Their Uses.**

| General Product | Finish to Use | Instructions | Comments |
|---|---|---|---|
| PAINTS | Alkyd paints | Apply alkyd primer and 2 finish coats | Alkyds are quick drying, blister resistant and can be applied self-primed. Oil-base paints are not blister resistant unless applied over a zinc-free primer. Seal back of siding with water repellent. |
| | Oil-base paints | Use a zinc-free primer plus 2 finish coats | |
| | Latex paints | same as above | Product development in this field rapid. Follow manufacturer's instructions. |
| STAINS | Heavy-body, oil-base stain | 1 or 2 coats. Brush, dip or spray | Particularly suited for rough and saw-textured products. |
| *Solid, but somewhat soft color. Shows wood texture, but little grain.* | Semi-transparent oil base stain | 2 brush applications. May be sprayed and smoothed with brush. | A natural for rough or saw-textured sidings. Gives transparent color which is durable and long lasting. |
| | Creosote stains | 1 or 2 brush applications | A durable type finish. Some brands suitable for subsequent painting after several years of weathering, if desired. Allows grain show-through. |
| *Light coloring, emphasis on wood grain show-through.* | Semi-transparent resin stains | 2 brush applications | Fast drying with good penetration and durability. |
| WEATHERING AGENTS | Commercial Bleaches | Brush 1 or 2 coats. Renew in 3 or 5 years if necessary. | Will give natural wood a weather appearance. |
| REPELLENTS | Water repellent | 2 coats. Dip before installation, brush after. | Excellent for retaining the natural wood look. Pigmented or dye stain may be added. |

though you may have to touch up a few spots with a brush.

Your paint dealer can recommend the best finish for your particular climate. If you are planning to plant against the fence, watch for mildew deposits. You might use a mildewcide in your finish. Remember that some garden sprays will stain painted finishes. Flush the fence with water immediately if spray gets on it.

Fences in the country are often spray painted, but this method is inadvisable in the city. Wind can carry the paint droplets some distance and deposit them on neighbors' cars and windows. Spray painting often does not give the lasting surface that a skillfully handled brush can provide. A surface that has been spray painted must be repainted more often.

### Water Repellents

There are certain advantages to using a *water repellent* preservative when allowing the wood to weather. The water repellents do not alter the natural appearance of the wood, and they can be applied rapidly and easily. Water repellent modifies the natural weathering process so that the initial stage of darkening, which frequently occurs, is eliminated. The wood gradually changes from its original color and stabilizes at lighter shades. The water repellents also tend to minimize occurrence of watermarks or surface checks on exposed wood.

This is an economical, easy-to-maintain type of treatment for exterior surfaces. In new construction the water repellent may be used as a back, end, and edge primer as well as a face treatment. It may be applied by giving the siding a 3-minute dip. If dipping is not feasible, apply the water repellent liberally with a brush to the face, back, and ends of the boards. In either event freshly cut surfaces that develop during construction should be given a liberal brush coating. The second application of the water repellent should be made after the siding is in place.

Begin with a two-coat application for existing construction. Subsequent maintenance coats need be applied only when the wood no longer shows ability to shed water. No special surface preparation is needed prior to application, and one coat is sufficient.

The cost of the material is considered economical, even in comparison with the low-cost natural finishes.

Paints, stains, or bleaches may be used over the paintable water repellents without difficulty if you decide to change the exterior finish effect of the fence. Paintable water repellents contain a mildewcide. Typical brands are Wood-Tox and Seal-Treat or other products that meet the requirements of Federal Specification TT-W-572 Type II, Composition A.

### Bleaches

Use a *bleach* if you want a gray, long-weathered look without waiting the time necessary to achieve it through unassisted weathering. A bleach will hasten the natural color changes in the wood and will provide a more uniform appearance than occurs when the wood is untreated. It will also eliminate the initial darkening of the natural process in many woods. This is another easy-to-maintain finish effect employing a chemical action to accelerate the natural color change of the wood to the final driftwood gray or other tone.

Use one or two coats of bleach according to the manufacturer's recommendations for the original application. Typical brands are Cabot's Bleaching Oil No. 241 and Olympic's Bleachtox. These are used primarily for cedar siding.

Reapplication of the bleaching oil is necessary only if the wood shows a tendency to darken. No surface preparation is necessary before reapplication other than washing off dirt. Because the bleaching application depends both on moisture and sunlight, it's helpful to spray the surface with water occasionally. To eliminate the possibility of streaky areas developing after a rainstorm, flush the siding from top to bottom with a hose. Occasionally flushing also will clean off dirt and grime.

### Masonry Finishes

Concrete masonry walls can be painted with a

special portland cement base paint available at most building material outlets. Follow directions on the scan.

The masonry surface must be clean of oil, dirt, or any substance that could prevent the paint from adhering. Check the wall thoroughly for cracks and repair them before painting the surface.

Spray the wall with a garden hose. Make sure that it's uniformly damp but not soaked. Mix your paint by adding water as recommended by the manufacturer. Make sure it's thoroughly mixed before and during application to avoid settling. Apply with a stiff brush. See that the paint gets into the pores of the concrete block. Exterior concrete walls should be given two coats.

Cement base paints must cure slowly. To keep your wall's paint from drying out too fast in the sun, keep the first coat moist for at least 12 hours and the second coat moist for about 48 hours.

## REPLACING ROTTEN FENCE POSTS

Most fences can be repaired more easily and economically than they can be replaced (Fig. 13-8). All it takes is a few tools and some know-how.

Fig. 13-8. Parts from old fences can often be used to decorate new fences (photo by Val Ramos).

Because of the highest combination of moisture and oxygen, posts usually rot right at ground level. Preventive maintenance steps include using pressure-treated posts and crowning the posthole fill, so water runs off easily and doesn't collect at the base of the post.

The easiest way to replace a rotten fence post is to add a reinforcement post next to it and cut the old one off above the rot. Use scrap lumber to prop the rotting post into place. Dig the old posthole out and remove the bad section of the post. Lay the new post aside it, pour and pack concrete for the new posthole, then attach the two posts with lag screws or carriage bolts. Remove the supports and you're back in business.

## MAINTAINING PICKET FENCES

Picket fences are pretty to look at but a pain to maintain. If you catch a fence in time, a minor touch-up may be enough. Give healthy posts a coat of penta, especially around the base, and repaint.

If your picket fence is in rough shape, you can still save it with some work on a Saturday. Set up an outside work area if it's good weather, or open up the garage and clear a space if it's not. A 4×8 sheet of plywood on sawhorses makes an excellent worktable for picket fence sections. You can lay two sections out at a time.

Check each picket, rail, and post for rot. If the material is either dry and brittle or wet and soggy, replace it. Remove it from the lineup. Hopefully the fence was built of standard dimensional lumber, and the picket design isn't too fancy to duplicate. Fancy cuts can be copied with a handsaw, radial arm saw, or saber saw using the technique outlined in Chapter 5.

Replace or reinforce all rotten posts (Fig. 13-9). Rails rarely rot. Use preservative on the new and old materials as needed. Apply the first coat of paint to the picket fence before installing it. Dig new postholes or pull out the casings in the old

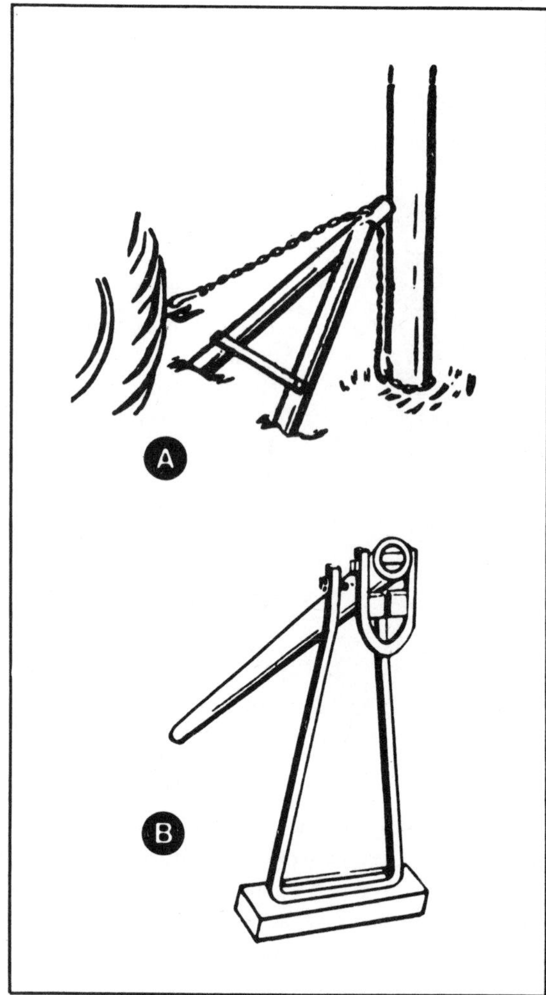


Fig. 13-9. Post pullers. (A) Tractor-powered. (B) Hand-operated.

ones. Place your fence and attach temporary supports until the concrete is poured and cured (Figs. 13-10 and 13-11). Apply the second coat of paint to your renewed picket fence.

## REPAIRING MASONRY WALLS

If a brick masonry wall is properly constructed, it requires little maintenance or repair. The proper repair of old masonry can be more expensive than the complete removal and replacement of the disintegrated portion. The use of good mortar, proper finishing joints, and adequate flashing adds little to the initial costs and reduces the cost of maintenance throughout the life of the masonry.

*Tuck-pointing* involves cutting out all loose and disintegrated mortar to a depth of at least ½ inch and replacing it with new mortar. If leakage is to be stopped, all the mortar in the affected area should be cut out and replaced with new mortar. Tuck-pointing is done as routine maintenance only.

To prepare the mortar joint, all dust and loose material should be removed by brush or by a water jet after the cutting has been completed. A chisel with a cutting edge of about ½ inch wide is suitable for cutting. If water is used in cleaning the joints, no further wetting is required. If not, the surface of the joint must be moistened.

The mortar to be used for tuck-pointing should be portland-cement-lime, prehydrated type S mor-

Fig. 13-10. A temporary support can be placed against a weak fence until repairs can be made (photo by Val Ramos).

Fig. 13-11. Temporary supports are used to lift a fallen fence into position for repair (photo by Val Ramos).

tar, or prehydrated prepared mortar made from type II masonry cement. The prehydration of mortar greatly reduces the amount of shrinkage.

Sufficient time should be allowed for absorption of the moisture used in preparing the joint before the joint is filled with mortar. Filling the joint with mortar is called *repointing* and is done with a pointing trowel. The prehydrated mortar that has been prepared is packed tightly into the joint in thin layers about ¼ inch thick and finished to a smooth concave surface with a pointing tool. The mortar is pushed into the joint with a forward motion in one direction from a starting point to reduce the possibility of air pockets forming.

## REPAIRING GATES

If your gate sags, binds, or won't latch, check the hinge post to see if it is still solid and plumb. Sometimes a wire from the hinge post to a more solid post down the line will correct the tilt. If the gate still binds, see if the hinges pulled out slightly. When posts and hinges are in good order, try tightening the turnbuckle or wedging up the wood brace.

Sometimes a poorly latching gate is caused by a sagging gate frame. The whole gatepost may sink slightly, causing the latch bar to miss the catch. Reset either the hinges or the latch. If screws and nails pull out of the wood, remove the gate and hinges, fill the holes with a strong glue, and reset the hinges when the glue is dry, or change the location of the hinges using longer screws.

A wooden gate may bind in wet weather and work fine when it's dry. Plane off a little of the latch post or gate frame. You can frequently restore an old gate by simply replacing a wooden brace with a wire and turnbuckle brace.

## GROUNDING METAL FENCES

Many owners of metal fences should consider installing a *lightning protector,* especially on fences in areas where lightning is a problem. Livestock can be killed instantly if near an ungrounded or improp-

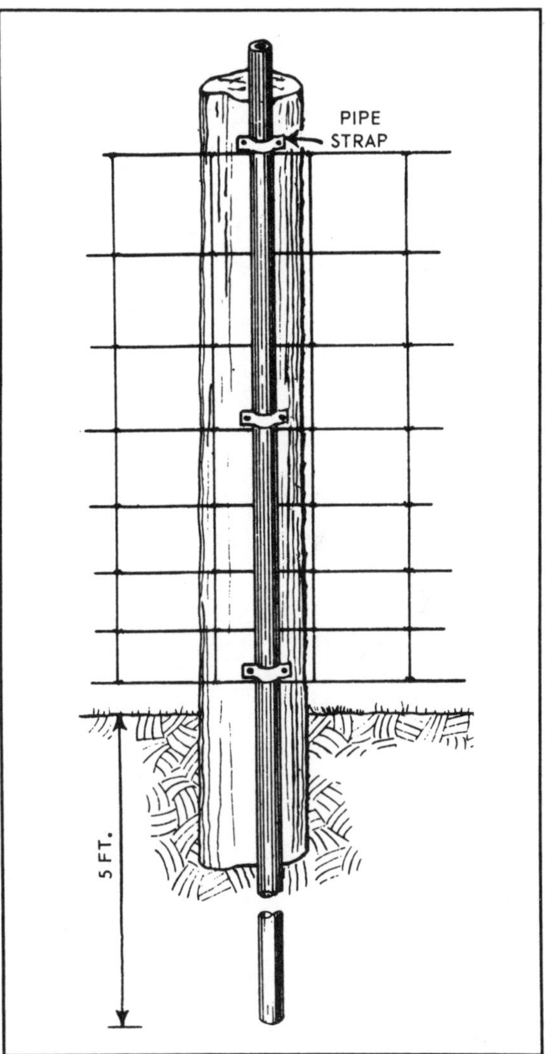


Fig. 13-12. Grounding of woven wire fence with wood posts.

erly grounded wire fence that receives a lightning discharge. Wire fences attached to trees and buildings are most likely to receive lightning discharges, but any wire fence can be a hazard.

Properly grounded fences greatly reduce the chance of electrocution. Because lightning is so highly erratic, there will always be some danger.

All steel fence posts will ground a wire fence if they are in contact with wet or moist soil. Unless you can be sure that your posts are in contact with wet soil, you should either use extra long posts set at least 5 feet in the ground or install special ground rods as recommended for wood posts below.

Figure 13-12 shows the recommended method of grounding a wire fence with wood posts. Drive the ½- or ¾-inch steel rod at least 5 feet into the ground. Allow it to extend a few inches above the post. Fasten the rod to the post with the pipe straps so that it touches all the wires. Ground the fence in this manner every 150 feet. Another way to ground the fence is to use an extra long steel post, set 5 feet into the ground, every 150 feet.

# Chapter 14

# Fence Landscaping

FENCES AND WALLS ARE ELEMENTS OF LANDscaping (Fig. 14-1). Besides their functional purposes of protection and privacy, fences can also become the backdrop or even an integral part of your yard's design (Figs. 14-2 through 14-9). This chapter looks at the fence's related elements within the yard and how they can work together: trees, shrubs, hedges, climbers, flowers, ground cover, rocks, and man-made decorations (Figs. 14-10 through 14-12).

## CONSIDERATIONS

There are four considerations in planning landscaping around and with your fence: *nature, harmony, concealment,* and *maintenance.*

Considering nature in your fence landscaping project means looking at the natural elements to decide what effect they will have. Will the fence, trees, or shrubs change the amount of sunlight received within your yard? Will they increase shade? Will they redirect or stop the wind? How much and during what part of the year? Is this change a benefit or a liability to your yard's intended use?

Will a planned tree drop leaves into the pool? Will a tall, windbreaking fence cast too much shade into your garden area? Will the shrubs next to the fence receive adequate light and water?

The main idea of landscaping is harmony of purpose and of design. Will the ground cover blend in with your stone wall or will it detract? Are the colors of the flowers complementary to your fence and home?

Concealment applies to those landscape elements that cover something else: a fence, rock, or a view. Ivy might be grown to conceal a fence. A tree may be planted to conceal a view. Make sure that the concealment is intended. It's a waste of time and money to install a quality fence and then plant climbers that completely cover it.

Maintenance is important because whether the landscape element is a fence, hedge, or ground cover, it should not require undue maintenance. Some ivies can take over a yard in a couple seasons and be a chore to maintain. Other plants can thrive on neglect.

Fig. 14-1. A well-designed and built fence can be a beautiful addition to your landscaping (courtesy Western Wood Products Association).

There are other considerations such as soil, water, and local growing conditions. Nature, harmony, concealment, and maintenance directly relate to fence landscaping.

## TREES

*Trees* act as a natural barrier that adds beauty and function to a fenced yard (Figs. 14-13 and 14-14). Trees can offer both effective noise control and shade.

Keep in mind the mature height and spread of the tree. Shade trees ideally should be sturdy, long-lived species that grow relatively fast and produce the size and shape desired. If yours is a one-story house on a small lot, you should plant small trees. The following can be recommended for small properties:

- Trident maple (*Acer buergerianum*).
- Hornbeam maple (*Acer carpinifolium*).
- Full moon maple (*Acer japonicum*).

- Manchurian maple (*Acer mandschuricum*).
- Nikko maple (*Acer nikoense*).
- European hornbeam (*Carpinus betulus* "Globosa").
- American hornbeam (*Carpinus caroliniana*).
- Eastern redbud (*Cercis canadensis*).
- Flowering dogwood (*Cornus florida*).
- Russian olive (*Elaeagnus angustifolia*).
- Balkan ash (*Fraxinus holotricha*).
- Flowering ash (*Fraxinus ornus*).
- Golden rain tree (*Koelreuteria paniculata*).
- Sourwood (*Oxydendrum arboreum*).
- Chinese elm (*Ulmus parvifolia*).

If you have space for a large tree, you might want one of the following:

- European beech (*Fagus sylvatica*).

Fig. 14-2. Brick fences offer security, privacy, and beauty (courtesy Brick Institute of America).

Fig. 14-3. Wood fences blend well with natural landscaping (courtesy Weyerhaeuser Company).

- Sugar maple (*Acer saccharum*).
- Littleleaf linden (*Tilia cordata*).
- Red maple (*Acer rubrum*).
- Northern red oak (*Quercus borealis*).
- Tulip tree (*Liriodendron tulipifera*).
- Pin oak (*Quercus palustris*).
- White oak (*Quercus alba*).
- Cucumber tree (*Magnolia acuminata*).

Fig. 14-4. The split rail fence is a popular landscaping accent (photo by Val Ramos).

Consider the planting site and its soil type, compaction, and drainage. Select only those trees that will be hardy enough to survive summer heat and winter cold in your area. Many species when planted north of their adapted range are killed by early fall or late spring frosts. United States Agriculture Handbook 425, *Shade Trees for the Home*, gives the adaptive range of shade tree species. Your local garden shop or landscaper can give you additional information.

Protection of newly planted trees is another matter. After you have selected and planted new trees, you have the job of maintaining and protecting them.

The most frequent cause of death to newly established trees is the lack of ample water. There is a critical period following transplanting before an adequate root system is established to maintain the plant. Ample water must be provided during this period to allow maximum efficiency for those roots that are functional.

The soil around each tree should be saturated deeply but not flooded. The number of times you

Fig. 14-5. A split rail fence easily follows land contours (photo by Val Ramos).

Fig. 14-6. A fence can be an outdoor room divider (photo by Val Ramos).

Fig. 14-7. Fences serve as a backdrop for landscaping (photo by Val Ramos).

Fig. 14-8. Landscaping can be segmented by fencing (photo by Val Ramos).

water will depend on rainfall and the soil conditions. It may be necessary to water twice a week for the first two months following planting. Soil around the root system should be kept moist. A mulch around the tree consisting of organic material (course peat moss, pine bark, tan bark, ground corncobs, or peanut hulls) will help prevent water loss through evaporation.

Fig. 14-9. Landscaping and fences should reflect the mood of your home (photo by Val Ramos).

Even after your plants are established, you will have to water them during periods of drought. Permanent irrigation systems are recommended in arid regions.

In newly established yards it's a good idea to fertilize your plants every year until they are established. Liquid premixed fertilizers are available at garden centers. These fertilizers are advantageous in that they are available immediately to the plant, and no fertilizer residue is left to burn the plants roots or grass. Follow the directions on the label in applying these fertilizers.

## SHRUBS

*Shrubs* can be planted in the same way as trees to define your property, reduce noise, and increase beauty in your yard (Figs. 14-15 and 14-16). Evergreen plants generally keep their leaves year-round and often make the best hedges. Semievergreens may lose some of their foliage during the fall and winter. Deciduous plants drop their leaves during colder months and are used where winter shade is not needed.

Fig. 14-10. Rocks and shrubs highlight this masonry and wood fence (photo by Val Ramos).

Fig. 14-11. Shrubs and trees can be contained with a rustic fence (photo by Val Ramos).

Fig. 14-12. A fence, tree, and a shrub (photo by Val Ramos).

Fig. 14-14. These trees were planted here to accent the vertical lines of the fence (photo by Val Ramos).

Fig. 14-13. Deciduous trees are best for the south side of your home (photo by Val Ramos).

## Evergreen Shrubs

- Bog rosemary (*Andromeda polifolia*).
- Aucuba (*Aucuba japonica*).
- Korean boxwood (*Buxus microphylla koreana*).
- Bottlebrush (*Callistemon citrinus*).
- Natal plum (*Carissa grandiflora*).
- New Jersey tea (*Ceanothus americanus*).
- Blue blossom (*Ceanothus thyrsiflorous*).

Fig. 14-15. Shrubs should not be planted too close to fences and walls (photo by Val Ramos).

- Heather (*Erica canaliculata*).
- Japanese aralia (*Fatsia japonica*).
- Cape jasmine (*Gardenia jasminoides*).
- Veitch wintergreen (*Gaultheria veitchiana*).
- Japanese holly (*Ilex crenata*).
- Common juniper (*Juniperus communis*).
- Mountain laurel (*Kalmia latifolia*).
- Sweet bay (*Laurus nobilis*).
- Oleander (*Nerium oleander*).
- Chinese photinia (*Photinia serrulata*).
- Japanese andromeda (*Pieris japonica*).
- Japanese pittosporum (*Pittsoporum tobira*).
- Yeddo hawthorn (*Raphiolepis umbrellata*).
- Japanese skimmia (*Skimmia japonica*).
- Athel tree (*Tamarix aphylla*).
- Canada yew (*Taxus canadensis*).

Fig. 14-16. Shrubs should be chosen carefully to make sure they don't grow over fences (photo by Val Ramos).

#### Semievergreen Shrubs

- Glossy abelia (*Abelia grandiflora*).
- Spanish jasmine (*Jasminum grandiflorum*).
- Common white jasmine (*Jasminum officinale*).
- Creeping mahonia (*Mahonia repens*).

#### Deciduous Shrubs

- Shablow, service berry (*Amelanchier canadensis*).
- Japanese barberry (*Berberis thunbergii*).
- Butterfly bush (*Buddleia davidii*).
- Summer sweet (*Clethra alnifolia*).
- Cornelian cherry (*Cornus mas*).
- Fragrant daphne (*Daphne odora*).
- Russian olive (*Elaeagnus angustifolia*).
- Silverberry (*Elaeagnus pungens*).
- Winged euonymus (*Euonymus alata*).
- Early forsythia (*Forsythia ovata*).
- Large fothergilla (*Fothergilla major*).
- Spring witch hazel (*Hamamelis vernalis*).
- Shrub althaea (*Hibiscus syriacus*).
- Beauty bush (*Kolkwitzia amabilis*).
- Amur privet (*Ligustrum amurense*).
- Winter honeysuckle (*Lonicera fragrantissima*).
- Tatarian honeysuckle (*Lonicera tatarica*).
- Cinquefoil (*Potentilla fruticosa*).
- Flowering currant (*Ribes sanguineum*).
- French pussy willow (*Salix caprea*).
- Bridal wreath spiraea (*Spiraea prunifolia*).
- Late lilac (*Syringa villosa*).
- Arrowwood (*Viburnum dentatum*).
- Wayfaring tree (*Viburnum lantana*).
- European cranberry bush (*Viburnum opulus*).
- Cranberry bush (*Viburnum trilobum*).
- Chaste tree (*Vitex agnus-castus*).

Plant evergreen shrubs in the fall or spring and deciduous shrubs in the spring.

### VINES

A climbing *vine* can add a sense of permanence to any fence, wall, or trellis. Vines grow quickly, are easy to care for, and can provide shade, privacy, and beauty.

Your choice of vines depends partly on the location of the barrier you want the vines to climb (Fig. 14-17). Some varieties thrive best in the direct sun while others prefer shade. Here are the most popular climbing vines:

#### Sun Vines

- Coral vine (*Antigonon leptopus*).
- Evergreen clematis (*Clematis armandi*).
- Morning glory (*Ipomoea purpurea*).
- Scarlet kadsura (*Kadsura japonica*).
- Sweet honeysuckle (*Lonicera caprifolium*).
- Chilean jasmine (*Mandevilla suaveolens*).
- Passion flower (*Passiflora caerulea*).
- Scarlet runner bean (*Phaseolus coccineus*).
- Plumbago (*Plumbago capensis*).
- Rambler rose (*Rosa*).
- Japanese wisteria (*Wisteria floribunda*).

Fig. 14-17. A lattice screen is the perfect place to plant a rose bush or ivy plants (photo by Val Ramos).

## Partial Shade Vines

- Five-leaf akebia (*Akebia quinata*).
- Blueberry climber (*Ampelopsis previpedunculata*).
- Dutchman's pipe (*Aristolochia durior*).
- Cross vine or trumpet vine (*Bignonia capreolata*).
- American bittersweet (*Celastrus scandens*).
- Wintercreeper (*Euonymus fortunei*).
- Creeping fig (*Ficus pumila*).
- Carolina jasmine (*Gelsemium sempervirens*).
- Climbing hydrangea (*Hydrangea petiolaris*).
- White jasmine (*Jasminum officinale*).
- Burmese honeysuckle (*Lonicera hildebrandiana*).
- Hall's honeysuckle (*Lonicera japonica*).
- Virginia creeper (*Parthenocissus quinquefolia*).
- Kudzo vine (*Pueraria thunbergiana*).
- Horse brier (*Smilax rotundifolia*).
- Star jasmine (*Trachelospermum jasminoides*).
- Glory grape (*Vitis coignetiae*).

## Shade Vines

- English ivy (*Hedera helix*).

## Espaliers

An *espalier* (e-*spal*-yer) is a trellis on which shrubs are trained to grow flat (Fig. 14-18). The trellis can actually be a fence, wall, woven latice trellis, or even a mound of dirt or rock. Espalier plants are trimmed and trained to the desired shape. Common espalier plants include:

- Japanese camellia (*Camellia japonica*).
- Chinese rosebud (*Cercis chinensis*).
- Chinese quince (*Chaenomeles sinensis*).
- Border forsythia (*Forsythia intermedia spectabilis*).
- Winter jasmine (*Jasminum nudiflorum*).
- Korean stewartia (*Stewartia koreana*).
- Spreading English yew (*Taxus baccata repandens*).
- Japanese yew (*Taxus cuspidata*).

Espaliers can be grown in the ground or in containers placed close to the fence or other support. Shoots can be trained with string tied between nails or hooks on the fence or wall. They can also be shaped by pruning.

Fig. 14-18. An espalier where a plant is trained to decorate a trellis (photo by Val Ramos).

## FLOWERS

Fences can be emphasized or camouflaged with the beauty and color of *flowers*. You can tie together the colors of the house and outdoor living area, or you can separate them with the appropriate selection of perennials, annuals, and bulbs.

*Perennials* are long-lived, strong growers that produce richly colored flowers. Popular perennials include: aster, baby's breath, chrysanthemum, columbine, delphinium, carnation, primrose, hibiscus, iris, lily of the valley, peony, sunflower, and violet.

*Annuals* can bring colorful blooms to your yard on little notice, especially during seasons when perennials are dormant. Common annuals include: African daisy, baby blue-eyes, California poppy, everlasting, forget-me-not, French marigold, nasturtium, petunia, snapdragon, sweet pea, and tassel flower.

*Bulbs* are the trumpets of spring offering bright colors and varied designs. Common bulbs are: crocus, dahlia, glory-of-the-snow, hyacinth, lily of the nile, narcissus, star-of-Bethlehem, tulip, and windflower.

Fig. 14-20. Sometimes an ivy or other ground cover decides to take over a fence (photo by Val Ramos).

## GROUND COVERS

*Ground covers* serve as natural carpeting for outdoor activities and help fill in landscaping with easy-maintenance beauty (Fig. 14-19). Ground covers include bog-rosemary, carmel creeper, cinquefoil, creeping mahonia, dwarf rosemary, English ivy, ground holly, ground ivy, Hall's honeysuckle, ice plant, periwinkle, rock spray, Scotch heather, star jasmine, sweet fern, thyme, wild strawberry, and wintercreeper (Fig. 14-20).

Fig. 14-19. Ground covers are easy-maintenance landscape elements (photo by Val Ramos).

The most popular ground cover is lawn grasses. They are classified into two groups: cold-season (for areas with winter frost and snow) and subtropical (for areas with milder winters). Cold-season grasses include bents, blue grasses, clover, coarse fescues, fine fescues, red top, and rye grasses. Subtropical grasses include Bermuda grasses, Saint Augustine grass, and zoysia grasses.

When planting grasses or ground cover near fences, make sure that the fence will not interfere with subsequent maintenance and cutting of the covers as they grow (Figs. 14-21 and 14-22).

## ROCKS

*Rocks* can be used as landscaping elements in many ways (Figs. 14-23 and 14-24). They can be grouped to form rock gardens. Flat rocks can be

Fig. 14-21. Low shrubs and ground cover should periodically be trimmed back (photo by Val Ramos).

buried to become the tops of walkway steps. Rocks can be the central point of a landscape design (Fig. 14-25).

A true rock garden is not a haphazard collection of rocks sprinkled with plants, but it has distinctive characteristics. The principal rocks should be native to your locality and blended with natural plants.

A large rock can be set in front of a tall board fence to break the monotony of the design. You can add ground cover around to accent the rock.

Sometimes you'll run across a large rock in building your fence that can be integrated into the fence's design. Go over or around the rock rather than remove it as long as your fence remains within your property line.

## MAN-MADE DECORATIONS

A fence lends itself to many decorative possibilities, especially when it serves as the wall of an

Fig. 14-22. A simple bed of ground cover accents a well-built fence.

Fig. 14-23. Rocks are an easy-to-find landscape element (photo by Val Ramos).

Fig. 14-24. Rocks can be used to build a short retaining wall for your fence (photo by Val Ramos).

Fig. 14-25. Footbridge (photo by Val Ramos).

Fig. 14-26. Accent can be added with man-made designs or living plants (photo by Val Ramos).

outdoor room. The decoration adds color, interest, and makes the fence seem more like a real wall, extending the size and function of the home. Many man-made decorations can be used in beautifying your fence (Fig. 14-26).

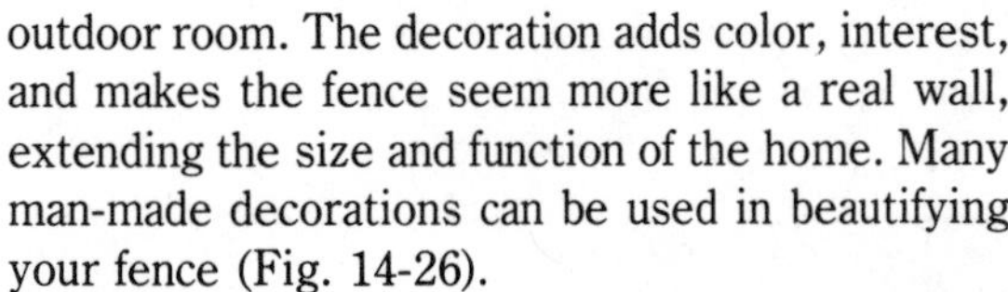

There are some real differences between decorating indoor and outdoor areas. A picture that is just the right size for a wall in your home may look too small on a 40-foot fence. You normally sit farther away from a fence than you do an indoor wall, so your outdoor decorations should be larger.

Another consideration is weathering. You should select decorative material that will take extremes of sun, wind, rain, and temperature change well. It doesn't have to remain unweathered. The material need only be predictable and beautiful in its discoloration. Wood, copper, brass, bronze, and brick become more beautiful as they weather.

The materials available for decorating fences and walls are limitless. They can be of wood, metal, plastic, concrete, tile, stone, clay, or other materials. Some unique decorations used on fences and walls include old farm implements, scrap metals, glass floats, clay tiles, used brick, plywood scraps, wire, cans, pottery, cast blocks, and plastics. Your imagination is your only limitation.

## LIGHTING

One of the most dramatic decorations you can add to your fence and yard is *lighting* (Figs. 14-27 and 14-28). You can use your fence as the backdrop or screen for many shadows and designs by running underground wires and setting spotlights. You can accent the wood or masonry texture, silhouette plants or decorations, spotlight a fountain, or even add color lighting for special effects.

Electric wiring for outside lighting must be weatherproof in accordance with the National Electrical Code and local regulatory agencies.

Incandescent lamps or fixtures are simple and inexpensive for outside the home. The "gooseneck" fixture, a porcelain reflector fastened to a pipe curved like a gooseneck, is still in use and is mounted to the vertical side of buildings or poles.

New installations use a floodlight holder for incandescent lamps with built-in reflectors. Some types completely shield the lamp, permitting the use of indoor lamps. Others shield only the lamp base, and outdoor or weatherproof lamps must be used. Although not as efficient as other types of higher wattage lamps, incandescent lamps are used where the lamps are turned off and on frequently or where color rendition is important.

Tungsten-halogen incandescent lamps have a longer life and are used in larger wattage floodlights. Tungsten-halogen is normally a tubular lamp with electric contacts at each end, although some are available in reflector types with regular screw bases.

Fig. 14-27. Floodlights help accent landscaping (photo by Val Ramos).

Fluorescent lamps can be used for outdoor lighting provided that a weatherproof fixture is used, the lamps are enclosed with a transparent cover for temperatures below 50 degrees, and that special ballasts or fixtures are used for operation at below freezing temperatures. A fluorescent lamp's light output efficiency at indoor temperatures is normally two to three times that of an incandescent. The efficiency is only slightly more than incandescent lamps for outdoor temperatures of freezing or below.

Torches burning kerosene or similar fuels are decorative and portable for occasional outdoor use in patios and gardens. For frequent use or unattended operation, camping lanterns are preferred because of convenience and safety in operation. Open torches should be kept remote from combustible materials.

## HIRING A LANDSCAPER

You may decide to have some or all of the landscaping done for you by professionals. You may design it yourself and have a landscape contractor do the work, or you may have it drawn up by a landscape architect or designer and let him subcontract the job to a landscaper.

The cost of full landscaping is usually figured at

Fig. 14-28. Lamp post offer both decoration and outdoor lighting (photo by Val Ramos).

about 5 percent of the home's value. A $75,000 home will probably need about $7,500 in landscaping to bring it up to the quality of the home. This figure may be on the high side depending on the size of the lot, whether the construction of a fence or masonry walls is included, and what outdoor structures are planned.

### Investigate the Contractor

Make sure the firm that will be landscaping your property is reputable and has experience. Ask for references, both client and business. Make sure the contractor is bonded and has adequate liability insurance in case your property is damaged or any workman is hurt on the job within your property.

### Get It in Writing

Know what you're getting. A reputable landscape contractor, designer, or architect will have detailed plot drawings, artist renditions, and a list of plants, shrubs, and trees that will be installed. Make sure you have in the contract when work will begin, when it will be completed, what happens if it isn't completed on time (forfeiture of partial funds), how it will be paid for and who has final say-so. Depending on the complexity of the job and total price, you may want a lawyer to look over the contract. Some contracts are simple forms that can be understood by many laymen.

### Follow the Job

While no contractor likes a "sidewalk supervisor," most will work more conscientiously if they know you're nearby. Also, they may have a question that you can answer which will help them do the job faster or more to your liking.

## Appendix A

# Grading Dimension Lumber and Boards

THIS APPENDIX WILL ASSIST BUYERS AND users in properly specifying and identifying the grades of western softwood dimension lumber and boards to best suit their needs. The material is from *Western Wood Product Species Book*, Vol. 1: *Dimension Lumber* and Vol. 2: *Selects-Finish/ Commons-Boards*, courtesy of Western Wood Products Association (WWPA), Yeon Building, Portland, OR 97204.

Western softwood species commonly manufactured into dimension lumber include western hemlock, Engelmann spruce, larch, western cedars, and all pines and firs. Many of these species are grown, harvested, manufactured, and marketed together. They have similar performance properties that make them interchangeable in use, grading, and grade marking. Douglas fir and larch are grouped together as "Douglas fir-larch." Western hemlock combines with true firs as "hem-fir." The "white woods" include Engelmann Spruce, all true firs, hemlocks, and pines. "Ponderosa pine" is an individual species.

## SPECIFICATIONS

Dimension lumber is surfaced lumber of nominal thickness from 2 to 4 inches. It is used for structural support and framing including studs, joists, and rafters.

National grading rules classify dimension lumber in three width categories and four use categories. *Structural Light Framing* and *Light Framing* are 2 to 4 inches wide. *Studs* are 2 to 6 inches wide. *Structural Joists and Planks* are 5 inches and wider.

The categories of Structural Light Framing and Structural Joists and Planks each contain four grades, indicating a range of allowable characteristics and manufacturing imperfections affecting strength, stiffness, and appearance.

Select Structural is the highest grade in Structural Light Framing and Structural Joists and Planks. It indicates a piece recommended where good appearance is required along with strength and stiffness.

The No. 1 grade is recommended where good appearance is desired but is secondary to strength and stiffness. The No. 2 grade is recommended for most general construction uses. The No. 3 grade is appropriate for general construction where high strength is generally not a factor.

The Light Framing category contains three grades indicating a range of allowable characteristics and manufacturing imperfections that affect strength, stiffness, and appearance.

Construction is the highest grade in Light Framing. This indicates a piece widely used for general framing, with a good appearance but graded primarily for strength and serviceability. Some pieces in this grade would be No. 1 or better in Structural Light Framing.

Standard grade is customarily used for the same purpose or with construction grade, providing good strength and excellent serviceability.

Utility grade is recommended where economies are desired for studding, blocking, plates, and bracing.

Stud grade is a separate grade. Pieces are suitable for all stud uses including load-bearing walls. Restrictions on crook, wane, and edge knots make this one of the most popular grades for wall construction. Lengths, however, are limited to 10 feet.

Economy grades are also available in all three categories of Structural Light Framing, Light Framing, and Structural Joists and Planks.

## GRADE STAMP

The Western Wood Products Association grade stamp contains five elements identifying the manufacturer, grade, species, moisture content, and certification (Figs. A-1 and A-2).

**Manufacturer.** The originating mill is identified by an assigned number or by the firm's name or brand.

**Grade.** The grade is shown by the grade name or its abbreviation. Dimension grade names include: CONST (Construction), STAND (Standard), UTIL (Utility), STUD (Stud), SEL STR (Select Structural), 1 (No. 1), 2 (No. 2), and 3 (No. 3).

**Species Mark.** Species or species grouping is indicated by an appropriate symbol.

**Moisture Content.** Moisture content at the time of surfacing is shown by appropriate abbreviation: S-GRN (Surfaced Green, standard size unseasoned lumber with moisture content of 20 percent or more); S-DRY (Surfaced Dry, Standard size lumber dried to moisture content of 19 percent or less); MC 15 (Moisture Content 15 percent, Standard size lumber dried to a specific moisture content of 15 percent or less).

**Certification.** A piece bearing this mark has been graded under supervision of Western Wood Products Association.

## CHARACTERISTICS

Grades are determined primarily by the natural characteristics of the log that appear in a given piece of lumber and have an effect upon its strength, stiffness, and appearance. Manufacturing imperfections, no matter what the cause, also affect the grade.

The grade is calculated on a complex formula

12 STAND
& BTR
S-DRY
HEM FIR

Fig. A-1. Typical grade stamp (courtesy Western Wood Products Association).

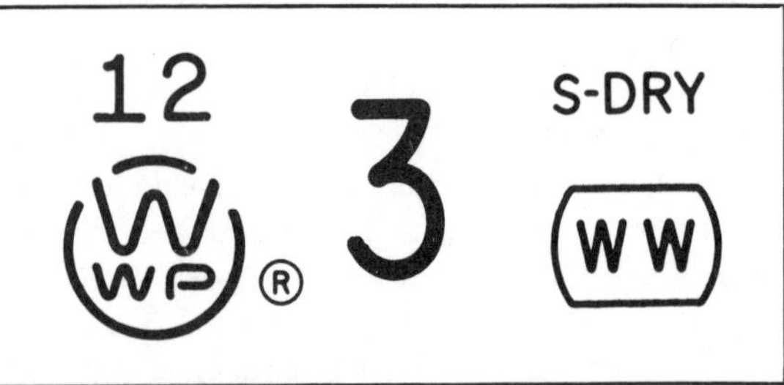


Fig. A-2. Grade stamp for Structural Light Framing lumber (courtesy Western Wood Products Association).

that considers type, size, closeness, frequency, and location of all characteristics and imperfections within the piece. It is the responsibility of the grader to judge visually the total effect of the various combinations according to limitations set forth in the grading rules for each grade and species.

*Knots* are the most frequently encountered characteristic. Knot terms include: round, sound, encased, intergrown, spike, tight, and watertight.

*Wane* is the presence of bark or lack of wood on the edge or corner of a piece of lumber.

*Shake* is a lengthwise separation of the wood that usually occurs between or through the annual growth rings.

*White speck* and *honeycomb* are caused by a fungus in the living tree. White speck is small white pits or spots. Honeycomb is similar, but the pits are deeper or larger. Neither is subject to further decay unless used under wet conditions.

*Decay* is a disintegration of the wood substance due to action of wood-destroying fungi. It may also be called dote, rot, or unsound wood.

*Checks* are separations of the wood fibers. They normally occur across or through the annual growth rings and usually as a result of seasoning.

*Splits* are similar to checks except the separations of the wood fibers extend completely through a piece, usually at the ends.

*Bow* is a deviation from a flat plane of the wide face of a piece of lumber from end to end.

*Crook* is a deviation from a flat plane of the narrow quality, with one hole per lineal foot.

LIGHT FRAMING (DF-L, HEM-FIR, PP, WW)

*Construction*—Sound, firm, encased, and pith knots are tight and limited to no larger than 1½ inches. Unsound or loose knots or holes are limited to 1 inch, one per 3 lineal feet.

*Standard*—Knots are not restricted as to quality up to 2 inches anywhere on the wide face. Holes are limited to 1¼ inches, one per 2 lineal feet.

*Utility*—Knots are not restricted to quality up to 2½ inches anywhere on the wide face. Holes are limited up to 1½ inches, one per lineal foot.

*Stud*—Knots are not restricted as to quality, but they must be well-spaced. Sizes are up to what is allowed in Utility grade. Lengths are limited to a maximum of 10 feet.

STRUCTURAL JOISTS & PLANKS (DF-L, HEM-FIR, PP)

*Select Structural*—Knots are limited to sound, firm, encased, and pith knots, if tight and well-spaced, with one unsound or loose knot or hole per 4 lineal feet. Center line knots range from maximums of 1½ inches on 5-inch widths to 3¼-inch-on-14-inch widths. Edge knots range from maximums of 1-inch-on-4-inch widths to 2⅜-inches-on-14-inch widths. Unsound or loose knots or holes range from maximums of ⅞-inches-on-5-inch face of a piece of lumber from end to end.

*Twist* is a deviation from the flat planes of all four faces by a spiraling or torsional action. It is usually the result of seasoning.

*Cup* is a deviation from a flat plane, edge to edge.

*Manufacturing imperfections* include chipped, torn, raised, or loosened grain, skips in surfacing, undersize, mismatch, wavy dressing and machine-caused burns, chips, bite, or knife marks.

*Other characteristics* include burl, compression wood, pitch, slope of grain, pitch streak, pith, pocket, sapwood, and stain.

## DIMENSION LUMBER GRADES

STRUCTURAL LIGHT FRAMING (DF-L, HEM-FIR, PP)

*Select Structural*—Sound, firm, encased and pith knots are limited up to ⅞ inch and are tight and well-spaced. Unsound or loose knots or holes are limited up to ¾ inch, one per 4 lineal feet.

*No. 1*—Knots must be of the same type as in the Select Structural grade, up to 1½ inch. Unsound or loose knots or holes are limited up to 1 inch, one per 3 lineal feet.

*No. 2*—Well-spaced knots of any quality are allowable up to 2 inches, with one hole per 2 lineal feet.

*No. 3*—Knots can be up to 2½ inches of any widths to 1¼-inches-on-14-inch widths, one per 4 lineal feet.

*No. 1*—Knots must be of the same type as in

**Table A-1. Design Values/WWPA Standard Grading Rules (courtesy Western Wood Products Association).**

**STRUCTURAL JOISTS and PLANKS and APPEARANCE—**
**2" to 4" Thick, 5" and Wider**
**Design Values in Pounds Per Square Inch***

**Grades Described in Sections 62.00 and 50.00. Also Stress Rated Boards. See Section 30.60 WWPA Grading Rules.**

| Species or Group | Grade | Extreme Fiber Stress in Bending "Fb" | | Tension Parallel to Grain "Ft"** | Horizontal Shear "Fv" | Compression | | Modulus of Elasticity "E" |
|---|---|---|---|---|---|---|---|---|
| | | Single | Repetitive | | | Perpendicular "Fc ⊥" | Parallel to Grain "Fc" | |
| DOUGLAS FIR-LARCH | Select Structural† | 1800 | 2050 | 1200 | 95 | 385 | 1400 | 1,800,000 |
| | No. 1†/Appearance | 1500 | 1750 | 1000 | 95 | 385 | 1250/1500 | 1,800,000 |
| | No. 2† | 1250 | 1450 | 650 | 95 | 385 | 1050 | 1,700,000 |
| | No. 3/Stud | 725 | 850 | 375 | 95 | 385 | 675 | 1,500,000 |
| DOUGLAS FIR SOUTH | Select Structural | 1700 | 1950 | 1150 | 90 | 335 | 1250 | 1,400,000 |
| | No. 1/Appearance | 1450 | 1650 | 975 | 90 | 335 | 1150/1350 | 1,400,000 |
| | No. 2 | 1200 | 1350 | 625 | 90 | 335 | 950 | 1,300,000 |
| | No. 3/Stud | 700 | 800 | 350 | 90 | 335 | 600 | 1,100,000 |
| HEM-FIR | Select Structural | 1400 | 1650 | 950 | 75 | 245 | 1150 | 1,500,000 |
| | No. 1/Appearance | 1200 | 1400 | 800 | 75 | 245 | 1050/1250 | 1,500,000 |
| | No. 2 | 1000 | 1150 | 525 | 75 | 245 | 875 | 1,400,000 |
| | No. 3/Stud | 575 | 675 | 300 | 75 | 245 | 550 | 1,200,000 |
| MOUNTAIN HEMLOCK | Select Structural | 1500 | 1700 | 1000 | 95 | 370 | 1100 | 1,300,000 |
| | No. 1/Appearance | 1250 | 1450 | 850 | 95 | 370 | 1000/1200 | 1,300,000 |
| | No. 2 | 1050 | 1200 | 550 | 95 | 370 | 825 | 1,100,000 |
| | No. 3/Stud | 625 | 700 | 325 | 95 | 370 | 525 | 1,000,000 |
| MOUNTAIN HEMLOCK-HEM-FIR | Select Structural | 1400 | 1650 | 950 | 75 | 245 | 1100 | 1,300,000 |
| | No. 1/Appearance | 1200 | 1400 | 800 | 75 | 245 | 1000/1200 | 1,300,000 |
| | No. 2 | 1000 | 1150 | 525 | 75 | 245 | 825 | 1,100,000 |
| | No. 3/Stud | 575 | 675 | 300 | 75 | 245 | 525 | 1,000,000 |
| WESTERN HEMLOCK | Select Structural | 1550 | 1800 | 1050 | 90 | 280 | 1300 | 1,600,000 |
| | No. 1/Appearance | 1350 | 1550 | 900 | 90 | 280 | 1150/1350 | 1,600,000 |
| | No. 2 | 1100 | 1250 | 575 | 90 | 280 | 975 | 1,400,000 |
| | No. 3/Stud | 650 | 750 | 325 | 90 | 280 | 625 | 1,300,000 |
| ENGELMANN SPRUCE-ALPINE FIR (Engelmann Spruce-Lodgepole Pine) | Select Structural | 1200 | 1350 | 775 | 70 | 195 | 850 | 1,300,000 |
| | No. 1/Appearance | 1000 | 1150 | 675 | 70 | 195 | 750/900 | 1,300,000 |
| | No. 2 | 825 | 950 | 425 | 70 | 195 | 625 | 1,100,000 |
| | No. 3/Stud | 475 | 550 | 250 | 70 | 195 | 400 | 1,000,000 |
| LODGEPOLE PINE | Select Structural | 1300 | 1500 | 875 | 70 | 250 | 1000 | 1,300,000 |
| | No. 1/Appearance | 1100 | 1300 | 750 | 70 | 250 | 900/1050 | 1,300,000 |
| | No. 2 | 925 | 1050 | 475 | 70 | 250 | 750 | 1,200,000 |
| | No. 3/Stud | 525 | 625 | 275 | 70 | 250 | 475 | 1,000,000 |
| PONDEROSA PINE-SUGAR PINE (Ponderosa Pine-Lodgepole Pine) | Select Structural | 1200 | 1400 | 825 | 70 | 235 | 950 | 1,200,000 |
| | No. 1/Appearance | 1050 | 1200 | 700 | 70 | 235 | 850/1000 | 1,200,000 |
| | No. 2 | 850 | 975 | 450 | 70 | 235 | 700 | 1,100,000 |
| | No. 3/Stud | 500 | 575 | 250 | 70 | 235 | 450 | 1,000,000 |
| IDAHO WHITE PINE | Select Structural | 1150 | 1300 | 775 | 70 | 190 | 950 | 1,400,000 |
| | No. 1/Appearance | 975 | 1100 | 650 | 70 | 190 | 875/1050 | 1,400,000 |
| | No. 2 | 800 | 925 | 425 | 70 | 190 | 725 | 1,300,000 |
| | No. 3/Stud | 475 | 550 | 250 | 70 | 190 | 450 | 1,200,000 |
| WESTERN CEDARS | Select Structural | 1300 | 1500 | 875 | 75 | 265 | 1050 | 1,100,000 |
| | No. 1/Appearance | 1100 | 1300 | 750 | 75 | 265 | 950/1100 | 1,100,000 |
| | No. 2 | 925 | 1050 | 475 | 75 | 265 | 800 | 1,000,000 |
| | No. 3/Stud | 525 | 625 | 275 | 75 | 265 | 500 | 900,000 |
| WHITE WOODS (Western Woods) | Select Structural | 1150 | 1300 | 775 | 70 | 190 | 850 | 1,100,000 |
| | No. 1/Appearance | 975 | 1100 | 650 | 70 | 190 | 750/900 | 1,100,000 |
| | No. 2 | 800 | 925 | 425 | 70 | 190 | 625 | 1,000,000 |
| | No. 3/Stud | 475 | 550 | 250 | 70 | 190 | 400 | 900,000 |

*These design values were calculated in accordance with ASTM standards. For information about use of these values, see Sections 100.00 through 170.00 in WWPA Grading Rules.

**Tabulated values apply to 5" and 6" widths. For 8" width, use 90% of tabulated tension parallel to grain value for Select Structural and 80% for all other grades. For 10" and wider widths, use 80% of tabulated tension parallel to grain value for Select Structural and 60% for all other grades.

†For Dense values, see Table 6 in the WWPA Grading Rules.

**BEAMS and STRINGERS—5" and Thicker**
**Width More Than 2" Greater Than Thickness**
**Design Values in Pounds Per Square Inch**

**Grades Described in Section 70.00 WWPA Grading Rules**

| Species or Group | Grade | Extreme Fiber Stress in Bending "Fb" | Tension Parallel to Grain "Ft" | Horizontal Shear "Fv" | Compression | | Modulus of Elasticity "E" |
|---|---|---|---|---|---|---|---|
| | | Single Members | | | Perpendicular "Fc ⊥" | Parallel to Grain "Fc" | |
| DOUGLAS FIR-LARCH | Select Structural | 1600 | 1050 | 85 | 385 | 1100 | 1,600,000 |
| | No. 1† | 1350 | 900 | 85 | 385 | 925 | 1,600,000 |
| DOUGLAS FIR SOUTH | Select Structural | 1550 | 1050 | 85 | 335 | 1000 | 1,200,000 |
| | No. 1 | 1300 | 850 | 85 | 335 | 850 | 1,200,000 |
| HEM-FIR | Select Structural | 1250 | 850 | 70 | 245 | 925 | 1,300,000 |
| | No. 1 | 1050 | 725 | 70 | 245 | 775 | 1,300,000 |
| MOUNTAIN HEMLOCK | Select Structural | 1350 | 900 | 90 | 370 | 875 | 1,100,000 |
| | No. 1 | 1100 | 750 | 90 | 370 | 750 | 1,100,000 |
| MOUNTAIN HEMLOCK—HEM-FIR | Select Structural | 1250 | 850 | 70 | 245 | 875 | 1,100,000 |
| | No. 1 | 1050 | 725 | 70 | 245 | 750 | 1,100,000 |
| WESTERN HEMLOCK | Select Structural | 1400 | 950 | 85 | 280 | 1000 | 1,400,000 |
| | No. 1 | 1150 | 775 | 85 | 280 | 850 | 1,400,000 |
| ENGELMANN SPRUCE—ALPINE FIR (Engelmann Spruce-Lodgepole Pine) | Select Structural | 1050 | 700 | 65 | 195 | 675 | 1,100,000 |
| | No. 1 | 875 | 600 | 65 | 195 | 550 | 1,100,000 |
| LODGEPOLE PINE | Select Structural | 1150 | 775 | 65 | 250 | 800 | 1,100,000 |
| | No. 1 | 975 | 650 | 65 | 250 | 675 | 1,100,000 |
| PONDEROSA PINE-SUGAR PINE (Ponderosa Pine-Lodgepole Pine) | Select Structural | 1100 | 725 | 65 | 235 | 750 | 1,100,000 |
| | No. 1 | 925 | 625 | 65 | 235 | 625 | 1,100,000 |
| IDAHO WHITE PINE | Select Structural | 1000 | 700 | 65 | 190 | 775 | 1,300,000 |
| | No. 1 | 850 | 575 | 65 | 190 | 650 | 1,300,000 |
| WESTERN CEDARS | Select Structural | 1150 | 775 | 70 | 265 | 875 | 1,000,000 |
| | No. 1 | 975 | 650 | 70 | 265 | 725 | 1,000,000 |
| WHITE WOODS (Western Woods) | Select Structural | 1000 | 700 | 65 | 190 | 675 | 1,000,000 |
| | No. 1 | 850 | 575 | 65 | 190 | 550 | 1,000,000 |

## Table A-1. Design Values/WWPA Standard Grading Rules (courtesy Western Wood Products Association) (continued from page 216).

**POSTS and TIMBERS—5" x 5" and Larger**
**Width Not More than 2" Greater Than Thickness**
**Design Values in Pounds Per Square Inch***

Grades Described in Section 80.00 WWPA Grading Rules

| Species or Group | Grade | Extreme Fiber Stress in Bending "Fb" | Tension Parallel to Grain "Ft" | Horizontal Shear "Fv" | Compression | | Modulus of Elasticity "E" |
|---|---|---|---|---|---|---|---|
| | | Single Members | | | Perpendicular "Fc ⊥" | Parallel to Grain "Fc" | |
| DOUGLAS FIR-LARCH | Select Structural[1] | 1500 | 1000 | 85 | 385 | 1150 | 1,600,000 |
| | No. 1[1] | 1200 | 825 | 85 | 385 | 1000 | 1,600,000 |
| DOUGLAS FIR SOUTH | Select Structural | 1400 | 950 | 85 | 335 | 1050 | 1,200,000 |
| | No. 1 | 1150 | 775 | 85 | 335 | 925 | 1,200,000 |
| HEM-FIR | Select Structural | 1200 | 800 | 70 | 245 | 975 | 1,300,000 |
| | No. 1 | 950 | 650 | 70 | 245 | 850 | 1,300,000 |
| MOUNTAIN HEMLOCK | Select Structural | 1250 | 825 | 90 | 370 | 925 | 1,100,000 |
| | No. 1 | 1000 | 675 | 90 | 370 | 800 | 1,100,000 |
| MOUNTAIN HEMLOCK—HEM-FIR | Select Structural | 1200 | 800 | 70 | 245 | 925 | 1,100,000 |
| | No. 1 | 950 | 650 | 70 | 245 | 800 | 1,100,000 |
| WESTERN HEMLOCK | Select Structural | 1300 | 875 | 85 | 280 | 1100 | 1,400,000 |
| | No. 1 | 1050 | 700 | 85 | 280 | 950 | 1,400,000 |
| ENGELMANN SPRUCE-ALPINE FIR (Engelmann Spruce-Lodgepole Pine) | Select Structural | 975 | 650 | 65 | 195 | 700 | 1,100,000 |
| | No. 1 | 800 | 525 | 65 | 195 | 625 | 1,100,000 |
| LODGEPOLE PINE | Select Structural | 1100 | 725 | 65 | 250 | 850 | 1,100,000 |
| | No. 1 | 875 | 600 | 65 | 250 | 725 | 1,100,000 |
| PONDEROSA PINE—SUGAR PINE (Ponderosa Pine-Lodgepole Pine) | Select Structural | 1000 | 675 | 65 | 235 | 800 | 1,100,000 |
| | No. 1 | 825 | 550 | 65 | 235 | 700 | 1,100,000 |
| IDAHO WHITE PINE | Select Structural | 950 | 650 | 65 | 190 | 800 | 1,300,000 |
| | No. 1 | 775 | 525 | 65 | 190 | 700 | 1,300,000 |
| WESTERN CEDARS | Select Structural | 1100 | 725 | 70 | 265 | 925 | 1,000,000 |
| | No. 1 | 875 | 600 | 70 | 265 | 800 | 1,000,000 |
| WHITE WOODS (Western Woods) | Select Structural | 950 | 650 | 65 | 190 | 700 | 1,000,000 |
| | No. 1 | 775 | 525 | 65 | 190 | 625 | 1,000,000 |

*These design values were calculated in accordance with ASTM standards. For information about use of these values, see Sections 100.00 through 170.00 in WWPA Grading Rules.

**LIGHT FRAMING and STUDS—2" to 4" Thick, 2" to 4" Wide**
**Design Values in Pounds Per Square Inch***

Grades Described in Sections 40.00 and 41.00. Also Stress Rated Boards. See Section 30.60 WWPA Grading Rules.

| Species or Group | Grade | Extreme Fiber Stress in Bending "Fb" | | Tension Parallel to Grain "Ft" | Horizontal Shear "Fv" | Compression | | Modulus of Elasticity "E" |
|---|---|---|---|---|---|---|---|---|
| | | Single | Repetitive | | | Perpendicular "Fc ⊥" | Parallel to Grain "Fc" | |
| DOUGLAS FIR-LARCH | Construction[1] | 1050 | 1200 | 625 | 95 | 385 | 1150 | 1,500,000 |
| | Standard[1] | 600 | 675 | 350 | 95 | 385 | 925 | 1,500,000 |
| | Utility[1] | 275 | 325 | 175 | 95 | 385 | 600 | 1,500,000 |
| | Stud | 800 | 925 | 475 | 95 | 385 | 600 | 1,500,000 |
| DOUGLAS FIR SOUTH | Construction[1] | 1000 | 1150 | 600 | 90 | 335 | 1000 | 1,100,000 |
| | Standard | 550 | 650 | 325 | 90 | 335 | 850 | 1,100,000 |
| | Utility | 275 | 300 | 150 | 90 | 335 | 550 | 1,100,000 |
| | Stud | 775 | 875 | 450 | 90 | 335 | 550 | 1,100,000 |
| HEM-FIR | Construction[1] | 825 | 975 | 500 | 75 | 245 | 925 | 1,200,000 |
| | Standard | 475 | 550 | 275 | 75 | 245 | 775 | 1,200,000 |
| | Utility | 225 | 250 | 125 | 75 | 245 | 500 | 1,200,000 |
| | Stud | 650 | 725 | 375 | 75 | 245 | 500 | 1,200,000 |
| MOUNTAIN HEMLOCK | Construction[1] | 875 | 1000 | 525 | 95 | 370 | 900 | 1,000,000 |
| | Standard[1] | 500 | 575 | 275 | 95 | 370 | 725 | 1,000,000 |
| | Utility | 225 | 275 | 125 | 95 | 370 | 475 | 1,000,000 |
| | Stud | 675 | 775 | 400 | 95 | 370 | 475 | 1,000,000 |
| MOUNTAIN HEMLOCK-HEM-FIR | Construction | 825 | 975 | 500 | 75 | 245 | 900 | 1,000,000 |
| | Standard | 475 | 550 | 275 | 75 | 245 | 725 | 1,000,000 |
| | Utility | 225 | 250 | 125 | 75 | 245 | 475 | 1,000,000 |
| | Stud | 650 | 725 | 375 | 75 | 245 | 475 | 1,000,000 |
| WESTERN HEMLOCK | Construction[1] | 925 | 1050 | 550 | 90 | 280 | 1050 | 1,300,000 |
| | Standard | 525 | 600 | 300 | 90 | 280 | 850 | 1,300,000 |
| | Utility | 250 | 275 | 150 | 90 | 280 | 550 | 1,300,000 |
| | Stud | 700 | 800 | 425 | 90 | 280 | 550 | 1,300,000 |
| ENGELMANN SPRUCE-ALPINE FIR (Engelmann Spruce-Lodgepole Pine) | Construction[1] | 700 | 800 | 400 | 70 | 195 | 675 | 1,000,000 |
| | Standard[1] | 375 | 450 | 225 | 70 | 195 | 550 | 1,000,000 |
| | Utility[1] | 175 | 200 | 100 | 70 | 195 | 375 | 1,000,000 |
| | Stud | 525 | 600 | 300 | 70 | 195 | 375 | 1,000,000 |
| LODGEPOLE PINE | Construction[1] | 775 | 875 | 450 | 70 | 250 | 800 | 1,000,000 |
| | Standard[1] | 425 | 500 | 250 | 70 | 250 | 675 | 1,000,000 |
| | Utility[1] | 200 | 225 | 125 | 70 | 250 | 425 | 1,000,000 |
| | Stud | 600 | 675 | 350 | 70 | 250 | 425 | 1,000,000 |
| PONDEROSA PINE-SUGAR PINE (Ponderosa Pine-Lodgepole Pine) | Construction[1] | 725 | 825 | 425 | 70 | 235 | 775 | 1,000,000 |
| | Standard[1] | 400 | 450 | 225 | 70 | 235 | 625 | 1,000,000 |
| | Utility[1] | 200 | 225 | 100 | 70 | 235 | 400 | 1,000,000 |
| | Stud | 550 | 625 | 325 | 70 | 235 | 400 | 1,000,000 |
| IDAHO WHITE PINE | Construction[1] | 675 | 775 | 400 | 70 | 190 | 775 | 1,200,000 |
| | Standard[1] | 375 | 425 | 225 | 70 | 190 | 650 | 1,200,000 |
| | Utility[1] | 175 | 200 | 100 | 70 | 190 | 425 | 1,200,000 |
| | Stud | 525 | 600 | 300 | 70 | 190 | 425 | 1,200,000 |
| WESTERN CEDARS | Construction[1] | 775 | 875 | 450 | 75 | 265 | 850 | 900,000 |
| | Standard[1] | 425 | 500 | 250 | 75 | 265 | 700 | 900,000 |
| | Utility[1] | 200 | 225 | 125 | 75 | 265 | 450 | 900,000 |
| | Stud | 600 | 675 | 350 | 75 | 265 | 450 | 900,000 |
| WHITE WOODS (Western Woods) | Construction[1] | 675 | 775 | 400 | 70 | 190 | 675 | 900,000 |
| | Standard[1] | 375 | 425 | 225 | 70 | 190 | 550 | 900,000 |
| | Utility[1] | 175 | 200 | 100 | 70 | 190 | 375 | 900,000 |
| | Stud | 525 | 600 | 300 | 70 | 190 | 375 | 900,000 |

*These design values were calculated in accordance with ASTM standards. For information about use of these values, see Sections 100.00 through 170.00 in WWPA Grading Rules.

[1] Fb, Ft and Fc design values apply only to 4" width of these grades. See also Tables 1a and 1b in the WWPA Grading Rules.

Select Structural grade. They can be slightly larger with one unsound or loose knot or hole permitted per 3 lineal feet.

*No. 2*—Well-spaced knots of any quality are allowable, with one hole from any cause per 2 lineal feet.

*No. 3*—Well-spaced knots of any quality are allowable, with one hole from any cause per lineal foot.

## BOARD LUMBER

Western softwood species commonly manufactured into board lumber include Douglas fir, western larch, ponderosa pine, lodgepole pine, sugar pine, Engelmann spruce, Idaho white pine, western red cedar, incense cedar, western hemlock, and true firs (Table A-1).

Many of these species are grown, harvested, manufactured, and marketed together. Some have similar appearance and performance properties that make them interchangeable in use. This applies to western hemlock and the five true firs that are grouped together as hem-fir. Similar marketing groups include western cedars (incense and western red cedar), and white woods (Engelmann spruce, any true firs, any hemlocks, and any pines).

## GRADE CLASSIFICATIONS

*Select* and *Finish* grades of western region woods are used for many appearance applications. Grading is based on a 1×8-inch by 12 foot piece with the number and extent of characteristics in larger or smaller pieces varying in proportion.

Select grades are determined from the better side or face and separated into three grades: B & BTR., C Select, and D Select. (With Idaho white pine these three grades are called, respectively, Supreme, Choice, and Quality.)

B & Btr. Select grade is the ultimate in appearance. It is the highest quality of Select grade lumber. Many pieces are absolutely clear.

C Select grade is recommended for all finishing uses where fine appearance is essential. Its appearance ranks only slightly less than B & BTR. grade.

D Select grade has many of the fine appearance features of C Select grade. It is suitable where the needs for finishing are less exacting.

Finish grades are determined from the better side or face and from both edges on pieces 5 inches and narrower, and from the better side or face and edge on pieces 6 inches and wider. Finish grades are Superior, Prime, and E.

Superior is the highest grade of Finish lumber. Many pieces are absolutely clear.

Prime grade exhibits a fine appearance, although it is less restrictive than Superior grade.

E Finish can be ordered where pieces can be crosscut or ripped to obtain cuttings of Prime or better quality.

There are five grades of boards referred to as Commons and five Alternate Board Grades. Grade levels of boards referred to as Commons are not identical to those of Alternate Board Grades. Overlapping levels provide customers with a broader choice of grade variations.

Common board grades, as determined from the better face, are 1 Common, 2 Common, 3 Common, 4 Common, and 5 Common. The usual practice is to combine 1 Common with 2 Common and market the mixture as 2 & Better Common. Idaho white pine grades are called respectively Colonial, Sterling, Standard, Utility, and Industrial.

The No. 1 Common grade is not usually carried in stock in large quantities, but may be ordered when the ultimate in fine appearance of knotty material is required.

The No. 2 Common grade is intended primarily for use in paneling, shelving, and other uses calling for knotty lumber with fine appearance.

The No. 3 Common grade is widely used for shelving, paneling, and siding as well as fences, boxes, crating, sheathing, and industrial applications.

The No. 4 Common grade is more widely used than any other grade for general construction such as subfloors, roof and wall sheathing, concrete forms, low-cost fencing, crating, etc.

The No. 5 Common grade is intended for use in economical construction where appearance and strength are not basic requirements.

*Alternate Board Grades,* determined from bet-

**Table A-2. Grade Selector Charts (courtesy Western Wood Products Association).**

| APPEARANCE GRADES | | |
|---|---|---|
| | **SELECTS** | B & BETTER (IWP—SUPREME)<br>C SELECT (IWP—CHOICE)<br>D SELECT (IWP—QUALITY) |
| | **FINISH** | SUPERIOR<br>PRIME<br>E |
| | **PANELING** | CLEAR (ANY SELECT OR FINISH GRADE)<br>NO. 2 COMMON SELECTED FOR KNOTTY PANELING<br>NO. 3 COMMON SELECTED FOR KNOTTY PANELING |
| | **BEVEL OR BUNGALOW SIDING** | SUPERIOR<br>PRIME<br>(Refer to WWPA "Wood Siding" Catalog for other siding grades) |
| **GENERAL PURPOSE BOARDS** | | NO. 1 COMMON (IWP—COLONIAL)<br>NO. 2 COMMON (IWP—STERLING)<br>NO. 3 COMMON (IWP—STANDARD)<br>NO. 4 COMMON (IWP—UTILITY)<br>NO. 5 COMMON (IWP—INDUSTRIAL) |
| | | **ALTERNATE BOARD GRADES**<br>SELECT MERCHANTABLE<br>CONSTRUCTION<br>STANDARD<br>UTILITY<br>ECONOMY |

**SPECIFICATION CHECK LIST**

- ☐ Grades listed in order of quality.
- ☐ Include all species suited to project.
- ☐ Specify lowest grade that will satisfy job requirement.
- ☐ Specify surface texture desired.
- ☐ Specify moisture content suited to project.
- ☐ Specify (WW) grade stamp. For finish and exposed pieces, specify stamp on back or ends.
- ☐ See publication A-2 "Lumber Specification Information."

**Western Red Cedar**

| | |
|---|---|
| FINISH PANELING AND CEILING | CLEAR HEART<br>A<br>B |
| BEVEL SIDING | CLEAR — V.G. HEART<br>A — BEVEL SIDING<br>B — BEVEL SIDING<br>C — BEVEL SIDING |

## Dimension/Stress-Rated Framing Lumber 2"x2" Through 4"x16"

| | | |
|---|---|---|
| **LIGHT FRAMING**<br>2x2 Through 4x4 | CONSTRUCTION<br>STANDARD<br>UTILITY | This category for use where high strength values are **NOT** required; such as studs, plates, sills, cripples, blocking, etc. |
| **STUDS**<br>2x2 Through 4x6<br>10' and Shorter | STUD | An optional all-purpose grade limited to 10 feet and shorter. Characteristics affecting strength and stiffness values are limited so that the "Stud" grade is suitable for all stud uses, including load bearing walls. |
| **STRUCTURAL LIGHT FRAMING**<br>2x2 Through 4x4 | SELECT STRUCTURAL<br>NO. 1<br>NO. 2<br>NO. 3 | These grades are designed to fit those engineering applications where higher bending strength ratios are needed in light framing sizes. Typical uses would be for trusses, concrete pier wall forms, etc. |
| **STRUCTURAL JOISTS & PLANKS**<br>2x5 Through 4x16 | SELECT STRUCTURAL<br>NO. 1<br>NO. 2<br>NO. 3 | These grades are designed especially to fit in engineering applications for lumber five inches and wider, such as joists, rafters and general framing uses. |

## Timbers 5" and thicker

| | | | |
|---|---|---|---|
| **BEAMS & STRINGERS**<br>5" and thicker<br>Width more than 2" greater than thickness | SELECT STRUCTURAL<br>NO. 1<br>NO. 2**<br>NO. 3** | **POSTS & TIMBERS**<br>5" x 5" and larger<br>Width not more than 2" greater than thickness | SELECT STRUCTURAL<br>NO. 1<br>NO. 2**<br>NO. 3** |

**Design values are not assigned.

## Decking 2x4 Through 4x12

(See "Standard Patterns" for Shape and Sizes).
See page 110 of the WWPA Grade Rules for design values.

| Selected Decking | Commercial Decking |
|---|---|

ter face, are: Select Merchantable, Construction, Standard, Utility, and Economy.

Select Merchantable grade is intended primarily for use in housing and light construction where it is exposed as paneling, shelving, and where knotty-type lumber with the finest appearance is required.

Construction grade is recommended and widely used for subfloors, roof and wall sheathing, concrete forms, and similar types of construction.

Standard grade is most widely used for general construction purposes where it is seldom left exposed.

Utility grade is judged primarily on serviceability instead of appearance to provide an inexpensive lumber for general construction purposes.

Economy grade is suitable for low grade sheathing, crating, bracing, temporary construction, and similar uses. See Table A-2.

## Appendix B

# Common Wood Preservatives

MATERIAL IN THIS APPENDIX IS FROM *PRESERvative Treatment of Fence Posts and Farm Timbers,* U.S. Department of Agriculture, Farmers Bulletin 2049.

### COAL-TAR CREOSOTES

*Coal-tar creosote,* which is a brownish-black heavy oil that is practically insoluble in water, is the most widely used preservative in agriculture and industry. Its advantages are high toxicity against decay fungi and insects; permanence under a wide variety of conditions, including use in fresh and salt water; ease of determining the depth of penetration in treated wood; freedom from corrosive action on metals and wood; and comparatively low cost when bought in large quantities. The disadvantages of creosote are its odor, which is often objectionable in buildings and around foodstuffs; its oily nature and the tendency of wood treated with it to bleed, which makes the treated wood objectionable to handle and difficult to paint over; its irritating effect on the skin of some workers, particularly those of light complexion; and its complicated and variable chemical composition.

The lighter, more easily evaporated oils of creosote present in treated wood until it has been in use for some time may permit the treated wood to catch fire more easily than untreated wood. After these light oils have evaporated from the wood or have been removed by weathering, the wood may actually be less likely to catch fire than untreated wood.

Coal-tar creosotes vary considerably in quality. Satisfactory results may be obtained from any good grade, provided enough is put into the wood and the wood is well-penetrated. Creosotes containing a high percentage of oils that boil at a comparatively low temperature are not so suitable for uses around the home and farm as those that contain less of these oils. A considerable part—perhaps up to 20 percent—may evaporate during treatment. This loss of oil may be largely offset, however, by the lower prices for low-boiling creosotes. The increase in price for the higher boiling creosotes will generally not be more than 25 to 35 percent. When considerable creosote is needed, it can be bought to meet specifications. Quality specifications for coal-tar creosote have been set up by the U.S. government and the American Wood Preservers' Association.

### ANTHRACENE OILS (CARBOLINEUMS)

*Carbolineums* (anthrancene oils) are coal-tar products that are heavier and contain less low-boiling (easily evaporated) material than ordinary coal-tar creosote. They usually cost more, but this is offset to some degree by the absence of the low-boiling materials that cause some loss through evaporation. Carbolineums are usually sold under trade names. Their properties and effectiveness as preservatives are similar to those of creosote.

### WOOD-TAR CREOSOTES

*Wood-tar creosotes,* made from wood tar rather than coal tar, are not produced in large quantities. They have not been so widely used. When of good quality and thoroughly applied, they have good wood-preserving properties. Service tests show them to be less effective than coal-tar creosote.

### COAL TAR

*Coal tar* is not a good preservative for home or farm use. It is not as poisonous to decay fungi as creosote and does not penetrate wood well.

### WATER-GAS TAR AND WATER-GAS-TAR CREOSOTE

*Water-gas tar* a product coming from the petroleum oils used in making water gas, is an inexpensive preservative, although it is not readily obtainable. It should be reasonably free of water; otherwise, foaming can be expected during heating. The tar should also not be too viscous to penetrate the wood. Water-gas-tar creosote is also a good preservative, although it is not as poisonous to fungi as coal-tar creosote. It is effective if the wood is well-penetrated and retains good quantities of the preservative.

### CREOSOTE MIXTURES

Coal-tar creosotes are usually so poisonous to decay fungi that they can be diluted with less effective oils and still give good protection to wood. In cases where the cost of straight creosote places it out of reach, it may be mixed with an equal amount of cheaper oils. Many treatments have been made with such mixtures. For reasons of cost and supply, the heavier petroleum oils have been employed by large users of treated wood such as the railroads. Creosote solutions containing the heavier petroleum oils have had a good record of performance with crossties. Creosote solutions made with domestic fuel oil have been used in the cold-soaking process because of their low viscosity. Information is lacking, however, on the effectiveness of these solutions with lighter domestic fuel oils. You should not anticipate the service that you can expect from wood treated with straight creosote.

The heavier oils and the coal tars, water-gas tar, and water-gas-tar creosote, which are sometimes mixed with creosote, may not penetrate wood so readily as straight creosote. They can be recommended only for woods that are penetrated readily and for treatments involving heating, which are carefully managed to insure good penetration.

Tar mixtures, when applied as treatments, leave the wood with a black coating that makes it objectionable to handle in post form. This condition is not considered a handicap in items like railroad crossties.

Creosote-petroleum solutions are naturally less poisonous to fungi than straight creosote, and in most cases they are even less poisonous than the proportion of creosote in the mixture would indicate. Frequently, during periods of creosote shortage, petroleum oils added to creosote have been fortified with pentachlorophenol or copper naphthenate to maintain the mixture's effectiveness. Some mixtures of creosote and petroleum oil cause a sludge that interferes with penetrating and may block pipelines and pumping systems. This sludge should be allowed to settle after thoroughly stirring the mixture. It should then be removed.

### PENTACHLOROPHENOL

Some years ago the Forest Products Laboratory indicated that the higher chlorinated phenols were very poisonous to wood-destroying fungi. Field tests on stakes and posts started in 1936 indicated one of these chemicals, *pentachlorophenol*, provided good protection against decay and termites. Since 1945 this preservative has come into fairly wide use in the treatment of telephone and power line poles.

The chlorinated phenols were first used in quickly evaporating solvents, such as mineral spirits, for dipping treatments of window sash and millwork where a clean, nonswelling, and paintable treatment was required. Plenty of wood was treated with various oils containing pentachlorophenol based on the early favorable results in post and stake tests. The oils used have ranged from the mineral spirits type to the heavier oils commonly used in commercial creosote-petroleum solutions. Diesel-type oils are often employed in solutions of pentachlorophenol used in the cold-soaking and hot-and-cold-bath processes.

Pentachlorophenol is available in three forms—dry flake, concentrated solution, and ready-to-use solution. When bought dry, it is in the form of dark gray flakes or crystals having a slight odor. When handled in this form, the chemical has a tendency to give off dust. The dust is irritating to the eyes, nose, and throat. Goggles and dust masks are recommended for anyone mixing the solution. Special heating and agitating equipment, along with a knowledge of the solubility and other properties of the solvents used, is ordinarily needed in making solutions from the dry chemical.

If you don't have special mixing equipment, it is generally easier to buy either a ready-to-use solution or a concentrated solution of pentachlorophenol and dilute it with the desired oil. Concentrates are mixed with 2 to 12 or more parts of solvent (by volume) to make a 5-percent solution. Concentrates are either dark or light-colored depending on the use for which they are intended and the strength of the pentachlorophenol in the concentrate. Light-colored concentrates usually contain less preservative than those that are darker. To meet special requirements as to color, paintability, and heating, pentachlorophenol solutions should be selected carefully. The supplier of the preservative should furnish information as to suitable petroleum diluents.

## COPPER NAPHTHENATE

*Copper naphthenate* is supplied either in ready-to-use solutions or in a concentrated solution for mixing with petroleum oils to make effective treating solutions. Copper naphthenate, based on stake tests, provides good protection against decay and termites when thoroughly applied to the wood and when used in petroleum oil solutions containing a copper metal equivalent of at least 0.5 percent. A copper metal equivalent of not less than 1.0 percent is recommended for nonpressure treatment.

## ZINC CHLORIDE

The principal advantages of *zinc chloride* are relative cheapness, uniformity of quality, cleanliness, lack of odor, ease of shipment, and that it isn't a fire hazard. Zinc chloride's chief disadvantage is its tendency to leach out of wood in contact with water or soil. The water added to wood with the preservative adds considerably to its weight and, in order to avoid shrinkage troubles, must be dried out before the wood is used in buildings.

When injected into wood in the usual amounts (1 pound to 1½ pounds per cubic foot), zinc chloride has a slight effect in reducing flammability. A higher retention of 3 pounds of the salt per cubic foot does have a considerable effect in reducing flammability.

Zinc chloride is shipped either in the solid form (fused or granulated) or in concentrated solutions. When the freight haul is not too great, the concentrated solution, usually about 50-percent strength, is shipped in drums or tank cars. The salt is shipped in solid form in airtight drums for long freight hauls. The airtight containers are necessary because solid zinc chloride attracts moisture from the air. For use in treating wood, water solutions of 3 to 20 percent (by weight), depending on the process used, are prepared from the concentrated material.

## CHROMATED ZINC CHLORIDE

*Chromated zinc chloride* is a wood preservative developed by a manufacturer of zinc chloride based on experiments by the Forest Products Laboratory and intended as an improvement over straight zinc chloride. Chromated zinc chloride is usually sold in the granular form containing approximately 18 percent commercial sodium bichromate and 82 percent commercial zinc chloride.

Chromated zinc chloride is claimed to be more resistant to leaching than zinc chloride and to give equal protection against termites and greater protection against decay. Tests on posts do not always support these claims. Chromium salts do not leach readily from wood.

## PROVEN TRADE NAME PRESERVATIVES

Some patented preservatives are available that have been designed and promoted by their manufacturers for effective treating procedures, principally pressure impregnation. Forest Products Laboratory Report R149, Wood Preservatives, describes some of these standardized preservatives. Many preservatives, based on the performance of wood treated with them to date, have qualified as efficient wood preservatives.

## MATERIALS OF LOW PRESERVATIVE VALUE

Crude petroleum, fuel oil, and gas oil have been used in many tests. The results show that petroleum oils used alone do not generally stop decay fungi. They cannot be recommended unless they are mixed at least with an equal quantity of creosote or are fortified with a good oil-soluble preservative such as pentachlorophenol or copper naphthenate.

You cannot prevent decay by applying paint, linseed oil, whitewash, asphalt, water repellents, or similar coatings to fence posts or other timber in contact with the ground. These materials do not penetrate the wood deeply, and as a rule they are not poisonous to wood-rotting fungi. Some people believe that coatings can prevent decay by preventing fungi or moisture from getting into the wood, but no economical coating is known that comes close to doing so. Wood is seldom painted on all sides, so usually you will find moisture and the fungi getting in through an unpainted part. The spores of fungi are commonly present on wood surfaces, or they can get to the wood whenever the painted film cracks or peels off. Tests have shown many times that paint films do not prevent moisture changes; they merely slow them up. It is quite common to see wood decaying beneath a coat of paint.

## Appendix C

# Specification for Galvanized Steel Chain Link Fence Materials

THESE STANDARDS AND SPECIFICATIONS ARE offered by the Chain Link Fence Manufacturers Institute and by the International Fence Industry Association. Copies of ASTM publications are obtainable from the American Society for Testing and Materials, 1916 Race Street, Philadelphia, PA 19103.

### 1. PURPOSE

1.1 The purpose of this specification is to provide a nationally recognized standard of quality for galvanized steel chain link fence fabric.

### 2. SCOPE

2.1 This specification gives the nomenclature, definitions, and general requirements for galvanized steel chain link fence fabric.

### 3. DEFINITIONS

**3.1 Chain Link Fence Fabric.** Chain link fence fabric is a fencing material made from wire helically wound and interwoven so as to provide a continuous mesh without knots or ties, except in the form of knuckling or of twisting the wires' ends to form the selvage of the fabric.

**3.2 Knuckling.** Knuckling is the term used to describe the type of selvage obtained by interlocking adjacent pairs or wire ends and bending the wire ends back into a closed loop.

**3.3 Twisting.** Twisting is the term used to describe the type of selvage obtained by twisting adjacent pairs of wire ends together in a close helix of 1½ machine turns, which is equivalent to three full twists.

### 4. REQUIREMENTS

**4.1 Materials.**

**4.1.1 Base Metal.** The base metal of the fabric shall be a good commercial quality steel wire of the gauges specified in Table C-1. The wire shall withstand the following breaking loads: No. 6 gauge, 2,170 pounds; No. 9 gauge, 1,290 pounds;

and No. 11 gauge, 850 pounds. The break strength of the wire shall be determined in accordance with the requirements of 5.5.1.

**4.1.2 Zinc Coating.** The fabric shall be zinc-coated by the hot-dip process after fabrication, or it shall be fabricated from wire zinc-coated by the electrolytic or hot-dip process. The weight of zinc coating shall be not less than 1.2 ounces per square foot of the actual surface covered when tested in accordance with 5.5.2. The zinc used for the coating shall conform to the grades specified in ASTM Designation B6 Standard Specifications for slab zinc.

**4.2 Fabric Sizes.** The height, size of mesh, and wire diameters of chain link fabric shall be as given in Table C-1. The methods of measurement and tolerances are given in 4.2.1, 4.2.2, and 4.2.3 respectively.

**4.2.1 Height of Fabric.** The height of the fabric shall be the overall dimension from ends of barbs or knuckles. The tolerance on the nominal height shall be plus or minus 1 inch.

**4.2.2 Mesh Sizes.** The size of mesh shall be determined by measuring the minimum clear distance between the wires forming the parallel sides of the mesh, measured in either direction. The tolerance in the size of 1¾- and 2-inch mesh shall be plus or minus ⅛ inch and for 1-inch mesh it is plus or minus 1/16 inch.

**4.2.3 Wire diameter.** The diameter of the coated wire shall be determined as the average of two readings measured to the nearest 0.001 inch taken at right angles to each other on the straight portion of the mesh's parallel sides. The tolerance in the diameter of the coated wire shall be plus or minus 0.005 inch.

**4.3 Selvage.** Fabric 60 inches high and under in 2-inch mesh shall be furnished with knuckling at each selvage. Fabric over 60 inches high in 2-inch mesh shall be furnished with knuckling at one selvage and twisting at the other. All fabric less than 2-inch mesh shall be furnished with knuckling at both selvages. Special selvages may be specified by the purchaser.

**Table C-1. Fabric Sizes.**

| Height of fence fabric (inches) | Size of mesh | Gauge, coated wire | Nominal diameter of coated wire |
|---|---|---|---|
| | Inches | Number | Inch |
| 36, 42, 48, 60, 72, 84, 96, 108, 120, 144 | 2 | 6 | 0.1920 |
| 36, 42, 48, 60, 72, 84, 96, 108, 120, 144 | 2 | 9 | .1483 |
| 36, 42, 48, 60, 72, 84 | 2 | 11 | .1205 |
| 96, 108, 120, 144 | 1¾ | 11 | .1205 |
| 36, 42, 48, 60 | 1 | 13 | .0915 |

**4.4 Workmanship.** The chain link fence fabric shall be made of high-grade materials and with good workmanship. The zinc coating shall be applied in a continuous process and shall not be applied to the fabric in roll form. Excessive roughness, blisters, sal ammoniac spots, bruises, and flaking shall be noted. These and other obvious defects, if present to any considerable extent, may provide a basis for rejection.

## 5. INSPECTION AND TESTING

**5.1 General.** The tests given herein are intended primarily for use as production tests in conjunction with manufacturing processes, inspection methods, and with other tests if needed, according to 5.2, so as to insure the conformity of the chain link fabric with the requirements of this specification.

**5.2 Production Inspection and Testing.** The manufacturer shall make such inspections and tests during the manufacturing process as are needed to maintain the quality of the product so as to be consistently in conformity with this specification. The inspection and tests given herein (see 5.3 and 5.5) shall be made regularly during production for all chain link fabric furnished as being in conformity with this specification.

**5.3 Inspection.** The chain link fabric shall be visually inspected to determine its conformance with the workmanship, design, and dimensional requirements of this standard.

**5.4 Sampling.** One roll from every 50 rolls or fraction thereof shall be selected at random for test purposes, but in no case shall less than three rolls be selected from a shipment. The specimens for test purposes shall consist of individual pieces of wire taken from the outside end of the sample rolls.

**5.5 Test Procedures.**

**5.5.1 Breaking Strength.** The break-strength of the fabric shall be determined in accordance with the method described in ASTM Designated E8 Tension Testing of Metallic Materials, using one specimen from each sample roll. Specimens to establish conformance to this requirement shall constitute individual pickets from a section of hte fence fabric to a sufficient length so as to measure 15-18 inches after straightening. The straightened portion of the specimen shall be inside the jaws of the tensile testing machine, so the actual test is performed on the undeformed section between the jaws. If fracture takes place other than between the grips, the test shall be discarded.

**5.5.2 Weight and Zinc Coating.** The weight of zinc coating on the fabric shall be determined in accordance with the method described in ASTM Designation A90, Weight of Coating on Zinc-Coated (Galvanized) Iron and Steel Articles, using one piece of wire removed from the fabric of each sample roll. The specimen tested may be of any continuous length over 12 inches, but it preferably should be about 24 inches long.

**5.6 Noncompliance.** If any specimen tested fails to meet the requirements specified, two additional specimens shall be taken from the sample roll and tested. Both shall meet the requirements in every respect. Otherwise, the material represented by that sample roll shall be considered as not being in compliance with this standard.

## INDUSTRIAL STEEL SPECIFICATIONS FOR FENCE POSTS, GATES, AND ACCESSORIES

**1. Materials.** Posts, gate frames, braces, rails, stretcher bars, and truss rods shall be of steel. Reinforcing wires shall be of high carbon steel. Gate hinges, post caps, barbed wire supporting arms, stretcher bar bands, and other parts shall be of steel, malleable iron, ductile iron, or similar material, except that ties and clips may be of aluminum (Fig. C-1).

Posts, gate frames, rails, and braces shall conform to the dimensions and weights shown in Table C-2.

**2. Zinc Coating.** All steel and iron parts shall be zinc-coated after fabrication, using zinc grade "E" in accordance with Federal Specification QQ-Z-351.

The weight of the zinc coating per square foot of actual surface area shall average not less than 1.2 ounces. No individual specimen shall show less than 1.0 ounces.

**3. Gates.** Gates shall be swing or sliding as specified, complete with latches, stops, keepers, hinges or rollers, and roller tracks, and when so specified, with provision for three strands of barbed wire above the fabric.

3a. *Gate Frames* shall be constructed of tubular members (round or square) welded at all corners or assembled with fittings. On steel, welds shall be painted with aluminum-based or zinc-based paint. Where corner fittings are used, gates shall have truss rods of ⅜-inch nominal diameter to prevent sag or twist. Gate leaves shall have vertical intermediate bracing as required, spaced so that no members are more than 8 feet apart. Gate leaves 10 feet or more shall have a horizontal brace or one ⅜-inch, diagonal truss rod. When barbed wire top is specified (see 6.2), the end members of the gate frames shall be extended 1 foot above the top horizontal member to which three strands of barbed wire, uniformly spaced, shall be attached by use of bands, clips, or hook bolts. Dimensions and weights of gate frames shall be as shown in Table C-2. Gate filler shall be of the same fabric as specified for the fence and shall be attached securely to the gate frame at intervals of 15 inches.

3b. *Fabric* shall conform to the current CLFMI specification and shall be the same type as used in the fence construction. The fabric shall be attached securely to the gate frame at intervals not exceeding 15 inches.

3c. *Hinges* shall be of adequate strength for the gate and with large bearing surfaces for clamping in position. The hinges shall not twist or turn under the action of the gate. The gate shall be capable of being opened and closed easily by one person.

3d. *Latches, stops, and keepers* shall be

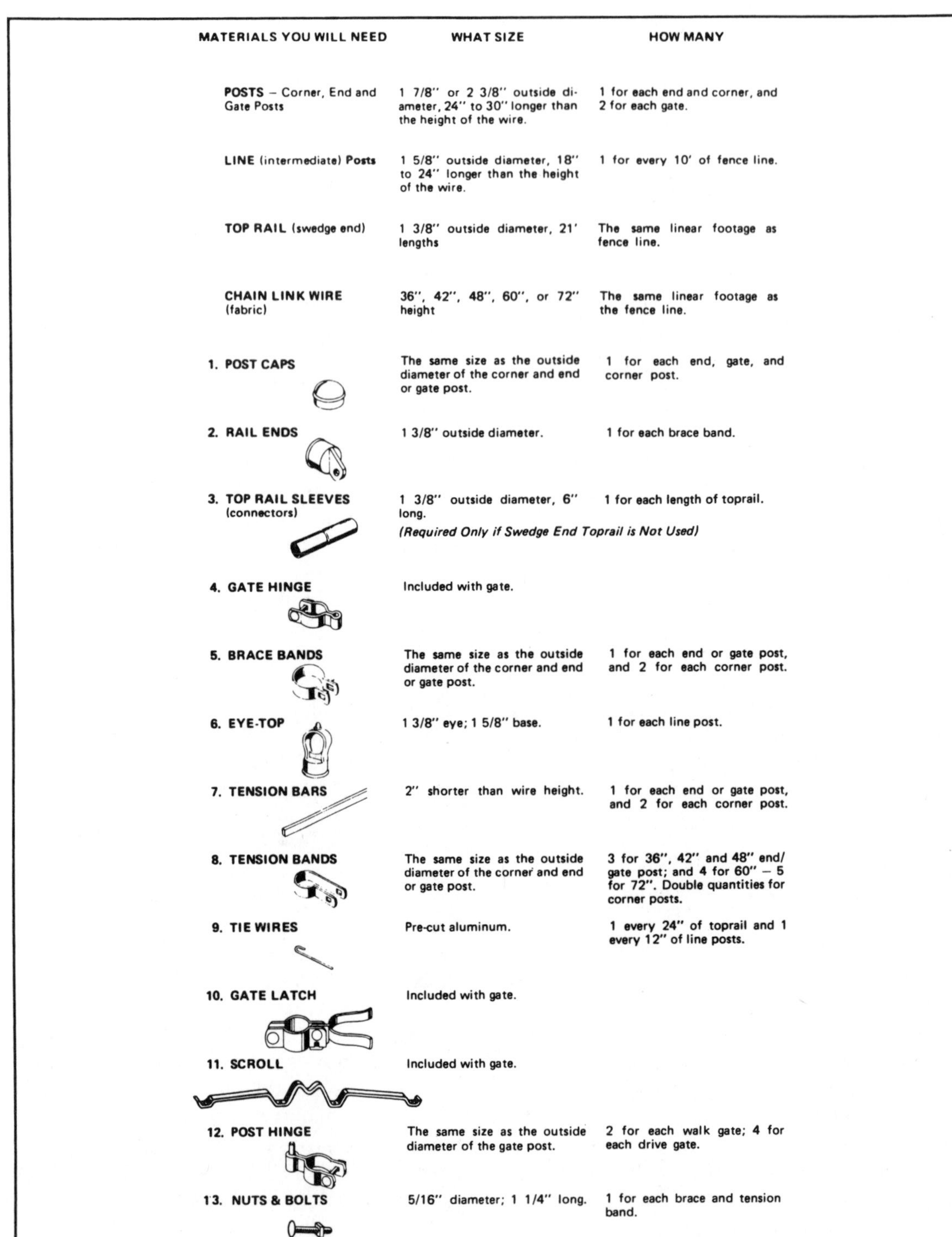

| MATERIALS YOU WILL NEED | WHAT SIZE | HOW MANY |
|---|---|---|
| **POSTS** – Corner, End and Gate Posts | 1 7/8" or 2 3/8" outside diameter, 24" to 30" longer than the height of the wire. | 1 for each end and corner, and 2 for each gate. |
| **LINE** (intermediate) **Posts** | 1 5/8" outside diameter, 18" to 24" longer than the height of the wire. | 1 for every 10' of fence line. |
| **TOP RAIL** (swedge end) | 1 3/8" outside diameter, 21' lengths | The same linear footage as fence line. |
| **CHAIN LINK WIRE** (fabric) | 36", 42", 48", 60", or 72" height | The same linear footage as the fence line. |
| 1. **POST CAPS** | The same size as the outside diameter of the corner and end or gate post. | 1 for each end, gate, and corner post. |
| 2. **RAIL ENDS** | 1 3/8" outside diameter. | 1 for each brace band. |
| 3. **TOP RAIL SLEEVES** (connectors) | 1 3/8" outside diameter, 6" long. *(Required Only if Swedge End Toprail is Not Used)* | 1 for each length of toprail. |
| 4. **GATE HINGE** | Included with gate. | |
| 5. **BRACE BANDS** | The same size as the outside diameter of the corner and end or gate post. | 1 for each end or gate post, and 2 for each corner post. |
| 6. **EYE-TOP** | 1 3/8" eye; 1 5/8" base. | 1 for each line post. |
| 7. **TENSION BARS** | 2" shorter than wire height. | 1 for each end or gate post, and 2 for each corner post. |
| 8. **TENSION BANDS** | The same size as the outside diameter of the corner and end or gate post. | 3 for 36", 42" and 48" end/gate post; and 4 for 60" – 5 for 72". Double quantities for corner posts. |
| 9. **TIE WIRES** | Pre-cut aluminum. | 1 every 24" of toprail and 1 every 12" of line posts. |
| 10. **GATE LATCH** | Included with gate. | |
| 11. **SCROLL** | Included with gate. | |
| 12. **POST HINGE** | The same size as the outside diameter of the gate post. | 2 for each walk gate; 4 for each drive gate. |
| 13. **NUTS & BOLTS** | 5/16" diameter; 1 1/4" long. | 1 for each brace and tension band. |

Fig. C-1. Common chain link fence parts.

**Table C-2. Dimensions and Weights.**

| Use and Section | | Outside Diameter or Dimensions, Nominal | Weight Per Foot, Nominal |
|---|---|---|---|
| End, corner, and pull posts (tubular) for fabric heights: | | Inches | Pounds |
| 6 feet and less: | Round | 2.375 | 3.65 |
| | Square | 2.00 | 3.60 |
| Over 6 feet: | Round | 2.875 | 5.79 |
| | Square | 2.50 | 5.70 |
| Gate posts for nominal width of gate, single, or one leaf of double 6 feet and less: | Round | 2.875 | 5.79 |
| | Square | 2.50 | 5.70 |
| Gate width 13 feet and less: | Round | 4.00 | 9.10 |
| | Square | 3.00 | 9.10 |
| Gate width over 13 feet to 18 feet, incl.: | Round | 6.625 | 18.97 |
| Gate width over 18 feet: | Round | 8.625 | 24.70 |
| Gates: exterior frames for fabric heights: 6 feet and less, and leaf widths not exceeding 8′: | Round | 1.660 | 1.806 |
| | Square | 1.50 | 1.90 |
| Over 6 feet, or gate leafs over 8′ width: | Round | 1.90 | 2.72 |
| | Square | 2.00 | 2.10 |
| Internal gate bracing: | Round | 1.660 | 1.806 |
| | Square | 1.50 | 1.90 |
| Rails and post braces (tubular): | Round | 1.660 | 1.806 |
| Intermediate posts for fabric heights: 6 feet and less: | | | |
| Tubular (round) | | 1.90 | 2.72 |
| H-Section | | 1.875 x 1.625 x .113 | 2.70 |
| Over 6 feet: | | | |
| Tubular (round) | | 2.375 | 3.65 |
| H-Section | | 2.25 x 1.95 x .143 | 4.10 |

Note: Where no tolerances are specified in this table or elsewhere in this specification, standard commercial tolerances shall apply. Note#4 of ASTM A-120 shall apply to weight tolerances.

provided for all gates. Latches shall have a plunger bar arranged to engage the center stop, except that for single gates of openings less than 10 feet wide a forked latch may be provided. Latches shall be arranged for locking. Center stops shall consist of a device arranged to be set in concrete and to engage a plunger bar of the latch of double gates. No stop is required for single gates. Keepers shall consist of a mechanical device for securing the free end of the gate when in the full open position.

**4. Posts.** Posts shall be of the lengths specified and shall be tubular, except that line posts may be H-beam (Fig. C-2).

**5. Post Braces.** Post braces shall be provided for each gate corner, pull, and end post for use when the top rail is omitted or with fabric 6 feet or more in height. A post brace shall consist of a round tubular brace extending to each adjacent line post at approximately mid-height of the fabric, and a truss consisting of a rod not less than ⅜ inch in nominal diameter from the line post back to the gate, corner, pull, or end post, with a turnbuckle or other equivalent provision for adjustment.

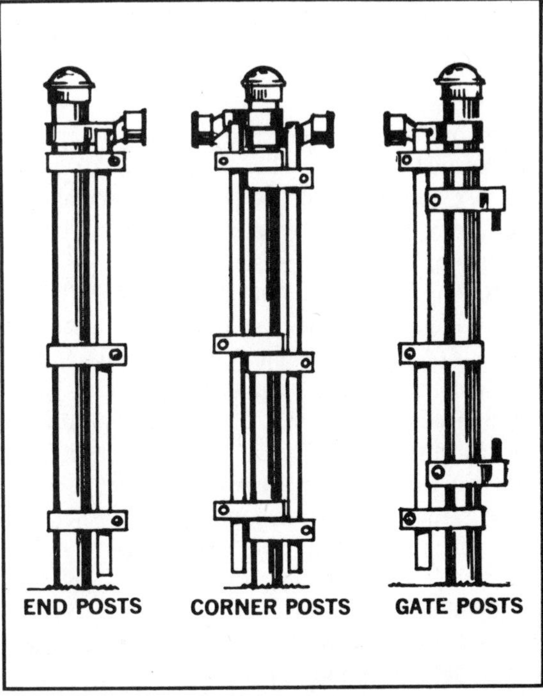


Fig. C-2. End posts, corner posts, and gateposts (courtesy Builders Fence Co., Inc.).

**6. Post Tops.** Post tops shall consist of ornamental tops or combination tops with barbed wire supporting arms as specified. When so specified or when a top rail is to be provided, the top shall be provided with a hole suitable for the through passage of the top rail. The post tops shall fit over the outside of posts and shall exclude moisture from tubular posts.

**7. Barbed Wire Supporting Arms.** When specified to be furnished, these arms shall be at an angle of approximately 45 degrees or vertical as specified. They shall be fitted with clips or other means for attaching three strands of barbed wire. With 45-degree arms the top wire shall be approximately 12 inches horizontally from the fence line, and the other wires are spaced uniformly between the top of the fence fabric and the outside strand. The barbed wire arm shall be of sufficient strength to withstand a weight of 200 pounds applied at the outer strand of barbed wire. Six line barb wire V arm may be specified if desired.

**8. Top Rails.** Top rails shall be round (tubular), in lengths not less than 18 feet, and shall be fitted with couplings for connecting the lengths into a continuous run. The couplings shall be not less than 6 inches long, with .070 minimum wall thickness, and they shall allow for expansion and contraction of the rail. Open seam outside sleeves shall be permitted only with a minimum wall thickness of .100 inches. Enough suitable ties or clips shall be provided for attaching the fabric securely to the top rail at intervals not exceeding 2 feet. Means shall be provided for attaching the top rail to each gate, corner, pull, and end post.

**9. Stretcher Bars.** These bars shall be no less than 3/16 by ¾ inch and no less than 2 inches shorter than the full height of the fabric with which they are to be used. The stretcher bars shall be arranged for attaching the fabric to all terminal posts by threading through the fabric, by bands, or by other positive mechanical means. One stretcher bar shall be provided for each gate and end post, and two bars are for each corner and pull post.

**10. Ties or Clips.** Ties or clips of adequate strength shall be provided for attaching the fabric to all line posts at intervals not exceeding 15 inches.

**11. Bands or Clips.** Bands or clips of adequate strength shall be provided for attaching the fabric and stretcher bars to all terminal posts at intervals not exceeding 15 inches. Tension bands and brace bands shall be formed from flat or beveled steel and shall have a minimum thickness of .115 ± .005 after galvanizing with a minimum width of ⅞ inch ± .015.

**12. Tension Wire.** If the top rail is not specified, a top tension wire shall be provided. Spiraled or crimped tension wire shall be not less than No. 7 gauge plus or minus 0.005 inch in diameter. Ties or clips shall be provided for attaching each wire to the fabric at intervals not exceeding 2 feet. Zinc coating shall be a minimum coating of .80 ounces per square foot of surface area.

**13. Barbed Wire.** Barbed wire shall consist of two strands of 12½-gauge wire with 14-gauge, four-point barbs spaced approximately 5 inches apart. All wire shall be zinc-coated with a minimum coating of .80 ounces per square foot of surface area on 12½-gauge wire and .60 ounces per square foot of surface area on 14-gauge wire.

## COMMERCIAL STANDARD FOR INDUSTRIAL ALUMINUM ALLOY CHAIN LINK FENCING

Here is information on the commercial standard for industrial aluminum alloy chain link fencing.

### 1. Purpose

1.1 The purpose of this commercial standard is to provide a nationally recognized standard of quality for aluminum alloy chain link fencing to promote fair marketing practices and a better understanding between manufacturers, distributors, and users of this fencing. It will also assist ultimate users in determining the types and sizes of fencing that are standard within the industry.

### 2. Scope and Classification

**2.1 Scope.** This standard covers the design, construction, and the minimum chemical and mechanical requirements of the component parts and accessories for industrial aluminum alloy chain link fencing intended primarily for installation on the premises of any dwelling, building, or structure as a boundary line or for the protection of property.

### 3. Requirements

**3.2 Materials.**

**3.2.1 Fabric.** Aluminum alloy chain link fence fabric of 1-inch mesh size shall be made of wire conforming to the requirements of Alloy 6061-T94 of ASTM Designation B211. Fabric of 1¾- and 2-inch mesh size shall be made of wire conforming to the requirements of Alloy 6061 or of any alloy having equivalent strength and corrosion resistance of the same specification, except that the minimum tensile strength of the wire after weaving shall be 50,000 psi.

**3.2.2 Pipe.** The aluminum alloy pipe shall conform to the requirements for Alloy 6063, Temper T6, of ASTM Designation B241.

**3.2.3 Extruded Shapes.**

**3.2.3.1 Square Tubing.** The aluminum alloy square tubing shall conform to the requirements for Alloy 6063, Temper T6, of ASTM Designation B235.

**3.2.3.2 H-Beam.** The aluminum alloy H-beam sections shall conform to the chemical and mechanical property requirements of ASTM Designation B221. The sections shall comply with the dimensional tolerance requirements of this specification as applicable.

**3.2.3.3 Accessories.** The accessories shall be made of the aluminum alloy materials specified in Table C-3.

**Table C-3. Nomenclature, Size, and Material of Fencing Accessories**

| Accessories | | Diameter or dimensions (nominal) | Aluminum alloy | |
|---|---|---|---|---|
| Nomenclature | Type of material | | Alloy & Temper | ASTM Designation |
| | | inches | No. | No. |
| Tension bars | Bar | ¼ × ¾[1] | 6063-T5 or T6 | B221 |
| | Bar | 3/16 × ½ or ¼ × ⅜[2] | 6063-T5 or T6 | B221 |
| Brace and tension bands | Bar | ⅛ × ⅞ | 6063-T5<br>3003-H14<br>3105-H14 | B221<br>B221 |
| Extension arms<br>Arm-line post | Bar | 0.080 (thick) | 6061-T4<br>5052-H34 | B221<br>B209 |
| Arm-corner & end post[3] | Castings | To fit posts & bases | SG70A, ZG61A<br>ZG61B, ZC81A | B26<br>B26 |
| Bases | Castings | To fit posts | ZG70A<br>SG100B, S12B | B108<br>B85 |
| Rail and brace ends, post tops, and turnbuckles | Castings | To fit posts & rails | Same as for above castings | Same as for above castings |
| Rail couplings—outside | Pipe | 6 × 0.078 | 6063-T6 | B241 |
| Rail couplings—inside | Pipe | 6 × 0.062 | 6063-T6,<br>5052-H34,<br>3105-H18 | B241<br>B241<br>B241 |
| Truss rods | Rod | 0.375 | 6061-T6<br>6063-T6 | B221<br>B221 |
| Barbed wire—double strand | Wire | 0.110 | 5052-H38 | B211 |
| Barbed wire—barbs | Wire | 0.080 | 5052-H38 | B211 |
| Tension wire | Wire | 0.192 | 6061-T6<br>5052-H38 | B211<br>B211 |
| Hog rings | Wire | 0.105 | 6061 | B211 |
| Fabric ties | Wire | .144 | 3105-EC-F or 1100-H14 | B211 |
| Bolts and nuts | Wire | 5/16 | 2024-T4,<br>6061-T6 | B211<br>B211 |
| Rivets | Wire | 5/16 | 1100-F | B211 |

[1] Intended for use with 1¾ and 2 inch mesh.
[2] Intended for use with 1 inch mesh.
[3] Bar 0.105 inch thick (nominal) of Alloy 6061,Temper 4, of ASTM Designation B221 may also be used for arm.

**3.3 Construction.**

**3.3.1 Chain Link Fabric.** The chain link fabric shall be made from wire helically wound and interwoven so as to provide a continuous mesh without knots or ties, except in the form of knuckling or of twisting the selvage of the fabric.

**3.3.1.2. Fabric Sizes.** The height, size of mesh, and wire diameters of the chain link fabric shall be as given in Table C-4. The methods of measurement and tolerances are given in 3.3.1.3 and 3.3.1.4 respectively.

**3.3.1.3 Height of Fabric.** The height of the fabric shall be the overall dimension from ends of barbs or knuckles. The tolerance on the nominal height of 1¾- and 2-inch mesh size fabric shall be plus or minus 1 inch, and for 1-inch mesh size it is plus or minus ½ inch.

**3.3.1.4 Mesh Sizes.** The size of mesh shall be determined by measuring the minimum clear distance between the wires forming the parallel sides of the mesh, measured in either direction. The tolerance in the size of 1¾- and 2-inch mesh shall be plus or minus ⅛ inch, and for 1-inch mesh it is plus or minus 1/16 inch.

**3.3.1.5 Selvage.** Fabric 60 inches high and under in 2-inch mesh shall be furnished with knuckling at each selvage. Fabric more than 60 inches high in 2-inch mesh shall be furnished with knuckling at one selvage and twisting at the other. All fabric less than 2-inch mesh shall be furnished with knuckling at both selvages. Special selvages may be specified by the purchaser.

**3.3.2 Posts, Top Rails, and Braces.** The fence posts, top rails, and braces shall be made of aluminum alloy pipe (see 3.2.2) or extruded shapes (see 3.2.3) of the sizes shown in Table C-5 for the specified height of fabric and application. See Table C-4.

**3.3.3 Gate Posts and Frames.** The gateposts and gate frames shall be made of aluminum alloy pipe (see 3.2.2) or square tubing (see 3.2.3.1) of the sizes shown in Table C-6 for the specified opening and swing of gate.

**3.3.3.1 Gates.**

**3.3.3.1.1 Gate Frames.** Assembly of gates shall be accomplished by using properly designed

**Table C-4. Fabric Sizes.**

| Height of fence fabric (nominal) | Size of mesh | Nominal wire[1] diameter |
|---|---|---|
| inches | inches | inches |
| 36, 42, 48, 60, 72, 84, 96, 108, 120, 144 | 2 | 0.192 |
| 36, 42, 48, 60, 72, 84, 96, 108, 120, 144 | 2 | .148 |
| 96, 108, 120, 144 | 1¾ | .120 |
| 36, 42, 48, 60 | 1 | .095 |

[1] Tolerance, plus or minus 0.0015 inch.

**Table C-5. Sizes of Pipe and Extruded Shapes for Posts, Top Rails, and Braces**

| Fabric height | Application | Pipe sizes[2] | | Square tubing sizes | | H-beam sizes | |
|---|---|---|---|---|---|---|---|
| | | Nominal size | Outside diameter (nominal) | Dimensions (nominal) | Weight per foot (nominal) | Dimensions (nominal) | Weight per foot (nominal) |
| feet | | inches | inches | inches | pounds | inches | pounds |
| 6 to 12, incl. | End, corner, & pull posts | 2½ | 2.875 | 3.00 × 3.00 | 2.00 | - | - |
| 6 to 12, incl. | Line posts | 2 | 2.375 | - | 1.26 | 2.25 × 1.95 | 1.253 |
| 6 to 12, incl. | Top rails, braces | 1¼ | 1.660 | - | .78 | - | - |

[1] Limiting values for the nominal dimensions and weights are given in the applicable ASTM specifications.
[2] Schedule 40, nominal weight. Standard commercial tolerances shall apply.

**Table C-6. Size and Pipe and Square Tubing for Gatepost and Frames**

| Application | Gate opening | | Pipe sizes[2] | | Square tubing sizes | |
|---|---|---|---|---|---|---|
| | Single swing | Double swing | Nominal size | Outside diameter (nominal) | Dimensions (nominal) | Weight per foot (nominal) |
| | feet | feet | inches | inches | inches | pounds |
| Gateposts | 6 and under | 12 and under | 2½ | 2.875 | 3.00 × 3.00 | 2.00 |
| | Over 6 to 12, incl. | Over 12 to 24 incl. | 3½ | 4.000 | | 3.15 |
| | Over 12 to 18, incl. | Over 24 to 36, incl. | 6 | 6.625 | | |
| | Over 18 to 32, incl. | Over 36 to 44, incl. | 8 | 8.625 | | |
| Gate frames | All | All | 1½ | 1.900 | 2.00 × 2.00 | 0.94 |

[1] Limiting values for the nominal dimensions and weights are given in the applicable ASTM specifications.
[2] Schedule 40, nominal weight. Standard commercial tolerances shall apply.

fittings or by welding. Gates shall operate freely through a minimum arc of 180 degrees. Where corner fittings are used, gates shall have intermediate members and/or diagonal truss rods as necessary to provide rigid construction of ample strength that is free from sag and twist.

**3.3.3.1.2 Hinges, Latches, Center Stops, and Holdbacks.** Hinges shall be aluminum alloy castings conforming to the latest issue of ASTM Designations B108 or B26 or made of malleable iron or steel and hot-dip galvanized. Hinges shall be designed not to twist or turn under gate action. They shall allow the gate to swing a full 180 degrees to lie along and parallel to the fence line. Latches, stops, and keepers shall be provided for all gates. Double gate latches shall be a combination fulcrum-type latch with center drop rod or of the plunger bar of the latch of double gates. Keepers engage the gate stop. Single gate openings may be furnished with a fulcrum type of latch or other suitable type latch. Center stops shall consist of a device arranged to be set in concrete and to engage a plunger bar of the latch of double gates. Keepers shall consist of a substantial mechanical device for securing and supporting the free end of the gate when in full open position. All latches, stops, and keepers shall be made of aluminum alloys as specified for hinges or galvanized malleable iron or pressed steel.

**3.3.5 Workmanship.** All parts of the aluminum fencing shall be uniform in quality and temper. The exterior and interior surfaces of parts and pipe shall be clean, smooth, and free from slivers, laminations, folds, grooves, cracks, and other injurious defects within the limits consistent with best commercial practice.

## 4. Inspection and Testing

**4.1 Production Inspection and Testing.** The manufacturer shall make such inspections and tests during the manufacturing process of all components as are needed to maintain the quality of the product consistently in conformity with this standard.

**4.2 Inspection.** All parts of the aluminum fencing shall be visually inspected to determine their conformance with the workmanship, design, and dimensional requirements of this standard.

## STANDARDS FOR CHAIN LINK FENCE INSTALLATION

**Installation.** All materials and workmanship

shall be first class in every respect and done in a neat, workmanlike manner (Fig. C-3).

**Post Spacing.** Line posts shall be spaced at intervals not to exceed 10 feet on the average when measured from center to center between terminal posts. In determining the post spacing the measurement generally will be made parallel to the slope of the natural ground. All posts shall be placed in a vertical position except where designated otherwise by the owner or the owner's representative.

**Post Setting.** All posts shall be set in holes of appropriate diameter and depth. After the post has been set and plumbed, the hole shall be filled with 2,000 psi (four-sack mix) concrete. The exposed surface of the concrete shall be crowned to shed water.

Using mechanical devices for the setting of fence posts is acceptable under this specification, provided the mechanical device develops a strength in the ground equal or superior to the strength developed by the concrete settings as specified earlier.

Where solid rock is encountered without an overburden of soil, line posts shall be set a minimum depth of 12 inches. End, corner, gate, and pull posts shall be set a minimum of 18 inches into the solid rock. The hole shall have a minimum width of 1 inch greater than the largest dimension of the post section to be set.

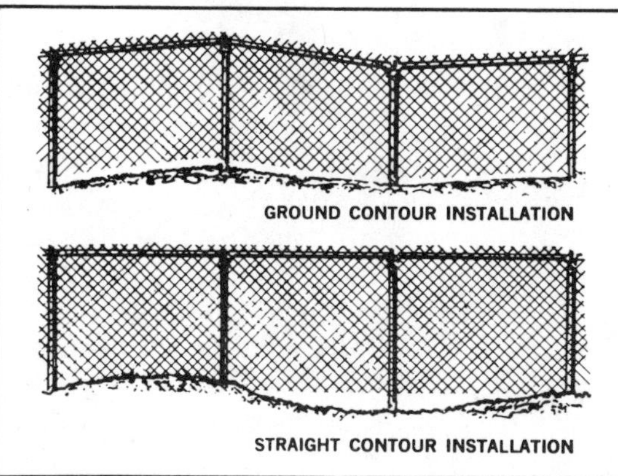


Fig. C-3. Contouring chain link fencing (courtesy Builders Fence Co., Inc.).

After the post is set and plumbed, the hole shall be filled with grout consisting of 1 part portland cement and 3 parts clean, well-graded sand. Other grouting materials may be used if they are approved or specified by the owner. The grout shall be thoroughly worked into the hole so as to leave no voids. The grout shall be crowned to carry water from the post.

Where solid rock is covered by an overburden of soil or loose rock, the posts shall be set to full depth unless the penetration into solid rock reaches the minimum depths specified earlier, in which case the depth of penetration may be terminated. Concrete footings shall be constructed from the solid rock to the top of the ground. Grouting will be required on the portion of the post in solid rock.

**Terminal Post.** End, corner, gate, and pull posts shall be set as shown heretofore. They shall be braced to the nearest post with a galvanized pipe horizontal brace used as a compression member, and a galvanized ⅜-inch steel truss rod and truss tightener used as a tension member. On fences 3-5 feet in height where a top rail is required, no braces needed. Bracing will always be required on all fences 6-11 feet high. A center rail is recommended on a fence 12 feet high. If the center rail is omitted, two truss braces will be required in lieu of one at each terminal. Regardless of height, all fences installed without a top rail must have braces on all terminals. All changes in direction of the fence line of 30 degrees or more shall be considered corners. Pull posts shall be used at all abrupt changes in grade.

**Chain Link Fabric.** It shall be placed on the side of the fence as designated by the owner or his representative. The fabric shall be stretched taut approximately 2 inches above the ground and securely fastened to the posts. The fabric shall be cut, and each span shall be attached independently at all terminal posts. Fastening to terminal posts shall be with stretcher bars and fabric bands spaced at maximum 15-inch intervals. Fastening to the line post shall be with tie wire, metal bands, or other approved material attached at maximum 15-inch intervals. The top edge of the fabric wire with wire ties at intervals not exceeding 24 inches. The bottom edge of the fabric shall be fastened to the bottom tension wire with wire ties at intervals not exceeding 2 feet. Rolls of wire fabric shall be joined by weaving a single strand into the ends of the rolls to form a continuous mesh.

**Insurance and Permits.** The fence contractor shall provide and pay for workmen's compensation insurance; public liability insurance, bonds, where required; permits; and other requirements of national, state, and local governments.

# Index

# Index